DA
500
.G52

100843

GIPSON

BRITISH EMPIRE...

LAWRENCE HENRY GIPSON

AUTHOR

JARED INGERSOLL: A STUDY OF AMERICAN LOYALISM
IN RELATION TO BRITISH COLONIAL GOVERNMENT

STUDIES IN CONNECTICUT COLONIAL TAXATION

THE MORAVIAN INDIAN MISSION ON WHITE RIVER

LEWIS EVANS

THE COMING OF THE REVOLUTION, 1763–1775

THE BRITISH EMPIRE BEFORE THE AMERICAN REVOLUTION

THE BRITISH EMPIRE
BEFORE THE AMERICAN REVOLUTION

VOLUME XII

THE TRIUMPHANT EMPIRE:

BRITAIN SAILS INTO THE STORM

1770–1776

THE BRITISH EMPIRE
BEFORE THE AMERICAN REVOLUTION
VOLUME XII

THE

TRIUMPHANT EMPIRE:

BRITAIN SAILS INTO THE STORM
1770-1776

BY

LAWRENCE HENRY GIPSON

MCMLXVII
ALFRED A. KNOPF
NEW YORK

L. C. catalog card number: 58–9670

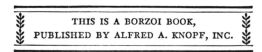

THIS IS A BORZOI BOOK,
PUBLISHED BY ALFRED A. KNOPF, INC.

PUBLISHED, DECEMBER 1965
SECOND PRINTING, APRIL 1967

To HARVEY ALEXANDER NEVILLE, *who after a distinguished career as Professor of Chemistry was successively Director of the Institute of Research, Dean of the Graduate School, Vice-President and Provost, and President (now President Emeritus) of Lehigh University—for his scholarly interest, warm encouragement, and effective support across the years.*

Preface

As has been made clear in the preface to Volume XI, the present volume was written as an immediate continuation of that one as well as forming part of the Book—*The Triumphant Empire*—that also embraces Volumes IX and X and will include part of Volume XIII. In the preface to Volume X, I sought to point out the nature and proportions of the task facing me in defining and interpreting the fundamental issues which arose within the Empire after the conquest of Canada in 1760 and finally produced a crisis that was to break the bonds which had long held the thirteen older North American colonies to the mother country. In the introductory chapter—"Colonies Ripe for Revolt"—of that volume, I emphasized the degree of political, economic, and social maturity of these colonies at the end of the Great War for the Empire. The present volume is concerned with the culmination of the crisis generated in great part by this sense of maturity.

In commenting on the connection that had long been maintained between the colonies and the parent state, and also in strongly defending the steps taken by Great Britain to secure obedience to the legislative authority of Parliament and the laws designed to bind the Empire, Peter Orlando Hutchinson, editor of *The Diary and Letters of His Excellency Thomas Hutchinson* (Boston, 1884), made the following pertinent observation (p. 15):

> "Yet the Americans were not wholly wrong, and the Mother Country not entirely right. The parent was treating her grown-up child as if it were still in the nursery. That is the secret of the whole quarrel."

Granted that Hutchinson was right in his discovery of "the secret of the whole quarrel," certain questions arise (if we may also take the liberty of pursuing the parent-child analogy, despite the objections of the political scientists). When, if ever, should a mature person be given freedom of action by a parent? Was the old Roman law of *patria potestas*, bestowing upon the head of a family almost unlimited authority over his offspring and even their children, a sound principle? Should the decision rest solely with the parent? Should the parent, in justifying the continuance of such authority, point to the manifold indulgences and other benefits showered upon the offspring during the period of immaturity? Or, should the parent simply command strict obedience from his offspring, even those well prepared to assume personal responsibility in life? When such a situation arises, is it natural or unnatural for such mature offspring to resent the attempt to interfere with their freedom of action and determine to stand on what they consider to be their personal rights even if these conflict with the parental rights?

Such questions as the above inevitably come to mind as one turns to consider the course of events within the Old British Empire during the critical years of the 1760's and 1770's. The answer to them may now, happily, be viewed dispassionately—something that was not possible then on the part of those personally involved in the crisis, whether on the side of the parent or of the offspring. Their conflicting views, I have felt, should be presented with fairness and considerable fullness, as an important contribution to an understanding of one of the most momentous events in modern history, especially in view of the ultimate impact of the American Revolution upon the world in the eighteenth and succeeding centuries. My attempt to do so has necessitated a two-volume work, especially since issues other than those that produced the revolutionary movement—such as the sharp intercolonial rivalries, the intracolonial conflicts of interest, and the problems involved in the westward movement stressed in Volume XI—occupied much of the attention of American colonials.

Developments of an interimperial nature, occurring far beyond British North America, also demand attention. Such was the contest between Great Britain and Spain over the Falkland Islands, which, for a time, brought the threat of a new international war. Later came the financial crisis of the United East India Company, the solution of which had a most important bearing upon the colonial policy of the British Ministry and Parliament, especially in connection with the Tea Act. These form part of the subject matter of the present volume. Then, too, although an earlier plan of this series stated that it would present the history of the First British Empire up to the outbreak of hostilities in North America in 1775, it has seemed obligatory to go beyond this date. For a proper culmination of the work must trace the development of the trend toward American independence—which was not the original objective of the revolutionary movement in the minds of most colonials —down to the Declaration of Independence by the Continental Congress in 1776.

As for those parts of the Empire which did not join in the movement to throw off dependence upon Great Britain, their story must be reserved for Volume XIII. Therefore the chapter of the present volume dealing with the Coercive Acts will not include a discussion of the passage of the Quebec Act, on the ground that this subject more properly belongs to that province's internal history.

Acknowledgment of the archives and other depositories which have been consulted for this volume appears at the end of the preface to Volume XI, as does my debt of gratitude to Lehigh University for its support of my project over the past forty years, to the foundations which have given me financial aid during the writing of the series, and to specific individuals who have assisted me while the work was in progress.

Lawrence Henry Gipson

The Library
Lehigh University
Bethlehem, Pennsylvania
December 7, 1964

Contents

The Financial Crisis of the East India Company

CHAPTER II

MASSACHUSETTS BAY FOMENTS REBELLION

CHAPTER III

TEA AND THE CLIMATE OF SEDITION

CHAPTER IV

PARLIAMENT ACCEPTS THE CHALLENGE:

THE COERCIVE ACTS

Chapter V

MASSACHUSETTS BAY RESISTS

CHAPTER VI

OTHER COLONIES PREPARE TO RESIST:

NEW ENGLAND AND THE MIDDLE COLONIES

CHAPTER VII

OTHER COLONIES PREPARE TO RESIST:

MARYLAND AND VIRGINIA

CHAPTER VIII

OTHER COLONIES PREPARE TO RESIST:

THE CAROLINAS AND GEORGIA

CHAPTER IX

THE GATHERING OF THE FIRST CONTINENTAL CONGRESS

Chapter X

A CRUCIAL DECISION

CHAPTER XI

REPUDIATION OF CHATHAM'S PLAN OF CONCILIATION

CHAPTER XII

OPEN REBELLION

Chapter XIII

FAILURE OF THE OLIVE BRANCH PETITION

CHAPTER XIV

INDEPENDENCE

Maps, Views, and Plans

CHRONOLOGY

General Background

1740: a British naval base in the South Pacific is recommended; 1760: the accession of George III; 1764: the British set out to survey the Falkland Islands; the French land on East Falkland; 1765: West Falkland is claimed for Great Britain and a settlement established at Port Egmont; the Stamp Act Congress is held at New York; 1766: a British colonizing expedition fortifies Port Egmont; the Stamp Act is repealed, the Declaratory Act passed; the affairs of the East India Company produce a crisis; the formation of the Pitt Ministry; 1767: the French settlement at East Falkland is delivered to the Spanish; passage of the Townshend American Revenue Acts; 1768: reorganization of the British Ministry and Grafton succeeds Chatham as the King's chief minister; Massachusetts Bay incites the other colonies to protest the Townshend Acts; British troops land at Boston Harbour to support the customs service; 1769: the British commander at the Falklands issues an ultimatum to Spanish surveyors; the rise of John Wilkes signals the social, economic, and political discontent in England; the spread of the non-importation movement signals the discontent of colonials with parliamentary taxation and regulation, as does the burning of the revenue ship *Liberty* at Newport; 1770: the British garrison at Port Egmont surrenders to a Spanish expedition; inter-imperial rivalries reach a climax with the threat of war between Spain and England over the Falkland Islands; Lord North succeeds the Duke of Grafton as the King's chief minister; the partial repeal of the Townshend Acts; the collapse of the colonial non-importation movement; Great Britain increases its armed services; General Gage in America is warned of a potential rupture between Britain and Spain and of plans to attack first at New Orleans; the Massachusetts Bay House of Representatives challenges the authority of the Lieutenant Governor to prorogue the Assembly to Cambridge or to remove provincial troops from Castle William to garrison it with British regulars.

1771

Jan. 22 Peaceful negotiations end the threat of war between Britain and Spain over the Falkland Islands.

March 14 Thomas Hutchinson succeeds Sir Francis Bernard as Governor of Massachusetts Bay.

June 19 The Massachusetts Bay Assembly protests the Governor's use of royal instructions (in the issue over the Governor's salary) as an infringement of charter rights.

July 4 The Massachusetts Bay House of Representatives again denies the power of a royal instruction in conflict with its claimed charter rights when the Governor refuses approval to a provincial act that would tax officers of the Crown.

5 The Massachusetts Bay Assembly protests the Governor's denial of their right to make grants to their London agents.

The destruction of a revenue vessel in the Delaware River emphasizes the hostility of colonials to the customs service and vice-admiralty courts.

1772

Jan. 21 The King announces the restoration of West Falkland to Great Britain.

June 9 The burning of the customs schooner *Gaspee*.

July 14 Governor Hutchinson returns the sittings of the Massachusetts Bay Assembly to Boston.

Aug. 14 The Earl of Dartmouth succeeds the Earl of Hillsborough as Secretary of State for the colonies.

21 The Privy Council authorizes a board of inquiry to investigate the *Gaspee* affair.

Sept. 2 The King appoints a commission on the *Gaspee* investigation.

Oct. 28 Hutchinson is charged with despotism for his refusal to call an Assembly at the request of a Boston town meeting or otherwise to yield his prerogatives.

Nov. 2 A Boston town meeting approves a statement of rights and a "List of Infringements"; initiates the provincial committees of correspondence.

Dec. News reaches Rhode Island of the proclamation appointing a commission of inquiry on the *Gaspee* affair; the press protests the royal investigation.

Many Massachusetts Bay towns pass resolutions in line with those of Boston concerning colonial rights.

1773

Jan.–
March
: Widespread agitation in the colonial press over the *Gaspee* affair.

The commission to investigate the burning of the *Gaspee* meets at Newport.

Jan. 6
: Governor Hutchinson addresses the newly called General Court of Massachusetts Bay and defends the supremacy of Parliament.

25
: The reply of the Massachusetts Bay representatives challenges the principle of parliamentary supremacy.

Feb.
: The beginning of the controversy in North Carolina over "Tryon's Court Law."

March 2
: The East India Company notifies the British government of its inability to meet the requirements of the recent acts of Parliament governing its affairs.

6
: The Governor prorogues the Massachusetts Bay General Court; the House of Representatives petitions the King.

12
: The Virginia House of Burgesses creates the intercolonial committee of correspondence system in reaction to the royal investigation of the *Gaspee* affair.

March–
May
: Parliamentary debates on the need for reform in the internal affairs of the East India Company and for external financial help.

April 8
: The Governor dissolves the Massachusetts Bay General Court and calls a new election.

May 10
: Passage of the Tea Act of 1773.

19
: The East India Company advises the House of Commons of its insolvency.

28
: The new Massachusetts Bay General Court acts on Virginia's proposals for intercolonial committees of correspondence.

June 2–16
: Debates begin in the Massachusetts Bay Assembly on the intercepted Hutchinson-Oliver-Whately correspondence.

21
: The act for regulating the affairs of the East India Company becomes law.

22
: Termination of the inquiry on the *Gaspee* affair produces none of the feared results.

23
: The Massachusetts Bay Assembly petitions the King to remove Hutchinson and Oliver from office.

26
: Governor Hutchinson seeks a leave of absence to go to England.

29
: The Governor prorogues the Massachusetts Bay General Court.

July   1 The Loan Act for relief of the East India Company becomes
              law.
Aug.   21 London agent Benjamin Franklin forwards the Massachu-
              setts Bay petition to remove the Governor to Lord Dart-
              mouth for presentation to the King.
Oct.–   The Tea Act reaches the colonies and is widely publicized in
Nov.   the press.
Oct.   15 New York is first to react to the Tea Act.
          18 Philadelphia merchants pass strong resolutions against the
              Tea Act.
          21 Through the intercolonial system of committees of correspon-
              dence Boston urges other colonies to prevent the landing
              of East India Company tea shipments.
Nov.   15 Governor Hutchinson informs the British Ministry of his lack
              of Council support and helplessness to maintain order.
          18 The tea consignees refuse the demands of the Boston town
              meeting to resign their commissions.
          28 The first tea ship arrives in Boston.
          29 The Boston town meeting votes to return the tea ship.
              Principal gentlemen of New York sign an "Association of the
              Sons of Liberty" to protest the Tea Act.
          30 Governor Hutchinson's proclamation on the cessation of un-
              lawful proceedings is ignored.
              Tea-ship owners in Boston agree to return the tea to England.
Dec.   The arrival of the other tea ships at Boston Harbour and
              unsuccessful negotiations precipitate a crisis.
          16 Boston Harbour is the scene of the "Boston Tea Party"
          22 Chests of tea landed at Charleston are seized and stored in
              the custom house.
          25 Philadelphians refuse to receive tea shipments and send the
              tea ship back to England.

1774

Jan.   4 Benjamin Franklin appears before the Privy Council in a
              preliminary hearing on the petition to remove Hutchinson
              and Oliver from office.
          13 Parliament reconvenes.
          25 The tarring and feathering in Boston of customs officer John
              Malcom.
          28 The continuation of the Privy Council hearings on the Massa-
              chusetts Bay petition; Solicitor General Wedderburn casti-

gates Franklin for his part in sending the Hutchinson-Oliver letters to Boston.

Jan.–Feb. The Cabinet Council considers methods of punishing Boston. The issue over the judges' salaries in Massachusetts Bay.

Feb.   1   A Massachusetts Bay committee takes steps to replenish the province's powder stock.

       7   The Privy Council rejects the Massachusetts Bay petition to remove its Governor.

      11   The Massachusetts Bay Assembly attempts to impeach the Chief Justice in the issue over royal salaries of the judges.

March 16   Inhabitants of Massachusetts Bay hold military exercises.

      31   Passage of the Boston Port Act.

April 7   Thomas Gage is commissioned Governor-in-Chief of Massachusetts Bay.

      18   The tea ship arriving in New York is returned to London, the consignees having resigned.

      19   Edmund Burke's great speech in the House of Commons endorses repeal of the tea duty.

      22   The New York "Tea Party"

May   10   News of the Boston Port Act reaches Massachusetts Bay.

      13   Governor Gage is welcomed at Boston.

      17   A town meeting at Providence, Rhode Island, recommends the holding of an intercolonial congress.

      20   Passage of the second and third Coercive Acts.

      26   Virginia burgesses, meeting at Raleigh Tavern, sanction the idea of a continental congress.

June   2   The enactment of the fourth Coercive Act.

       8   The plan for a Solemn League and Covenant for non-importation is launched in Boston.

      17   The proposal in the Massachusetts Bay Assembly for Philadelphia as the site of the continental congress.

      22   Passage of the Quebec Act.
           Resolves taken at Annapolis support aid to Boston and a trade embargo.

July–Aug. The thirteen older North American colonies hold town meetings, local conventions, and provincial congresses to approve aid to Boston, a non-importation movement, and the sending of delegates to a continental congress.

Sept. 5   The First Continental Congress gathers at Carpenter's Hall, Philadelphia.

      17   The Continental Congress approves the Suffolk County Resolves adopted in Massachusetts Bay on the 9th.

      28   Joseph Galloway proposes a plan of union to the Congress.

      30   The dissolution of Parliament and the call for a new one as a test of public sentiment in Great Britain.

Oct.   7 The Massachusetts Bay House of Representatives becomes a Provincial Congress.

      14 Adoption of a Declaration of Rights by the Continental Congress.

      19 The burning of the ship *Peggy Stewart* at Annapolis.

      20 The Continental Congress signs the Continental Association.

      26 The Massachusetts Bay Provincial Congress creates a committee of safety.

          Before its adjournment, the First Continental Congress approves an address to the people of Great Britain, a memorial to the colonists represented in the Congress, an address to the inhabitants of Quebec, and a petition to the King.

Nov.–Dec. The King and the Cabinet Council face the prospects of war in America.

Dec.   14 The garrison at Fort William and Mary, New Hampshire, is overwhelmed by colonial raiders.

1775

Jan.   19 Parliament reconvenes.

      20 The Earl of Chatham denounces the Ministry; he urges removal of troops from Boston.

      21 The Cabinet Council resolves to abate taxation of the colonies upon prior acceptance by them of parliamentary supremacy.

Jan.–Feb. The petition movement of British merchants in towns trading to North America, as an economic pressure weapon, fails to prove the effectiveness in England of the non-importation association.

Feb.   1 Chatham's reconciliation plan presented to the House of Lords.

  1–16 The second Provincial Congress of Massachusetts Bay meets at Cambridge to become a revolutionary, military government.

      2 Lord North advocates enforcement of obedience by the colonies before considering their grievances.

      7 Parliament agrees to support the measures to bring the colonies to obedience.

 12–13 Augmentation of British sea and land forces.

     20 The Cabinet Council's conciliatory resolution is submitted to the House of Commons.

March 8 Defeat of David Hartley's humanitarian amendment to the New England Restraining Bill in Parliament.

22 Edmund Burke's speech on reconciliation in the House of Commons.

27 David Hartley's conciliation plan for an American revenue by requisition is ignored by the Commons.

28 General Gage reports to the Ministry on the failure of his mission.

30 Passage of the New England Restraining Act.

March–
April
The second Massachusetts Bay Provincial Congress, sitting at Concord, approves a militia, Minute Men, and taxation to buy war supplies.

April 13 Passage of the bill for restraining the trade of the colonies south of New England.

16 General Gage receives a command to action from Lord Dartmouth to stop further rebellious action.

18 British regulars are sent to destroy a colonial military supply depot at Concord.

19 The British order the dispersal of an assemblage of Minute Men at Lexington and fire upon the men.

The colonials attack the British force at Concord; additional Minute Men harass the Redcoats on their retreat to Boston.

20 Boston becomes a besieged town.

May 10 The Second Continental Congress meets at Philadelphia.

Capture of the King's fort at Ticonderoga by the Green Mountain Boys and some Massachusetts Bay troops.

11 Capture of Crown Point by colonial forces.

17 Lord Camden presents to the House of Lords a petition from the Protestant settlers of Quebec appealing for repeal of the Quebec Act.

The Continental Congress resolves to boycott American colonies not supporting the Continental Association.

18 Defeat in the House of Commons of a motion to repeal the Quebec Act.

26 Parliament is prorogued after the King signs a large money bill to provide for the service of 1775.

The House of Commons plan of conciliation is laid before the Continental Congress.

29 The Continental Congress sends a letter of appeal to the inhabitants of Canada.

June 9 The Continental Congress assumes authority for determining the shape of civil government in Massachusetts Bay.

14 Formation by the Congress of the American continental army.

15 George Washington is chosen Commanding General of the continental forces.

17 British forces at Boston capture Breed's Hill.

22 The Continental Congress assumes the sovereign power of authorizing the emission of bills of credit.

27 Congress makes the decision to invade Canada.

July 6 The American Congress issues "A Declaration on the Causes and Necessity of their taking up Arms."

7 Congress sends the Olive Branch Petition to the King.

Aug. The Olive Branch petition, refused by the King, is delivered to the British press.

Sept. American forces move forward and clear the way to Montreal.

Oct. At the new session of Parliament the King denies the sincerity of the Olive Branch Petition.

Nov. 13 American forces under Montgomery enter Montreal without resistance and proceed toward Quebec.

14 Benedict Arnold's forces camp on the Plains of Abraham.

16 Edmund Burke presents his peace-plan bill seeking parliamentary recognition of the Continental Congress.

20 Lord North presents the Prohibitory Bill along with last-ditch proposals to restore peace.

Dec. 2 The Arnold and Montgomery forces join in the siege of Quebec.

22 Passage of the Prohibitory Act.

30 Americans fail to storm Quebec; the death of General Montgomery and wounding of General Arnold.

1776

Publication in London of *The Rights of Great Britain Asserted against the Claims of America* . . .

Jan. 10 Thomas Paine's *Common Sense* appears from the Philadelphia press to spark the colonial movement for independence.

24 The Continental Congress approves the preparation of an address to the "United Colonies," denying that independence is being sought.

Word of passage of the Prohibitory Act reaches the Congress.

Feb. 13 The address of the Continental Congress to the United Colonists is tabled.

15 The Continental Congress votes to send a mission to Canada to persuade the French inhabitants to join the American union.

25 The Loyalist uprising is crushed at Moore's Creek in North Carolina.

29 The House of Commons approves three treaties for the use of German troops in America, despite strong opposition stands.

March 1 Silas Deane is commissioned to purchase military supplies in France.

5 The House of Lords approves the use of German troops.

15 Major General William Howe evacuates Boston.

23 Congress authorizes the use of American privateers.

26 South Carolina repudiates all its ties to Great Britain as a royal colony.

April Failure of the American mission to Canada.

6 Congress agrees to permit importation of goods in foreign vessels from places outside the British Empire.

13 North Carolina delegates to the Congress are empowered to join in declaring independence.

15 A Georgia provincial congress votes to elect a President and a Council of Safety to advise him.

May 6 American forces raise the siege of Quebec and retreat to Montreal.

6–15 A Virginia convention meeting at Williamsburg votes to declare the United Colonies free and independent states.

June 7 In the Continental Congress, Richard Henry Lee moves three resolutions: for independence, for foreign alliances, and for a plan of confederation.

12 The Virginia Convention issues its Declaration of Rights.

29 Virginians adopt a constitution as a commonwealth.

July 2 The Continental Congress approves Lee's resolutions and declares the United Colonies to be free and independent states.

4 The formal Declaration of Independence.

THE BRITISH EMPIRE
BEFORE THE AMERICAN REVOLUTION

VOLUME XII

THE TRIUMPHANT EMPIRE:

BRITAIN SAILS INTO THE STORM

1770–1776

CHAPTER I

The Empire in a Period
of Crisis

THE preceding volume dealt with the problems of colonization, land speculation, and internal problems in the expanding North America of the second half of the eighteenth century. These were but a part of the larger problems involved in the great sweep of Empire as men went out from the British Isles in ever widening circles of exploration and adventure. In the 1770's Great Britain, by exploiting the geographic and other scientific discoveries made by Captain James Cook and his companions, was laying the foundation for extending the Empire into the Pacific.[1] The colonization of Australia, Tasmania, and New Zealand and the establishment of control over other islands in this great ocean cannot be treated within the scope of the present series. Nevertheless, one aspect of this expansion must be given consideration—the settlement of the Falkland Islands—for it brought the threat of another war with Spain and France at a time when the government was faced with crises in both domestic and foreign affairs.

The Falkland Islands Crisis

The Falkland Islands and their islets, some one hundred in number, lie about 250 miles east of the southern coast of the present state

---

[1] The student should consult in this connection V. T. Harlow: *The Founding of the Second British Empire, 1763–1793* (2 vols., London, New York, and Toronto, 1952, 1964), I. Volume II, *New Continents and Changing Values*, was completed by F. McC. Madden. For the debate on the state of the nation in the House of Lords on January 22, 1770—the speech by Rockingham emphasizing the "universal discontent of the people" over domestic and foreign issues, the defence of the government by Grafton, and Chatham's view that there was no need to "look abroad for

of Argentina and slightly northeast of the Straits of Magellan. They cover 6,500 square miles—a total land area a little larger than Connecticut and Rhode Island. Only two of the islands have importance: East Falkland, with a length of 95 miles and a breadth of about 40, and West Falkland, 80 miles long and some 25 wide. Although such plants as fuchsias and pelargoniums flourish in the reasonably mild temperature, the winds blow almost continuously over the treeless islands, and rain and mist prevail much of the time. Thus neither the climate nor the limited mineral resources of the islands would attract colonization except by the hardiest types of people, yet pasturage abounds for sheep and cattle, and the sheep flourish there. However, at the time the British became seriously interested in the Falklands it was because of their highly strategic location athwart the entrance to the Pacific Ocean.

In 1740, during the war with Spain, Commodore George Anson (later made Admiral of the Fleet and raised to the peerage) sailed through the Straits of Magellan to fall upon Spanish commerce and Spanish-American towns. Out of this adventure came his well-known *A Voyage Round the World. . . .*[2] In this volume Anson strongly recommended that Great Britain take over an island or islands to the south of Brazil, similar to the Falklands, where a fleet could be stationed in time of need to patrol these waters and be ready to intercept Spanish ships. After the conclusion of the Great War for the Empire the first steps in this direction were taken when, in 1764, Commodore John Byron was sent to the islands "in order to make better surveys thereof . . . and to determine a place or places, most proper for a new settlement or settlements thereon."[3] Reaching West Falkland early in 1765, he went ashore at a place he named Port Egmont, made surveys, and took possession of this island in the name of His Majesty George III.[4] When sending out Byron to these islands

---

grievances" when "the grand capital mischief is fixed at home . . . The constitution has been grossly violated"—see *Parliamentary History*, XVI, 741–55.

[2] First published in London in 1748, this compilation of Lord Anson's papers was prepared by Richard Walter.

[3] For the secret instructions given to Byron see P.R.O., Admiralty Papers, 2:1332. These have been printed by B. G. Corney in Vols. I and II of *The Quest and Occupation of Tahiti . . . 1772–1776* (London, 1913–14), II, 432–7. These are Vols. XXXII and XXXVI of the 2nd series of works issued by the Hakluyt Society.

[4] See John Byron: "An Account of the Voyage Round the World, in the Years MDCCLXIV, MDCCLXV, and MDCCLXVI," in John Hawkesworth: *An Account of the Voyages Undertaken by the Order of His present Majesty for Making Discoveries in the Southern Hemisphere . . .* (3 vols., London, 1773), I, 53–7. See map opposite p. 41.

the government of Great Britain had assumed that they were uninhabited. However, a year before the British commodore reached West Falkland, Louis Antoine de Bougainville—whose career as an aide-de-camp to Montcalm in New France has been dealt with in an earlier volume of this series[5]—had landed on East Falkland with a small group of refugee Acadians (who had been carried to France from Nova Scotia). Entering what is now called Berkeley Sound, his party had built huts, established a fort, and erected an obelisk bearing a medallion of Louis XV and an inscription testifying that these islands—called by the French Isles Malouines—were colonized by the King of France.[6] Leaving the little colony under command of Captain de Nerville early in April, Bougainville returned to France. In January 1765 he went back to the islands with supplies and additional settlers. It was then that he saw Commodore Byron's vessels. But, according to Bougainville's account, after Byron had surveyed the islands and had taken possession of them in the name of the King of Great Britain, he had sailed for the Pacific without leaving any settlers and without having discovered the presence of the French.[7]

When Byron's account of his taking possession of the Falklands reached England, the government decided to colonize the islands. Meanwhile, news of the French settlement had also been received in England. Instructing the Admiralty on July 20, 1765, on the colonization expedition, the Secretary of State for the Southern Department, Henry Seymour Conway, stated: "And if, contrary to Expectation, the subjects of any Foreign Power in Amity with Great Britain, should under any real and [or] pretended authority, have taken upon them to make any settlement . . . upon . . . the said Falkland's or Pepys' Islands, the commanders of His Majestys ships . . . are directed to warn them off the said Islands. . . ."[8] The importance of the step being taken was made clear to others in the government. The Earl of Egmont, First Lord of the Admiralty, writing

---

[5] See Volume VII of this series.

[6] [L. A. de Bougainville]: *Voyage autour du Monde, par la Frégate du Roi La Boudeuse, et la Flûte L'Étoile* . . . (Paris, 1771), pp. 50–1. It may be noted that Bougainville signed the preface to this volume.

[7] *Ibid.*, pp. 51–3.

[8] Conway to the Admiralty Board, July 20, 1765, quoted by Julius Goebel, Jr.: *The Struggle for the Falkland Islands. A Study in Legal and Diplomatic History* (New Haven, 1927), p. 235. This book is an exceedingly important contribution to the history of British eighteenth-century expansion. For briefer accounts see V. T. Harlow: *op. cit.*, I, 22–32, and Cecil Headlam's chapter "International Relations in the Colonial Sphere, 1763–1783" in the *Cambridge History of the British Empire* (8 vols., Cambridge and New York, 1929–40), I, 698–703.

to the Duke of Grafton, Secretary of State for the Northern Department, called the Falklands *"the key to the whole Pacifick Ocean.* This Island [that is, both Falklands] must command the Ports and trade of . . . all the Spanish Territory upon that sea. . . . Your Grace will presently perceive the prodigious use hereafter to be made of an establishment in this place by that nation who shall first fix a firm footing there."[9]

Early in January 1766, a colonizing expedition under command of Captain John McBride (MacBride) arrived at Port Egmont and built fortifications.[10] Not until the end of that year, however, was the French post on East Falkland discovered, at which time McBride notified the French of the British claims. But Captain de Nerville, still in command there, let it be known that he was prepared to defend his post if attacked. McBride returned to his own island without taking action.[11]

Meanwhile the Spanish court, apprised of the foothold that the French had secured in the islands, took deep exception to this move as a violation of the Bourbon Family Compact. Very reluctantly therefore the Duc de Choiseul agreed to release the islands to Spain.[12] In March 1767 a joint French and Spanish fleet arrived at East Falkland with Bougainville aboard. On April 1 in a formal ceremony he delivered the settlement, Port Louis, into the hands of the Spaniards, who named it Puerto de la Soledad.[13] The British at Port Egmont on West Falkland were now faced by the Spanish. Even before this transfer took place, the Spanish ambassador in London, Prince de Masserano, had written in August 1766 to his court recommending that the English settlement should be destroyed without delay. When the Court of Louis XV was made fully aware of this advice, its ministers counselled moderation on the part

---

[9] Egmont to Grafton, July 20, 1765, quoted by Julius Goebel, Jr.: *op. cit.,* p. 236.

[10] The Spaniards were made very curious and suspicious by reports from their ambassador to the Court of St. James, Prince Fieschi de Masserano, about the activities of the British in the region of the Falkland Islands. In 1767 the ambassador sent information secured from a master's mate, who had been with McBride, that there were two batteries of six 24-pounders each defending the entrance to Port Egmont with twelve other batteries further within the inlet and eight more to be constructed, while 200 men were working constantly throwing up ramparts. See Julian de Arriaga to Don Manuel de Amat, November 13, 1767, G. B. Corney: *op. cit.,* I, 101–4.

[11] For McBride's secret instructions given September 26, 1765, see B. G. Corney: *op. cit.,* II, 441–5; for McBride's visit to the French post on East Falkland see *ibid.,* I, 125–6n.

[12] For a detailed account of the above negotiations, as a result of which Bougainville was reimbursed his expenses, see Julius Goebel, Jr.: *op. cit.,* pp. 226–30.

[13] See [Bougainville]: *op. cit.,* p. 46.

of Spain—feeling that France was not prepared to support her ally in another war. Nevertheless, the Spanish ambassador, in his conversations with the British ministers, did not fail to stress the encroachment of the British on territory belonging to the Crown of Spain. In turn, it was reported that the Earl of Shelburne, now Secretary of State for the Southern Department, denied that Great Britain had ever acknowledged the southern seas to be possessions of the Spanish Crown but, rather, insisted on the right of navigating these waters and, by implication, the right to use the uninhabited islands lying within them.[14]

It was not until November 1769 that anything noteworthy took place in the area of the Falklands.[15] In that month a vessel sent out by the Governor of Soledad to survey the islands fell in with the British ship *Tamar*, Captain Hunt, which had sailed out of Port Egmont. After messages had been exchanged, Hunt bluntly informed the Spaniard that the islands belonged to His Britannic Majesty and warned him that the settlement on East Falkland must be evacuated within six months.[16] The Spanish vessel therewith made its way to Buenos Aires to report Hunt's defiance. As a result, Captain General Francisco P. Bucareli determined to send out an expedition of three vessels to overawe the British at Port Egmont and rid the island of the intruders. Entering the sound on February 20, 1770, the Spanish commander, Fernando de Rubalcava, warned Hunt by letter that the British were there in violation of treaties and cautioned him and the settlers to depart peacefully. He then returned to Buenos Aires. Soon after his departure Hunt sailed to England to make a report.[17]

---

[14] This was embodied in the report sent by French *chargé d'affaires* Durand to Choiseul from London on September 26, 1766; for this see Julius Goebel Jr.: *op. cit.*, p. 246. For an extensive discussion of the diplomacy of this period involving the Falklands see *ibid.*, pp. 246–72.

[15] In the absence of Lord Harcourt, British ambassador to the French court, the Hon. Robert Walpole, as minister plenipotentiary and *chargé d'affaires*, figured prominently in the opening scenes of the crisis over the Falklands. See *British Diplomatic Instructions, 1689–1789, VII, France, Part IV, 1745–1789* (ed. L. G. W. Legg, Royal Historical Society, London, 1934), Camden Third Series, XLIX, xix and 107.

[16] Hunt's written exchanges with Governor Felipe Ruiz Puente of Soledad and later with Rubalcava are embodied in *Papers Relating to the Late Negotiation with Spain and the taking of Falkland's Island from the English* (London, 1777).

[17] Hunt seems to have carried with him a rather long letter—written from Port Egmont on March 4, 1770, by a Thomas Coleman, apparently a lieutenant of the marines—which referred to the warning from the Spanish commander, who "said he should not act any further at present, but wait for further orders from his court." In the letter Coleman affirmed that there were 150 people at Puerto de la Soledad who were being constantly reinforced and supplied; by contrast, at Port Egmont

Captain General Bucareli now determined to take decisive action and settle the matter once for all. Accordingly, he sent an expedition against Port Egmont under command of Don Juan Ignacio de Madariaga on May 17, 1770, consisting of four frigates and a xebec (a three-masted Mediterranean-type vessel), carrying in all 1,400 troops. Arriving at the British settlement early in June, the Spanish commander threatened to use force unless the British should evacuate peacefully. At first the defenders rejected the surrender terms and even went so far as to order the Spaniards to withdraw. But after Don Madariaga fired on the blockhouse, Captain George Farmer, acting in the absence of Hunt, surrendered and the garrison at Port Egmont was evacuated.[18] The Spanish commander thereupon sailed directly to Madrid with the news of the surrender. His arrival was well in advance of the sloop *Favourite* bearing the British garrison from the Falklands, which only reached England late in September. It was therefore possible for Prince de Masserano to be the first to inform Lord Weymouth, now British Secretary of State for the Southern Department, of what had happened. When he did so he indicated that Bucareli had acted without authorization from the court of Spain. Weymouth, after consultation with George III, advised the Spanish ambassador that the King demanded a disavowal of the act and the restoration of the colony. These demands were also embodied in instructions sent to James Harris, British *chargé d'affaires* in Madrid. When Harris made his representation to the Spanish minister, the Marqués de Grimaldi, the Marqués voiced conciliatory phrases but tended to justify the steps taken by Bucareli. It now became obvious that the centre of negotiations must be in London, if war were to be avoided.[19]

---

there were but two British detachments of marines, one, his own, consisting of twelve men, and the other of nine under a "brother officer"; the only other defences the English settlement had were "two miserable little sloops." See *Grenville Papers* (ed. W. J. Smith, 4 vols., London, 1853), IV, 505–8.

[18] According to the Duke of Grafton, the Spanish commander of the expedition had the rudders of the two British vessels removed so as to delay the departure of the garrison and thereby keep the news from reaching England until after the Spaniards could arrive in Madrid. Grafton called it "one of the most outrageous insults ever offered from one nation to another." The rudders were later restored. See *Autobiography and Political Correspondence of Augustus Henry, third Duke of Grafton* (ed. Sir Willian Anson, London, 1898), p. 254, to be cited hereafter as Grafton's *Autobiography*.

[19] For the complicated negotiations between Spain and France and Spain and Great Britain see Julius Goebel, Jr.: *op. cit.*, pp. 272–94. For the diplomatic exchanges between the British ambassadors in Spain and France, and the instructions from Secretary of State Weymouth to Robert Walpole in Paris in the autumn of 1770, see

As early as September 28 the Earl of Hillsborough, Secretary of State for the Colonies, wrote to General Gage in America warning him that, unless the court of Spain repudiated this act of hostility committed in time of peace, and made proper restitution, war would come. Gage was therefore to be prepared for a rupture of relations.[20] When Parliament met on November 13, its third session having ended in May, the King in his speech from the throne declared that the Governor of Buenos Aires, "in seizing by Force One of my Possessions," had struck at the honour of the Crown and the security and rights of the nation. He declared that preparations were in hand to protect the national interest in case satisfaction was not provided by Spain.[21] On November 29 the House of Commons ordered that a bill be brought in for "the better Supply of Mariners and Seamen to serve in His Majesty's Ships of War . . . ,"[22] and on December 10 large increases in the ground forces were proposed.[23] The next day

P.R.O., S.P. 78, Nos. 281, 282, 283, as printed in British Diplomatic Instructions, Camden Third Series, XLIX, 114–23.

[20] The Correspondence of General Thomas Gage, with the Secretaries of State, 1763–1775 (ed. C. E. Carter, 2 vols., New Haven, 1931 and 1933), II, 117–18, cited hereafter as Gage Correspondence.

[21] Journals of the House of Commons, XXXIII, 3. For the debates that took place in both Houses of Parliament over the wording of the addresses of thanks, see Parliamentary History, XVI, 1034–81. In each House some members spoke bitterly against the Ministry but in neither was there a division on the question of upholding the honour of the Crown over the issue. However, there was a demand on the part of some of the opposition for all the pertinent papers to be placed before them. Although the ministers spoke against spreading such data before the world at the height of the crisis, after the situation became less tense some forty-three papers, covering November 30, 1769, to October 17, 1770, were laid before the House of Commons on February 4, 1771. For the list see Journals of the House of Commons, XXXIII, 138–9.

[22] This bill was presented on December 3, 1770, to the House of Commons, where— after its several readings, during the course of which some amendments were engrossed on December 3 as introduced at a meeting of the committee of the whole— it passed on December 6 and was sent to the House of Lords; after passage there it received the King's assent on December 17. See Journals of the House of Commons, XXXIII, 31, 33, 46, 48, 69. For a statement by Lord North to the King on November 28, that "The 40,000 seamen pass'd today without a division in the Hˢ of Commons," see The Correspondence of King George the Third from 1760 to December 1783 (ed. Sir John Fortescue, 6 vols., London, 1927–28), II, 173, cited hereafter as Correspondence of George III (Fortescue). Actually, Great Britain was weak in naval power in 1770. From the £2,800,000 voted in 1766 for the maintenance of the navy, the amount had been reduced to £1,800,000 in 1767 and to £1,500,000 in 1768. According to Lord Sandwich, First Lord of the Admiralty, referring to the situation in 1770: "We had not above fifteen ships fit for the sea, and I believe the French and Spaniards were then superior to us and were more forward in their preparations" (The Private Papers of John, Earl of Sandwich [eds. G. R. Barnes and J. B. Owen, 4 vols., Navy Records Society Publications], I, 24). See also Admiral Sir Herbert Richmond: Statesmen and Sea Power (Oxford, 1947), pp. 141–4.

[23] For the "Estimate of the Charge of an Augumentation proposed to be made to

Hillsborough again warned Gage of the preparations for imminent war, since Spain had not yet repudiated the action of Don Bucareli.[24] The Cabinet Council also laid plans for striking crippling blows at Spain's naval bases, such as those at Ferrol, and in her New World possessions. With a declaration of war, offensive operations would begin in America by an attack on New Orleans. When communicating this design to General Gage, Commander-in-Chief of British Forces in North America, the Earl of Hillsborough pointed out:

> "The Advantages that would attend the entire Possession of the Mississippi, both in point of Commerce and of Security to the rest of the King's Possessions in North America, have been fully . . . explained in the course of our Correspondence; and those Advantages, combined with the general Intelligence of the small Number of Troops left in Louisiana by General O Reilly [O'Reilly], the Indisposition, or rather Aversion, of the French Inhabitants to the Spanish Government, the great Extent and Weakness of the Defences of the Town of New Orleans, and the supposed Practicability of approaching it either on the side of West Florida or by the Rivers Ohio and Mississippi, have been the Grounds on which this Proposition has been adopted."[25]

The Spanish court, doubtless realizing how vulnerable to attack were many of its Crown possessions in America—also aware that France was not yet internally prepared for a new war and that Choiseul was therefore opposed to hostilities that would, under the Family Pact, involve his country—acceded to the British demands.[26] On January 22, 1771, after messengers had moved back and forth between London and Madrid, Prince de Masserano handed Lord

His Majesty's Land Forces, for . . . 1771," see *Journals of the House of Commons,* XXXIII, 35; see also p. 57.

[24] *Gage Correspondence,* II, 121–2.

[25] Hillsborough to Gage, January 2, 1771, *Gage Correspondence,* II, 122–3. In the Cabinet Council Lord Weymouth proposed "giving the most fatal Blow that could be given to France by attacking them in the East Indies. . . ." Lord Rochford, Secretary of State for the Northern Department, opposed this, however, and assured the King that a majority would be against such a step. See Lord Rochford to the King, December 6, 1770, *Correspondence of George III* (Fortescue), II, 174–5. Did not Weymouth have in mind the Spanish possessions rather than those of France?

[26] For an excellent analysis of the negotiations that took place between the three powers and the difficult position in which Choiseul found himself before his dismissal from office on December 24, 1770, see D. A. Winstanley: *Lord Chatham and the Whig Opposition* (Cambridge, 1912), pp. 375–402. An even fuller account of the diplomacy is to be found in Julius Goebel, Jr., *op. cit.,* pp. 326–405.

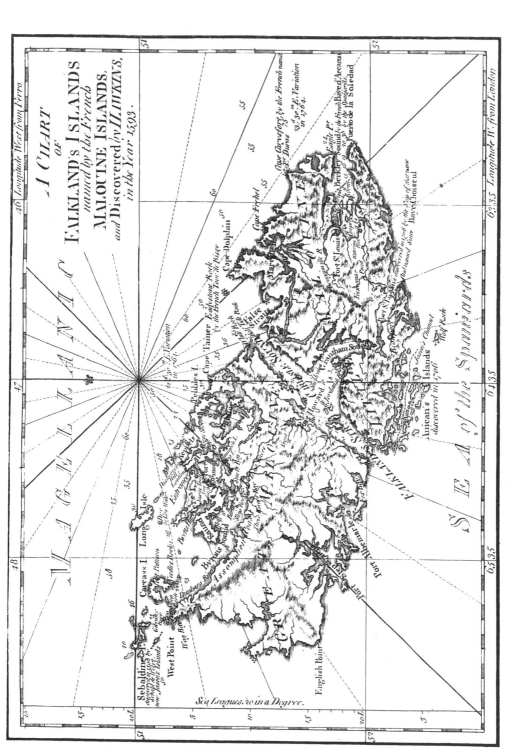

"A Chart of Falkland's Islands . . ." by J. Gibson, post 1764.

(From the Map Division, Library of Congress)

A View of the Barges conducting his DANISH MAJESTY from Whitehall to the Temple Sept. 23 1768 on his way to the Mansion House. Humbly Inscribed to his most Gracious Majesty CHRISTIAN VII. KING of DENMARK. &c. &c.

(From *Gentleman's Magazine*, 1768)

A view of London beyond the Thames, 1768.

Rochford a note in which His Catholic Majesty disavowed the "violent Interprise" of June 10, 1770, against the British settlement in the Falklands and declared that orders would be sent to deliver over to His Britannic Majesty Port Egmont together with all its stores and effects and the property of private individuals. However, the note pointed out that this resolution to seek a peaceful accommodation "cannot nor ought any wise to affect the Question of the prior Right of Sovereignty of the Malouine Islands, otherwise called Falkland's Islands."[27] In reply to this note Rochford was authorized to declare that the King would "look upon the said Declaration of Prince De Masserano, together with the full Performance of the said Engagement . . . , as a Satisfaction for the Injury done to the Crown of Great Britain."[28] By January 1772 the King was able to announce to Parliament that the King of Spain had fulfilled his engagement.[29] West Falkland had been restored to the British. Thus passed the threat of a new war. One cannot refrain from speculating on what might have been the history of the British Empire between 1770 and 1775 had hostilities taken place and had, for example, Spanish Louisiana been conquered and become British colonial territory. Would this have promoted or retarded the movement that was developing for colonial autonomy, if not independence? While this particular conjecture probably did not preoccupy the minds of those in London concerned with the administration of the Empire, the threat of war had undoubtedly been a serious concern, especially

---

[27] For the above translation of the Spanish note into English see *Journals of the House of Commons*, XXXIII, 88.

[28] For Rochford's reply see *ibid.* For the vote of thanks of the House of Commons to His Majesty for the solution of the crisis see *ibid.*, XXXIII, 160.

[29] *Ibid.*, XXXIII, 409. It may be noted that the government of Great Britain had advised Spain of its lack of real interest in the Falklands and had announced that, after reoccupying Port Egmont, it would evacuate the place. This step took place on May 20, 1774. However, before the garrison left, it affixed an inscription to the blockhouse declaring that the Falkland Islands were "the sole right and property of His Most Sacred Majesty, George the Third. . . ." Early in 1811 the Spaniards likewise abandoned Puerto de Soledad on East Falkland. During the wars for the independence of Spanish America, the revolutionary government of La Plata occupied the islands in 1820. But later, when Americans were obstructed in their whaling activities off these islands, came the action of 1831 when Commander Duncan of the *Lexington* landed at Soledad and broke up the settlement. Although the Argentinians returned, early in 1833 two British warships appeared before the port, now renamed Port Luis, and ordered them to depart. Since then Great Britain has continued to occupy the islands. These events are presented in great detail by Goebel (*Struggle for the Falkland Islands . . .*, especially pp. 410–68), who queries the validity of Great Britain's position in the eyes of international law, just as in an earlier portion of his volume he questioned the soundness of the British position between 1765 and 1771.

when added to other ominous problems facing the hard-pressed administration, such as the problems raised by the East India Company.

The Financial Crisis of the East India Company

Although the British Crown was not to acquire new territory in North America, there was to occur an expansionist movement in the opposite direction—the subcontinent of India. There the United East India Company, faced with near anarchy—especially in southern India, where the local princes were feuding among themselves—was beginning to assume greater responsibilities for territorial administration. This was so despite the efforts of the Directors of the Company in 1768 to warn their servants in India that there must be no additional expansion. "If we pass these bounds," they had declared, referring to the limited areas already controlled by the Company, "we shall be led on from one acquisition to another, till we shall find no security but in the subjection of the whole, which by dividing your force, would lose us the whole, and end in our extirpation from Hindoostan."[30]

Consideration of the problems of governing India after the departure of Clive in 1766 must be reserved for the final chapters of this series (which will be concerned with those parts of the Empire that did not renounce allegiance to the Crown in 1776). However, the affairs of the East India Company produced a critical situation which must be considered here, for the effort to maintain a semblance of order and security in India involved the company administrators in unexpectedly heavy expenditures. As has been stated in Chapter III of the preceding volume, in "A State of the Companys' Revenue for the Year 1766" it was estimated that the total net revenue—that is, after all expenses were paid—would amount to the sum of £2,136,977.5.[31] But by 1773 this vision of great prosperity had vanished. Indeed, George Johnstone, late Governor of East Florida, speaking for the East India Company before the House of Commons on May 19, 1773, made clear that the Company was in danger of bankruptcy, a plight brought about by the statutory neces-

---

[30] For an excerpt from this letter see Henry Beveridge: *A Comprehensive History of India* . . . (3 vols., London, 1858–72), II, 261.

[31] George Grenville Papers, Stowe Collection, Box 102, Huntington Library.

sity of paying the government an annual sum of £400,000,[32] as well as by the need to make good "the losses of Fort St. George, Fort St. David's, and two expensive wars, . . . the loss of a complete investment of £300,000, two sums alone amounting to £700,000, besides the expences of wars, . . . and besides the sum of £200,000 paid for the renewal of their charter . . ." In fact, Johnstone admitted, "during that period [that is, between 1765 and 1772] we run £800,000 in debt. . . ."[33] Nor was this the full extent of the financial embarrassments facing the United East India Company. In 1767, in addition to having engaged itself to pay the government the annual sum mentioned above, it had, with a view toward encouraging the sale of its great surplus of tea, committed itself to make good any loss in government revenues resulting from the abolishment for a period of five years of the inland duties on tea and the drawbacks of duties on this article re-exported to Ireland and the colonies.[34] Obviously it was impossible for the Company to meet the demands upon its treasury with available revenues. Thus on March 2, 1773, the proprietors felt it necessary not only to apply to the government for a loan of £1,500,000 at a low rate of interest, but also to request "that the Company be released from the heavy penal interest incurred by the non-payment of money due to the public, by virtue of the late acts of parliament respecting the indemnity on teas, and the agreement for payment of £400,000 per annum, for five years, from the 1st of February 1769, into the receipt of his Majesty's exchequer. . . ."[35]

It is unwarranted, at this point, to discuss in detail the debates over the East India Company that took place in Parliament from March until June 1773. Suffice it to say that the Company was strongly attacked for the mismanagement of its affairs by its servants in India as well as for their venality. It was also strongly defended.[36]

---

[32] The agreement between the government of Great Britain and the Company in 1767 was embodied in 7 Geo. III, c. 57; for the extension in 1769 for five years, see 9 Geo. III, c. 24.

[33] Parliamentary History, XVII, 885–6.

[34] 7 Geo. III, c. 56.

[35] Parliamentary History, XVII, 800.

[36] In the account of these debates Lord North appears to advantage, despite his characteristic disposition to express a certain diffidence when approaching a problem such as that of maintaining a good relationship between the government and the East India Company. General Burgoyne, later to win fame in the War for American Independence, took the lead in the attack on the Company, and especially on Lord Clive, by introducing resolutions that would turn all the Company's acquisitions over to the state and appropriate to the state all gifts secured by Clive. Edmund Burke spoke at length in opposition to the government in its attack upon the Company. In

A Select Committee and a Secret Committee had been appointed by the House of Commons to investigate East India Company affairs; each issued a series of reports.[37] Out of this protracted and concentrated consideration, the need for reform in the internal affairs of the Company and for external financial help became clear. The result was the passage of three acts: first, "An Act to allow a Drawback of the Duties of Customs on the Exportation of Tea to any of his Majesty's Colonies or Plantations in America; to increase the Deposit on Bohea Tea to be sold at the India Company's Sales; and to impower the Commissioners of the Treasury to grant Licences to the East India Company to export Tea Duty-free" (the Tea Act, 13 George III, c. 44);[38] second, "An Act for establishing certain Regulations for the better Management of the Affairs of the *East India* Company, as well in *India* as in *Europe*" (the Regulating Act, 13 George III, c. 63); and, third, the act which provided for loans to keep the Company solvent (the Loan or Relief Act, 13 George III, c. 64).[39] It is only the first of these laws that need concern us at this point.

On April 27, 1773, a series of resolutions in the House of Commons had been offered by the committee of the whole House for the relief of the East India Company. These embodied, among other things, three resolutions that were to become the basis for the Tea Act of 1773.[40] On this occasion Lord North is reported to have declared that, were the Company to be allowed to export to America from its warehouses in London such amounts of tea, free of duty, as it thought proper, it would be "prodigiously to the advantage of the

turn Solicitor General Wedderburn, although holding a post in the government, rose to the defence of Clive and denounced the reports of the Secret Committee indicting the Company as narrow and invidious. Finally, Clive defended his conduct while at the head of affairs in India. Out of these debates came the legislation that produced a temporary settlement of East India Company affairs and first involved the government in active management of the Company through the Treasury, a subject that will be discussed in full in the final chapters of the series. For the debates in Parliament see *ibid.*, XVII, 799–831, 840, 848–931.

[37] For the five reports of the Select Committee of the House of Commons published in the House of Commons *Reports, II* (London, 1772) see *Parliamentary Papers, 1731–1800*, Vol. 32 of the *General Collection*. For the nine reports of the Committee of Secrecy published in 1772–3, see *ibid.*, Vols. 32–3, *British Sessional Papers, House of Commons, 1731–1800* (ed. E. L. Erickson), Readex Microprint.

[38] *Statutes at Large*, VIII, 228–30. This bill received the King's approval on May 10, 1773.

[39] *Ibid.*, VIII, 248–57. The circumstances under which the Regulating Bill and the Loan Bill were passed, which established parliamentary supremacy over the affairs of the East India Company, will be dealt with in Volume XIII of this series.

[40] For these resolutions see *Journals of the House of Commons*, XXXIV, 286.

Company, as they have at present above 17,000,000 pound[s] by them. The converting a part of it into money would greatly ease them, and be attended with these good consequences which are now so necessary to re-establish their affairs. . . ."[41] Even earlier a writer in the *Gentleman's Magazine* had pointed out that, in addition to the 17,000,000 pounds of tea on hand, thirteen ships from China would bring in 8,000,000 pounds of tea in the course of 1773 and ten ships, returning home in 1774, would bring in 6,000,000 additional pounds—making a total of 31,000,000 pounds—with the prospect of selling only 13,000,000 pounds in the course of these two years, thus leaving an enormous surplus in the warehouses of the distressed Company.[42] That the tea could not be sold cheaper abroad under current restrictions seemed to be clear to the same writer, who asserted that it was priced 15⅓ per cent cheaper than the tea sold by the French East India Company (La Compagnie des Indes Orientales) at L'Orient, France, 34⅔ per cent cheaper than in Holland, and 46⅓ per cent lower than at Gothenburg (Göteborg), Sweden, but could not be brought into competition. To move this present and vast future surplus, he pleaded that the government give the Company the same privileges of free exportation as were enjoyed by competing foreign companies. Another factor that had been contributing to the precarious situation of the East India Company's trade and its surpluses of tea in British warehouses was the problem of smuggling. In the British Isles the smugglers had built a veritable commerce of their own, especially in tea; for there was a brisk trade in the cheaper Bohea species brought from Holland to most of the English port towns.[43] Similarly, there existed in North America a

---

[41] *Parliamentary History*, XVII, 840–1.

[42] Benjamin Franklin, writing from London to Thomas Cushing on January 5, 1773, observed that "the India Company is so out of Cash, that it cannot pay the bills drawn upon it, and its other Debts; and at the same time so out of Credit, that the Bank [of England] does not care to assist them, when they find themselves obliged to lower their Dividend; the Apprehension of which has sunk their Stock from 280 to 160, whereby several Millions of Property are annihilated, occasioning private Bankruptcies and other Distress, besides a loss to the Public of £400,000 per Annum . . ." (*Writings of Benjamin Franklin* [ed. A. H. Smyth, 10 vols., New York, 1905–7], VI, 2–3). An item under date-head London, July 6, in the *Pennsylvania Gazette* of September 8, 1773, reported that the Company, being "vastly overstocked with goods, which are absolutely spoiling, some having lain in their warehouses for seven years, particularly tea," was "determined to take up this year into their service no more than twelve ships."

[43] *Gentleman's Magazine*, December 1772, XLII, 547–50. For the effect of the smuggling trade on the economy of the British Isles, particularly in tea, see G. D. Ramsay: "The Smugglers' Trade . . . ," Royal Historical Society *Transactions*, 5th

thriving illicit commerce in tea, especially the Dutch variety. This illegal trade was to become an important key in the events surrounding colonial resistance to the implementation of the Tea Act.[44] For this smuggling of tea from Holland was made amply clear to the East India Company and was used by them, and those seeking to establish connections with them, as a strong argument for anticipating success in wiping out the illicit trade by selling their product at a cheaper rate in the colonies.

As has been mentioned, what had become clear was that the Company, far from being in the prosperous condition it had anticipated in 1767, was by 1773 apparently on the verge of collapse—an eventuality with highly dangerous potential consequences to the nation on account of the Company's size and the amount of public investment in it. Now, with the passage of the legislation permitting the export of tea, in addition to the Regulating Act and the Loan Act, a prospect was held out for restoring the East India Company's one-time prosperity. For embodied in the Tea Act was a new feature. Heretofore, the Company's tea had been sold—"openly and fairly, by Way of Auction, or by Inch of Candle, within the Space of three Years from the Importation thereof"—to those who bought in quantity and who either resold it within Great Britain to retailers or exported it to Ireland or America, under existing restrictions, where it was likewise disposed of to retailers. Now it was possible for the Company to secure a licence from the Treasury to take out

---

ser., II, 131–57, and W. A. Cole: "Trends in Eighteenth-Century Smuggling," *Economic History Review*, 2nd ser., X, 395–410. For the efforts made to control smuggling activities based on the Isle of Man see Volume X of this series, pp. 194–9.

[44] For a broad account of the legal and illegal importation of tea into the colonies between the years 1770 and 1773 see A. M. Schlesinger: *The Colonial Merchants* . . . (New York, 1918), pp. 245–51 and 264–7. According to figures compiled from the customs reports, as presented by O. M. Dickerson (*The Navigation Acts and the American Revolution* [Philadelphia, 1951], p. 89), the average yearly legal import of tea between 1763 and 1768 was 328,125 pounds, whereas from 1768 to 1772 (after the Townshend Revenue Acts) it was 295,876 pounds. Between 1768 and the end of 1772 the ports of New England, New York, and Philadelphia imported legally 1,479,382 pounds of tea with New England bringing in the bulk, that is, 895,847 pounds. See *ibid.*, p. 99. Despite the implications of these figures, Professor Dickerson draws different conclusions with respect to the illegal trade in Dutch tea, which he maintains (pp. 91, 100, 101) was chiefly a matter of rumor circulated by government partisans or those seeking advantage with the East India Company. For a table of tea importations by the American colonies, 1761–75, compiled by Professor L. A. Harper from the English Inspector General's Ledgers, P.R.O., Customs 3, see *Historical Statistics of the United States*, . . . *Colonial Times to 1957* (Washington, D.C., 1960), pp. 750, 767, and, for a discussion of the value of exports to and imports from England by the American colonies, 1697–1776, see *ibid.*, p. 744.

of the warehouses whatever quantity it pleased—always reserving, however, 10,000,000 pounds for a possible national emergency— and, without submitting it to public sale, export it to appointed agents in the British colonies or to foreign ports and there sell it "discharged from the Payment of any Customs or Duties whatsoever. . . ."[45]

After the passing of the Tea Act on May 10, 1773, the East India Company immediately began negotiations for putting into effect a plan to export 600,000 pounds of tea to the chief American ports, Boston, New York, Philadelphia, and Charleston. Within the next few weeks the Company's Directors had received numerous applications from merchants in London trading to the colonies seeking to arrange for factors in America to distribute the tea. In the course of these negotiations the Company had also placed before it by these same men recommendations as to which species of tea might best be introduced into America, methods for accomplishing this, and a comprehensive report on the state of the tea trade in America.[46] This collective report—in the form of extracts from letters, chiefly from Boston, written between April 29, 1771, and February 25, 1773—made clear that the Bohea teas imported illegally from Holland had been ruining the market for the legal colonial importers of tea from England to such a degree that both New York and Pennsylvania were importing no English tea and Rhode Island very little. The report also compared the consumption of tea at Boston,

---

[45] *Statutes at Large*, VIII, 230.

[46] For the letter of William Palmer (a merchant who claimed to have "been concerned in a great part of the tea which has been shipped to America since . . . 1767") to the East India Company's Directors stating his desire to ship an assortment of Congou, Souchong, Hyson, and the several species of Singlo teas, see *Tea Leaves: Being a Collection of Letters and Documents Relating to the Shipment of Tea to the American Colonies in the Year 1773, by the East India Tea Company* (ed. F. S. Drake, Boston, 1884), p. 190, see also pp. 241–2; for Palmer's second plan, which indicates that he may have been seeking to become an exclusive agent for the Company, see *ibid.*, pp. 205–7. For the "State of the Tea Trade in America" see *ibid.*, pp. 191–8.

Tea Leaves, it may be noted, is a very important work of scholarship and is indispensable to the student concerned with the subject of the attempts to put the Tea Act of 1773 into operation. Benjamin W. Labaree, who in 1963 was engaged in writing his volume on the tea crisis, gave an illuminating talk before the Colonial Society of Massachusetts in the spring of that year, in which he stressed the point that many documents relating to the crisis that should be among the United East India Company papers in the Public Record Office are not to be found there; in fact, the only evidence of their existence is their reproduction in *Tea Leaves*. See in this connection B. W. Labaree *The Boston Tea Party* (New York, 1964), p. 283. Unhappily this new work, which appears to be an exhaustive and richly documented study of the subject, was published too late for adequate use in this volume.

Charleston, and New York, and gave a detailed account of the methods used by the Dutch traders.[47]

A memorial to the Directors of the East India Company from the Philadelphia merchant Gilbert Barkly (Barkley, Barclay), sent on May 26, 1773, proposed that the Company should open a branch "in one of the principal, & central cities, of North America." The memorial also elaborated a scheme for undercutting the smugglers by providing a speedy supply of tea for the American market, which was estimated to consume annually 5,703,125 pounds of leaves.[48] By June 25 the "Committee of Warehouses" of the Company had received a sufficient number of petitions from merchants in London offering to advance security for shipment to the consignees in America recommended by them—for which security they would charge interest—to warrant calling a preliminary meeting at the East India House on that date.[49] However, before July 17, when a second meeting was called[50] to confirm the appointment of the agents in the colonies to receive the tea, the Chairman of the Company had apparently received an unsigned report suggesting that "if a proper application was made to the ministry, . . . it might produce a relaxation of that disagreeable and fatal duty of 3d. pr lb.," and calling attention to previous colonial resolutions not to import tea until the duty should be removed. "There is another difficulty," this communication continued, "and that is, there is not so much specie in the country as would pay for the quantity [of tea] . . . intended to be exported." In conclusion it warned that "there may be an opposition made by some of the Provinces upon a surmise that Government is aiding in this plan, and mean to establish [both] principle and right of taxation, for the purpose of a revenue, which at present is very obnoxious . . . great care should be had not to employ either paymaster, collector, or any other gentleman under the immediate service of the Crown, to receive the money."[51] Thus, it

---

[47] *Tea Leaves*, pp. 191–8.

[48] *Ibid.*, p. 199. In a later letter of June 29, 1773, Barkly suggested that the Company absorb the duty of threepence per pound; he also pointed out that "the Americans have not money to pay for those goods" (sterling, that is), but opined that there would be ample foreign silver and gold, together with bills of exchange, received from foreign trade to enrich the Company, *ibid.*, pp. 216–17. For Grey Cooper's endorsement of Barkly see *ibid.*, pp. 211–12; see also the Hon. Thomas Walpole's proposal for making Philadelphia the centre of colonial distribution, *ibid.*, pp. 203–5.

[49] *Ibid.*, p. 215.

[50] *Ibid.*, p. 235.

[51] For these undated "Thoughts upon the East India Company's Sending out

would appear that the Company had at least some warning of how the Tea Act would be received in America but that its Directors chose to ignore these potential threats. Instead they saw only the optimistic outlook indicated by the eager vying of the London merchants for the Company's American trade. For these men continued to push their business with the Company and to anticipate their profits, as may be seen, for example, by William Kelly's letter of July 5, 1773, to the Committee of Warehouses, showing the terms under which the factors were to do business with the Company.[52]

As for the government itself, it continued to be faced with pressing problems—whether over domestic issues, foreign affairs, or the growing-pains of Empire. The relative ease with which the administration had been able to handle the crisis with Spain over the Falkland Islands, as well as the financial aspects of the East India Company's crucial relationship to India, may well be contrasted to the baffling complexity of the problems with which it was faced in the crises that followed in rapid succession in the American colonies in 1773 and thereafter.

The Crisis over Enforcement of Trade Regulations in America

It is clear from evidence presented earlier in the two preceding volumes of this series that a new colonial viewpoint had begun to crystallize by 1765. The colonial position that taxation without representation was unconstitutional was gradually being expanded into

---

Teas to America," submitted to the Company's chairman, see *ibid.*, pp. 218–21. See also John Norton's statement of July 6, 1773, as a prominent American merchant in London: "I advised the gentlemen [in the India Direction] not to think of sending their Tea till Government took off the duty, as they might be well assured it would not be received on any other terms. . . ." This statement is to be found in Norton's letter to the Virginia committee of correspondence, after he had been selected by it to act in something of the capacity of a London agent. See *John Norton & Sons, Merchants of London and Virginia, . . . Papers . . . 1750–1795* (ed. F. N. Mason, Richmond, 1937), p. 337.

[52] For Kelly's letter see *Tea Leaves*, pp. 224–5. The terms given were on a commission basis of 6 per cent of the gross sales after paying "the cartage, warehouse rent, brokerage, and other charges incidental to the sale." For their part the Company agents in London, according to this letter, hoped to get preferential treatment in the use of their ships to carry the tea, which was to be done at the risk and expense of the Company. Kelly, a native New Yorker, had been a resident of London for some years. For his testimony during the great debate on the Stamp Act in 1766 see the article by L. H. Gipson in *Pennsylvania Magazine of History and Biography*, LXXXVI, 32.

a general challenge of the authority of Parliament to legislate for America. Coupled with this was the view that Americans should enjoy all the rights of Englishmen. Among other such rights demanded was that of trial by jury, especially in cases having to do with the enforcement of the trade and navigation acts. Although in England men accused of violating the trade acts were entitled to this right, in the plantations similar cases might, at the option of the prosecution, be tried in a court of vice-admiralty, which, functioning under civil law rather than common law, made no provision for a jury.[53] This became the ground for a serious colonial grievance against the mother country. In its Declaration of Rights, the Continental Congress in 1774 resolved: "That the respective colonies are entitled to the common law of England, and more especially to the great and inestimable privilege of being tried by their peers of the vicinage, according to the course of that law."[54] Yet it must be pointed out that eighteenth-century English officials were aware from experience that local juries would seldom convict one of their community of smuggling or any other violation of the trade laws.[55] As a result, in England such cases were usually transferred by the customs officials to the Court of Exchequer in London, where jury trials were less prejudiced.[56] In America, with the passage of the comprehensive Trade and Navigation Act in 1696 (7 and 8 William III, c. 22), a system of vice-admiralty courts was established for the colonies.[57] Very naturally, customs officials, given the choice proffered by this statute, could and did resort to these courts without juries.

In preceding volumes of this series, emphasis has been placed on the efforts of the British government between 1764 and 1767 to strengthen the American customs system and vice-admiralty jurisdiction so as to make them more effective agencies for the enforce-

---

[53] See Volume XI of this series, Chap. 4.

[54] *Journals of the Continental Congress, 1774–1789* (eds. W. C. Ford *et al.*, 34 vols., Washington, 1904–37), I, 69.

[55] However Professor L. A. Harper, in his *The English Navigation Laws: A Seventeenth-Century Experiment in Social Engineering* (New York, 1939, p. 195), presents figures to indicate that seventeenth-century American juries made a creditable record of convicting trade violators.

[56] For a thorough treatment of the Court of Exchequer in relation to violations of the trade acts see *ibid.*, pp. 109–23.

[57] For the beginning of vice-admiralty courts in the colonies see Helen J. Crump: *Colonial Admiralty Jurisdiction in the Seventeenth Century* (London, 1931); see also the "Introduction" written by Professor C. M. Andrews for the volume edited by Dorothy S. Towle: *The Records of the Vice-Admiralty Court of Rhode Island, 1715–1752*.

ment of the trade laws. In so far as this was accomplished, it added to the intensity of the dislike engendered in American traders for both the customs service and the vice-admiralty courts. The hatred —as reflected by the populace in the chief ports of entry, especially after 1770—may best be illustrated by events that took place in the Delaware River and Narragansett Bay.

In November 1771, only a few months after the setting up in Philadelphia of the new Court of Vice-Admiralty for the Middle District,[58] an attempt was made by customs official John Musket, acting under orders of the collector at this port, to bring a condemnation case before the court. The case concerned a pilot boat which Musket had seized as it moved up the Delaware River after the crew had refused to open the hatches for inspection. The boat had been found to contain a cargo of wine and tea not covered by proper entrance papers. After the revenue schooner conveyed it some distance up the river, Musket ordered anchors cast for the night. Some time afterwards in the darkness a second pilot boat drew up with thirty heavily armed men aboard dressed as sailors and with blackened faces. They boarded the revenue vessel, wounded Musket and two of his assistants, and threw them and the rest of the crew into the hold of the schooner, which they then conveyed to a sand-bar and left to its fate, after cutting the sails and rigging. Thereupon they took possession of the seized pilot boat with its illegal cargo and disappeared.[59] Although Lieutenant Governor Richard Penn issued a proclamation offering a reward of £200, together with a pardon to any person implicated in the attack who would furnish information leading to the arrest and arraignment of the offenders,[60] no one ventured to provide the information. There were other instances of militant objections on the part of colonials to the condemnation cases brought by the customs service before the vice-admiralty courts,[61] but the most glaring example of the hostility

---

[58] The four district courts of vice-admiralty for North America were actually created under the Great Seal in 1768, but there was delay in setting up the court in Philadelphia. See Volume XI in this series, Chap. 4.

[59] For an account of this episode see *Pennsylvania Gazette*, December 12, 1771.

[60] *Ibid.*

[61] For additional cases of colonial opposition in this period see O. M. Dickerson: *The Navigation Acts . . .* , and Carl Ubbelohde: *The Vice-Admiralty Courts and the American Revolution* (Chapel Hill, N.C., 1960). For the active smuggling trade to Philadelphia and the precarious position of the customs officers there and in the waters leading to this port as early as 1769, see William Sheppard's letter to the Commissioners of Customs in Boston of April 1, 1769, Massachusetts Historical Society *Collections*, 4th ser., X, 611–17; see also A. S. Martin: "The King's Customs: Philadelphia, 1763–1771," *William and Mary Quarterly*, 3rd ser., V, 201–16.

of the public to those involved in enforcing the trade and navigation acts occurred in Rhode Island waters the year following the attack on Musket's customs vessel.

All students of the history of the American colonies of this period have been confronted by the fact that there are no available statistics to indicate the extent to which illicit trade was carried on by the people of Rhode Island. One can assume that it was widely practiced, if the trading operations of the Brown brothers of Providence were typical.[62] Even in time of war, both in 1757 and in 1762, the merchants of this little colony had been singled out by the commanding generals of the British Forces in North America and accused of trading with the enemy.[63] The deep hostility of the traders to those customs officers whom they could not corrupt and to the enforcement service itself was already manifest in the 1760's, as was shown in a previous volume of this series.[64] At that time there occured successively the abortive seizure of the *Rhoda* early in 1764, the attempt to destroy the revenue schooner *St. John* in July of that year,[65] and in 1765 the seizure of the *Wainscott* and the *Nelly* for running contraband and the attempt to seize the *Polly*.[66]

The next important event which took place in Rhode Island waters was on July 17, 1769, with the destruction of H.M. *Liberty*, a sloop commanded by Captain William Reid (Read). Reid had seized a

---

[62] J. B. Hedges: *The Browns of Providence Plantations. Colonial Years* (Cambridge, Mass., 1952), pp. 43–6 *et seq.* For the memorial signed in 1750 by the London agents of Jamaica, Barbados, St. Christopher, and Montserrat and over fifty planters and merchants, pointing to Rhode Island as the leading colony engaged in contraband trade, see P.R.O., C.O. 323:13, O. 59–60; see also this series revised Volumes II, 255–7, and III, 59–62.

[63] The Earl of Loudoun to Governor William Greene, October 9, 1757, Loudoun Papers, No. 4615, Huntington Library; Jeffrey Amherst to Governor Hopkins, May 7, 1762, *Rhode Island Colonial Records* (10 vols., ed. J. R. Bartlett, Providence, 1856–65), VI, 317–18.

[64] See Volume X, 242–4.

[65] The affair began when Lieutenant Thomas Hill of the *St. John* seized 93 hogsheads of sugar illegally landed from the *Basto*, a vessel from Monte Christi, and subsequently the vessel itself. See *Acts of the Privy Council, Col. Ser., 1745–1766*, pp. 690–2, for reports on this incident; see also *Rhode Island Colonial Records*, VI, 427–30, for extracts of letters from Rear Admiral Lord Colville, Commander-in-Chief of the British naval forces in North American waters, with a copy of Lieutenant Hill's report of the incident. One extenuating circumstance was that three of the crew of the *St. John* were accused of stealing; one had already been arrested and the other two were sought. When the Rhode Island authorities boarded H.M.S. *Squirrel*, which protected the *St. John*, her lieutenant promised to deliver the sailors. However, the matter of theft by the sailors was surely only incidental in creating the hostility displayed against the customs service.

[66] See Volume X in this series, pp. 243–4.

brig and a sloop, both from Connecticut, and conducted them to Newport for condemnation on charges that the brig was engaged in illicit trade and that the sloop had contraband on board. According to the published accounts, while Captain Reid was on shore, the commander of the brig, Captain Packwood, returned by harbour boat to his vessel in order to get certain possessions. He was rebuffed by the customs-service sailors, but after discovering that the objects of his search had been removed to the *Liberty*, he managed to get back into the harbour boat with two of his hands and row to shore, despite being under musket fire from the *Liberty*. In view of the behaviour of his crew, and at the insistence of the crowd, Reid ordered his men ashore to answer for their misconduct. This was no sooner accomplished than the cables of the government vessel were severed by those who planned its destruction. They brought the sloop to the wharf, cut down the mast, and threw overboard everything of value, including the armament. Soon afterward the *Liberty* drifted to Goat Island, where, during the night, it was burnt. Meanwhile, the two vessels that had been seized sailed away.[67]

Although the matter was considered sufficiently serious to come before the Privy Council, no action was taken,[68] probably because of confusion within the Cabinet Council, the decline in prestige of the Duke of Grafton, and the increasing influence of Lord North, who became the King's chief minister early in 1770. The British government's failure to take any steps to bring to justice those who had destroyed the *Liberty* undoubtedly added to the feeling of confidence of Rhode Islanders and others that they could threaten with impunity any of the King's ships that seriously interfered with their trade.[69]

[67] *Providence Gazette; and Country Journal,* July 22, 1769; *Pennsylvania Gazette,* August 3, 1769; *Rhode Island Colonial Records,* VI, 593–6, and VII, 59. Very full reports of the destruction of the *Liberty* are among the Treasury Papers in the Public Record Office. See P.R.O., Treas. 1:471, ff. 200–26 and 289–93; for the American Board of Customs report on Commander Reid's memorial see *ibid.,* 1:482, f. 206.

[68] *Acts of the Privy Council, Col. Ser., 1766–1783,* p. 227.

[69] In a report to the King dated June 22, 1773, the royal commission appointed in 1772 to investigate the destruction of the *Gaspee* listed among the probable causes of the late defiance of the royal authority in Rhode Island the following: "The great impatience of some people, in this colony, under any restraint of trade, however illicit; the check which Your Majesty's navy officers have put to such trade . . . ; the plundering and burning a sloop, called the *Liberty,* in this harbor [Newport], in July, 1769, then employed in Your Majesty's revenue service, and commanded by William Reid, liberating a vessel and cargo, then under seizure by said commander, and in a violent and outrageous manner assaulting and detaining him in this town,

In March 1772 H.M. *Gaspee,* a schooner commanded by Lieutenant William Dudingston, appeared in Rhode Island waters. It is extremely difficult to get a true picture of this ship's activities at this period. Those hostile to its commander asserted that he "boarded, searched, and maltreated every Vessel" he met with, "not shewing any Commission or Authority, for so doing. . . ."[70] Chief Justice Stephen Hopkins of the Superior Court—a most popular person who had been repeatedly elected Governor of the colony—when asked by the Deputy Governor for his opinion of the activities of Dudingston in Rhode Island waters, took the position "that for any person, whatever, to come into this colony, and in the body thereof, to exercise any authority . . . without showing his commission to the Governor, and, if a custom house officer, without being sworn to his office [by the Governor], was guilty of a trespass, if not piracy."[71] This opinion, of course, implied that these formalities were a prerequisite for any of the King's vessels appearing off the coast of the colony for the purpose of helping to enforce the trade acts. That, upon his arrival, Lieutenant Dudingston had duly waited upon Governor Joseph Wanton and notified him of his purpose was not disputed. Dudingston, in answer to the charges levelled by the Governor on March 22 and on complaint of others that he was acting "in a most illegal and unwarrantable manner," replied that when he had waited upon Wanton in person he had his commission in hand to show, if so required. The charges were contained in a letter from the Governor carried by the high sheriff of Newport County with the request that Dudingston present his commission and instructions without delay. The Lieutenant answered that he did not feel bound by duty or custom to do anything more than send one of his officers, a man qualified to provide "any information relative to my proceeding."[72]

---

in duress, till the accomplishment of the above facts; the same night, dragging two boats, belonging to said sloop, through the streets, and burning them; and the perpetrators of the above outrage, escaped with impunity; not one person being so much as apprehended on this occasion" (*Rhode Island Colonial Records,* VII, 180).

[70] See the article by "Providentia" in the *Providence Gazette,* January 9, 1773. See also D. S. Lovejoy: *Rhode Island Politics and the American Revolution* (Providence, 1958), pp. 158–9, for a very unfavourable account of the activities of Dudingston.

[71] *Rhode Island Colonial Records,* VII, 180; see also Deputy Governor Sessions to Governor Wanton, March 21, 1772, *ibid.,* VII, 60–1.

[72] See Wanton to "the Commanding Officer [Dudingston] of a Schooner near Brenton's Point," March 22, 1772, *ibid.,* VII, 61, and Dudingston to Wanton, March 23, 1772, *ibid.* Writing to Rear Admiral J. Montagu on May 22, 1772, Dudingston,

There is little doubt that Dudingston was actively pursuing his mission by attempting to stamp out smuggling in the area of his assignment. In doing so, however, he was faced by the hostility not only of the trading element in Rhode Island but also of the chief officers of the government. Although the crew of his vessel was accused of "stealing sheep, hogs, poultry etc.,"[73] this was not mentioned by the royal commission of investigation as one of the causes of the incident which subsequently took place, even though the chairman of the board of inquiry, the Governor of the colony, would surely have seen that any lawless activity by the personnel of the *Gaspee* had not gone uncensured in the report. The board later stressed two points: (1) the possible influence on the minds of the people of the previously mentioned opinion of Chief Justice Hopkins, and (2) that there was "too much reason to believe, that in some instances Lieutenant Dudingston, from an intemperate, if not a reprehensible zeal to aid the revenue service, exceeded the bounds of his duty."[74] How far the trading element of the colony was determined to go to thwart the *Gaspee* by armed force—as they had done in the case of the *Liberty*—if a vessel were actually seized, was never made clear. However, Admiral Montagu informed Governor Wanton by letter on April 8, 1772, that he had received word that "the people of Newport talk of fitting out an armed vessel to rescue any vessel the King's schooner may take carrying on an illicit trade,"[75] which Wanton declared was "without any foundation and a scandalous imposition. . . ."[76]

Early in May the sloop-of-war *Beaver* was assigned to support the *Gaspee* in patrolling the waters off the colony.[77] That same month Dudingston seized a rum-laden ship, the property of the firm

---

in an attempt to reproduce his conversation with the Governor the morning after his ship had arrived at Newport, quotes himself as beginning the interview by stating: "Sir, I command His Majesty's schooner Gaspee, and am ordered into this government by Admiral Montagu, to assist the revenue" (*ibid.*, VII, 65).

[73] *Providence Gazette*, January 9, 1773; see also Henry Marchant to Benjamin Franklin, Newport, November 19, 1772, Marchant Letter Book, Newport Historical Society, quoted by D. S. Lovejoy: *Rhode Island Politics and the American Revolution, 1760–1776* (Providence, 1958), p. 158. In this letter Marchant wrote that Dudingston "suffered his People to commit many Outrages upon the Possessions and Property of the Inhabitants on Shore. . . ."

[74] *Rhode Island Colonial Records*, VII, 180.

[75] *Ibid.*, VII, 63. Montagu's letter warned the Governor that if a Rhode Island ship should attack the *Gaspee*, and any of the people involved should be captured, "I will hang them as pirates."

[76] Wanton to Montagu, May 8, 1772, *ibid.*

[77] *Providence Gazette*, May 9, 1772.

of Green & Co. of Warwick. Unwilling to rely on a court in Rhode Island to condemn the vessel, he sent it to Boston for condemnation in the district court of vice-admiralty.[78] According to an act passed by Parliament late in 1767 and approved by the King in March of the following year (8 George III, c. 22), the action was permitted legally, although denounced by Governor Wanton as an illegal act.[79] This step by the commander of the *Gaspee* would appear to have filled to the brim the cup of resentment of the trading people against him.[80] The opportunity to get revenge on Dudingston was afforded on June 9, 1772. On that day he left Newport for Providence to take on board some seamen due there from Boston.[81] The *Hannah*, Captain Thomas Lindsey, had left Newport shortly before for the same destination. According to Lindsey, his packet was pursued by Dudingston until the *Gaspee* ran aground at Namquit Point, some six miles from Providence.[82] As soon as the *Hannah* reached Providence, Lindsey hastened to inform John Brown, one of the famous Brown family trio of Rhode Island merchants, that the *Gaspee* was at last in their power and would remain so until the tide should rise some hours later.[83] Brown, a man of great decisiveness, acted at once. He ordered one of his ship-masters to collect

[78] *Boston Gazette*, August 10 and 17, 1772; see also Carl Ubbelohde: *op. cit.*, p. 156 and *n.*

[79] See *Statutes at Large*, VIII, 60–1; see also Wanton to the Earl of Hillsborough, May 20, 1772, *Rhode Island Colonial Records*, VII, 67. The act was passed in anticipation of the creation of the four district courts of vice-admiralty and gave these courts both concurrent and appeal jurisdiction within the district over cases of trade violations, as is discussed in Volume XI of this series, Chap. 4. It is clear that had Dudingston acted illegally in sending the vessel to Boston, the report of the board of inquiry would have mentioned that fact.

[80] See Dudingston to Admiral Montagu of June 12, 1772, written while suffering from a serious wound received in the capture of the *Gaspee*, in which he reported the sheriff as having told him that, unless he would agree to pay for the rum sent to Boston for condemnation, he should not have back any of his personal possessions taken from the *Gaspee* before it was burnt. See *Rhode Island Colonial Records*, VII, 86–7.

[81] Affidavits of Bartholomew Cheever, John Johnson, and William J. Caple on June 10, 1772, *ibid.*, VII, 78–9.

[82] Dudingston apparently had evidence that the *Hannah* was engaged in smuggling. At least General Gage, writing to Sir Jeffrey Amherst on July 1, stated that the *Gaspee* was in pursuit "of [a] Smuggling Vessel, which by that accident escaped being taken" (Amherst Papers, Canadian Archives transcripts).

[83] Whether or not the destruction of the *Gaspee* had long been planned is not certain. It was pictured as a spontaneous act by most contemporaries. However, a man named Charles Dudley, writing to an unknown person on July 23, 1772, stated: "The attack upon the Gaspee was not the effect of sudden passion and resentment, but of cool deliberation and fore-thought. . . . It had long been determined she should be destroyed" (*Rhode Island Colonial Records*, VII, 92).

at Fenner's wharf eight of the largest long-boats of five oars each that could be found in the harbour and to muffle the oars. Soon after sunset a drummer hurried through the town to notify the inhabitants of the plight of the *Gaspee* and to call upon those who would aid in its destruction to gather at Sabin's Inn near the wharf. There the men assembled, most of them heavily armed.

About ten o'clock that night they entered the boats, in each of which (according to the account left by one of the participants, Ephraim Bowen) a sea captain in command acted as steersman. Although Brown was present, one of his captains, Abraham Whipple, was in general charge of the operation. The boats moved forward in the stillness of the night. They were some sixty yards from the *Gaspee* when a sentinel challenged them twice. No answer came from the darkness. Hearing the challenge, Dudingston, only partially clad, rushed on deck and twice more hailed the dark objects in the water. In reply Whipple called out (still following Bowen's testimony): "I am the sheriff of the county of Kent, G–d d––n you. I have a warrant to apprehend you, G–d d––n you; so surrender, G–d d––n you." While Whipple was thus addressing the commander, a man in one of the boats fired at the Lieutenant and wounded him. He fell to the deck. Pushing the boats alongside the *Gaspee*, the volunteers now clambered aboard the vessel, whose crew retreated below. After Dudingston's wound had been dressed, all occupants of the schooner were ordered to collect their personal belongings and abandon the doomed vessel in their own boats. After this was accomplished and Dudingston removed from it, the *Gaspee* was set afire. It burned to the water's edge.[84]

On June 12 Governor Wanton, following the advice of the Council, issued a proclamation offering a reward of £100 sterling to any who could discover the perpetrators of the "atrocious Crime." The

---

[84] For this eye-witness account by Bowen, who was in the long-boat with the nephew of Chief Justice Hopkins, Captain John B. Hopkins, in charge, see S. G. Arnold: *History of the State of Rhode Island and Providence Plantations* . . . (2 vols., New York, 1859–60), II, 318–20. This account also gives the names of the most prominent men identified with the attack on the *Gaspee*. For an additional report by a participant in the attack, see the account left by Dr. John Mawney, who was in the long-boat commanded by Captain Joseph Tillinghast; it was published in *The Documentary History of the Destruction of the Gaspee* (ed. W. R. Staples, Providence, 1845), pp. 9–10. According to Mawney's record, John Brown was a participant and seems to have taken charge of things on board the *Gaspee* after it was boarded. See also J. B. Hedges: *op. cit.*, p. 209. For a concise account of the incident see *Providence Gazette*, June 13, 1772.

reward was to be paid upon the conviction of any one or more of them.[85] It is worth noting that Wanton's merchant firm at the time had intimate business connections with the Browns of Providence, who had also supported him for the office of Governor.[86] If indeed the man who organized the assault on the King's ship actually remained unknown to Wanton, it is paradoxical that after the Governor had issued his proclamation he undertook no further effort to uncover the instigator or others guilty of the crime.

On June 12, 1772, Admiral Montagu wrote to Lord Hillsborough about the conduct of "the lawless and piratical people of Rhode Island . . . this nest of daring smugglers [who] have wounded . . . Lieut. Dudingston, and burnt the King's schooner Gaspee, under his command, for no other cause, except his being diligent in the discharge of his duty, by giving every proper assistance to the fair trader, and using every endeavor to suppress the illicit trade that is carried on to a great degree, in that province. . . ."[87] Four days later Wanton also wrote to Hillsborough deploring the attack on the Gaspee, yet strongly criticizing the activities of the officers of the naval patrol for insulting the inhabitants "without any just cause."[88] These letters were transmitted to the Attorney General and the Solicitor General by Hillsborough, who was still Secretary of State for the Colonies. But even before the law officers could issue an opinion, he drafted a letter on August 7 to the Governor and Company of Rhode Island directing them to "exert themselves most actively for the discovery of the offenders," and enclosing "An Act for the better securing and preserving his Majesty's Dock Yards, Magazines, Ships, Ammunition, and Stores," which provided among other things that any person who set fire to one of the King's ships should be "adjudged guilty of Felony, and shall suffer Death . . . without Benefit of Clergy." The second clause of this act stated that if this crime should be committed in any place out of the realm the accused might "be indicted and tried for the same, either in any Shire or County within this Realm, . . . or in such Island,

---

[85] For the proclamation see *ibid.;* see also *Rhode Island Colonial Records,* VII, 81.

[86] The firm was that of Joseph & William Wanton. Only in 1775 did the intimate relations between the Wantons and the Browns decline, when Wanton at last decided to adhere to the Loyalist cause, in which his two sons, Joseph, Jr., and William, had become active. See J. R. Bartlett: *History of the Wanton Family of Newport, Rhode Island* (*Rhode Island Historical Tracts,* No. 3, Providence, 1878), pp. 81–112.

[87] *Rhode Island Colonial Records,* VII, 89. In this letter Montagu enclosed copies of letters to and from Dudingston and also to and from Governor Wanton.

[88] Wanton to Hillsborough, June 16, 1772, *ibid.,* VII, 90–2.

Country, or Place, where such Offence shall have been actually committed, as his Majesty . . . may deem most expedient for bringing such Offender to Justice; any Law, Usage, or Custom notwithstanding."[89] However, after the swearing in of Lord Dartmouth as Hillsborough's successor on August 14,[90] this communication, it may be noted, was withdrawn and cancelled during a Cabinet meeting held on the 20th, at which it was also agreed that all the papers concerning the *Gaspee* affair be laid before the King, including the opinion and report made by the Attorney General and the Solicitor General on the 10th. The following day the matter came before the Privy Council and, as a result, this body ordered the law officers to prepare a commission by which Governor Wanton, Chief Justice Daniel Horsmanden of New York, Chief Justice Frederick Smythe of New Jersey, Chief Justice Peter Oliver of Massachusetts Bay, and Robert Auchmuty of Boston, judge of the district court of vice-admiralty, were appointed commissioners for a board of inquiry to investigate the destruction of the *Gaspee* and report their findings to the secretaries of state.

The Board of Inquiry was to have full power to examine witnesses and records in order to secure evidence for the civil authorities that would lead to conviction. The Attorney General and the Solicitor General were also ordered to prepare a proclamation—offering among other things a reward of £500 and a pardon to any concerned in the attack on the *Gaspee* who would give information leading to the conviction of other participants—which received the great seal on the 26th.[91] The commission was appointed by the King on

[89] 12 Geo. III, c. 24. For the passage of this bill, introduced by Lord North and both the Attorney General and the Solicitor General on March 23, 1772, see *Journals of the House of Commons*, XXXIII, 608, 630, 637, 656, 667, 669, 675, 696, 701. For Hillsborough's action see *Manuscripts of the Earl of Dartmouth, Vol. II, American Papers, Historical Manuscripts Commission, Fourteenth Report, Appendix, Part X*, 86, to be cited as *Dartmouth Manuscripts*, II, throughout this chapter.

[90] When Dartmouth became Secretary of State he continued to hold his office of First Lord of Trade, an office which had previously caused him to be sought out hopefully by American patriot leaders, as in the joint letter of Bowdoin, Pemberton, and Warren of March 23, 1770, seeking the removal of troops after the Boston Massacre; see *ibid.*, II, 72. Franklin's account of his own possible influence on the appointment of Dartmouth (*Writings of Benjamin Franklin* [Smyth], V, 413–14) leaves no doubt that he and other Americans welcomed Dartmouth's appointment. That John Pownall, brother of Governor Thomas Pownall and Under Secretary of State for the Colonies since the inception of that post, probably carried the brunt of the work in Great Britain involved in the *Gaspee* affair seems indicated by his letter to Dartmouth (*Dartmouth Manuscripts*, II, 87–95 *passim*) and from his report prepared for the August 20 meeting (A. C. Wedderburn Papers, Clements Library).

[91] *Dartmouth Manuscripts*, II, 88–90; see also the formal proceedings of the Privy Council in *Acts of the Privy Council, Col. Ser., 1766–1783*, pp. 356–7. Only

September 2 and two days later royal instructions were sent to Governor Wanton and the other commissioners.[92] Among the directions was one requiring the commission to communicate to the civil officers and magistrates such information as might lead to the arrest of those responsible for the plunder and destruction of the government ship and their delivery into the custody of Admiral Montagu for transportation to England to stand trial; another instruction provided that, in view of "the outrages . . . committed within our said colony of Rhode Island, by numbers of lawless persons," should insults and violence be directed against the members of the board, notice thereof was to be given to the Commander-in-Chief of the British Forces in North America, who would be required to send such military forces into the colony as might be necessary to provide protection and to aid the court magistrates in preserving the peace. The instructions also directed that the royal commission was "to be read and published . . . with such solemnity as are due to the authority from which it proceeds."[93]

The first official news of the royal proclamation and the appointment of the commissioners of inquiry reached Rhode Island in the latter part of November 1772.[94] However, as early as October 24, the *Providence Gazette* had published word of the Privy Council's actions and, by the time the commissioners met, Governor Wanton had made public a private letter to him from Lord Dartmouth, which was printed throughout New England in such a way as to place the most unfavourable light upon the government's plan of action.[95] When additional information was made public in the colony

two people were excluded from potential pardon: the person who called himself the "head sheriff" and the one who was called "captain" of the expedition. For a copy of the proclamation see *Rhode Island Colonial Records*, VII, 107–8; for the commission setting up the Board of Inquiry see *ibid.*, VII, 108–10.

[92] See C.O. 5:1284, ff. 279 and 373; see also *Dartmouth Manuscripts*, II, 94. The seriousness with which the *Gaspee* episode was viewed by British officials—the Attorney General considered it "five times the magnitude of the Stamp Act" (*ibid.*, II, 91)—is witnessed by the fact that the directions and instructions to the commissioners for the investigation went out over the Great Seal of the Crown.

[93] For the royal instructions see *Rhode Island Colonial Records*, VII, 110–12. See also the Earl of Dartmouth to General Gage, September 4, 1772, directing him to furnish the necessary military support to suppress any "Riots or Insurrection," whenever so called upon by the commissioners. *Gage Correspondence*, II, 149.

[94] *Providence Gazette*, November 21, 1772.

[95] For Governor Wanton's explanation of his action see the letter of Chief Justice Horsmanden to Dartmouth, February 20, 1773, *Rhode Island Colonial Records*, VII, 182–3. For the details of the exploitation in the colonial press of the creation of the *Gaspee* commission, as presented in an excellent examination of the wider implications of the *Gaspee* affair, especially the constitutional aspects, see W. R. Leslie: "The

the following month, the stories were often incorrect and misleading. It is therefore not surprising that the reaction of the inhabitants was vociferous. The attitude of the Rhode Island seafaring and commercial public toward the investigation of the crime may doubtless be judged from the following statement which appeared in the December 21, 1772, issue of the *Newport Mercury:*

> "Ten thousand deaths, by the *halter* or the *ax*, are infinitely preferable to a miserable life of slavery, in chains, under a pack of worse than Egyptian tyrants, whose avarice nothing less than your whole substance and income will satisfy; and who, if they can't extort that, will glory in making a sacrifice of you and your posterity, to gratify their master, the d – – – l, who is a tyrant, and the father of tyrants and of *liars.*"

The press re-echoed the hue and cry. Reference was made to

> "the very extraordinary Measures adopted by Government for . . . punishing the Offenders. . . . These devoted Persons . . . are to be transported to England, where they are to be tried for high Treason. . . . In this Situation of Affairs, every Friend to our violated Constitution cannot but be greatly alarmed.—The idea of seizing a Number of Persons, under the Points of Bayonets, and transporting them Three Thousand Miles for Trial, where, whether guilty or innocent, they must unavoidably fall Victim alike to Revenge or Prejudice, is shocking to Humanity, repugnant to every Dictate of Reason, Liberty and Justice, and in which Americans and Freemen ought never to acquiesce."[96]

Another writer quoted from the law passed in Rhode Island on March 1, 1663/4: "That no Freeman shall be taken, or imprisoned, . . . or be outlawed, or exiled, or otherwise destroyed, . . . but by the lawful Judgment of his Peers, or by the Law of this Colony." He also pointed out the way to deal with the commission that was soon to convene at Newport by citing a prior event. In 1664, he noted, Sir Robert Carr and three others were commissioned by the King to examine and determine all causes military, criminal, and civil in the colonies. Going to Massachusetts Bay to perform this duty, they had to face the Great and General Court, which, following the sound of trumpet, pronounced to the public: "In his Majesty's

Gaspee Affair: A Study of Its Constitutional Significance," *Mississippi Valley Historical Review,* XXXIX, 233–56.
[96] *Providence Gazette,* December 19, 1772.

Name, and by his Authority to us committed, by his Royal Charter, we declare to all the People of this Colony, that in Observance of their Duty to God and to his Majesty . . . we cannot consent unto, or give our Approbation of, the Proceedings of the abovesaid Gentlemen. . . ."[97] To stir up the people further, "Americanus" in the December 26, 1772, edition of the *Providence Gazette,* warned of the setting up of a

> "court of inquisition, more horrid than that of Spain and Portugal, . . . vested with exorbitant and unconstitutional power. . . . Is there an American, in whose breast there glows the smallest spark of publick virtue, but must be fired with indignation and resentment, against a measure so replete with the ruin of our free constitution? To be tried by one's peers is the greatest privilege a subject can wish for; and so excellent is our constitution, that no subject shall be tried, but by his peers."

In the same paper there appeared an extract of a letter from a "gentleman of character in England" to a friend of Boston, in which he declared: "Our tyrants in administration are greatly alarmed with the late manoeuver of the brave Rhode-Islanders, . . . they have determined to vacate the charter of that colony." Still more alarming was a letter from Boston asserting that Admiral Montagu would shortly sail for Newport determined to lay it and Providence "in ashes."

The commissioners met at the Newport court house early in January 1773. On the 9th of that month a letter appeared in the *Providence Gazette* breathing defiance to the commission under which the investigators were acting. It began by quoting the resolves of the Rhode Island Assembly taken on October 25, 1769, and closely patterned upon the resolves passed by the Virginia House of Burgesses on the 16th of May of that year, which stated that all trials for treason, felony, or any crime whatsoever committed within the colony by anyone residing therein ought to be held within the colony and that the seizing and sending of any resident of the colony beyond the sea to be tried was "highly derogatory of the Rights of British Subjects."[98] The Rhode Island writer declared: "we can assure our

---

[97] *Ibid.* For the royal commission of 1664, see G. L. Beer: *The Old Colonial System, 1660–1754* (2 vols., New York, 1912), II, 247–51.

[98] For the Virginia resolves of 1769 see *Journals of the House of Burgesses of Virginia* (eds. J. P. Kennedy and H. R. McIlwaine, 13 vols., Richmond, 1905–13), *Journals . . . , 1766–1769,* p. 214. These were passed as a reply to resolutions of the two Houses of Parliament that the statute relating to treason enacted in the reign of

Brethren of the other Colonies, that we will in no Instance, give up the least Tittle of our just and dear-bought Right to any Power on Earth."

The fear that the commissioners would resort to drastic action began to subside soon after they had assembled. While the judges on the Board of Inquiry were loyal servants of the Crown, they were, except for Chief Justice Smyth, native-born Americans; moreover, they were all learned in the law and deeply committed to the principles and procedures embodied in the common law; in addition they were men of property within their respective colonies and were closely associated with many people who feared that if an American were ever sent to England to be tried it would be the end of that measure of self-government which colonials had enjoyed and the end of American freedom. As Chief Justice Oliver confessed to the Rev. Ezra Stiles, the people of Massachusetts Bay were so much against him as a commissioner that he felt obliged to make clear to them the limitations of the power he and his fellow commissioners held in bringing to justice those responsible for the burning of the *Gaspee*—limitations that the Board of Inquiry had placed on itself.[99] As for the popularly elected Governor Wanton, presiding officer of the board, it was inconceivable that he would endanger his standing as a public official and as head of a prosperous mercantile firm by giving his official support to any measure that would carry an inhabitant of his colony to Great Britain to stand trial.

At the initial meeting of the commissioners for the purpose of laying down their procedures, they apparently had gone into consultation with Deputy Governor Sessions[100] and Chief Justice Hopkins. Out of this meeting and pursuant to instructions came the tacit understanding that they themselves would not assume the responsibility "to take up and commit to the Admiral alone and by themselves," but would rely for such action upon the "internal Justiciary Authority of this Colony."[101] In other words, if any who

Henry VIII—providing that those accused of committing treason in foreign parts could be tried at the King's pleasure in any county in England and before any persons duly commissioned under his Great Seal—should be in force. See 26 Henry VIII, c. 13, Par. 4, and 35 Henry VIII, c. 2.

[99] *The Literary Diary of Ezra Stiles* (ed. F. B. Dexter, 3 vols., New York, 1901), I, 382–3.

[100] Darius Sessions, while Wanton was acting on the commission, was accorded the title of "Governor."

[101] Ezra Stiles to the Rev. Elihu Spencer, Newport, February 16, 1773, *ibid.*, I, 346–7. The close relationship at this period of Judge Oliver with Stiles is indicated in the latter's *Diary*, which is a storehouse of information. For a recent biography of

might be accused were to be sent to England for trial, it would be by decision of the Rhode Island Superior Court, with that ardent patriot and most influential member of the bench, Stephen Hopkins, as its presiding officer.[102]

Admiral Montagu, who doubtless expected to play a leading role in the dramatic situation, in reality found himself on the outside with little or no power to act. It is true that he produced a witness, one Aaron Briggs, a mulatto, who claimed to have been with the party that boarded the *Gaspee* and who sought to identify certain of the participants in the attack on the King's ship.[103] But other testimony tended so to discredit it that Briggs's story could not be admitted as evidence; nor was any other testimony more satisfactory to the commissioners. Furthermore, the refusal of three lawyers to appear before the King's commissioners—despite the subsequent appearance of two of them—brought into focus the issue which arose over the jurisdiction of the Board of Inquiry acting as a court.[104] The work of the commissioners was therefore terminated on June 22, 1773, without producing any of the results anticipated by the government of Great Britain.[105]

But there were consequences from the royal commission that the British Ministry had not anticipated; for it could not have known that setting up a Board of Inquiry would result in such violent reaction over the legal and jurisdictional issues involved, nor that the repercussions would be so widely disseminated by the colonial press. Purdie and Dixon's *Virginia Gazette* was especially active in spreading alarm among Americans concerning the serious implications of the developments.[106] In its issue of February 25, 1773, the *Virginia Gazette* quoted in full the article defying the commission for the inquiry that had appeared in the *Providence Gazette* for January 9, 1773, as presented earlier in this chapter, and, most significantly, emphasized the report made by the Boston Committee of Correspondence on the replies it had received from other towns

---

this distinguished colonial, see E. S. Morgan: *The Gentle Puritan: A Life of Ezra Stiles* (New Haven and London, 1962).

[102] The standard life of Hopkins is W. E. Foster: *Stephen Hopkins, a Rhode Island Statesman . . .* (*Rhode Island Historical Tracts*, No. 19, Providence, 1884).

[103] For the Briggs deposition of January 14, 1772, see *Rhode Island Colonial Records*, VII, 136–9.

[104] *Ibid.*, VII, 155–8, 170, 172–3.

[105] See "Report of the Commissioners to the King," *ibid.*, VII, 178–82.

[106] See issues of November 5 and December 10, 1772, of January 21 and 28, and of February 18 and 25, 1773.

in Massachusetts Bay "as to the rights of the colonials" in the issues that had arisen between that province and the government of Great Britain. It is therefore not surprising—especially in view of its strong resolution of 1769—that the Virginia House of Burgesses should on March 12, 1773, have adopted some important resolutions based on the premise that "various Rumours and Reports of proceedings tending to deprive them of their ancient, legal and constitutional Rights" were disturbing because of the ties between that colony, the mother country, and neighbouring colonies. Therefore, to establish communications between them, they resolved to set up an eleven-man committee of correspondence and inquiry consisting of such members of the House as Richard Bland, Richard Henry Lee, Patrick Henry, and Thomas Jefferson, who were to obtain early information of government action affecting the American colonies and keep in correspondence with similar committees that the Burgesses therewith recommended be appointed in other colonies. This was followed by an additional resolution instructing "the said Committee . . . without delay, [to] inform themselves particularly of . . . a *Court of Inquiry*, said to have been lately held in *Rhode Island*, with Powers to transmit Persons, accused of Offences committed in America, to places beyond the Seas, to be tried."[107]

The aim of the intercolonial committees of correspondence was to bring about a unity of mind and purpose, at least among those who were responsible for guiding the work of the various colonial assemblies, in order to lay a solid foundation for opposing the efforts of the British government to subordinate colonials throughout the Empire to the sovereign will of Parliament. In the words of "a Gentleman of Distinction," writing on March 14 from Virginia to his friend in Boston, ". . . by the enclosed Resolutions, . . . we are endeavouring to bring our Sister Colonies into the strictest Union with us; that we may resent, in one Body, any Steps that may be taken by Administration to deprive any one of us of the least Particle of our Rights and Liberties."[108] This objective was echoed by an

---

[107] For the resolves of March 12, 1773, see the *Journals of the House of Burgesses, 1733–1776*, pp. xi–xii, 28; see also the *Virginia Gazette*, March 18, 1773. For the origins of the Virginia committee see Jefferson's "Autobiography," *Writings of Thomas Jefferson* (ed. P. L. Ford, 10 vols., New York, 1892–99), I, 7–9; see also the two-part article by E. I. Miller: "The Virginia Committee of Correspondence, 1759–1770" and "1773–1775," *William and Mary Quarterly*, 1st ser., XXII, 1–19 and 99–113.

[108] *Virginia Gazette* (Purdie and Dixon), May 13, 1773. In this connection, see also Richard Henry Lee to John Dickinson, April 4, 1773, urging "that every colony

"American gentleman for some years a resident in London," when he wrote to his Newport correspondent on April 12, 1773 that the appointment of the *Gaspee* commissioners of inquiry was "a dangerous, arbitrary, and unconstitutional proceeding" which was designed to render Americans "as miserable slaves as ever existed." He also mentioned that an effort was being made to have "a general meeting of Americans who are in here in London" who will agree to support any American who may be sent over by the Board of Inquiry to stand trial.[109]

The response of the popular branches of the various colonial assemblies to Virginia's invitation to follow the example of its House of Burgesses and provide for intercolonial committees of correspondence and inquiry was impressive. On May 7 Rhode Island voted to create such a committee; so did Connecticut on May 21, followed by New Hampshire on May 27 and Massachusetts Bay on the 28th; South Carolina fell into line on July 8, Georgia on September 10, Maryland on October 15; Pennsylvania on October 16, Delaware on October 23, North Carolina on December 8, New York on January 20 of the new year, and New Jersey on February 8.[110] As for Pennsylvania, the reply by the Speaker of the Assembly, Joseph Galloway, on September 25, 1773, to the letter sent by the Virginia Committee of Correspondence, stated that the Assembly "esteem it

---

on the Continent will adopt these Committees of correspondence and enquiry" as a means of maintaining "large and thorough union counsels . . . to defend ourselves from . . . designs for destroying our constitutional liberty" (*Letters of Richard Henry Lee* [ed. J. C. Ballagh, 2 vols., New York, 1911–14], I, 84). It is also noteworthy that Lee first broached this subject to Dickinson on July 25, 1768 (*ibid.*, I, 29), as the result of his brother Arthur's encouragement and contact with Dickinson, as was the case when he first wrote to Samuel Adams on February 4, 1773 (*ibid.*, I, 82), on "the cause of union."

[109] For an extract of this letter see *Providence Gazette*, June 26, 1773. That the "American gentleman in London" may have been Arthur Lee can be shown by comparison of the above letter to one written by Lee from London to his brother, Richard Henry, on February 14, 1773, which reads: "The Commissioners lately sent over to bring hither for trial, those who are suspected of having burnt his Majesty's Sloop of War at Rhode Island, is the most dreadful violation your Liberties, that can be offer'd. It is big with every evil that can be dreaded from a general Warrant to the most cruel oppression." See Arthur Lee Papers, 2:2, Harvard College Library.

[110] For the replies of the speakers of the various colonial assemblies see the *Journals of the House of Burgesses, 1773–1776*, pp. 47–64 and 143–59; and *Votes and Proceedings of the House of Representatives of the Province of Pennsylvania* (Philadelphia, 1774), p. 509. The *Journal of the House of Representatives* (Boston, 1773) shows May 28 to be the proper date for the vote to set up a committee of correspondence for this province rather than May 27 as given in the Virginia source.

a Matter of the greatest Importance to cooperate with the Representatives of the other Colonies in every wise and prudent Measure, which may be proposed for the Preservation and Security of their general Rights & Liberties, and that it is highly expedient and necessary a Correspondence should be maintained between the Assemblies of the several Colonies."[111] The feeling thus expressed—that it was "a Matter of greatest Importance to cooperate with the Representatives of the other Colonies . . . for the Preservation and Security of their general Rights & Liberties"—was to lead directly to the concept of an American political union. Undoubtedly the address "to the Americans" by "Sidney" that appeared in the *Providence Gazette* for June 12, 1773, reflected the contemporary views of many leading Americans, especially in the statement:

> "The Union of the Colonies which is now taking Place, is big with the most important Advantage to this Continent. From this Union will result our Security from all foreign Enemies; for none will dare to invade us against the combined Force of these Colonies, nor will a British Parliament dare to attack our Liberties, when we are united to defend them. . . . In this Union, every Colony will feel the Strength of the Whole; for if one is invaded All will unite their Wisdom and Power in her defence. In this Way the weakest will become strong, and America will soon be the Glory of the World, and the Terror of the wicked Oppressors among the Nations. . . ."

Thus, the investigation of the *Gaspee* incident in Rhode Island may be said to have caused the Virginia House of Burgesses to instigate the intercolonial committees of correspondence[112]—an action that was then but a breeze, to signal the brewing storm. The centre of this storm lay in Massachusetts Bay, where it had been

[111] *Journals of the House of Burgesses, 1773–1776*, pp. 39–64, especially p. 56.

[112] For an account of the intercolonial committees see E. D. Collins: "Committees of Correspondence of the American Revolution," American Historical Association *Annual Report* (1901), I, 245–71. Despite a few minor inaccuracies it contains much useful data and stresses the point that the concept of intercolonial unity of action through committees of correspondence was not a new one in 1773, for it had been proposed in other colonies as early as 1764. In it Dr. Collins seeks to prove (*ibid.*, I, 246–7) that "it was correspondence, with cooperation at the terminal points, that brought about the Revolution," and that the question of which "inventive political genius" originated the committees of correspondence was of secondary importance. For E. I. Miller's statement that Franklin had suggested such a means of communication in 1754, and evidence of the use of the new system of intercolonial correspondence for other than revolutionary purposes, see his previously cited article, *William and Mary Quarterly*, 1st ser., XXII, 106.

gathering force since 1760, and where it was to remain up to the outbreak of hostilities in 1775. The intercolonial committees of correspondence were to prove an extraordinarily effective instrumentality to the Bay colony in its attempts to draw within its orbit all the colonies from New Hampshire down to Georgia.

CHAPTER II

Massachusetts Bay Foments Rebellion

ESTIFYING before the Lords of the Committee of the Privy Council on June 27, 1770, Sir Francis Bernard, Governor of Massachusetts Bay, stated that from August 2, 1760, when he took office in the colony, until July 1765, "every thing was regular and orderly, and no Governor lived better with the people." Adding that thereafter began a period of disorders and opposition to the government which continued and grew in intensity, he went on to note:

"That the Doctrine of the Colonies not being Subject to Parliament was till then unknown. That the Right of Parliament to Tax the Colonies had been admitted in Mr. Otis's Book . . . and frequently when Mr. Otis disputed the Right of Parliament in the Assembly to Tax the Colony, a Member produced his own pamphlet against him in which he Admitted that Right—That they used to make a Distinction, between the Kings Instructions and Acts of Parliament holding themselves bound by the latter and not by the former—That these new Doctrines were adopted with great vehemence—That they set out with making a Distinction between external and Internal Taxes—that he understood at first they Admitted the Right of Parliament to Impose port Duties, which they afterwards denied and Construed every duty into an Internal Tax. . . . That it is the opinion of the best people there that the Disturbances are grown too strong for Government, unless parliament interferes. . . . That they Reckon about one fighting Man in five, . . . which amounted to about 40,000—That every Body is Armed, by Law and the Town [Boston] had about 800 stand of Arms."[1]

---

[1] *Acts of the Privy Council, Col. Ser. 1766–1783*, pp. 256–9.

When Governor Bernard gave his testimony, he had been repudiated by both the House of Representatives and the Council, and had returned to England on orders of the King "to lay before him a state of the Province."[2] On June 27, 1769, the House had voted to petition the King that Sir Francis "may be *forever* removed from the government of this province." In it they accused him of having charged both houses of the Assembly "with oppugnation against the royal authority," of having exercised the royal prerogative by negativing the election of certain men to the Council,[3] of having interfered with the choice of a London agent for the colony, of having sent back to England secret reports on individual colonials, and of having misrepresented to the King the loyalty of his subjects in Massachusetts Bay; he was also accused of falsely disclosing a plan to seize Castle William. The petition further claimed that the Governor's misrepresentations had resulted in bringing reproach and hardship to the people of the province, with the advent of troops to enforce law and order. The final charge was that the Governor had attempted to overthrow the "constitution of government" in the colony and to deprive the people of their charter rights; therefore, the petition read, "he has rendered his administration odious to the whole body of people. . . ."[4]

In answer to these charges Bernard might well have replied that he had done nothing a loyal servant of the King in his position should not have been expected to do. It is clear today that he was certainly a man of ability whose sole desire was an orderly administration. As Professors Channing and Coolidge of Harvard stated, when editing a body of his papers: "Had Bernard's career in Massachusetts been in other times, it is conceivable that he might have had a pleasant and profitable term of office, for his scholarly tastes would have been in harmony with his surroundings."[5] But it was his misfortune to have been obliged to preside over the most dynamic and revolutionary of

---

[2] Governor Bernard to Lord Barrington, May 30, 1769, *Barrington-Bernard Correspondence . . . 1760–1770* (eds. Edward Channing and A. C. Coolidge, Cambridge, Mass., 1912), p. 203.

[3] See F. G. Walett: "The Massachusetts Council, 1766–1774: The Transformation of a Conservative Institution," *William and Mary Quarterly*, 3rd ser., VI, 605–27, particularly pp. 608–9.

[4] *Speeches of the Governors of Massachusetts Bay . . . and other Public Papers* (ed. [Alden Bradford], Boston, 1818), pp. 188–91; hereafter cited as [Bradford]: *Massachusetts State Papers.*

[5] *Barrington-Bernard Correspondence,* p. xix.

the American colonies during a period of crisis and to have had to make the cruel choice of either violating his royal commission and instructions or adhering to them while bearing all the odium that would, and inevitably did, attach itself to such an unpopular course of action. When the Governor left Boston for England in the summer of 1769, never to return, Lieutenant Governor Hutchinson took over the administration. From the beginning to the end of his term of office, he too was faced with an impossible situation.

It was doubtless felt by the Ministry that if any man were qualified by place of birth, experience, and talent to deal with the explosive situation in Massachusetts Bay, that man was Thomas Hutchinson. A son of early-seventeenth-century settlers, Harvard graduate, member of the Congregational Church, deep student of the history of his colony, and a highly competent official in matters of public business (as indicated by his extraordinary success in handling the complicated finances of the colony before, during, and after the period of the Great War for the Empire), Hutchinson enjoyed the confidence of the General Assembly above other men for his ability to protect the interests of the province during the boundary dispute with New York (which was finally settled in May 1773). Despite all these outstanding assets, Hutchinson also possessed certain serious handicaps. At a time of growing resentment over multiple office-holders—not that the emoluments of these offices were large, even when lumped together—he was held to be one such. He was especially unfortunate, in this connection, for having accepted the office of chief justice of the superior court, since it apparently had been promised by two earlier Governors to one of the popular leaders, Colonel James Otis, father of the more celebrated Otis. Again, although he had been elected more than once to the speakership of the House of Representatives, he had since lost favour with that body because of his unswerving fidelity toward maintaining the constitution of the province as he and other royal officials interpreted it and because of his great influence in the Bernard administration. On the other hand, these drawbacks were probably considered assets by the Ministry. Therefore, when the decision was finally reached to replace Sir Francis as Governor, Hutchinson was commissioned and sworn to that office on March 14, 1771,[6] at the very time when events were

---

[6] Hutchinson's commission was dated April 13, 1770; for this commission see P. R. O., C. O. 5:765, pp. 96–113. His instructions were dated a year later, that is, on April 13, 1771; see C. O. 5:203, pp. 481–511, and C. O. 5:920, pp. 364–405.

heading toward a critical period in the relations of Massachusetts Bay with the mother country.

Of all the colonies, Massachusetts Bay was an acknowledged leader during the 1760's and 1770's in the stand taken on colonial constitutional rights. This was not illogical. As the most mature and among the most highly integrated of the colonies, the Bay province seemed predestined to take the leadership. Virginia, although enjoying considerable prestige in the eyes of Americans, was still predominantly rural, and its social and nationality cleavages were as pronounced as were the sectional differences between the English slave-holding élite of the older settled Tidewater, the Piedmont people, and the Ulster-Scot and German settlers of the newer Valley of Virginia.[7] Pennsylvania, a flourishing colony with many thriving towns, was beset with sharp politico-religious problems as well as those arising out of the mixed nature of its population; New York, more rural than Pennsylvania, was in constant turmoil as a result of the political rivalries of its great aristocratic land-owning families and the dissatisfaction of the tenant farmers; Connecticut, filled with towns, as was Massachusetts Bay, was in some respects much more conservatively oriented than its neighbours; Rhode Island, though radically inclined, lacked influence among its sister colonies; in South Carolina the popular leaders, looking elsewhere in North America for inspiration and example, found it, as a rule, in the Bay colony. It would therefore not be exaggerating the position of this colony to say that from 1761 to the outbreak of hostilities in 1775 the eyes of most colonials were upon it. The amount of space in the newspapers of other colonies devoted to articles concerning events in Massachusetts Bay gives ample evidence of this fact.

What we witness in the Province of Massachusetts Bay during the period under consideration are the actions or reactions of the people of an adult commonwealth—no longer willing to be treated as an infant colony. But there was no place for adult commonwealths in the orbit of the eighteenth-century British Empire, with its constitution premised on colonial dependence and the rule by command and obedience typical of the relationship of parent to immature offspring. Cries of "tyranny" and "despotism" resounded when the will of the

---

[7] See Carl Bridenbaugh: *Myths and Realities: Societies of the Colonial South* (Baton Rouge, 1952), Chap. 1; see also F. H. Hart: *The Valley of Virginia in the American Revolution, 1763–1789* (Chapel Hill, N. C., 1942), Chaps. 1–2, and, in this series, Volume II, revised, Chap. 1.

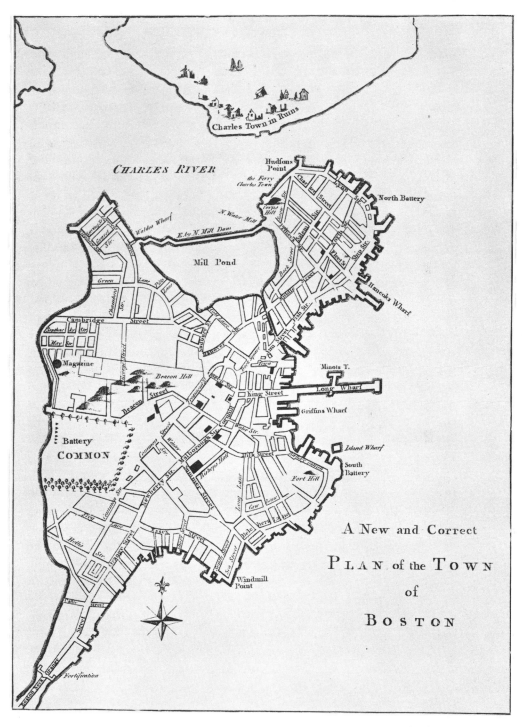

"A New and Correct Plan of the Town of Boston."

(From *Gentleman's Magazine*, 1775)

"A Map of 100 Miles round Boston." (From *Gentleman's Magazine*, 1775)

e opposed the desires of this colony—itself, be it noted, the mother or other colonies.

When, after the so-called Boston Massacre in the spring of 1770, Lieutenant Governor Hutchinson, in obedience to his instructions, had issued a proclamation for the General Court to meet in Cambridge rather than in the Town House at Boston, both the House of Representatives and the Council protested this action as a violation of their charter rights. In reply Hutchinson told the Council: "I must consider myself as a servant of the King, to be governed by what appears to me to be his Majesty's pleasure. . . ."[8] In the course of the dispute the Lieutenant Governor again stated to the Council that in taking the action of proroguing the Assembly to meet in Cambridge he had done no more than the charter of the province authorized him to do. He further pointed out to the Council members that, in taking the position they had, ". . . you have explained away all the prerogative, and removed it from the King and his representative, and made yourselves and the people the judges, when it shall be exercised. . . ."[9] Still later, with the General Court unwilling to proceed to business, Hutchinson addressed the two chambers and pointed out that it was the opinion of the Attorney General and the Solicitor General of Great Britain "That the sole Power of dissolving, proroguing or adjourning the General Court or Assembly, either as to Time or Place, is in his Majesty's Governor. . . ."[10] But this had no effect upon the stand persisted in by the two bodies that their interpretation of charter rights must prevail. Another issue arose over the violation of the charter on September 27, when the Lieutenant Governor addressed the General Court, still being held at Cambridge, and disclosed that His Majesty had seen fit to order the provincial troops at Castle William to be withdrawn and the fort to be garrisoned solely by British regulars.[11] The House of Representatives thereupon raised the question whether the Lieutenant Governor's announcement indicated that he, although acting as Governor, had been divested of the gubernatorial powers conferred upon him by the charter. Hutchinson replied that he had in no way

---

[8] Hutchinson to the Council, March 21, 1770, [Bradford]: *Massachusetts State Papers*, p. 198.

[9] Hutchinson to the Council, June 15, 1770, *ibid.*, p. 227.

[10] Hutchinson to the Council and House of Representatives, July 25, 1770, *Journal of the House of Representatives* (Boston, 1770–1), p. 58.

[11] *Ibid.*, p. 81.

given up any power attached to his office. Nevertheless, on November 20 the House of Representatives sent a message to him declaring: ". . . that your Honor has . . . merely in Obedience to Instructions, divested yourself of a Power of governing, which, by the Charter, is vested in you for the safety of the People; and that it is a Precedent of the most dangerous tendency."[12]

A third issue that involved the charter, according to the claims of the House of Representatives, was Hutchinson's refusal when he became Governor in the spring of 1771 to assent to a bill providing for a grant of £325 as partial compensation for his services as Lieutenant Governor, or to two other bills, one providing £506 as additional compensation for his services as Lieutenant Governor, and the other for a grant of £1,300 "to enable your Excellency, as Governor, to carry on the affairs of this province." Furthermore, the message concerning this matter pointedly asked him whether any provision was made for his support "as Governor of this province, independent of his Majesty's Commons in it"—thus giving the House of Representatives a new and more significant title.[13] To this Hutchinson answered: "I must observe to you, that the King, Lords, and Commons, our supreme Legislature, have determined it to be expedient to enable his Majesty to make a certain and adequate provision for the support of the civil government in the colonies, as his Majesty shall judge necessary."[14] Out of this on June 19 came the following protest by the House against the royal instructions: "By the Charter, the Governor, with other Civil Officers, is to be supported by the free Gift of the General Assembly; and, it would be dangerous for so important a Trust as that of convening, adjourning, proroguing or dissolving the General Assembly to be placed in any one, who is not thus supported by the free Grants of the People."[15] To the above issues involving the integrity of the charter, a fourth one was added when the Governor received an engrossed bill for apportioning and assessing a tax of £15,000. As in the case of acts annually passed "of late years," the assessors in the several towns were called upon to tax the officers of the Crown resident in such towns. But the instructions to the Governor expressly forbad him to give his assent to any such

---

[12] *Ibid.*, pp. 94–5, 99–100, 100, 112, 172.
[13] Message to the Governor, April 25, 1771, [Bradford]: *Massachusetts State Papers*, p. 298. It should be noted that the Governor at the time of the message had neither assented to nor rejected the two bills involving his salary.
[14] *Ibid.*, p. 299.
[15] *Journal of the House of Representatives.* (Boston, 1771–2), pp. 63–4.

act. In his message to the House on July 4, 1771, Hutchinson explained that the bill should be so construed as to "extend no farther than to Commissions which peculiarly relate to this Province; otherwise any of his Majesty's Servants who may occasionally reside here for a short Term may be taxed for the Profit which they receive from their Commissions and Places in Great Britain, and every other part of his Majesty's Dominions."[16] Again, the House denied the power of a royal instruction designed to deprive it of rights which it insisted were embodied in the charter, and declared that "for your Excellency to withhold your Assent to this Bill, merely by Force of Instruction, is effectually vacating the Charter and giving Instruction the Force of Laws within this province."[17] Finally, there was the issue over the support of London agents William Bollan and Dennys De Berdt, who had been appointed respectively by the Council and the House without the Governor's approval. When bills providing grants to them had been refused by Hutchinson, the two houses remonstrated on July 5, 1771. Their position was that "the great Principle of self Defence . . . makes it unfit and unreasonable that the Governor should refuse his Assent to Grants made to such Agents. . . ."[18] In reply, Hutchinson declared that their remonstrance failed to alter his objections to such independent appointments, which "are rather increased than lessened."[19]

These various disagreements actually resolved themselves into one issue: the extent to which the Crown and Parliament could intervene in those activities of the colony which the General Court, by its own interpretation, considered to be reserved to the colony by charter right. Writing about the situation as it existed in 1772, Hutchinson maintained in his *History of the Province of Massachusetts Bay* that in "no independent state in the world could the people have been more happy, than they were in the government of Massachusetts Bay." He affirmed that those in the colony who desired to destroy the beneficial relationship that had long existed between the colony and the mother country were therefore obliged to instill fears as to what the future, not the present, held in store for colonials. The arguments of such enemies of the constitution of the Empire, he contended, were based upon the position that self-interest would lead the supreme authority in Great Britain

[16] *Ibid.*, p. 107
[17] House of Representatives to Hutchinson, July 5, 1771, *ibid.*, p. 109.
[18] *Ibid.*, p. 113.
[19] *Ibid.*, p. 117.

"to distinguish America from the other parts [of the Empire], by imposing on her an unequal share of the burdens, and debarring [her] from an equal share of the benefits of government.—The people of England had it in their power to change their rulers, whenever they abused the trust reposed in them.—The Americans had no remedy.— The one were subjects, the other were slaves.—The Americans imagined themselves owners of estates, which were in reality the estates of the people of England; for how can a man be said to have a property in any thing which is at the disposal of another? . . . Troops had been sent to suppress tumults, and unlawful assemblies, as pretended; but the real design was, to take possession of the province, and . . . to secure obedience to an absolute, unlimited power, and give success to the plans of despotism."

In rebuttal the Governor asserted:

"It was not easy to devise a system of subordinate government less controlled by the supreme, than the governments in the colonies. Every colony had been left to frame its own laws, and adapt them to the genius of the people, and the local circumstances of the colony. Massachusetts, in particular, was governed by laws varying greatly from, though not repugnant to, the laws of England."

As examples of this freedom he cited the penal laws of the colony, the forms of administering justice, the inheritance laws, and the establishment of a form of worship (Congregationalism) "which, at most, might be said to be only tolerated in England." As to colonial resistance to the attempts by Parliament to raise a revenue in America, he affirmed that the colonies had received every consideration possible or desirable from the government—repeal of the Stamp Act, removal of other duties, assurances that no further duties or taxes would be levied. Speculating upon the probability of attaining independence, even if it were warranted, he asked: "As soon as we shall appear in open rebellion, is not the power of Britain sufficient to crush us at one stroke?"[20]

In 1772 one of the grievances of the General Court was removed when on July 14 Hutchinson—after seeking the Council's advice as to whether, under the terms of his instructions, he was justified in returning the sittings of the Assembly to Boston, and obtaining their assurances that he was—adjourned the Assembly to its customary seat. But another basis for opposition to the government of Great

---

[20] *The History of the Colony and Province of Massachusetts-Bay* (ed. L. S. Mayo, 3 vols., Cambridge, Mass., 1936), III, 252–5.

Britain arose soon after this conciliatory step. A report was circulated in the province that the salaries of the judges of the superior court were to be paid out of the import duties. Although the General Court was not then sitting, the towns, headed by Boston, took up the cry that such a provision for the judiciary tended "rapidly to complete that System of Slavery" projected by the British government against the colonials.[21] On October 28 the Boston town meeting sent a message to the Governor requesting him to confirm or deny the report. When Hutchinson replied that it was improper for him to lay his official correspondence before that body, the town meeting immediately petitioned him to call a meeting of the Assembly at once, so that it might deliberate on a matter so "important and alarming" that even the most distant thought of such an establishment filled their "Minds with Dread and Horror." To this new request the Governor answered that he had already reached the determination to delay the gathering of the General Court and that for him to change his plans at the request of the town would be for him to yield a part of the prerogative vested in him by the King. But the members of the Boston town meeting voted that the Governor's reply was unsatisfactory and resolved that they not only had the right to petition the King or his representative "for Redress of Grievances" but also the right "to Communicate their Sentiments to other Towns."[22]

Other Massachusetts Bay town meetings joined the Boston protest and expressed an intense fear of "repeated Attacks on our Constitution" which could—in the words of the Plymouth town meeting —make the province "a Prey of Vultures and Harpies, who riot in the Spoils of it." They saw in the fixing of the judges' salaries "the last Seal of the Despotism they have so long endeavoured to establish here."[23] But it was the Boston town meeting that continued to lead the opposition to the colonial policy of Great Britain. Out of its deliberations in November 1772 came a notable document embodying a statement of "the Rights of the Colonists, and of this Province

[21] For the proceedings of the Boston town meeting of October 28, see *Boston Evening-Post*, November 2, 1772.

[22] For the actions of the town meeting relating to the judges' salaries and Hutchinson's responses see *The Votes and Proceedings of the Freeholders and other Inhabitants of the Town of Boston, in Town Meeting Assembled . . .* (Boston, [1772]), Appendix, pp. 37–43, cited hereafter as *Votes and Proceedings of the Boston Town Meeting, 1772.*

[23] A petition on the part of one hundred inhabitants of Plymouth, November 13, 1772, *Boston Evening-Post*, November 23, 1772.

in particular, as Men, as Christians, and as Subjects." This document was prepared by a committee of correspondence of twenty-one which included such leading radicals as James Otis, Samuel Adams, and Dr. Joseph Warren. Adams and Otis prepared the statement of rights, and Warren an additional list of infringements and violations of them.[24] To understand better the revolutionary movement in Massachusetts Bay it is important to study their report and the reactions it produced throughout the colony. For the formation of the committee of twenty-one on November 2 marked the beginning of the Massachusetts Bay committees of correspondence that were to prove so powerful a force in binding together the towns and counties of that province into a great potential resource for the revolutionary movement.[25]

The statement of rights emphasized those of life, liberty, and property as natural rights. On this subject, the report of the committee quoted with approval John Locke's statement: "The *natural* Liberty of Man is to be free from any superior Power on Earth, and not to be under the Will or Legislative Authority of Man; but only to have the Law of Nature for his Rule. . . . it is the greatest Absurdity to suppose it in the Power of one or any Number of Men, at the entering into Society, to renounce their essential natural Rights, or the Means of preserving those Rights." As to the rights of Englishmen, it was asserted that all persons born in the British colonies "are, by the Laws of God and Nature, and by the common Law of England, . . . well entitled . . . to all the natural, essential, inherent and inseparable Rights, Liberties and Privileges of Subjects born in Great-Britain, or within the Realm." Then, striking at the powers of Parliament and the King, it stated: "The Legislative has no Right to absolute arbitrary Power over the Lives and Fortunes of the People: Nor can Mortals assume a Prerogative, not only too high for Men, but for Angels. . . ." In fact, the report added, the so-called "Supreme Power" claimed by government is a limited one in that it "cannot justly take from any Man, any Part of his Property without his Consent, in Person or by his Representative." Also

---

[24] See *Votes and Proceedings of the Boston Town Meeting, 1772*, pp. iii–iv. For an analysis of the impact of the formation of the committee of twenty-one, as the nucleus of a network of committees of correspondence, and for Dr. Warren's part in the events leading up to the preparation of the "List of Infringements," see John Cary: *Joseph Warren: Physician, Politician, Patriot* (Urbana, Ill., 1961), pp. 112–15.
[25] *Ibid.*

stressed were the rights of colonials as Christians and as Englishmen, subjects of the King.[26]

In drawing up the "List of Infringements and Violations of Rights," Warren and the other members of the committee appointed for this purpose made it so comprehensive that it is difficult to see how Parliament or the King was expected to exercise any real power over the inhabitants of the colonies. This series of indictments reads as follows:

"1st. The British Parliament have assumed the Powers of Legislation for the Colonists in all Cases whatsoever, without obtaining the Consent of the Inhabitants, which is ever essentially necessary to the rightful Establishment of such a Legislative. 2dly. They have exerted that assumed Power, in raising a Revenue in the Colonies without their Consent; thereby depriving them of that Right which every Man has to keep his own Earnings in his own Hands until he shall, in Person, or by his Representative, think fit to part with the Whole or any Portion of it. . . . 3dly. A Number of new Officers [the customs officers], unknown in the Charter of this Province, have been appointed to superintend this Revenue. . . . 4thly. These Officers are by their Commissions invested with Powers altogether unconstitutional, and entirely destructive to that Security which we have a right to enjoy. . . . 5thly. Fleets and Armies have been introduced to support these unconstitutional Officers in collecting and managing this unconstitutional Revenue. . . . 6thly. The Revenue arising from this Tax unconstitutionally laid . . . has been in part applied to the most destructive purposes. . . . 7thly. We find ourselves greatly oppressed by Instructions sent to our Governor from the Court of Great Britain. . . . 8thly. The extending of power of the Courts of Vice-Admirality . . . deprives the people in the colonies, in a great measure, of their inestimable right to trials by juries. . . . 9thly. The restraining us from erecting Slitting-Mills for manufacturing our iron . . . is an Infringement of that Right with which God and Nature have invested us. . . . And we look upon the Restraint laid upon the Manufacture and Transportation of Hats to be . . . grievous. . . . 10thly. The Act passed in the last Session of the British Parliament, intituled, An Act for the better preserving his Majesty's Dock-Yards, Magazines, Ships, Ammunition and Stores, is, as we apprehend, a violent Infringement of our Rights. . . . 11thly. As our Ancestors . . . particularly desired to be freed from the Prelates . . . we cannot see without concern,

[26] For the extended statement of colonial rights see *Votes and Proceedings of the Boston Town Meeting, 1772*, pp. 1–12.

the various attempts . . . made, and are now making, to establish
an American Episcopate. . . . [Such attempts are] justly looked upon
a great Grievance. . . . 12thly. Another Grievance under which we
labour is, The frequent Alteration of the Bounds of the Colonies by
by Decisions before the King and Council, Explanatory of former
Grants and Charters. . . ."[27]

The Boston town meeting not only adopted the committee's report on colonial rights and violations thereof, but also approved a
letter to be sent with six hundred copies of the report to other towns
in the province, thus initiating the effective action of the committee
of correspondence. This letter stressed the point that "the Plan of
Despotism . . . is rapidly hastening to a completion . . . under a
constant, unremitted, uniform Aim to inslave us. . . ."[28] On December 8 Marblehead responded by passing some very strong resolves,
although ten days later twenty-nine people signed a protest against
them as being untrue to fact.[29] This was followed by the Plymouth,
Roxbury, and Cambridge resolves, adopted severally on the 14th,[30]
with those of both Plymouth and Roxbury framed in very high terms.
Then came the Charlestown resolves on the 28th.[31] Other towns
also fell in line—for example, Newburyport and Ipswich—until one
third of all the towns in the province had taken steps to support the
Boston resolves.[32]

It is small wonder that Governor Hutchinson was "greatly alarmed"
at these unexpected developments or that he was persuaded that the
principles embodied in the resolves were to be used "to justify
the colonies in revolting, and forming an independent state; and such
instances were given of the infringement of their rights by Parliamentary authority as . . . would justify an exception to the authority
in all cases whatsoever. . . ."[33] As a man with a sense of intense
loyalty to duty, he felt most keenly the difficulty of his position.
"By sitting still," he noted in his *History*,

"he had reason to think he would bring upon himself a charge of
conniving at proceedings, the unwarrantableness whereof he ought to

---

[27] For the list of infringements see *ibid.*, pp. 13–29.

[28] *Ibid.*, pp. 30–6.

[29] For the Marblehead town meeting resolves and the protest against them see
Boston Evening-Post, December 14 and 28, 1772.

[30] For these resolves see *ibid.*, December 21, 1772.

[31] For the Charlestown resolves see *ibid.*, January 4, 1773.

[32] See Hutchinson: *op. cit.*, III, 265n, for excerpts of the inflammatory resolves
of the towns of Petersham and Marlborough.

[33] *Ibid.*, III, 262–5.

have exposed, and the progress whereof to have checked, by every means in his power. By bringing the matter before the assembly, he knew, from past experience, he must bring on an altercation, . . . and that they [the members of the Assembly] would charge him with raising a flame in the province, under pretence of endeavouring to suppress it. The danger of this charge, and the abuse which he expected to follow it, both in England and America, he did not think would excuse a neglect of plain duty."[34]

He therefore decided to face the situation head on.

To the end that there should be no delay in attempting to block the action of the committee of correspondence or the town meeting as a means of bypassing the Assembly, the Governor determined to call the General Court to meet at a date earlier than previously planned and to make plain to the members and the people of the province in general how dangerous was the drift of public affairs. When he stood before the two houses on January 6, 1773, he appeared as the most eminent of Americans supporting the policies of Great Britain. John Adams remarked in his *Diary* that he and Samuel Adams concurred in the view "that the Liberties of this Country had more to fear from one Man, the present Governor Hutchinson, than from any other Man, nay than from all other Men in the World." This statement was recorded as being "founded in their Knowledge of his Character, his unbounded Ambition and his unbounded Popularity."[35]

The long address delivered by the Governor represented without doubt his greatest effort to reconcile his fellow countrymen to the British concept of the constitution of the Empire. It was calm and deliberate. In referring specifically to the resolves of a number of towns, Hutchinson stressed the point that "some of them deny the supreme Authority of Parliament, and are so repugnant to the Principles of the Constitution . . . as have a direct Tendency to alienate the Affections of the People from their Sovereign who has ever been most tender of their Rights. . . ."[36] He observed that "so much of

---

[34] *Ibid.*, III, 266.

[35] *The Adams Papers*, 1st ser., *Diary and Autobiography of John Adams* (eds. L. H. Butterfield *et al.*, 4 vols., Cambridge, Mass., 1961), II, 55, cited hereafter as *Adams Papers* (Butterfield), 1st ser.

[36] Among the Hutchinson papers are undated notes and drafts of the speech that indicate the great pains he took in the formation of the ideas he sought to bring home to the people. See the Massachusetts Archives, 25:433–6, State House. For the speech of January 6 see *Journal of the House of Representatives* (Boston, 1772–3), pp. 138–43; see also *Boston Gazette*, January 11, 1773.

the spirit of Liberty breathes through all Parts of the English Constitution that although from the nature of government there must
be one supreme authority over the whole, yet the Constitution will
admit of subordinate Powers with legislative and executive, greater
or less according to local and other circumstances." It was under
this constitution, he continued, that "for more than one hundred
years the Laws both of the supreme and subordinate authority were,
in general, duly executed. . . . At length the constitution has been
called in question and the authority of the Parliament to make and
establish Laws for the Inhabitants of this Province has been, by
many denied. . . ." In the face of this challenge to the constitution
he solemnly declared:

> "I know no Line that can be drawn between the supreme Authority
> of Parliament and the total Independence of the Colonies: It is im-
> possible there should be two independent Legislatures in one and
> the same State, for although there may be but one Head, the King,
> yet the two Legislative Bodies will make two Governments as dis-
> tinct as the Kingdoms of England and Scotland before the Union."[37]

The Governor's able and lengthy speech was answered on January
25 by the Council and by the House of Representatives with equally
able and extended replies. The Council took the position that

> "Supreme or unlimited Authority can with Fitness belong only to the
> Sovereign of the Universe: If then from the Nature and End of Gov-
> ernment, the supreme Authority of every Government is limited, the
> Supreme Authority of Parliament must be limited. . . . Life, Liberty,
> Property, and the Disposal of that Property with our own Consent,
> are natural Rights. . . . The Preservation of these Rights is the great
> End of Government. . . . Independence, as your Excellency rightly
> judged, we have not in Contemplation."[38]

---

[37] Ibid.; see also The Speeches of His Excellency Governor Hutchinson, to the
General Assembly . . . with the Answers of His Majesty's Council and the House
of Representatives [Published by Order of the House] (Boston, 1773), pp. 1–14,
cited hereafter as Governor Hutchinson's Speeches to the Assembly, 1773.

[38] For the reply of the Council see ibid., pp. 15–32. As to its authorship, Hutchinson wrote on February 1 to an unknown correspondent: "I can now cover the
answer of the Council & H. of Rep. . . . The first [that is, the answer of the Council]
is the draft of Mr. Bowdoin who supposes himself to be supported by what was
advanced in Parliament by Lord Camden & Mr. Pitt. The other [that is, the answer
of the House of Representatives] discovers the principles upon which the people
of this Prov. & the Opposers of the Supremacy of Parl^t in the other N. England
colonies ground their Opposition and they are such as I dare say their friends in
Parl^t will not avow" (Massachusetts Archives, 27:444). In a letter to Sir Francis
Bernard of February 3, Hutchinson wrote defending his speech to the General

The reply to the Governor from the House of Representatives, which was given its finished form by John Adams, may well be considered one of the most important papers issued in the colonies prior to the outbreak of hostilities in 1775.[39] Denying that the disturbed state of affairs in Massachusetts Bay was caused by the adoption on the part of the people of the province of unconstitutional principles, the message asserted that the situation was occasioned rather "by the British House of Commons assuming and exercising a Power inconsistent with the Freedom of the Constitution, to give and grant the Property of the Colonists, and appropriate the same without their Consent." The reply went on to trace the history of the relations of the colony to the mother country in order to show that the supreme authority of Parliament over the colony was never pretended; that, moreover, "one of the Liberties of free and natural Subjects" was, in the Governor's own words, to be governed "by

Assembly and said, in referring to the replies to it: "The papers I enclose will shew what we are about. [Samuel] Adams brought above 80 Towns to declare openly against the authority of Parl[t] & I question whether ten Towns in the Prov. would have stood out if I had not called upon the two Houses just as I did. You will think they [the two houses in their replies] have made miserable work of it & yet you have the utmost effort of Bowdoin . . . in one House & Hawley, & Adams in the other. What will Parliament say to this?" (*ibid.*, 27:456).

[39] Realizing the great importance of an effective reply, an effort was made by the House of Representatives, according to Hutchinson, to enlist the services of Daniel Dulany of Maryland, author in 1765 of the very important *Considerations on the Propriety of Imposing Taxes in the British Colonies, for the Purpose of raising a Revenue, by Act of Parliament.* A messenger was therefore sent to him by the Speaker of the House with a request that he prepare the answer to the Governor's speech. Dulany refused the offer and so informed the Rev. Jonathan Boucher, rector of St. Anne's in Annapolis, who later returned to England as a Loyalist and there reported the incident to Hutchinson (see Hutchinson: *op. cit.,* III, 268–9n). The messenger was requested (still following the Governor's account), if Dulany refused, to apply to John Dickinson, author in 1768 of the celebrated *Letters from a Farmer in Pennsylvania to the Inhabitants of the British Colonies.* Dickinson also declined the task (see C. J. Stillé: *Life and Times of John Dickinson,* Historical Society of Pennsylvania *Memoirs,* XIII, 103–4). W. V. Wells, in his *The Life and Public Services of Samuel Adams* (3 vols., Boston, 1865), argued in a long footnote (II, 31–40) that this could not have been true. The task was thereupon undertaken by Samuel Adams and Joseph Hawley. A draft was then submitted to John Adams, who, in going over it, found it "full of very popular talk and with those democratical Principles which have since done so much mischief in this Country." Having expunged them, he then (according to the account in his *Autobiography*) "furnished the committee with the Law Authorities, and the legal and constitutional Reasonings that are to be seen on the part of the House in that Controversy." (*See Adams Papers* [Butterfield], 1st ser., III, 305.) W. V. Wells (*op. cit.,* II, 31–40) argues at great length to prove that any aid received by Samuel Adams in the drafting of the reply to the Governor's speech was incidental.

For J. E. Alden's article establishing the fact that a Boston edition of the Dulany pamphlet mentioned above was published by John Mein in January 1766, see *New England Quarterly,* XIII, 705–11.

Laws made by Persons in whose Elections they from Time to Time have a Voice." But the right of representation in the English Parliament, it was foreseen, could not be exercised by the people of this colony, and a legislature was accordingly constituted within it and authorized to make all laws not repugnant to the laws of England. As to acts of Parliament made expressly to refer to the colony, the message read: "We are . . . at a Loss to conceive where your Excellency finds it 'provided in the same Charter.'" Concerning that part of the King's dominions not a part of the realm, to which our ancestors removed, "Parliament lost no Authority over it, having never had such Authority; and the Emigrants were consequently freed from the Subjection they were under [to Parliament] before their Removal: The Power and Authority of Parliament being constitutionally confined within the Limits of the Realm and the Nation collectively, of which alone it is the Representing and Legislative Assembly." Then, turning to the crucial point made by the Governor that he knew "of no Line that can be drawn between the Supreme Authority of Parliament and the total Independence of the Colonies," the House message replied:

> "If there can be no such Line, the Consequence is, either that the Colonies are the Vassals of the Parliament, or, that they are totally Independent. As it cannot be supposed to have been the Intention of the Parties in the Compact, that we should be reduced to a State of Vassalage, the Conclusion is, that it was their Sense, that we were thus Independent. . . . May we not then further conclude, that it was their Sense that the Colonies were by their Charters made distinct States from the Mother Country?"

In conclusion the following most pertinent point was raised:

> "If your Excellency expects to have the Line of Distinction between the Supreme Authority of Parliament, and the total Independence of the Colonies drawn by us, we would say it would be an arduous Undertaking; and of very great Importance to all the other Colonies: And therefore, could we conceive of such a Line, we should be unwilling to propose it, without their Consent in Congress."

To these replies the Governor made answer in due course, and the controversy over rights continued until the 6th of March.[40] On

---

[40] For the reply of the House of Representatives see *Governor Hutchinson's Speeches to the Assembly, 1773*, pp. 33–58. For the continuation of the arguments between the two houses and the Governor see *ibid.*, pp. 58–99. Writing to General

that date Hutchinson made a final speech to the Assembly—in which he sought to answer the arguments of the two houses, but especially those of the House of Representatives—and thereupon prorogued the General Court to April 21.[41] Throughout it all the utmost decorum in language was observed and respect for persons maintained. It was a debate on constitutional principles in the best British tradition with neither side retreating from the position it had assumed and was to continue to support.[42] The great importance of this discussion lies in the fact that nowhere else and at no other time before the outbreak of the War for American Independence were so clearly stated and so openly debated the issues that were to divide Americans into the two camps of Loyalist and patriot.

Despite the gravity of the constitutional issue at stake, the affairs of the government of Massachusetts Bay moved along in a relatively smooth fashion for a period of some weeks. Then, on April 8, the Governor dissolved the General Court and ordered a new election. Early in May the town of Boston selected as its representatives to the new Assembly Thomas Cushing, Samuel Adams, John Hancock, and William Phillips, and called upon them to work to protect the people's rights; in this connection it referred to "the black Catalogue of abuses which the Colonies have been subjected to for several

---

Gage on March 7, Hutchinson explained why he continued the debate as he did: "I had determined to make no reply until I closed the Session," he wrote, "but the few friends to Government pressed me to it by urging that if I gave no oportunity for considering the reply the construction among the people would be that I was afraid of their remarks upon the reply" (Massachusetts Archives, 27:461-2). See also J. K. Hosmer: *The Life of Thomas Hutchinson, Royal Governor of the Province of Massachusetts Bay* (Boston and New York, 1896), pp. 363–428, Appendix B, for Hutchinson's speech of January 6 and February 16, 1773, and the replies of the Council and House of Representatives to them.

[41] For the Governor's speech of March 6 see *Governor Hutchinson's Speeches to the Assembly, 1773*, pp. 114–26. That Hutchinson put great effort into his final rejoinder to the two houses of the Assembly is indicated by his letter dated February 1 to an unknown correspondent. In it he wrote: "I purpose before I close the Session to give them a very full Answer and shew the principles of the English Constitution and from their own Acts & Resolves the relation they stand in, to their Mother Country in so full a manner as would leave them without any room for a rejoinder" (Massachusetts Archives, 27:444). In a letter to Sir Francis Bernard, dated March 10, 1773, Hutchinson wrote: "The late messages of the House & Council if you have the patience to read them will leave you at a loss to determine which are the most nonsensical. Those of the Council are the production of Bowdoin. The House of S. Adams with the aid of Hawley & the Lawyer [John] Adams & they have such an opinion of them that they have ordered the whole Controversy to be printed in a pamphlet for the benefit of posterity" (*ibid.*, 27:465).

[42] In recounting this episode in his *History* (III, 267–76), Hutchinson presents at some length with candour and, all in all, with fairness the arguments of the opponents, at the same time voicing objections to certain of them.

years past," and added: "that we have suffered them so long is disgraceful to us. . . ."[43]

In contrast, the House of Representatives on the very day that it was prorogued, preceding its dissolution, addressed a petition to the King couched in language of deference and loyalty but adhering to the position that certain liberties and rights granted to the people of Massachusetts Bay by both charters were essential to a free people, and beseeching His Majesty to restore the Governor and the judges "to the footing upon which they were originally placed by the Royal Charter, and that the Rights and Liberties therein conceded upon the Word and promise of your Majesties Royal Predecessors may be faithfully observ'd."[44]

This petition was sent to Benjamin Franklin, the London agent of the House. Accompanying it went a long letter addressed to the Secretary of State for the Colonies, the Earl of Dartmouth, which followed very closely the lines of the Boston statement of the preceding year respecting the rights of colonials in general but particularly of those in Massachusetts Bay. The letter claimed that the position of dependence of the Governor and the judges upon the people was established by charter and could not be changed without the violation of rights; it also declared that the appointment of a Board of Customs Commissioners to reside in America was "a very dangerous Innovation" in view of the fact that they were invested "with Powers unconstitutional, and destructive of that Security we have a Right to enjoy"; likewise, the "enormous Extension of the Powers of Courts of Admiralty in America is an intollerable Grievance," and the instructions to the Governor by the Ministry "if persisted in will intirely destroy our Liberties and subvert our happy Constitution." Further, the question was asked whether the establishment of the office of Commander-in-Chief of the military forces in North America, independent of the civil power within the colonies, was "not repugnant to Law & must not be very alarming to all who have any regard for the Liberties of the Constitution either of Great Britain or of the Colonies." These, together with other grievances against what were considered to be innovations in the

---

[43] For the proceedings of the Boston town meeting of May 5, see *Boston Evening-Post*, May 10, 1773. For the instructions to the representatives see *A Report of the Record Commissioners of the City of Boston, containing the Boston Town Records, 1770 through 1777* (Boston, 1887), pp. 131–4, cited hereafter as *Boston Town Records*.

[44] For this petition, signed by Speaker Cushing, see the Arthur Lee Papers, 2:7, Harvard College Library.

government of the colonies, indicate clearly how incompatible were the demands of the Massachusetts representatives for freedom of action, untrammelled by limiting regulations, with the type of colonial administration that seemed necessary to the government of Great Britain for the smooth functioning of the Empire as a whole.[45]

On May 26 the General Court met and organized. That Hutchinson was still on cordial terms with the Council members and others is evident from the report that the Board and "a number of principal gentlemen of the town" at noon on that day waited upon the Governor to congratulate him on the anniversary of the day appointed by charter for the convening of the General Court, and "together they partook of a collation."[46] In the afternoon the members of the Council were elected. Hutchinson refused his consent only to John Adams and two others of those chosen. On the 28th, as recounted in the preceding chapter, the resolves of the Virginia House of Burgesses— condemning the government's action in the case of the *Gaspee* and recommending intercolonial committees of correspondence—were formally received and strongly approved and a committee was appointed to represent the House in this intercolonial activity.[47] The comparative quiet of the Assembly proceedings was further broken when on June 2 Clerk of the House Samuel Adams, after the galleries had been cleared of spectators, acquainted the members "that Letters of an extraordinary Nature had been written and sent to England, greatly to the Prejudice of the Province," which he had obtained, but under restrictions on the part of the person from whom he had received them that they should neither be printed nor copied. It was therefore moved that the letters be read. This was done. They were a group of thirteen letters written by Massachusetts Bay officials which Benjamin Franklin had sent to Speaker of the House Cushing in December 1772.[48]

---

[45] Speaker Cushing to the Earl of Dartmouth, March 6, 1773, *ibid.*, 2:5–6.

[46] *Boston Evening-Post*, May 31, 1773.

[47] For the proceedings of the House of Representatives, May 26–28, 1773, see *Journal of the House of Representatives* (Boston, 1773–4), pp. 3–14.

[48] *Ibid.*, pp. 26–7. On December 2, 1772, Benjamin Franklin, London agent for the House of Representatives, wrote to Speaker Thomas Cushing to say that he had obtained possession of "a Correspondence, that I have reason to believe laid the Foundation of most if not all our present grievances. I am not at Liberty to tell thro' what Channel I receiv'd it; and I have engag'd that it shall not be printed, nor Copies taken . . . ; but I am allow'd to let it be seen by some Men of Worth in the Province, for their Satisfaction only. . . . I can only allow them to be seen by yourself, by the other Gentlemen of the Committee of Correspondence, by Messrs. Bowdoin and Pitts of the Council, and Drs. Chauncey, Cooper, and Winthrop, with a few such other Gentlemen as you may think fit to show them to.

Of the letters, six were written by Hutchinson, then Lieutenant Governor, four by Andrew Oliver, the secretary of the province, and one each by Robert Auchmuty (at the time judge of the Massachusetts Bay Court of Vice-Admiralty and later judge of the District Court of Vice-Admiralty), Charles Paxton (then surveyor of customs for the port of Boston and later one of the Board of American Customs Commissioners), and Nathaniel Rogers (a prominent Boston merchant who sought to obtain the post of provincial secretary should Oliver succeed to the office of Lieutenant Governor and Hutchinson to that of Governor). All the letters but one were addressed to Thomas Whately,[49] formerly secretary to the Treasury under Grenville but no longer in office, and fell between the dates May 7, 1767, and October 26, 1769. The exception was the one by Auchmuty to Hutchinson, dated September 14, 1768, in which he referred to "the infernal purposes of the sons of liberty, as they falsely stile themselves" and warned the Lieutenant Governor that "from the terrible threats and menaces by those Catilines against you, . . . your life is greatly in danger." The most interesting and revealing comment in the Hutchinson correspondence with his British friend of long standing is found in the letter of January 20, 1769, in which he expressed the hope that in the present crisis no greater "degree of severity" should be employed by the government than "is absolutely necessary to maintain . . . the *dependance* which a colony ought to have upon the parent state," and then affirmed:

> "if no measures shall have been taken to secure this dependance, or nothing more than some declaratory acts or resolves, *it is all over with us*. . . . The friends of anarchy will be afraid of nothing, be it ever so extravagant. . . . I never think of the measures necessary for the peace and good order of the colonies without pain. There must be an abridgement of what are called English liberties. . . . I doubt whether it is possible to project a system of government in which a colony 3000 miles distant from the parent state shall enjoy all the liberty of the parent state. I am certain I have never yet seen the projection. I wish the good of the colony when I wish to see some further restraint of liberty, rather than the connexion with the parent state should be

After being some Months in your Possession, you are requested to return them to me" (*Writings of Benjamin Franklin* [Smyth], V, 448–51; VI, 265–9).
[49] For the career of Whately see Sir Lewis Namier and John Brooke: *History of Parliament: The House of Commons, 1754–1790* (3 vols., London and New York, 1964), III, 627–8.

broken; for I am sure such a breach must prove the ruin of the colony."[50]

After resolving itself into a committee of the whole House and giving further consideration to the correspondence, the House voted by a majority of 101 to 5 "that the Tendency and Design of the Letters . . . was to overthrow the Constitution of this Government, and to introduce arbitrary Power into the province."[51]

How the letters ever came into the hands of Benjamin Franklin has never been completely explained.[52] Even with all possible delay

[50] *The Letters of Governor Hutchinson, and Lieut. Governor Oliver, etc. Printed at Boston. And Remarks Thereon. With the Assembly's Address, and the Proceedings of the Lords Committee of Council. Together with the Substance of Mr. Wedderburn's Speech Relating to those Letters* (London, 1774), pp. 12–13 and 15–17. These letters were first printed in Boston in the summer of 1773 under title: *Copies of Letters sent to Great-Britain, by his excellency Thomas Hutchinson, the Hon. Andrew Oliver, and several other persons, born and educated among us.* . . . (Boston, 1773). See also J. K. Hosmer: *op. cit.,* Appendix C; for an sympathetic account of Hutchinson's part in the episode see *ibid.,* Chap. 12, "The Affair of the Letters."

[51] *Journal of the House of Representatives* (Boston, 1773–4), p. 27.

[52] See *Writings of Benjamin Franklin* (Smyth), VI, 81–2, and Franklin's "Tract" on the subject, *ibid.,* VI, 258–89. In the Jared Sparks edition of Franklin's *Works,* the editor appends to the Tract (IV, 405–40) a lengthy "Note" (IV, 441–55) attempting to disprove the claim made by Dr. David Hosack in his *Biographical Memoir of Hugh Williamson* (New York, 1820), pp. 50–1, that Dr. Williamson had obtained the Hutchinson-Oliver letters by "a bold stratagem" and turned them over to Franklin. For a further discussion of the problem see J. H. deR. Hamilton: "Hugh Williamson," *Dictionary of American Biography,* XX, 299.

For Hutchinson's account of the matter see his *History* (Mayo), III, 282–4, 298–9n (together with *Additions to Thomas Hutchinson's "History of Massachusetts Bay"* edited by Catherine B. Mayo, and reprinted with the same pagination from American Antiquarian Society *Proceedings,* LIX [Worcester, Mass., 1949], pp. 60–2), and his brief explanation made to the King in July 1774 to be found in "Extracts from the Journal of Thomas Hutchinson, Governor of Massachusetts," Massachusetts Historical Society *Proceedings,* XV, 326–34, and also printed in *The Diary and Letters of his Excellency Thomas Hutchinson* (ed. P. O. Hutchinson, 2 vols., Boston, 1884), I, 157–75. In the *Diary* (I, 81–93) the editor also presents a lengthy discussion of how the letters came into Franklin's hands. See also "Thomas Hutchinson" in C. K. Shipton's *Sibley's Harvard Graduates* (12 vols., Boston, 1873–1962), VIII, 200–2. It will be noted that Dr. Shipton continued the writing of these "Biographical Sketches of Those Who Attended Harvard College" with Vol. VI (1712–21), utilizing funds left for this purpose by the original author, J. L. Sibley.

According to the *Boston News-Letter,* April 28, 1774, the letters written to Thomas Whately by Hutchinson were turned over to George Grenville, and upon his death went to John Temple, who in turn gave them to the Hon. Mr. Fitzherbert, at whose hands they came into the possession of Franklin.

George Bancroft's findings on the subject—which coincide with the *Boston News-Letter* account, except in suggesting that it was probably Lord Temple as Grenville's possible executor who turned the papers over to John Temple, and in not naming the member of Parliament who released them to Franklin—are confirmed in a paper presented in 1878 by R. C. Winthrop to the Massachusetts Historical Society; see its *Proceedings,* XVI, 41–9. For the argument that the member of

of transatlantic posts the letters must have been in the province for some months prior to June 2 and open to inspection by certain of the leaders, but without creating the slightest stir. In fact, it is generally agreed that, in the words of Hutchinson, these letters "contained nothing more upon the subject of the constitution of the colonies in general, than what had been published in his speeches to the Assembly, . . . and that none of them had any respect [reference] to the particular constitution of the province, derived from the charter."[53] It would seem therefore that the reaction to them on June 2 was part of a predetermined plan on the part of Samuel Adams and his supporters to widen, not narrow, the growing breach between the colonies and Great Britain. For the raising of an issue over the letters also appeared to be linked to the creation of the Massachusetts Bay intercolonial committee of correspondence and its objective of bringing about a union of the several colonies at a time, according to the resolves of the House, when "their just rights and liberties are systematically invaded." As the Governor was later to point out, the perpetuation of the activities of the House during recesses, through the dealings of its committee of correspondence, was "a most glaring attempt to alter the constitution of the colony" not only "by assuming to one branch of the legislature the powers of the whole; by continuing, by delegation, powers of government, after the authority from which the delegation was derived had expired," but also "by uniting in one body a number of bodies [the various colonial assemblies] which, by their constitutions, were intended to be kept separate and unconnected. It was an act," Hutchinson further contended, "which ought to have been considered as an avowal of independency, because it could be justified only upon the principle of independency."[54]

The violation of the pledge of secrecy regarding the letters and their subsequent publication came as the result of a report made by John Hancock on June 9[55] that he had received certain copies of letters which he supposed were copies of the letters before the

---

Parliament may have been Thomas Pownall, see C. A. W. Pownall's *Thomas Pownall* . . . (London, 1908), pp. 255–6.

[53] Hutchinson: *op. cit.*, III, 289.

[54] *Ibid.*, III, 285.

[55] Hutchinson's letter of June 18, 1768, which was among the letters secured, had to do with the seizure of Hancock's sloop—"for a very notorious breach of the acts of trade"—the placing of it under the guns of H.M. *Romney* on June 10, and the ensuing mob action. See *The Letters of Governor Hutchinson* . . . , pp. 1–3.

House; he then moved that they be compared. Consequently, it was voted, with the consent of the Speaker, that as copies had already appeared in print, the House could make whatever use of the originals it saw fit.[56] The printers Edes and Gill (publishers of the *Boston Gazette*) were thereupon ordered to print a sufficient number of copies of the letters for the perusal of the members.[57] Then on June 16 came the approval of a series of important resolves that brought the strained relations between the Governor and the House to a climax. Among the resolutions was one stating that the letters "had a natural and efficacious Tendency to interrupt and alienate the Affections of our most gracious Sovereign King George the Third, from this his loyal and affectionate Province [and] to excite the Resentment of the British Administration against this Province, . . . and to produce the severe and destructive Measures which have been taken against this Province." The last of the resolves read as follows:

> "That this House is bound in Duty to the King and their Constituents, humbly to remonstrate to his Majesty, the Conduct of his Excellency Thomas Hutchinson, Esq., Governor; and the Honorable Andrew Oliver, Esq., Lieutenant Governor of this Province; and to pray that his Majesty would be pleased to remove them forever from the Government thereof."[58]

There was a certain irony in the last resolve in view of the action taken the following day, when the House was invited by the Council to join in expressing thanks to those gentlemen of the province who had, so much to the credit of the colony, completed the long and difficult negotiations with New York over the common boundary— negotiations in which Hutchinson had played a decisive role at the invitation of the two houses.[59] Not to be swerved from its course, on June 23 the committee appointed by the House to prepare a petition to the King seeking the removal of Hutchinson and Oliver indicated that it was ready to report. A motion that the consideration of their report be delayed until the next session, so that the members could consult their constituents, was defeated by a vote of 73 to 13. After the report had been read and approved—with an additional

---

[56] *Journal of the House of Representatives* (Boston, 1773–4), pp. 41 and 44.
[57] *Ibid.*, p. 56.
[58] *Ibid.*, pp. 58–61.
[59] *Ibid.*, p. 63. See Volume XI of this series, Chap. 10, "Intercolonial Conflicts: New York and Its Rivals."

provision that Arthur Lee be appointed as counsel to assist Franklin —the Speaker was ordered to sign and transmit it to the London agent for presentation to the King.[60]

The petition of the House of Representatives called attention to the "mal-Conduct of persons *who have heretofore had the confidence and esteem of this people, and whom your Majesty has been pleased*, . . . to advance to the highest places of trust and authority in the Province." It then related that certain papers had lately reached the Assembly giving evidence that there had "long been a conspiracy of evil men" plotting to advance to power by destroying the charter of the province and "annihilating the rights and liberties of the American colonies." Singling out Thomas Hutchinson and Andrew Oliver as "the chief instruments in introducing a fleet and an army into this province to establish and perpetuate their plans," the petition laid at their door the responsibility for all the disharmony in government and "hateful discords and animosities between the several parts of your Majesty's extensive dominions," including "all that corruption of morals and . . . confusion, misery, and bloodshed, which have been the natural effects of posting an army in a populous town." As a result of their conduct, the petition concluded, Hutchinson and Oliver had rendered themselves "justly obnoxious to your loving subjects, and entirely lost their confidence." On these grounds the petitioners besought the King to remove the two high officials from their posts.[61]

After receiving the petition Franklin sent it to the Earl of Dartmouth, Secretary of State for the Colonies, on August 21, 1773, with an explanatory letter begging him to present it to the King and hoping for a favourable reply.[62] By December 3 John Pownall signified that Dartmouth had presented the petition to the King, who directed that it be laid before the Privy Council.[63] On January 3, 1774, the Privy Council also received a petition from Israel Mauduit, in behalf of the Governor and the Lieutenant Governor, praying that he might be heard through counsel relative to the petition.[64] This was granted, and on January 4 Franklin and the London agent for the Council, William Bollan, together with Alexander Wedder-

[60] *Journal of the House of Representatives* (Boston, 1773–4), p. 75.
[61] For the petition see *Letters of Governor Hutchinson* . . . , pp. 67–70, and *Acts of the Privy Council, Col. Ser., 1766–1783*, pp. 387–8.
[62] *Letters of Governor Hutchinson* . . . , p. 65.
[63] *Ibid.*, p. 66.
[64] *Ibid.*, p. 71.

Franklin Before the Lords in Council, 1774, after the painting by C. Schuessele.
(From J. M. Butler's *Franklin Before the Privy Council, White Hall Chapel, London, 1774,* 1859)

The Boston Tea Party, a nineteenth-century copy of the contemporary English print.

(American Antiquarian Society)

burn, counsel for Mauduit, appeared before the Privy Council at a preliminary hearing.[65] Further proceedings took place on January 28 in the Privy Council chamber in the presence of the Lord President and thirty-five other Lords. It was on this occasion that Wedderburn delivered his philippic against Benjamin Franklin and the petition of the Massachusetts House of Representatives. In print it covered more than thirty-five pages, even with the omission of the major portion that gave a history of events in the colony from 1764 to 1774.[66] The Solicitor General's aim was to brand Franklin as a leader who used thoroughly unscruplous methods in seeking to widen the breach between Massachusetts Bay and Great Britain.[67] According to Franklin, his chief desire in sending the letters had been to prove that the government of Great Britain did not instigate the harsh measures taken against Massachusetts Bay but that these measures—"the sending of troops to Boston, and other measures so offensive to the People of New England . . . were projected, propos'd & solicited by some of the principle & best esteemed of their own People."[68] However laudable may have been the reasons for Franklin's conduct, the Ministry deplored it, called his action disgraceful, and accordingly deprived him of his office of joint deputy postmaster-general of North America.[69]

[65] *Ibid.*, extra, asterisk-marked pp. 77–80.

[66] For Wedderburn's speech see *ibid.*, pp. 77–113; on an extra page, inserted and marked "79°," a series of asterisks covering part of the page indicates the omission of the portion having to do with the behaviour of Hutchinson in public office from 1764 to 1774 to prove "the very laudable and friendly part he acted on every occasion for the good of the colony." Letters in the London *Public Advertiser,* later reprinted in the *Boston Evening-Post,* charged that before the speech had been published it had been edited so as to soften the harsher words used by the Solicitor General. For example, Wedderburn was reported to have stated that the letters sent by Franklin were "for Purposes the most malignant, and procured by Means the most infamous and corrupt," and "that Dr. Franklin had *stolen* . . . the Letters in question." See *Boston Evening-Post,* Supplement, May 2, 1774.

[67] Franklin defended his conduct in his "Tract Relative to the Affair of Hutchinson's Letters," written in 1774 but not published until 1817. See Smyth's *Writings of Benjamin Franklin,* VI, 258–89, especially pp. 283–5 for the cause of the duel between William Whately, brother of Thomas Whately, and John Temple involving the letters, and for Franklin's statement, published in the *Public Advertiser,* that the letters were never in the possession of William Whatley but that he himself secured them from another and sent them to Boston.

[68] Franklin to Joseph Galloway, February 18, 1774, *Writings of Benjamin Franklin* (Smyth), VI, 195–6.

[69] *Ibid.* For additional details of Franklin's dismissal from office see London advices, January 29, *Boston Evening-Post,* April 25, 1774.

In this connection an anonymous letter written to Lord North on February 5, 1774, presents a view of the reaction to Franklin's loss of office: "As an *American,* give me leave to assure your Lordship that I think the dismissing of Dr. *Franklin* from the Postmaster General in *North America,* at this particular crisis, one of the

On February 7, 1774, the Privy Council made final disposition of the petition of the House of Representatives. Designating the resolutions contained in it as based on "False and Erroneous allegations," the Council reached the decision that, in view of the "groundless, vexatious and . . . seditious Purpose" of the contents, which did not "in any manner or any Degree, Impeach the Honour, Integrity or Conduct of the said Governor or Lieutenant Governor, . . . the said Petition ought to be dismissed."[70]

As for Thomas Hutchinson, in the course of writing to Lord Dartmouth on June 26, 1773, to present the facts about the letters, he pointed out that after four years in office, attended by every difficulty that could be imagined, the complaint made about him by the General Assembly could point to no one act of maladministration but was forced to have recourse to letters which he had written in his private capacity before assuming the office of Governor and which were "in ev[er]y p[ar]t true, & in no p[ar]t unfriend[ly] to the Prov[ince]." He therewith indicated his desire to go to England, even at his "advanced period of life," and begged Dartmouth to secure the King's approval of an absence from his post for six or nine months for purposes of regulating his private affairs and for His Majesty's service.[71]

In truth, Governor Hutchinson was by the summer of 1773 an isolated, lonely person in the performance of his public duties.[72] He

---

most fortunate events that could have happened for that country. The people there never liked the Institution, and only acquiesced in it out of their unbounded affection for the person that held the office. . . . And thus will happily end your boasted Post Office, so often given as a precedent for taxing the *Americans*" (*American Archives*, 4th ser., I, 500).

[70] *Acts of the Privy Council, Col. Ser., 1766–1783*, pp. 387–8. To Hutchinson the means employed to secure his private letters, to stir up the public over their supposed contents, and to make them public, were "infamous and detestable." See his letter to the Rev. Mr. Lyman of July 16, 1773, Hutchinson Correspondence, Massachusetts Archives, 27:514.

[71] Although Dartmouth's name is not given, internal evidence shows that the letter must have been addressed to him as Secretary of State for the Colonies. The original of this letter has not been found, but a transcript of the draft in the handwriting of Hutchinson's nephew, the Rev. Thomas Hutchinson, is among the Hutchinson Family Correspondence, Egerton Manuscripts, 2659:44–5, British Museum. The leave of absence was granted in August but Hutchinson did not receive notice of it until November 14. See his letter to Dartmouth, November 15, 1773, Massachusetts Archives, 27:570–1; see also Shelburne Papers, 88:3–9, Clements Library.

[72] In writing to the Secretary of the Board of Trade about the provincial resolutions seeking Hutchinson's dismissal, after his private correspondence had been made public, the Governor declared, with singular objectivity: "It is immaterial . . . whether their [the Council and House] resolves are true or not. They carry weight

especially felt the lack of the support of the Council. On July 10 he wrote: "They have lost all sense of their being his Majesty's Council . . . & there are some who are ready to go to all the lengths of the Chief Incendiary [Bowdoin], who is determined, he says, to get rid of every Governor who obstructs them in their course to Independency."[73] Faced with the hostility displayed by both houses of the General Assembly to the policy of government which he was seeking to uphold, Hutchinson on June 29 by proclamation prorogued the General Court to September 15 and again, on August 14, to November 3; on October 9 it was further prorogued to January 12, 1774, and once again, on December 1, to January 26, when it at last reconvened.[74]

However, prior to the meeting of the General Assembly in 1774 other developments in Massachusetts Bay in reaction to the passage of the Tea Act and other colonial grievances made the Governor's position utterly untenable. For the prospects of the implementation of the Act were beginning to precipitate a storm of debate in the press and a crisis which would cause alarming repercussions throughout the colonies. Thus, we must consider these developments in 1773 before turning to the inexorable progression of events in the Bay colony, as its leadership in the American revolutionary movement in the year 1774 became ever more dominant.

---

among the people. . . . I think it would be giving up Government entirely to comply with their request, yet I fear what they desire will be necessary in a short time . . . the Lieut.-Governor may remain; the resentment is against me . . . I have no doubt this plot originated in England . . . The leaders give out that they take no step without advice or direction from England. I have withstood them as long as I could, but I am now left without any support in the province. It was not in the power of human wisdom to guard against this last villany [the obtaining and making public of the Governor's correspondence]" (Hutchinson to J. P[ownall], July 3, 1773, *Calendar of Home Office Papers, George III, 1773–1775* [ed. R. A. Roberts, London, 1899], p. 63). However, Hutchinson might have anticipated treatment of this kind, had he recalled the action that followed the ordering of troops to Boston in 1768 and the publication of Governor Bernard's *Letters to the Ministry* . . . (Boston, 1769) along with those of General Gage and Commodore Hood.

[73] Hutchinson to ———, July 10, 1773, Massachusetts Archives, 27:512–13.

[74] For the four proclamations proroguing the Great and General Court see *Boston Evening-Post*, July 5, August 23, October 16, and December 27, 1773.

CHAPTER III

Tea and the Climate
of Sedition

ONCURRENTLY with the constitutional issues that were coming
to a climax in Massachusetts Bay as the duty-bound Governor reached an impasse in the conflict with the General
Assembly, other colonial grievances—especially as a result of the
Gaspee affair and the passing of the Tea Act of 1773—were also
reaching a stage where open, aggressive action was accompanied
by a war of words. In addition to the bold steps being taken by the
town meetings and the committees of correspondence, the outpour-
ings of the press—in newspapers and pamphlets—were serving as a
chief instrument for arousing the people to extreme measures. For
example, on December 3, 1772, in Boston John Allen delivered an
oration on the "Beauties of Liberty," in protest against the trial connected with the *Gaspee* affair[1] and against Parliament's stand on
supremacy. This was published the following year by popular request.[2] In dedicating this sermon to the Earl of Dartmouth, the
author protested the infringement of the rights of Rhode Islanders by
the British government in setting up a Board of Inquiry with im-

[1] For the burning of the armed schooner *Gaspee* and the aftermath of this action
see Chap. 1 of this volume.

[2] The title as printed in the fourth edition of this pamphlet in 1773 is *An Oration,
on the Beauties of Liberty, or the Essential Rights of the Americans. Delivered at
the Second Baptist-Church in Boston . . . Dec. 3d, 1772. Dedicated to the Right
Honourable the Earl of Dartmouth. Published by the earnest Request of Many.
Fourth Edition, carefully corrected by the Author. . . . By a British Bostonian*
(Boston, 1773). This was earlier attributed to Isaac Skillman, but the *Providence
Gazette* of December 19, 1772, carries the following news item from Boston dated
December 14: "Last Thanksgiving . . . Mr. Allen, a British Bostonian, preached a
sermon at the Rev. Mr. Davis's Meeting House, from these words, Micah vii, 3."
This is the Biblical text used in *Beauties of Liberty*. The pamphlet also went into three
editions in New London. See in this connection J. M. Bumsted and C. E. Clark: "New
England's Tom Paine: John Allen and the Spirit of Liberty," *William and Mary
Quarterly*, 3rd ser., XXI, 561–70.

proper jurisdiction as the aftermath of the burning of the *Gaspee*. All power, he pointed out, flows from the people; those who administer this power are but trustees. If this power is abused, then it is the people's right and duty

> "to resume that delegated authority . . . and call their trustees to *Account;* to resist the usurpation, and extirpate the tyranny. . . . Then surely it follows, that the K – – g, M – – – – – – y, and P – – – – – – – – t, are Rebels to God and mankind, in attempting to overthrow, by guns, by swords, and by the power of war, the laws and government of Rhode-Island. Have not the Rhode-Islanders as much right to the privileges of their own laws, as the King of England to his Crown? . . . Then surely that man must be a Tyrant in his soul that deems it rebellion in the Rhode-Islanders if they kill every man that attempts to destroy their lives, laws, rights, or liberties."

As to the burning of the *Gaspee*, the writer denied that any laws binding on the people of Rhode Island had been broken, for he failed to see how any American could "be said to break the laws of England." He saw it rather as a matter of the "laws of *America*" having been broken and urged that the offenders be tried accordingly. For he could find no more justification for the presence of an armed schooner sent by the King or the Ministry in Rhode Island waters than if one were to be sent on that same authority to a French port to make demands there. He concluded with the significant words: "Let all lovers of Liberty, truth and justice now unite as one man in recovering and firmly establishing the Liberties of America: That the *American* Parliament may enjoy every power and priviledge the *English* Parliament enjoy. . . ."[3]

It was in line with this general point of view that a writer signing himself "Z" in the October 11, 1773, number of the *Boston Gazette* asked:

---

[3] This theme was greatly expanded by Allen in his *The American Alarm, or the Bostonian Plea, for the Rights, and Liberties, of the People. Humbly Addressed to the King and Council, and to the Constitutional Sons of Liberty, in America. By the British Bostonian* (Boston, 1773), a pamphlet divided into four parts. The first thirty-five pages formed "An Address to the gentlemen of the provinces of America"; the next three sections were addressed respectively "To the king's most excellent majesty," "To his excellency the governor of the Province of the Massachusetts-Bay," and, finally, "To the honourable the people's Council, and House of Representatives, of the Province of the Massachusetts-Bay." This pamphlet also was attributed to Isaac Skillman, according to Charles Evans: *American Bibliography, 1629–1820* (2nd edn., 14 vols., New York, 1941–59), IV, 393, but is authenticated as Allen's on p. 66 of the 4th edn. of *Oration on the Beauties of Liberty.*

"How shall the colonies force their oppressors to terms? This question has been often answered by our politicians; viz., 'Form an independent State,—an American commonwealth.' This plan has been proposed, and I can't find that any other is likely to answer the great purpose of preserving our liberties. . . ."

With the Tea Act occupying the people's primary interest in the fall of 1773, writers in the Boston newspapers continued to lead the way in America in adopting an extreme position regarding the constitutional issues. Nor did another writer using the signature "Z" in the October 25 edition of the *Boston Evening-Post* succeed in moderating the torrent of denunciation of the British government when he pointed out the inconsistency of this outcry by asking the readers: "Have not large quantities of Teas for some years past been continually imported into this Province from England both on account of Dealers of Tea there, and the Merchants here, all of which have paid the American Duty?"[4] In the *Massachusetts Gazette; and the Boston Weekly News-Letter* of October 28, the question was raised: "What consistency is there in making a clamor about this small branch of revenue, whilst we silently pass over the articles of sugar, molasses and wine, from which more than three-quarter parts of the American revenue has and always will arise?" To this a writer in the *Boston Gazette* of November 1 replied: "We clamor against the tea . . . as a commodity the British Ministry have inflicted with the plague." "Causidicus," writing in the *Massachusetts Spy*[5] of November 4, declared: "Despotism with all its horrors stares us full in the face. . . . Taxation without consent and monopoly of trade, establishing itself together. . . ." What, he asked, must the consequence be if these become permanent? "What indeed, but the most dreadful train of intolerable evils that ever overwhelm a people!" In the same edition of this paper "A Committee Man" proposed a

---

[4] It is of interest to note that the tightly reasoned argument given in the article by "Z" pointing out some of the beneficial consequences that would attend the execution of the East India Company's plan for the sale of tea in the colonies, was apparently written by members of the firm of Richard Clarke & Sons, Boston tea consignees, and was printed in the *Boston Evening-Post* at their instigation, "by the assistance of a friend." For the letter from the Clarke firm establishing their authorship of the "Z" article—in which, the writers claimed, "every objection that has been stated against the Company's plan is fully answered"—addressed in November 1773 to Abraham Dupuis, the London merchant, see *Tea Leaves: Being a Collection of Letters and Documents Relating to the Shipment of Tea to the American Colonies in the Year 1773, by the East India Tea Company* (ed. F. S. Drake, Boston, 1884), pp. 279–82.

[5] The full title of this paper was *The Massachusetts Spy Or, Thomas's Boston Journal.*

drastic solution to deal with the tea commissioners (or consignees) after they had been approached peaceably to go along with the will of the people. "If after this fair declaration of the public sense, they still persevere in their resolution to destroy their country, all the world will applaud the spirit that, for the common preservation, will exterminate such malignant and dangerous persons." He was upheld by the statement of "XY" in the same issue of the *Spy:*

> "that whereas the peace of this community is inevitably destroyed, if the unconstitutional [customs] commissioners, etc., which for some years past have been intruded upon us, get leave to remain any longer here, That the Select men who are fathers of the town, assemble and go in a body to them, respectively declaring their apprehension, that the people are not safe while they reside among them, and setting a time for their departure. And in case they do not comply with the proposal, for the whole body of the people to rise and expel them, as infested and dangerous persons."

"Sydney," writing from "North America" in the November 11, 1773, number of the *Massachusetts Spy,* saluted his fellow North Americans as follows:

> "I ADDRESS YOU as the most virtuous, free and happy people who now inhabit the world. . . . Your *humanity* has hitherto restrained you, and shielded your enemies from just punishment—But how much longer shall your wicked oppressors riot on your hard earned wealth? . . . You are now millions strong, situated in the best part of the globe, and will you any more be insulted by a kennel of *tyrants,* or their hackeyed *tools?* . . . Shall the island *Britain* enslave this great continent of *America* which is more than ninety nine times bigger, and is capable of supporting hundreds of millions of . . . people?"

"Britannus Septentrionalis" addressed the "Patriotic Printers in Boston" also in the *Massachusetts Spy* for November 11. He asked them whether during the past eight years (that is, from 1765 to 1773) patriotic correspondents to their papers had aimed at doing anything more than "skinning over a cancer, leaving the main root at the bottom?" For his own part he thought that "no state can be sound and entire unless the full and absolute sovereignty, that is, legislative, executive and military power thereof, be lodged solely in itself." After referring to the charter granted by Charles I, the writer then turned to the one drawn up during the reign of William and Mary and affirmed: "The province was from its foundation intended a free and sovereign state, that is, a state having all the powers of ruling . . . and defending itself." Mentioning the so-called reserve powers included in the William and Mary charter, he asked: "Can any one shew more than the reservation of power, *from time to time to appoint and commission one Governor, one Lieutenant or Deputy Governor, one Secretary and one Judge of vice admiralty*, every one of these, to be governed, directed and supported by the legislative of this province?" He then turned his attention to the abuse of the sovereign powers of the Crown—presumably limited to the appointment of a few officers—manifested by the presence in the province of "all this legion of custom house officers, surveyors of woods, and no one knows what else. . . ." Was this not, he asked,

> "erecting a power within our government entirely independent of it in every shape; . . . is not another power assumed, which no trace of stipulation in the universe is pretended to warrant, to *bind us* in fetters of iron, and extort from us what share of our property it pleases . . . ? Are all those no intrusions, no encroachments, no invasions, no violations of our rights? Or can any state making such inroads on the constitution of another state, and even taking the whole of its government into its own hands, and supporting all these usurpations by a military force, expect that the aggrieved state can conceive itself bound, by any pact whatever, to look upon the former state as a mother, patronness and protector? . . . But what of all this, says a prerogative gentleman, this province is no such thing as a nation, a sovereign independent state; it is only a colony depending on the crown or mother state from the first planting to the present day."

Then, calling upon Vattel (*Droit des gens* . . . [Neuchâtel, 1758], p. 12) as his chief authority and admitting there was a dependence on the Crown of Great Britain, he declared: "Two sovereign (*self governing*) states may be subject to the same prince, without any dependence on each other, and each may retain all its national rights free and sovereign." To prove that Massachusetts Bay was really a nation and state, he again quoted Vattel, who noted (p. 6) that "nations or states are bodies politic, societies of men united together, to procure their mutual safety by means of their union."

The above views of the independent position of the province in its relationship to the parent country were endorsed in a later edition of the *Massachusetts Spy*[6] by "Massachusettensis," in his appeal "To

---

[6] *Massachusetts Spy*, November 18, 1773.

all Nations of Men, dwelling on the face of the whole Earth, especially those of Great Britain and Ireland, more especially the inhabitants of North-America, and particularly those of Massachusetts-Bay
in New-England." The writer went even further. All demands by
Parliament on the purse of the people of the colony were, he affirmed,
illegal and, if put into execution, robbery;

> "if the demand be made sword in hand, *it is robbery with murderous
> intentions!* Can any one excuse the British parliament, from the viola-
> tion of those most sacred bonds of human society? Have they not
> actually invaded the freedom of our persons pretending to bind us
> by laws to which our consent was never so much as asked? . . . Have
> they not utterly subverted the free consititition of our state by making
> our supreme magistrate a mere dependent on the minister of Great
> Britain . . . ? Have they not further interfered with our civil policy
> and intruded a set of officers upon us, entirely independent of the
> supreme power of the province, constituting the most dangerous and
> intolerable evil that ever was felt by a people . . . ?"

The writer therefore arrived at the conclusion that these "usurpers,
or *foreign emissaries,* being screened from the power of the laws,
have returned to a state of nature again with respect to this people,
and may justly be slain as wolves, tygers, or . . . private robbers and
murderers. . . ."

How fundamentally different were the views of the above writers
from those expressed by Benjamin Franklin, London agent for the
House of Representatives, when he assured the Earl of Dartmouth
as late as August 21, 1773, that "a sincere disposition prevails in the
people there to be on good terms with the Mother Country" and that
"the Assembly have declared their desire only to be put into the
situation they were in before the stamp act; they aim at no novel-
ties."[7] Although there were many other expressions of this desire to
return to the relationship between colony and mother country as it
existed in the first half of the 1760's, it may well be speculated that
this was an argument that lacked a realistic basis.

Furthermore, in emphasizing the utterances in the Massachusetts
Bay press of individuals who were shielded by anonymity, the point
should be made that these words probably represented the deep
convictions of large numbers of people in that province, in contrast
to the more cautious statements openly put forward or endorsed by

---

[7] For this letter see *Letters of Governor Hutchinson . . . ,* p. 65.

identifiable persons, especially those known to have an understanding of English constitutional law. Nevertheless, were even the more extreme of those assertions of the sovereign rights of the people of Massachusetts Bay quoted above, far removed from Franklin's views privately expressed even as early as 1766, when he wrote: "The sov^y of the British legislature out of Britain I do not understand," and, with reference to the nature of the connection of the American colonies with Great Britain, ". . . we are different States, Subject to the King";[8] or the view expressed by him in 1771 to Speaker Thomas Cushing of the House of Representatives of the province: "My opinion has long been that Parliament had originally no Right to bind us by any kind of Law whatever without our Consent"?[9]

Such, by 1773, was the climate of opinion in Massachusetts Bay regarding the issue of parliamentary supremacy. Yet the press did not maintain a high pitch of excitement at all times. For instance, the passage of the Tea Act in the spring of 1773, apparently without debate, aroused little or no comment in America at the time. The July 14 *Pennsylvania Gazette* and the July 19 *Boston Evening-Post* simply listed the Act. Nor did Edmund Burke—one of the most active critics of the government in the House of Commons and an equally active supporter there of American interests—find any cause for adverse comment on the Act when, in his capacity as London agent of the New York Assembly, he wrote to its committee of correspondence in the summer of 1773 and mentioned only the bill for regulating the East India Company.[10] However, Benjamin Franklin, writing to the Speaker of the House of Representatives of Massachusetts Bay in June, expressed serious reservations:

"It was thought at the Beginning of the Session, that the American Duty on Tea would be taken off. But now the wise Scheme is to take off so much Duty here, as will make Tea cheaper in America than Foreigners can supply us, and to confine the Duty there to keep up the Exercise of the Right. They have no Idea that any People act from any other Principle but that of Interest; and they believe, that

---

[8] For Franklin's notations made in 1766 in connection with the Stamp Act crisis, see V. W. Crane: "Benjamin Franklin and the Stamp Act," Colonial Society of Massachusetts *Transactions*, XXXII, 71–3.

[9] Franklin to Cushing, June 10, 1771, *Writings of Benjamin Franklin* (Smyth), V, 324.

[10] Burke to the New York committee of correspondence, July 3, 1773, *Correspondence of Edmund Burke* (ed. T. W. Copeland *et al.*, 5 vols.+, Cambridge and Chicago, 1958–65+), II, *Correspondence, July 1768–June 1774* (ed. Lucy Sutherland, 1960), pp. 438–42.

3d in a lb. of Tea . . . is sufficient to overcome all the Patriotism of an American."[11]

The colonial merchants did not actually become alarmed until late in August, when information reached Boston that the East India Company was availing itself of the privilege of exporting tea free of any export duty and would soon send a cargo to Boston (subject to the duty payable in America) "to be sold in that Place on their account; and they mean to keep America so well supplied, that the [colonial smuggling] Trade to Holland for that Article must be greatly affected."[12] In September news arrived of a more definite nature—word that the Company had decided to send loads of 600 chests of tea to Philadelphia, New York, and Boston and, further, that it was prepared to establish warehouses at these places from which to dispose of the tea four times a year at public auction.[13] As the East India Company had no ships of its own for this service, it was obliged to charter them through the London houses trading to America, which apparently were eager to solicit this business. A correspondent writing from London on August 7 declared, however, that certain New York and Philadelphia captains, when approached, refused to commit their vessels to this traffic.[14] Despite such reluctance there is ample evidence that the East India Company did not lack for applicants eager to transport the tea.[15]

What tended to accentuate the hostility of colonials to the shipment of tea to America was not only the maintenance of the three-

[11] Franklin to Cushing, June 4, 1773, *Writings of Benjamin Franklin* (Smyth), VI, 57. In a previous letter to Cushing of January 5, 1773, Franklin, noting that unmarketable goods valued at £ 4,000,000 were estimated to be in the East India Company's warehouses, stated that this showed "the great Imprudence of losing the American Market, by keeping the [import] Duty on Tea [shipped into the colonies], which has thrown that Trade into the Hands of the Dutch, Danes, Swedes, and French, who . . . now supply by smuggling the whole Continent [through American vessels], not with Tea only, but . . . with other India Goods, amounting, as supposed, in the whole to £ 500,000 Sterling per Annum" (*ibid.*, VI, 3).

[12] London advices, May 26, *Boston Evening-Post*, August 23, 1773.

[13] London advices, August 4, *Pennsylvania Gazette*, September 29, 1773; the same item appeared in the *Boston Evening-Post* on October 11, 1773.

[14] *Ibid.* The correspondent was, according to internal evidence, manifestly a colonial who naturally presented the colonial point of view when he further stated that the Company had sought to have a bill introduced in Parliament to drop the American import duty, but that Lord North "struck out the plan . . . hoping thereby to outwit us, and to establish that Act effectually, which will forever after be pleaded for a precedent for every imposition Parliament shall think proper to saddle us with.—It is much to be wished that Americans will convince Lord North, that they are not yet ready to have the yoke of slavery rivetted about their necks, and [will] send back the Tea again."

[15] See *Tea Leaves*, pp. 243, 245–6, 251–4.

pence import duty as a token of the supremacy of Parliament, but the prospect that almost every leading merchant along the Atlantic seaboard would be adversely affected by the new right of the East India Company to sell directly to colonial retailers. It was true—as Joseph Galloway pointed out in 1780, when a refugee in England—that the new arrangement would have been a benefit to all American consumers of tea. But colonials chose to ignore the fact that under the arrangement they were to provide profits only to the Company and to the shopkeeper who sold them the tea, whereas, under the prior-established system, they were obliged to pay the Company its profit, another profit to the London merchant who bought his tea at the Company auctions, still another to the American wholesaler who purchased the product from the English merchant, and, finally, the profit that the retailer must receive to remain in business.[16] In other words, consumers would have been able to get their tea for a fraction of the price they had been accustomed to pay even for smuggled tea —which apparently came to the colonies in enormous quantities— not to mention the imported tea on which the duty was paid. For it should be made clear that Boston merchants (including Thomas Hutchinson) had been importing fairly large quantities of tea and paying the duties on it under the terms of the Townshend Act from 1769 up to October 1773—a fact which was not widely known until published in the newspapers in November 1773.[17] Even John Hancock, who was to play a leading role in the Boston Tea Party, imported 300 whole chests and 55 half chests of tea.[18] It would therefore

---

[16] See Joseph Galloway: *Historical and Political Reflections on the Rise and Progress of the American Rebellion* (London, 1780), pp. 17–18.

[17] See "An Account of Tea imported into Boston, from London, which has paid the duty of 3d. sterling per pound"

		Chests	½ Chests	¼ Chests
In the year	1769	329	11	–
	1770	153	14	–
	1771	709	84	7
	1772	323	52	–
to Oct.	1773	349	25	–

The above is copied from an "Account certified by the Collector of the Customs in Boston." This account was published in *Rivington's New-York Gazetteer* on November 11, 1773, and reprinted in the *Pennsylvania Gazette* on November 17; see also *Boston Evening-Post*, November 15, 1773, for a similar report. In connection with legal and illegal tea shipments see A. M. Schlesinger's *Colonial Merchants*, pp. 245–51 (as cited in Chap. 1 of the present volume), along with other importation figures having to do with the smuggling trade.

[18] See Boston comptroller of customs Benjamin Hallowell to John Pownall, September 29, 1773, quoted by Schlesinger: *op. cit.*, p. 246; see also W. T. Baxter: *The House of Hancock: Business in Boston, 1724–1775* (Cambridge, Mass., 1945), p. 281.

seem to have been not so much the prospect of being required to pay the insignificant duty of threepence per pound on tea—which had been levied ever since the passage of the Townshend Revenue Act in 1767—that so deeply stirred the mercantile element in America in the fall of 1773, as it was the prospect of losing an established business in both legal and smuggled tea now threatened by the East India Company's plan to become the chief agency for supplying the needs of the petty retailers of that article.[19] Moreover, the threat that the East India Company agents would gain a monopoly of the colonial tea market was compounded by fears of a subsequent rise in prices. Thus an element of self-interest was clearly mingled with the growing colonial concern over rights and liberties.

It was not possible to publicize the Tea Act fully in Boston until a copy of it reached that port in October, when it was given the widest possible circulation in the press.[20] Even then, it was not the people of Boston who first reacted unfavourably to this legislation but those of New York and Philadelphia. On October 15, at a meeting of inhabitants of New York held at the Coffee House, thanks were voted to the captains of ships belonging to that port and to the local import merchants who had refused to accept shipments in London of East India Company tea destined for the "insidious Purpose of levying the Duty in America, and taking off a much greater in England, . . . being nothing less than to establish the *odious* Precedent of *raising a Revenue in America*."[21] A meeting held on October 16 at the State House in Philadelphia unanimously adopted a series of resolutions, chiefly aimed at the British Ministry and Parliament. These asserted that the "Claim of Parliament to tax America is, in other Words, a Claim of Right to levy Contributions on us at Pleasure." Further, the tea duty was held to be a tax on Americans without their consent and to have "a direct Tendency to render Assemblies useless, and to introduce arbitrary Government and Slavery." Therefore, "a virtuous and steady Opposition to this Ministerial Plan of governing America" was deemed "absolutely necessary to preserve even the Shadow of Liberty." In the light of this danger, the resolutions concluded:

---

[19] See Thomas Hutchinson's *History* . . . (Mayo), III, 303.

[20] For example, the *Boston Evening-Post*, October 25, 1773, printed the Act on the first page, as did the *Pennsylvania Gazette* on November 3, 1773.

[21] *New York Gazette: and the Weekly Mercury*, October 25, 1773; see also *Pennsylvania Gazette*, October 27, 1773.

"That whoever shall . . . countenance this Attempt, or in any wise aid or abet in . . . vending the Tea sent . . . while it remains subject to the Payment of a Duty here, is an Enemy to his Country."[22]

Yet, as previously mentioned, the tension over the Tea Act had been steadily mounting in Boston during the fall of 1773.[23]

In the latter part of October the report spread in the town that Richard Clarke & Sons, Benjamin Faneuil, Jr., and the sons of the Governor, Thomas and Elisha Hutchinson, had been appointed to receive the tea that was being shipped to Boston. On the 21st a writer in the *Massachusetts Spy* declared that upon its arrival this article would undoubtedly be returned to England "if the people do not insist on copying the resolutions of Philadelphia and New York to destroy it." Another correspondent hinted that it would be highly improper if those great cargoes should be carried back "without sending [with them], the Important Gentlemen whose existence depends on it." As to the protection that the Governor reportedly had promised the tea consignees, the question was raised: "would his Excellency be certain of protection for himself, should a betrayed people take it upon them to right themselves?"[24] On this same day the intercolonial committee of correspondence in Boston sent out an appeal to all the other colonies calling upon them to prevent the East India Company shipments of tea from landing in America.[25] The committee had now found an issue on which to begin the concerted action that would lead to ultimate intercolonial unity.

The first action of the people of Boston stemmed, it would appear, from decisions reached by the North End caucus of mechanics that met, as was customary, in the Green Dragon Tavern on the night of November 2. It was here that, under the leadership of the popular Dr. Joseph Warren, certain resolutions were adopted for presentation to the tea consignees the following day at a mass meeting to be held at the Liberty Tree.[26] Tea commissioner Clarke was roused

---

[22] The resolutions were eight in number and are to be found in the *Pennsylvania Gazette*, October 20, 1773.

[23] See in this connection B. W. Labaree: *op. cit.*, Chap. 1, "The Colonial Tea Trade," for a definitive account of the general background of events surrounding that crisis.

[24] *Massachusetts Spy*, October 21, 1773.

[25] Massachusetts Historical Society *Proceedings*, XIII, 162.

[26] John Cary: *Joseph Warren, Physician, Politician, Patriot* (Urbana, Ill., 1961), p. 130; see also John Almon: *A Collection of Interesting, Authentic Papers, Relative to the Dispute between Great Britain and America . . . from 1764–1775* (London, 1777), p. 251, more commonly known by its short title, *Prior Documents*, which will be cited hereafter. For an excerpt from the circular letter dated October 21, 1773, see

from his bed with an order that he and his associates were to appear at the Liberty Tree gathering. When the inhabitants of Boston and the neighbouring towns met at the appointed spot—to the accompaniment of bells tolling throughout the town—to hear the consignees publicly agree to resign their assignments, these agents of the Company did not appear. Instead, they assembled in Clarke's store. There a committee of the people waited upon them with the information that, as they had not seen fit to obey the summons, "the public would be warranted in looking upon them as the enemies of the people." The tea factors replied that they would pay no attention to any demand for their presence.[27] Their refusal led the selectmen to call a town meeting for the morning of November 5 at Faneuil Hall. With John Hancock acting as moderator, the meeting adopted certain resolutions[28] in which it asserted that the express purpose of the tea tax was "to introduce arbitrary government and slavery" in the colonies, and that "a virtuous and steady opposition to this ministerial plan of governing *America* . . . is a duty which every freeman in *America* owes to his country, to himself, and to his posterity." A committee was then appointed to approach those who were to receive the tea and to request them, not only as a matter of their own character but for "the peace and good order of this town and province, immediately to resign their appointment." The consignees Clarke & Sons and Faneuil replied that when they were acquainted with the moral and pecuniary obligations of their commission they would be better qualified to give a definite answer; while Thomas Hutchinson, Jr., sent word from Milton that he and his brother were not in a position to reply until they had actually received and examined the terms of their appointment as factors of the tea. The town meeting held both of these responses to be unsatisfactory.[29]

Governor Hutchinson wrote to the Earl of Dartmouth on Novem-

Tea Leaves, Introduction, p. 15; see also E. I. Miller: "The Virginia Committee of Correspondence, 1773–1775," *William and Mary Quarterly,* 1st ser., XXII, 106–7.

[27] See *Boston Evening-Post,* November 8, 1773, and *Boston Gazette,* November 15, 1773.

[28] These resolutions were preceded by a petition of a large number of inhabitants who up to that time had been importing teas and paying the duties on them and who appealed "that the trade upon which they depend for a subsistence is threatened to be totally destroyed," adding (perhaps very inconsistently in view of their previous payment of the duties) that "our liberties, for which we have long struggled, will be lost. . . ." *Boston Town Records, 1770–1777* (Boston, 1887), pp. 141–2. See also *Votes and Proceedings . . . Of the Boston . . . Town Meeting Assembled . . . the 5th and 18th days of November, 1773* (Boston, 1773); this may be found in *Early American Imprints, 1639–1800,* Readex Microprint, Evans No. 12692.

[29] For the replies to the town meeting and its response see *ibid.*

ber 15, 1773, that he was doing everything in his power to preserve "the Peace and good Order of the Town," but made it clear that he was without the support of the Council. That body, he reported, professed to disapprove "the tumultuous violent Proceedings of the People," yet approved their objectives and believed that the only way to pacify them was for the consignees to refuse to accept the tea shipments. The Council members of greatest influence, he affirmed, had taken the position that they would never countenance "a Measure which shall tend to carry into execution an Act of Parliament which lays Taxes upon the Colonies for the Purpose of a Revenue," while the reaction of the factors was that as long as they could be "protected from Violence to their Persons, they will not give way to the unreasonable Demands which have been made of them."[30]

On November 18, in reply to representations made to them by a committee from a town meeting held that morning, the tea consignees announced that they had received information that the engagements entered into on their behalf by agents in England were purely commercial in nature, a disclosure which, they made clear, "puts it out of our power to comply with the request of the town." This statement was voted to be unsatisfactory by the town meeting.[31] The next day the agents therefore petitioned the Governor and Council to be permitted "to resign themselves and the property committed to their care, to his Excellency, and their Honours, as guardians and protectors of the people" and asked "that measures be taken to land and secure the tea until they would be at liberty openly and safely to dispose of it or until they had received directions from their constituents."[32] This petition so startled the Council that it was the subject of deliberation at several sessions. As the members were unwilling to assume any responsibility for acting on it, their only recommendation was that the Governor call upon the local peace officers to be vigilant in executing their duties—a step that, under the circumstances, was meaningless.[33]

---

[30] "American Letters," September 1773 to January 5, 1774, Shelburne Papers, 88:3–9.

[31] Votes and Proceedings ... Boston Town Meeting, November 5th and 18th, 1773, previously cited.

[32] Massachusetts Spy, November 26, 1773.

[33] For a certified copy of the proceedings of the Council at its meetings on November 19, 23, 27, and 29, 1773, see the Gage Papers, American Series, No. 119, Clements Library. Among the papers is the report of a Council committee, headed by James Bowdoin, that was unanimously adopted on November 29. Though it dealt primarily with the petition of the tea consignees, it also went into the background of the crisis, with emphasis on the efforts of Parliament to draw a revenue from America,

This was the state of things when on November 28 one of the tea ships, the *Dartmouth,* Captain Hall, came to anchor near Castle William eight weeks out of London, bearing 114 chests of "that worst of plagues, the detested tea." The next morning the ship anchored at the Long Wharf. Simultaneously, a town meeting, called by the Boston Committee of Correspondence to assemble at Faneuil Hall, was adjourned to Old South Meeting House because of the size of the crowd. There the gathering voted that the tea must be sent back without the payment of duty and that the owner of the vessel and Captain Hall were to be warned "at their peril" that they were not to permit any of the cargo to be landed. Then, also, came the suggestion that the way to dispose of the tea was to throw it overboard.[34] Furthermore, a letter from the tea consignees was read in which they asked the town to try to understand the unexpected difficulties that they faced. It indicated that they were prepared to store the tea until orders were received for its disposition. But the gathering was unmoved by this plea and remained firm in its determination that no East India Company tea should be landed. Acting upon this decision, volunteer guards set up a system of watches and boarded the *Dartmouth.*[35]

In the face of the open resistance to the authority of the government of Great Britain, the Governor issued a proclamation on the following day calling upon the people, who had again assembled, to disperse and "at their utmost Peril" to cease their unlawful proceed-

whereby the people were deprived of a right "which they hold to be an essential one, that it cannot be taken away, or given up without their being degraded, or degrading themselves below the character of Men." The report then turned to the danger of creating monopolies, such as would result from the proposal of the East India Company to import its own tea. Finally, it pointed out that the use of the funds to be secured thereby for the purpose of supporting civil government in some of the colonies, would deprive the people of other rights guaranteed by charter. For a printed copy of the proceedings of the Council for the period November 14–29, 1773, see also *Boston Evening-Post,* December 27, 1773.

[34] *Tea Leaves:* Introduction, pp. 38–45. See also *Boston Evening-Post,* November 29, 1773, and a broadside published "By Order of the Committee of Boston" on December 1, 1773, and signed by William Cooper, town clerk of Boston, in which the crowd at the town meeting was estimated at 5,000 persons; this is reprinted in *Autograph Letters and Documents Relating to the History of America . . .* (Iowa City, 1956), pp. 11–12.

The proposer of this first public suggestion for dumping the tea may have been the chief speaker at the meeting, Dr. Thomas Young, a controversial figure who— along with Samuel Adams, Dr. Joseph Warren, and William Molineux—took a leading part in the coming events. See in this connection John Cary: *op. cit.,* pp. 133, 134, 135n.

[35] Massachusetts Historical Society *Proceedings,* XIII, 168–9.

ings. When this proclamation was read to the meeting by Sheriff Greenleaf, it was greeted with hisses, and a unanimous vote was taken forthwith to refuse to disperse. Later in the day the owner of the *Dartmouth*, Francis Rotch, appeared before the meeting and, after lodging a protest against the proceeding, agreed to return the tea, but made it clear that this was not a voluntary act on his part. Captain Hall also appeared and affirmed that he would not attempt to land the tea. The part owners of two other tea ships momentarily due in Boston pledged to follow the example of Rotch and Hall.[36]

On December 2 a rumour spread that a permit would be given by the custom house to land the East India Company tea. Immediately a notice was posted warning the public of the vote made at the Old South Meeting House on the 30th of November "that said tea should never be landed in this province or pay one farthing of duty and that any attempt to do so must betray an inhuman thirst for blood. . . ." The notice went on to assure the "public enemies of this country" (that is, the consignees) that upon any attempt to land the tea they would "be considered and treated as wretches, unworthy to live, and made the first victims of our resentment."[37] As to the other tea ships, the *Beaver*, Captain Coffin, arrived in Boston from London on December 7, followed shortly after by Captain Bruce in the *Eleanor;* a fourth vessel, the *William*, Captain Loring, likewise due in Boston with fifty-eight tea chests on board, was, however, cast up on the shore of Cape Cod.[38] All three vessels that reached the harbour were required to anchor at Griffin's Wharf in South Boston and were kept under constant armed guard supplied by the town.

---

[36] For the proceedings of November 29 and 30 see *Massachusetts Spy,* December 2, and *Boston Evening-Post,* December 6, 1773; see also Richard Frothingham: *Life and Times of Joseph Warren* (Boston, 1865), pp. 234–81, which gives in great detail every step taken from the beginning of the crisis up to and including the destruction of the tea, and likewise John Cary: *op. cit.,* pp. 131–3. Writing from Milton on November 30 to his son Elisha, then at the home of Chief Justice Oliver at Middleborough, the Governor informed him that on the preceding day all of the tea factors but Clarke, Sr., had gone to the Castle. As to the "monstrous demand" of the populace respecting the tea, he expressed the hope that the consignees "will not comply. . . . I have just sent Talbot to Town with a declaration to be read by the Sheriff if they will give him leave. This may possibly cause me to take my lodgings at the Castle also. I was in Town yesterday with the Council who could only do what is worse than nothing" (Hutchinson Family Correspondence, Vol. I, Egerton Manuscripts, 2659:50, British Museum).

[37] *Massachusetts Spy,* December 9, 1773. In this paper also was printed the resolves entered into by the towns of Brooklyne (Brookline) on November 26, of Dorchester on November 30, and of Charlestown on November 27 and December 4.

[38] News from Boston, dated November 29, appearing in the *Pennsylvania Gazette,* December 8, 1773, stated: "Capt. Hall informs, that 114 Chests of Tea were shipped in Captain Coffin, 116 in Capt. Bruce, and 58 in Captain Loring, all for this Port."

On December 14, on the grounds that Mr. Rotch "lingered in his preparation to return his ship to London," a meeting of committees of several towns took place in Boston.[39] The owner of the *Dartmouth*, when required to appear before the gathering to justify his conduct, explained that he could see no way on his own volition to comply with the demands put upon him without being ruined. The following day, accompanied by members of a committee chosen by the meeting, he went to the collector of the port to request a clearance for his ship. But the collector declared that before he could act he must consult the comptroller of customs. When Rotch repeated his request a day later, "compell'd at my peril by a body of people," the collector replied that since the *Dartmouth* had been formally entered on November 30 with dutiable articles on board for which the duty had not been paid, he could not, consistent with his obligations as collector, give the ship a clearance until it was properly discharged through the custom house. When this was reported to the general meeting at Old South Meeting House, Rotch, a virtual prisoner, was ordered to ask the Governor for a pass; at the same time he was notified that his vessel must leave port that very day. Upon returning from Milton early in the evening, Rotch reported to the meeting that the Governor's reply to his request had been that he would willingly grant anything "consistent with the laws[40] and his duty to the King, but that he could not give a Pass unless the Vessel was properly

---

[39] It may be noted that at the December 14 meeting Timothy Prout addressed a letter to the moderator moving that the town reconsider its earlier vote not to land the tea and accept the proposals of the consignees to land and store it, with the keys to the warehouse to be turned over to a committee of the town until the matter was finally determined; a further part of the motion was that "Application be made to the Honorable the East India Company for their Intrest in Parliament that the Duty on Teas be taken off." It ends with the observation "that the Town's Compliance herewith will have a tendency to establish Peace and secure our Rights in future" (Massachusetts Miscellaneous Manuscripts, 1769–1778, Library of Congress). It may also be noted in passing that on May 4, 1744, at a Boston town meeting, Prout's father, also named Timothy, together with Thomas Cushing, Thomas Hutchinson, and Andrew Oliver, were all elected as the town's representatives to the General Assembly. See R. F. Seybolt: *Town Officials of Colonial Boston, 1634–1775* (Cambridge, Mass., 1939), p. 237. Prout, a member of the Harvard class of 1741, was a Boston merchant, as was his father. Unlike many of the merchants of the town, he was opposed to smuggling as both harmful to trade and dishonest. When the war broke out he became a Loyalist. See C. K. Shipton: *Sibley's Harvard Graduates*, XI, 56–8.

[40] For the laws that bound all officers of the government see 11 Geo. I, c. 30, "An Act for more effectual preventing Frauds and Abuses in the Publick Revenues . . . ," and 12 Geo. I, c. 28, "An Act for the Improvement of his Majesty's Revenues of Customs, Excise and Inland Duties," *Statutes at Large*, V, 392–404 and 415–21.

qualified from the Custom-House. . . ."[41] Under these circumstances
Rotch refused to order the *Dartmouth* to return to England. Then,
in the words of the *Boston Evening-Post,* the people who had assembled, "having manifested an exemplary patience and caution in
the methods it had pursued to preserve the Tea, the property of the
East India Company, without its being made saleable among us,
which must have been fatal to the Common-wealth," now moved to
dissolve the meeting and this was done.[42] Then came the destruction
of the tea.

It is clear that all preparations for the boarding of the tea ships
had been carefully planned. The moment the December 16 meeting
was dissolved a band of men disguised as Mohawk Indians emerged
from the building occupied by the printers of the radical *Boston
Gazette.* Wrapped in blankets, brandishing hatchets, and shouting
war whoops, they rushed to Griffin's Wharf, where the tea ships were
now anchored. Each of the three vessels was boarded in turn; the
hatches were raised and some 342 chests of tea were lifted on deck,
broken open, and the contents poured into the water below. Nothing
else on board the ships was damaged or disturbed. Still under discipline, the actors in this drama marched through the town with fife
and drum before dispersing.

To John Adams, the destruction of the tea was "so bold, so daring,
so firm, intrepid and inflexible, and it must have so important Consequences, and so lasting, that I cant but consider it an Epocha in
History."[43] Writing to Arthur Lee on December 21, Samuel Adams
described the reactions of the people of Boston to the destruction
of the tea: "You cannot imagine the height of joy that sparkles in

---

[41] For an account of the transactions on December 13 and 14 involving Rotch, see
Boston Evening-Post, December 20, 1773. Hutchinson, writing to his son Thomas
from London on December 20, 1774, had the following to say about the incident of
the tea: "The charge against me by the Congress as being the cause of the destruction
of the Tea does me no harm here, where the circumstances are known, but it shews
great malice of the Boston men in so representing it to their Brethren. I think I have
heard that in the time of it one or more of these men said publickly they knew it was
not in my power to grant the Pass when it was applied for" (Hutchinson Family Correspondence, Egerton Manuscripts, 2659:131, British Museum).

[42] *Boston Evening-Post,* December 20, 1773. For minutes of the tea meetings, as
printed in the newspapers, edited by S. A. Green, see Massachusetts Historical Society
Proceedings, 1st ser., XX, 10–17. For further insight into the nature of the discussions
that took place from November 29 through December 16, as told in a dispassionate
and competent report of the meetings that preceded the dumping of the tea, see
"Proceedings of Ye Body Respecting the Tea," a document brought to light from the
Sewell Papers, Public Archives of Canada, by L. F. S. Upton and admirably edited
by him in the *William and Mary Quarterly,* 3rd ser., XXII, 287–300.

[43] *Adams Papers* (Butterfield), 1st ser., II, 85–6.

the eyes and animates the countenances as well as the hearts of all we meet on this occasion; excepting the disappointed, disconserted Hutchinson and his tools."[44] That same day a letter signed by the four Boston representatives to the General Assembly, headed by Speaker Cushing, was written to the London agent. It stressed the efforts of responsible people to preserve the tea, despite their unwillingness that it should be landed and "the obstinacy of the Consignees," as well as the desire of Bostonians to avoid "a second Effusion of Blood [referring to the Boston Massacre]" should an attempt be made by the customs officers, as was threatened, to place the tea on shore.[45]

In view of the clear defiance of the government of Great Britain on the part of those who boarded the tea ships, John Scollay, long a selectman of the town and a man of high standing, two days after the destruction of the tea sent a full account of the surrounding events to Arthur Lee in London. In it he spoke of the great patience of the people of Boston, noting that the disguised men really responsible for the act, who were said to be "from the country," had passed by where "the people were assembled and went on board the several vessels . . . and in a very short time, without noise or tumult, destroyed all the tea, by throwing it into the sea. . . ." He also gave as the basis for this action the apprehension that—under the terms of the law which prescribed that articles subject to duty must be landed within twenty days after entering and cleared through the customs or else be liable to seizure—the customs officers would do their duty and, under the protection of the King's armed vessels, land the tea.[46] As for Governor Hutchinson, writing to the Earl of Dartmouth on December 17, he confessed he could not determine what "influence this violence & outrage may have"; he mentioned that the event was attended by a concourse of people "more numerous than any before & consisted of the inhabitants of divers other towns as well as Boston."[47] He also wrote to the Directors of the East India Company, stating:

---

[44] For this letter see R. H. Lee: *Life of Arthur Lee* . . . (2 vols., Boston, 1829), II, 209, where the date is given as December 31, 1773.

[45] The December 21, 1773, letter signed by Thomas Cushing, Samuel Adams, John Hancock, and William Phillips is given as sent to Arthur Lee in the Massachusetts Historical Society *Collections,* 4th ser., IV, 377, but the Arthur Lee papers at Harvard Library seem to indicate that the letter went to Benjamin Franklin.

[46] *Ibid.,* IV, 379–86.

[47] Hutchinson to Lord [Dartmouth], December 17, 1773, Massachusetts Archives, 27:589.

"As double the quantities of Teas proposed to be ship'd by the Comp^y had been imported in a year & the duty p^d w^thout any disturb^e[,] I flattered myself for several months after . . . the intention to ship on acc^t of the Company [was known,] that I should find no more difficulties than when Teas have been ship'd by private merchants."[48]

The Governor now felt obliged to take some action. Despite his having failed in earlier efforts to bring the Council together, he sought its advice in a meeting held at Cambridge three days after the riot. While most of the members were persuaded that something must be done to vindicate law and order, they were divided on their views as to the proper step to be taken: whether a proclamation should be issued offering a reward for information leading to the conviction of any person informed against or whether Attorney General Jonathan Sewall should be directed to inquire into the affair and submit his findings to a grand jury. As a majority of those voting favoured the latter course, it was adopted. However, to Hutchinson it was but a feeble gesture. "I have reason to think there will be no prosecution by a grand jury," he wrote (apparently to Dartmouth). "I cannot find any persons who were at the meeting of the people willing to give any account in writing of the persons who were most active there or of any of their transactions."[49] Writing to the London agent of the Governor and Council at this same period, he gave a detailed account of all the events that took place after the news had reached Boston of the plan of the East India Company to ship its tea to America up to the time of the final destruction of the tea. He began his letter by stating: "There is no Tyranny so great as that which is exercised by the people when they take the Government from the hands of those who are intrusted with it by the Constitution."[50] Addressing former Governor Bernard in January 1774, he stated: "After the usurpers of government had tried every method they could to force the tea back to England, and all in vain, they left . . . Dr. Sewall's meeting-house, and . . . in two or three hours destroyed three hundred and forty chests." After referring to the "unfortunate event" as something that might have been supposed to

[48] Hutchinson to the Directors of the East India Company, December 19, 1773, *ibid.*, 27:597–8.

[49] Hutchinson to ———, December 24, 1773, *ibid.*, 27:603–4. In this letter Hutchinson referred to his previous letters and also mentioned the fact that some people had already gone and others were going to England "who were present at some of their meetings."

[50] Hutchinson to Mauduit, Boston, December —, 1773, *ibid.*, 27:604–6.

be impossible, since "so many people of property had made part of the meetings, and were in danger of being liable for the value of it," he observed: "It would have given me a much more painful reflection if I had saved it by any concession to a lawless and highly criminal assembly of men to whose proceedings the loss must be consequently attributed. . . ."[51]

To Hutchinson the issue presented by this crisis was simple: Should mob rule supplant the legal government within Massachusetts Bay and in the Empire? Should he as Governor give this lawless rule the slightest countenance? To the popular leaders in Boston the issue was equally plain: Should American rights and American liberty be weakly sacrificed before the manifest determination of the government of Great Britain to establish the principle of the supremacy of the statutes of Parliament throughout the Empire, including the right to secure a revenue? The increasing hostility toward the Governor at this juncture of affairs is shown in a long letter written early in January 1774 by Isaac Royall, a member of the Council for twenty years, to the Earl of Dartmouth. "I firmly believe," Royall wrote, "this People [of Massachusetts Bay] to be as truly loyal to his Majesty . . . as any of his Subjects, in all his extended Dominions." At the same time he pointed out that they were "Zealously tenacious of their inestimable Charter Rights and Priviledges, which they apprehend . . . have been greatly infring'd and broken in upon through the Machinations and Misrepresentations . . . from persons on this side the Atlantic, who, from an Insatiable Thirst after Power and Gain, are far from seeking the welfare of Great Britain and her Colonies." He then pointed the way to the restoration of the good feeling that had prevailed in the colony under the "mild and prudent Administration" of both Governors Shirley

---

[51] Hutchinson to Bernard, January 1, 1774, Massachusetts Historical Society *Proceedings*, XIII, 174. The Governor was even more explicit when making clear to his friend Samuel Swift (who was also an intimate friend of John Adams) why he had been obliged to act as he did. In acknowledging the favourable opinion Swift had expressed of him in a letter dated December 30, Hutchinson wrote: ". . . I think you will be satisfied of the propriety of my conduct in the particular instance you refer to, when I put you in mind that I have taken a solemn oath, as Governor, to do everything in my power that the acts of trade may be carried into execution. Now, to have granted a pass to a vessel which I knew had not cleared at the custom-house, would have been such a direct countenancing and encouraging the violation of the acts of trade, that I believe you would have altered your opinion of me, and seen me ever after in an unfavourable light. I am sure, if I could have . . . complied with the general desire of the people, consistent with the duty which my station requires, I would most readily have done it" (Hutchinson to Swift, January 4, 1774, *ibid.*, XIII, 174–5).

and Pownall, by recommending not only the repeal of the Revenue Act but the appointment of Pownall "or some other prudent, discreet Gentleman of like Disposition" to the office of Governor, an action through which, he was convinced, "the former most agreeable and much to be desir'd Harmony would once more be restor'd and subsist between us and our Mother Country."[52]

The news of the destruction of the tea in Boston Harbour spread like wildfire—carried first to New York and then to Philadelphia by Paul Revere[53]—as did the spirit of resistance, fanned by the widespread reprinting in the local press of news of the action taken in Massachusetts Bay and by the activities of the intercolonial system of committees of correspondence. The people of the principal seaports were quick to approve the Boston action in order to bolster their own determination to resist, which was not everywhere equally effective. On December 1–2, 1773, Captain Curling arrived at Charleston in the *London* with a cargo of 257 chests of tea.[54] According to William Henry Drayton, before the arrival of the *London* no exception to the importation of tea by private merchants on their own account had been taken by the people, as "such teas had always been landed [after the collapse of the non-importation movement in South Carolina in December 1770] and had paid the duties [levied by the Townshend Revenue Act]."[55] However, under the leadership of the radical planter-merchant Christopher Gadsden, the mechanics of Charleston now rallied; handbills were distributed,

[52] Royall to Dartmouth, January 18, 1774, *ibid.*, XIII, 179–82.

[53] See *Tea Leaves*, Introduction, p. 83; see also Esther Forbes: *Paul Revere & the World He Lived In* (Boston, 1942), pp. 205–8.

[54] See Lieutenant Governor William Bull to the Earl of Dartmouth, December 24, 1773, P.R.O., C.O. 5:396 (P.R.O. transcripts, Vol. 33, 1771–1773, South Carolina Archives Department), printed in *Tea Leaves*, pp. 339–42; see also *South-Carolina Gazette* (Peter Timothy), December 6, 1773.

[55] See *Memoirs of the American Revolution . . . to the Year 1776 . . . as Relating to the State of South Carolina . . .* (written by William Henry Drayton in 1773–6 and published by his son John, 2 vols., Charleston, 1821; cited hereafter as *Drayton's Memoirs*), I, 98, which also states that "parcels of Tea were landed as well from Captain Curling's ship, as from two other vessels, which were the property of private importers; [and] that the duties had been paid on them." According to Captain Hunt, who arrived in New York late in December, fifteen days from Charleston, 170 chests of East India Company tea were on board the *London*. See *New-York Gazette: and the Weekly Mercury*, December 27, 1773. (Since the *New-York Gazette: or, the Weekly Post-Boy* ceased publication in the late summer or fall of 1773, the first-named paper will be cited hereafter as the *New-York Gazette*.) It is therefore possible that the remainder, that is 87 chests, had passed into the hands of private Charleston merchants, although the account of Lieutenant Governor Bull and that of the Charleston comptroller of customs stated that all 257 chests were on board the *London*; see *Tea Leaves*, pp. 339–42.

and the gathering which took place on December 3 at the Exchange was so well attended that the "main beams" gave way. The merchants found themselves arrayed against not only the mechanics but also some of the principal planters and landholders. In the debate, continued on the 4th, the merchants took the position—according to Captain Hunt's report, quoting one who was in Charleston at the time and apparently attended the meeting—"that Tea has ever been spontaneously imported, and the Duty paid; that every subject had an equal right to send that article from the Mother Country into this Province, and therefore it was unreasonable to exclude the Hon. East India Company from the same Priviledge."[56]

As for the report in the *South-Carolina Gazette* a few days later, it made clear that the meeting of Charleston inhabitants and others on the 3rd came to an agreement "that the Merchants be desired to promise and agree to import no more Teas that would pay a Duty" —an agreement already subscribed to by "upwards of 50 respectable Names." The tea consignees—Roger Smith and Messrs. Leger and Greenwood—were then called before the meeting and persuaded to renounce their commissions; they did so, "declining to receive the tea as the people requested." When Captain Curling desired to know what his next step should be, he was informed that he should return to England with the tea on board his vessel; this he prepared to do. In the meantime, however, at the meeting on the 4th, fifty names were added to the basic agreement not to accept the tea and "the principal planters and landholders entered into a further agreement to boycott anyone who should import, buy or sell any such teas." As a consequence Curling did not attempt to unload the tea; instead, taking steps to protest the action of the consignees, he proposed to land all other articles, place the tea between decks, and, upon filling his ship with rice and other commodities, to set sail for London. But he could not put his plan into action because of the provisions of the customs collector's instructions, which required this officer to seize goods liable to duty if, within a period of twenty days after arrival, the duty on such merchandise had not been paid.[57]

---

[56] See Captain Hunt's report, previously cited, in *New-York Gazette,* December 27, 1773.

[57] The detailed newspaper reports appear in the *South-Carolina Gazette* (Peter Timothy), December 6, 1773, and the *South-Carolina Gazette; And Country Journal,* December 7, 1773; see also Bull to Dartmouth, December 24, 1773, C.O. 5:396 (*Tea Leaves,* pp. 339–42). For the reaction in other colonies to the steps taken in Charleston, see *South-Carolina Gazette; And Country Journal,* February 1, 1774; for that of the Secretary of State for the Colonies, see Dartmouth to Bull, February

Meanwhile, the Charleston merchants met on December 9 and organized a chamber of commerce,[58] but they could not come to an agreement among themselves to prohibit the landing of the tea. Yet, some bolder spirits took the step of sending anonymous letters to Curling threatening to burn the *London* unless she were moved from the wharf; other similar letters went to the owner of the wharf and to masters of ships lying close to the *London*. When this threat to public peace was called to the attention of Lieutenant Governor William Bull, it led him to call a meeting of the provincial Council at which both Curling and the South Carolina collector of customs, Robert Dalway Haliday, were present. The discussion disclosed that as Curling could not land the tea because of the resignation of the consignees,[59] it was incumbent upon the customs collector to seize, land, and store the consignment from the *London* at the end of the twenty-day period. Therefore, acting upon the advice of the Council, the Governor ordered the sheriff to hold himself at the disposal of the collector and to support him in the execution of his duty.[60] Early on

5, 1774, P.R.O., C.O. 5:396 (P.R.O. transcripts, Vol. 34, 1774, South Carolina Archives Department). For Curling's account, see again the *New-York Gazette* issue of December 27, 1773.

[58] According to the *South-Carolina Gazette*, December 13, 1773, a meeting of the trade was held at Mrs. Swallow's and a committee of twenty-one appointed to bring in proposals for a chamber of commerce. See Hennig Cohen: *The South Carolina Gazette* (Columbia, S.C., 1953), p. 24. For the disagreement of the merchants see Bull to Dartmouth, December 24, 1773, *Tea Leaves*, p. 340.

[59] See Council Journal (Ms), No. 38, pp. 8–9, South Carolina Archives Department. The resignation of the consignees was, according to Lieutenant Governor Bull, produced "by threats and flatterys" (*Tea Leaves*, p. 340). See for example the address of "Junius Brutus": "To the Freemen of South Carolina . . . As to the gentlemen who, it is said, are appointed *Commissioners* to receive and distribute the stampt Tea, they are so well known amongst us, (one of each house having been members of the late *General Committee*) that scarce a single inhabitant can be persuaded to believe, they will descend to an acceptance of the detestable commission" (*South-Carolina Gazette*, November 29, 1773). The "General Committee" here mentioned was formed in 1769 at the time of the non-importation agreement against the Townshend Acts. See *ibid.*, July 27, 1769, and August 23, 1770. See also Henry Laurens to Leo Appleby, January 17, 1774, indicating that the consignees were members "of the General Comm[itt]ee under the Live Oak" (Henry Laurens Papers, Vol. 7, p. 179, South Carolina Archives Department microfilm of Laurens Mss in the South Carolina Historical Society, Charleston). Laurens himself had been a member of the General Committee.

For help in determining the names of the Charleston tea consignees (nowhere mentioned in most accounts of this period) and additional details concerning them and the incident, I am deeply indebted to Director Charles B. Lee of the South Carolina Archives Department (Columbia, S.C.) and to his able and cooperative Editorial Assistant, Miss Ruth E. Green, and her resources of staff and outside contact.

In connection with the tea episode in Charleston, see also Richard Walsh: *Charleston's Sons of Liberty* (Columbia, S.C., 1959), pp. 60–1, and Leila Sellers: *Charleston Business on the Eve of the American Revolution* (Chapel Hill, N.C., 1934), pp. 223–4.

[60] Bull to Dartmouth, December 24, 1773, *Tea Leaves*, pp. 340–1.

the morning of December 22 the landing of the tea took place without the slightest opposition. The seized chests were placed under the Exchange in vaults rented for that purpose " 'till the collector shall receive further orders relative thereto."[61] There, along with later shipments so stored, the tea was destined to remain until in the course of the War for American Independence it was appropriated by the government of the new state of South Carolina and sold to support military activities.

In his letter to the Earl of Dartmouth two days after the tea had been seized and stored, Lieutenant Governor Bull made the following comment:

"It is my opinion that if the merchants who viewed this measure of importing tea in a commercial rather than in a political light, had shewn their disapprobation of the intended opposition to land it, by action rather than by a refusal to subscribe to a proposed association, and a contempt of the public meetings on this occasion, and the agents of the East India Company had not been so hasty in their declining to accept their trusts, all might have gone on well, according to the plan of the East India Company, and to our benefit in purchasing that article, now become one of the necessaries of life, at a much cheaper rate than at present."[62]

The Lieutenant Governor's reasoning is borne out by the fact that Charleston had continued to legally import dutied tea up to this time. This was also true of all the other leading American ports except New York and Philadelphia.[63] In fact, it would appear that by 1773 both Philadelphia and New York had become the chief American centres for tea smuggling. In 1768, according to the returns of the custom houses of the three leading northern ports, New England (that is, Boston) legally imported 282,267 pounds of tea and in 1772 the amount entered was 110,242 pounds; in New York in 1768 the duty was collected on 352,488 pounds and in 1772 on only 530 pounds; in Philadelphia in 1768 there was entered 146,768 pounds and in 1772 but 128 pounds.[64] This report would seem to throw light

---

[61] *Ibid.*, also p. 342.

[62] *Ibid.*, p. 341.

[63] See A. M. Schlesinger: *Colonial Merchants . . .* , pp. 245–6.

[64] For these figures, drawn from the customs books in the English Public Record Office, see O. M. Dickerson: *The Navigation Acts and the American Revolution* (Philadelphia, 1951), p. 100. In this connection, as was noted in Chap. 1 of this volume, it should be stated that Professor Dickerson takes an opposing view (*ibid.*, pp. 91, 100, 101) to that of this author and Professor Schlesinger with respect to the importance of the illegal trade in Dutch tea.

on the comment of Joseph Reed, a prominent Philadelphia lawyer and later a revolutionary leader, who wrote to the Earl of Darmouth on December 27, 1773, concerning smuggling as it related to the importation of tea into Pennsylvania: "From the best inquiry and computation I can make, the annual consumption of this Province now amounts to two thousand chests of tea, the profits of which have been totally lost to England for upwards of five years."[65] Whereas at Boston the legal importers of tea were alarmed at the possibility that the East India Company factors would absorb their business, at Philadelphia the illicit importers were most concerned. They doubtless feared that the Company would sell their tea at a price so low that it would no longer be profitable to spirit Dutch tea into the province. Does this not perhaps help to account for the violence of the resolutions passed at the State House on October 16[66] appealing to the people to uphold their liberties—resolutions so strong that they became a pattern for other colonies? Is it not likely that the illegal traders exerted an influence on the local press to keep their readers inflamed against Parliament and the Company by publishing extensive reports of developments elsewhere in the colonies? For example, on December 9 a special edition of the *Pennsylvania Gazette* was issued to inform the public of the proceedings in Boston on November 29 and 30; further, on December 24, when an express arrived from New York bringing the details of the destruction of the tea in Boston Harbour on the 16th, another special edition was issued.

But once alarmed over the possibility of the loss of their liberties and rights, whether justly or unjustly, most Pennsylvanians seem to have lined up solidly in opposition to the Tea Act. The dangers they faced were presented in very vivid terms. For instance, on

---

[65] See W. B. Reed: *Life and Correspondence of Joseph Reed* (2 vols., Philadelphia, 1847), I, 54–6.

[66] For the resolutions passed on October 16, see *Pennsylvania Gazette*, October 20, 1773; see also *Pennsylvania Magazine of History and Biography*, XV, 387–8. For a letter of October 30, 1773, from Thomas Wharton in Philadelphia to Thomas Walpole in London, describing the meeting as having been held "with the greatest decency and firmness, and without one dissenting voice," and the resolutions as "entered into" on October 18, see *Tea Leaves*, pp. 275–7. This same letter closed with the clear warning: "Should the tea be sent subject to the payment of the duty, I am satisfied it will not be suffered to be landed, and that it must return to London. . . ." For Wharton's own confirmation of this prediction, see his extensive accounts of the events surrounding the tea episode in "Selections from the Letter-Books of Thomas Wharton, 1773–1783," *Pennsylvania Magazine of History and Biography*, XXXIII, 319–29.

December 4, copies were distributed in the city of a handbill signed by "A Mechanic" and addressed "To the Tradesmen, Mechanics etc. of the Province of Pennsylvania." It warned that "a corrupt and prostituted Ministry are pointing their destructive machines against the sacred Liberties of the Americans, [so that] the Eyes of all Europe are upon us" and declared the grand design of the Ministry to be "by every Artifice to enslave the American Colonies and plunder them of their Property, and, what is more, their Birth-Right, *Liberty*."[67] Moreover, at a public meeting held in Philadelphia at this period a committee was appointed to inquire into the cause of the rise in the price of tea. This group reported at a subsequent meeting that not more than twenty-five chests of tea remained available for sale in the city and that the retailers and shop-keepers who had engrossed this supply, when made to realize that by advancing the price they were engaging in "a dangerous Tendency," had agreed not to ask more than six shillings or at most six shillings sixpence per pound for this article.[68]

During the suspenseful interim of waiting for the arrival of the tea ship destined for Philadelphia,[69] the people kept in correspondence with the other colonies and prepared to take action. On December 9 they were informed by the press that the ship *Polly*, Captain Ayres, from London carrying the East India Company tea had been sighted three days previously off Cape May.[70] But this proved to be a premature report. It was not until the 25th that news arrived by express that the ship had at last appeared off Chester, and not until early the following day did one of the consignees of the tea, Gilbert Barkly [Barkley, Barclay], who had come aboard the *Polly* as a passenger, arrive in Philadelphia. Pressure was immediately brought to bear upon him to resign his commission. The tea ship having cast anchor off Gloucester Point, about three and a half miles below Philadelphia, was obliged to remain there while Ayres was conducted to the city by members of the committee appointed for that purpose, followed

---

[67] This handbill also appeared in the local newspapers. See *Pennsylvania Gazette*, December 8, 1773.

[68] *Pennsylvania Gazette*, December 8, 1773; *Pennsylvania Chronicle*, December 13, 1773.

[69] On November 30, 1773, Thomas Wharton wrote to his brother in London: "By the Reports here spread, we are told, that the Tea-Ship for this port sailed the 27th September, and is therefore hourly looked for . . ." (see *Pennsylvania Magazine of History and Biography*, XXXIII, 319).

[70] Postscript to the *Pennsylvania Gazette*, December 9, 1773.

by a large body of people.[71] There the Captain was quickly made to realize how hopeless it would be to attempt to enter the tea. Nevertheless, when confronted by the consignees—Barkly, Thomas and Isaac Wharton, and Jonathon Brown—he did not hesitate to protest their refusal to receive the tea or to pay freight on it.[72] Clearly there was now nothing for the Captain to do but take his ship back to London. Leaving the city on December 28 in a pilot boat, he embarked on the *Polly* as it moved down the Delaware River.[73] But before this, he had been present at a vast but orderly gathering of people, some 8,000 in number, at the State House on the 27th at which they passed resolutions prohibiting the unloading of the tea ship, but permitting its commander to remain in the city long enough to provision his vessel for the return voyage. They also resolved their full approval of the Boston action of destroying the tea.[74]

No effort was made by the Pennsylvania government to support the Tea Act. On May 3, 1774, Deputy Governor John Penn wrote a revealing letter to his aunt—Lady Juliana Penn, the wife of Thomas, the Proprietor—recounting the reception accorded the tea ship at

---

[71] In an article on the Philadelphia opposition to the landing of tea prepared by Frederick D. Stone and printed in the *Pennsylvania Magazine of History and Biography*, XV, 385–93, there appear fascimiles of two broadsides, signed by the "Committee for Tarring and Feathering," warning the Delaware River pilots of the fate in store for them should they bring the *Polly* to the custom house.

[72] The meeting of Ayres with four of the consignees was at the home of Thomas Wharton, merchant prince, land speculator, and also a consignee who wrote a full account of the events connected with the coming of the tea to Philadelphia, as has been noted. For his letter to Thomas Walpole, dated December 27, 1773, see *ibid.*, XIV, 78–9. It was Thomas Wharton and his brother Isaac, together with Jonathon Brown, who advanced to Ayres the necessary funds for obtaining provisions and other necessaries for the return trip of the ship, which also carried Gilbert Barkly back to England. The firm of Abel James and Henry Drinker was also a consignee but neither member was present. They had already resigned.

[73] *Pennsylvania Gazette*, December 29, 1773.

[74] The last-mentioned resolution adopted by the open meeting had previously been rejected by a vote of ten against two in the committee hearing where it was initially proposed. It reads in part as follows: "That this Assembly . . . return their hearty Thanks to the People of Boston for their Resolution in destroying the Tea, rather than suffering it to be landed." According to Thomas Wharton, this resolution was opposed to the views of "the substantial thinking part" of those assembled at the State House but was carried as the result of an appeal to the people by the two members of the committee who had favoured it. See Wharton Letter-Book, 1773–1784, pp. 33–4, Historical Society of Pennsylvania; see also his letters published in the *Pennsylvania Magazine of History and Biography*, XXXIII, 329, and A. M. Schlesinger: *Colonial Merchants . . . ,* p. 291. For an extensive account of the proceedings from December 25 to 28 see *Pennsylvania Gazette*, December 29, 1773, and also *New-York Gazette*, January 2, 1774, which presents certain details not mentioned in the Philadelphia paper. The newspaper accounts also commended the action of the consignees for "generously sacrificing their private interest to the public good."

Philadelphia and excusing his own inaction on this occasion. In it he gave the following reason for not writing to Lord Dartmouth, Secretary of State for the Colonies, about it:

> "It was believed the Ministry would not interfere in the matter[;] indeed many letters came from England which said so & a Gentleman who came from thence last winter, said he knew Lord Dartmouth had declared that it was entirely the affair of the East India Company & Government had nothing to do with it, & what made this more easily believed was that no Instructions were sent to the Governors by the Secretary of State nor to the Collectors of the Customs. No Application was made to me by the Cap[t] of the ship nor the merchants to whom the Tea was consigned nor the Custom house nor indeed by anybody at all. I have wrote to Lord Dartmouth about it, with an excuse for not giving him notice of what happened upon this occasion."[75]

If the radicals of Philadelphia in 1773 were more powerful and determined than those of Charleston, the New York radicals under the leadership of the triumvirate of John Lamb, Isaac Sears, and Alexander McDougall were even more so. This had already been demonstrated during the the Stamp Act crisis when the resort to terror on the part of the New York group fell somewhat short of the methods used by the leaders of the Boston radicals, it is true, but went beyond the steps employed by the leaders of the mobs in Philadelphia and Charleston. The movement against the East India Company tea shipments was, as has previously been stressed, promoted in the first instance by traders—whether engaged in smuggling Dutch tea or in importing tea purchased in London on which they paid duty—who felt that their interests would thereby be adversely affected. To Governor Tryon of New York, writing to the Earl of Dartmouth on November 3, 1773, the propaganda against the

---

[75] The ostensible reason why the Deputy Governor wrote to Lady Juliana, rather than to the Proprietor, was that he desired to congratulate her on recovering from a serious illness. For this letter see *Pennsylvania Magazine of History and Biography*, XXXI, 232–3. Although John Penn failed to send word immediately to the Secretary of State after the episode of the tea ship, Joseph Reed, wrote to Dartmouth on December 27, 1773, giving a rather full account of what took place at Philadelphia. In this letter, written on the same day that a large meeting was held on the grounds of the State House, he stressed the fact that among the several thousand people present were "a great number of the most considerable both in rank and property, when the enclosed resolutions were proposed and agreed to without hesitation." In fact Reed's letter stated that the movement had "originated and been conducted by some of the principal inhabitants, and I may safely say countenanced and encouraged by all . . ." (W. B. Reed: *op. cit.*, I, 54–6).

East India Company, then already well under way, was designed to bring support to those

> "who are deepest concerned in the illicet Trade to Foreign Countries. They are certainly declarative of the extent to which smuggling is carried on in the single Article of Tea. . . . So that let the [East India Company] Tea appear free or not free of duty, those who carry on illicit Trade will raise objections, if possible, to its being brought on shore and sold."[76]

Nevertheless, as he wrote privately to Thomas Hutchinson, he was determined "to protect the King's subjects in the enjoyment of their liberties and properties." Tryon, in the eyes of the Massachusetts Bay Governor, had certain great advantages for taking this course which he himself did not possess. For example, the people of New York had become "habituated to the use of the King's troops employed . . . from time to time to guard the officers of the customs when seizures were made," while the people of Boston "threatened destruction to any person who should attempt to introduce soldiers in the town"; again, whereas Tryon had a Council "disposed to support him in measures for the King's service," the Council of Hutchinson's province was "entirely at devotion of the people."[77] Yet this military man, who had scattered the Regulators of North Carolina, found that he was helpless in the face of the hostility that by December 1773 had been generated among all classes of the people of New York by ceaseless propaganda against the East India Company and the government of Great Britain.

---

[76] *Documents Relative to the Colonial History of the State of New York* (eds. E. B. O'Callaghan and B. Fernow, 15 vols., Albany, 1853–1887), VIII, 400–1, cited hereafter as *New York Colonial Documents.* William Smith, a member of the New York Council, referring in his diary to the importation of tea into the colony, made the following comment on October 3, 1773: "The Fact is that ever since the Duty of 3d per Pound had been laid, by the 7 Geo. III, all tea had been Smuggled from Holland, to the great Detriment of the India House—And now the Sons of Liberty & the Dutch Smugglers set up the cry of Liberty" (*Historical Memoirs . . . 1763–1776 . . .* [ed. W. H. W. Sabine, New York, 1956], p. 156). Smith, at this period on intimate terms with Philip Livingston, quoted the latter at a meeting of the Council as stating "there was not a Man in Town that was not a Smuggler in some sense" (*ibid.,* p. 161). For the effects of the smuggling, and the small amount of tea legally imported into New York, see again O. M. Dickerson: *op. cit.,* p. 100; see also Virginia D. Harrington: *The New York Merchant on the Eve of the Revolution* (New York, 1935), pp. 344–7, and *Tea Leaves,* pp. 192–4.

[77] Hutchinson to Rear Admiral Montagu, in charge of the British naval forces in American waters, December 28, 1773, Massachusetts Archives, 27:601. In this letter Hutchinson refers to the assurances he had received from Tryon that the liberties and properties of the people of New York would be protected.

Even the conservative *Rivington's New-York Gazetteer*[78] was obliged by threats to print letters directed against those disposed to support the Tea Act. For example, a letter signed "Legion," left at the door of the printer, read:

"Let the enclosed be published in your next paper. In this fail not at your peril. Messers. Gaine, Parker and Anderson[79] are also desired to publish from your paper, or they may rest assured they shall not pass with impunity."

The "enclosed" was a letter signed "Cassius" addressed "To the friends of liberty and commerce" which must have proved very embarrassing to Tryon when it appeared in the edition of the *Gazetteer* published on November 11. After citing a resolution adopted by the inhabitants of the city of New York, based on a similar Philadelphia resolve, "that Whoever shall aid, or abet, the importation of any article subject to a duty, by act of Parliament, for the purpose of raising a revenue upon you . . . shall be deemed an enemy to the liberties of America," the letter directed attention to the betrayal of such liberties by William Kelly, a New York merchant who had been residing in London for some years and had secured a commission for the sale of East India Company tea to America. Kelly, according to "Cassius," had declared: "That there was no danger of the resentment of the people of New-York. . . . That . . . they [the importers] have Governor Tryon (a military man) . . . and he would cram the tea down their throats. . . ."[80]

The most serious public attempt in New York to stem resistance to measures of Parliament relating to America came from the pens

---

[78] *Rivington's New York-Gazetteer* was one of the most attractive, if not the most attractive, of newspapers published in America in the eighteenth century. The type was large, the printing clear, and the make-up artistic; it thus appealed to people of cultivation. As Isaiah Thomas noted in his *The History of Printing in America* (2 vols., Worcester, Mass., 1810, II, 315–16), ". . . no newspaper in the colonies was better printed, or was more copiously furnished with foreign intelligence."

[79] Referred to were Hugh Gaine, publisher of the *New-York Gazette: and the Weekly Mercury*, and Samuel F. Parker and John Anderson, publishers of the *New-York Gazette: or, the Weekly Post-Boy*.

[80] Kelly was hung in effigy with the Devil as his companion. A "card" inserted in the *New-York Gazetteer* of November 11 described the event. On December 22, 1773, Kelly received word, dated November 5, from the New York consignee, Abraham Lott, informing him of the "Cassius" attack and expressing the hope that the tea would arrive duty free, for—as an extract of a "Letter from a merchant in New York," also dated November 5, pointed out—"the introduction of the East India Company's tea is violently opposed here, by a set of men who shamefully live by monopolizing tea in the smuggling way" (*Tea Leaves*, pp. 269–71).

of two members of the faculty of King's College in New York—John Vardill, a tutor, and President Myles Cooper—who collaborated in writing the articles signed "Poplicola" that appeared in the November 18 and December 2 and 23 editions of the *New-York Gazetteer*. They were addressed in moderate language "To the worthy Inhabitants of the City of New-York."[81] Their theme was love of country or patriotism as a duty, with the reminder to the reader that "this or any other province is not your country but *the whole British Empire*," whose "strength and superiority over its rival neighbours are the strength and glory of every part of its dominions, and its injuries, the injuries of all." The English East India Company, "tottering on the verge of ruin" and face to face with powerful commercial rivals, should be supported by all men of true patriotism, in contrast to the practice of a few of our merchants who "have their stores crowded with teas from the Dutch Company." Should "a lover of his country, . . . an honest man," "Poplicola" asked, "encourage the *illicit trader,* who crams his coffers with wealth . . . to the support and exaltation of a foreign Company, which is a rival to that of his own country . . . ?" Although these appeals went unheeded among the people at large, such writers as "Legion," "Cassius," and "A Tradesman" berated "Poplicola" as a "ministerial hireling" and an enemy of liberty.

On November 29 in New York "a great number of the principal gentlemen of the city, merchants, lawyers, and other inhabitants of all ranks," signed a document called "The Association of the Sons of Liberty" as a testimonial of the unity of the province's protest against "the diabolical project of enslaving America." After a preamble the Association listed five resolutions providing in substance that anyone who aided or abetted in importing, landing, selling, or buying the tea would be deemed "an enemy to the liberties of America," that the duty was equally offensive to American liberties no matter where it was paid, and, finally, "that whoever shall transgress any of these resolutions, we will not deal with, or employ, or have any connection with him."[82] Two days later, on December 1, the question of the reception of the tea consigned to New York came before the Council. Since, on this same day, the consignees had

---

[81] All three of these articles were also issued by Rivington in 1773 as separate publications. See *Early American Imprints, 1639–1800* (ed. C. K. Shipton), Evans Nos. 12955–7.

[82] Hezekiah Niles: *Principles and Acts of the Revolution in America . . .* (Baltimore, 1822), pp. 188–9.

resigned and had petitioned the Governor to protect them,[83] the provincial government was confronted with the problem of what should be done with the shipment. All the Council members (according to one of them, William Smith) agreed that the government should land and store the tea either in the fort or in the barracks. Moreover, in view of the warning delivered to the pilots by the Sons of Liberty not to bring the tea ship into the harbour, they further agreed that the frigate *Swan* should be sent down to meet the vessel and escort it to the docks.[84] However, on the 7th of this month an express from Boston brought that town's resolves recommending that the tea should be returned in the same ships that brought it. As a result the Sons of Liberty—under the leadership of Philip Livingston, Captain Isaac Low, Sears, and McDougall—who had agreed at first that the cargo might be landed and stored, changed their point of view and now attempted to put pressure on the Governor whereby he would refuse to concern himself with the tea and it could be returned to England.[85] But Tryon, who enjoyed a very considerable degree of popularity, was not so easily persuaded. At a meeting of the Council on December 15 he made it clear that he was determined to land the tea, but would not use military force to do so; rather "he would throw himself at that Time into the Court of the Citizens" and would "run the risk of Brick Batts & Dirt." Appealing to the Council, he added: "I trust that you & others will stand by me."[86] But he was never to be brought to the test before his departure for England in April of the following year.[87]

[83] The consignees for the tea destined for New York—Henry White, a member of the Council, Abraham Lott, treasurer of the province and also New York City alderman, and Benjamin Booth—signed a memorial declining the agency for the tea, which came before the Council on December 1. See *Historical Memoirs . . . 1763–1776 of William Smith*, p. 157.

[84] Tryon to Dartmouth, December 1, 1773, *New York Colonial Documents*, VIII, 402.

[85] *The Historical Memoirs . . . 1763–1776 of William Smith*, pp. 157–8, show how intimately Smith, who later became a Loyalist, was working with certain leaders of the Sons of Liberty and how the influence of the Boston resolves operated to change the attitude of these leaders toward permitting the tea to be landed and stored.

[86] *Ibid.*, p. 159.

[87] At his departure Tryon was reputedly cheered by an "immense Crowd" (*ibid.*, p. 182). In its account of Governor Tryon's leave-taking, *Rivington's New-York Gazetteer* for March 24, 1774, printed the address presented to him by the General Assembly on March 19 in which this body declared: ". . . the grateful sense we entertain of the uprightness and integrity of your conduct, during your administration of this government: We think it our duty, as the representatives of a free and happy people, to pay this tribute of applause and acknowledgment to a Governor who has so eminently distinguished himself by his constant attention to their welfare and prosperity. . . ." This same issue also reported "the greatest and most respectable number

On December 17 John Lamb addressed a meeting held at the City Hall, at which letters were read from both the Boston and the Philadelphia committee of correspondence; a committee of fifteen was appointed to answer these letters, and the five resolutions of "The Association of the Sons of Liberty" were read and approved— but not so a letter from the Governor. Tryon's communication stated that when the tea should arrive at the port it was to be put into the fort in daylight, where it was to remain until the Council should advise that it be "delivered out" or until an order for its disposition should come from the King, the Company, or the owners of the tea. When Lamb asked if this plan of Tryon's was satisfactory there was a general cry of "No! No! No!"[88] The arrival of the news of Boston's destruction of the tea served to strengthen this determination not to permit the landing of the tea. Before this event Tryon was still optimistic that the tea could be landed and stored, but afterwards he was obliged to admit to the Earl of Dartmouth, in a letter of January 3, 1774, that "the landing, storing, and safe keeping of the Tea, when stored, could be accomplished, but only under the protection of the Point of the Bayonet, and Muzle of the Canon, and even then I do not see how the consumption could be affected."[89]

But the ship *Nancy*, Captain Lockyer, expected momentarily, was not destined to arrive until April 18, 1774. It was only then that the storm-tossed vessel—after losing a top-mast, suffering other damage, and making its way from the British West India island of Antigua— finally put in its appearance at Sandy Hook. Immediately it fell under control of a committee of the Sons of Liberty designated to prevent the landing of the tea. As had been the case with the commanders of the other tea ships at the ports of Boston, Charleston, and Philadelphia, Lockyer protested when, upon his arrival at Sandy Hook, a letter was placed in his hands announcing that the consignees were declining their commissions.[90] At the same time he

---

of the inhabitants of this city, ever known to be assembled on such an occasion, gave at the Exchange a very elegant entertainment to his Excellency, the Governor, on his approaching departure to Great-Britain."

[88] *Pennsylvania Gazette*, December 22, 1773; see also Hezekiah Niles: *op. cit.*, pp. 169–70.

[89] See Tryon to Dartmouth, *New York Colonial Documents*, VIII, 407–8. For the reactions of Dartmouth to the actions taken by Tryon see New-York Historical Society *Collections*, 1923, *The Letters and Papers of Cadwallader Colden*, VII, 201–3, 210–211, 214.

[90] For the correspondence between the agents at New York and Captain Lockyer see *Tea Leaves*, pp. 358–60. This discloses that the agents, Henry White, Abraham Lott & Co., and Pigou and Booth, mutually signed a letter to the Captain on Decem-

decided to return to London with his valuable cargo, since there was no longer any indication that the provincial government was disposed to land and store the tea. However, while his ship was still off Sandy Hook, an incident occurred that must have made a deep impression upon him. The afternoon of April 22 Captain Chambers came into the harbour in his ship *London* with eighteen boxes of rare Hyson tea, worth £2,000, secreted in its hold. News that he had paid duty on it in London together with the marks and numbers taken from the cocket had already been forwarded to the New York Sons of Liberty by Captain Hall of Philadelphia. Captain Laurence, who had arrived from London on the 20th, confirmed the fact. When Chambers denied he had any tea aboard, this evidence was produced. He was then forced to confess that he had brought it on his own account. The news of this violation of the resolutions of the Association of the Sons of Liberty brought thousands to the wharf where the *London* was docked. Boarding the vessel, a number of men emptied the tea into the water, but reserved the chests for making a bonfire near the Coffee House.[91] As for Chambers—who had earlier received the thanks of the New York Sons of Liberty for his refusal to carry tea belonging to the East India Company—after going into hiding for a while, he succeeded in getting aboard the *Nancy* as a passenger on its return trip to England.[92] Apart from this incident there was relative quiet in New York and men of moderation appeared to gain control of the situation.[93]

As for the Directors of the East India Company, by January 8, 1774, they were well aware that the consignees in all the American ports would "not only be interrupted in executing such commission for the Company, but also that prejudice hath marked some of them by name, and rendered them in some degree exposed to the effects

ber 27, 1773, addressed to reach him upon his arrival at Sandy Hook; it warned him of the unhappy incidents in the other ports, advised him that they could not receive the tea, and counselled him to return the cargo as soon as possible. For an excellent account of New York and "The Tea Episode" see Carl Becker: *History of Political Parties in the Province of New York* (2nd edn., Madison, Wisc., 1960), Chap. 4.

[91] *The Historical Memoirs . . . 1763–1776 of William Smith*, pp. 184–5; *New-York Gazetteer*, April 28, 1774.

[92] *Ibid.*

[93] For the report on the tea crisis in New York sent by Lieutenant Governor Cadwallader Colden to Dartmouth on May 4, 1774, see *American Archives*, 4th ser., I, 249, and Colden to Tryon, May 4, 1774, New-York Historical Society *Collections* for 1877, *Colden Letter Books*, II, 335. See also Carl Becker: *op. cit.*, p. 111n, for the state of affairs in New York by the fall of 1774, as reported to Conway by Colden.

of popular indignation." Nevertheless they addressed themselves to Governor Tryon, asking him to forward further instructions to their New York agents and entreating him, in vain, "to give such countenance to our said Agents as shall be consistent with the dignity of the high office which you hold under the Crown."[94]

By this time it was evident that the government of the Old British Empire was faced with a supreme crisis—one that it was not capable of meeting, except by decisions that would leave the Empire shattered. How it came to these decisions must be the concern of the chapter that follows.

[94] New-York Historical Society *Collections*, 1923, *The Letters and Papers of Cadwallader Colden*, VII, 203.

CHAPTER IV

Parliament Accepts the Challenge: The Coercive Acts

B Y the end of 1773 it must have been clear to any well-informed
contemporary observer that the triumphant British Empire of
1763, the greatest of all world powers of that age, was on the
threshold of disaster as the result of internal strains of a fundamental
nature. The constitution had served well for almost a century. But,
although it was properly formulated, according to seventeenth-century concepts of a strong parent nation with weak, immature offspring, it was no longer well adapted to cope with the relations of a
mother country with colonies now come of age and seeking freedom
of action consonant with the self-confidence, self-reliance, and aspirations that maturity brings.

When Parliament had declared in 1696,

> "That all Laws, Bye-Laws, Usages, or Customs at this Time, . . .
> in any of the said Plantations, which are in any wise repugnant to
> the before mentioned Laws, . . . so far as they do relate to the said
> Plantations, . . . or to any other Law hereafter to be made in this
> Kingdom, so far as such Law shall relate to and mention the said
> Plantations, are illegal, null, and void, to all Intents and Purposes
> whatsoever."[1]

no colonial assembly had ventured to challenge that body's competence to pass so sweeping a statute. It therefore remained a basic
feature of the constitution of the Old British Empire. As has been
indicated in Volume III of this series, when in 1741 Parliament
passed "An Act for restraining and preventing several unwarrantable
Schemes and Undertakings in his Majesty's Colonies and Plantations

---

[1] 7 and 8 Wm. III, c. 22, Par. 9, *Statutes at Large,* III, 587.

in America" (14 George II, c. 37), which extended to the colonies the restrictions of the so-called "Bubble Act" of 1718, there was no denial by colonials of the government's right to deal with an internal matter of this nature.[2] A further proof of the acceptance of parliamentary supremacy was provided when the General Court of Massachusetts Bay in 1758—in its dispute with Commander-in-Chief Loudoun over the quartering of troops—acknowledged this transcendent power of Parliament in the following words:

> "The Authority of all Acts of Parliament which concern the Colonies, and extend to them, is ever acknowledged in all Courts of Law, and made the Rule of all Judicial Proceedings in the Provinces.
>
> There is not a Member of the Colonial Court, and we know no Inhabitant within the Bounds of the Government, that ever questioned this Authority."[3]

But by 1773 such an acknowledgment of the authority of Parliament would not have been conceded by the assembly of either this colony or any other of the thirteen older colonies in North America. Nevertheless, it is well to point out that, before the passing of the Stamp Act, the lives and fortunes of American colonials had been affected most profoundly by Parliament's enactment of scores of laws which no colonial assembly at the time, with one exception, had attempted to question as being "unconstitutional."[4] In fact, according to the testimony of Sir Francis Bernard, Governor of Massachusetts Bay in the 1760's (cited in Chapter II of this volume), the objections to parliamentary supremacy were unknown before 1765. Yet the views expressed by Benjamin Franklin in 1771 that Parliament never had the right to bind the colonies without their consent—which was stressed in the preceding chapter—was gaining wide acceptance among colonials.

---

[2] See Volume III, revised, of this series, pp. 11–12.

[3] *Journal of the House of Representatives* (Boston, 1757–8), p. 256.

[4] See *Statutes at Large* (Eyre and Strahan), X, *Index* under the title "Plantations" for a listing of 79 acts or parts of acts that related to the colonies before the passage of the Stamp Act. The one exception was the reaction in 1762 of the House of Representatives of Massachusetts Bay to Parliament's extension to America of the writs of assistance, as the result of which the London agent of the colony was given private instructions by the House of Representatives—undoubtedly under the influence of James Otis—which embodied the following statement: ". . . The Liberty of all Men in society is to be under no legislative power but that established by Consent in the Commonwealth, nor under the Dominion of any Will or Restraint of any Law, but what such legislative [authority] shall enact. . . . " See Volume X of this series, pp. 130–1.

It should also be made clear that it was not the view of any British statesman, no matter how sympathetic he was to what he conceived to be legitimate colonial aspirations, that any colony or group of colonies could or should be placed outside the authority claimed by Parliament over all dependencies within the Empire.[5] Yet the idea of American representation in this body had been decisively rejected even by the rather conservatively inclined members of the Stamp Act Congress in 1765. Instead, charter rights, or natural rights, or the two combined, were put forward—together with the rights of Englishmen as supposedly embodied in Magna Carta—to block the efforts of the home government to exact colonial recognition of its sovereign power over them. In other words, the imperial crisis arose out of a fundamental defect in the constitution which was designed to bind the Empire together and to promote the interests of all its units, but which was, in reality, a body of statutes and other regulations ill-adapted by the 1760's to serve the needs of the more mature colonies.

Colonial leaders could sound all the notes on one specific grievance: that of taking money from the pockets of British subjects not represented in the legislative body which sought to exact financial support from all who enjoyed the protection the Empire afforded. But to over-emphasize that grievance in any analysis of the causes for the outbreak of the War for American Independence is to fail to understand the real attitude of those responsible for the break in the imperial ties. Many other grievances were as serious as that of taxation without representation but none offered such fruitful grounds for agitation and denunciation, since the people of the colonies had long acquiesced, no matter how reluctantly, in the competency of Parliament to regulate the affairs of the colonies.

Not until the oppressions under which colonials assertedly groaned were set forth in the Declaration of Independence as the voice of all the colonies, was an attempt made to lay bare in orderly, comprehensive fashion all the pent-up opposition to the general regulatory system that had been evolved for the Empire in the

---

[5] Burke, for example, in his great speech "On American Taxation," delivered in the House of Commons on April 19, 1774, declared with reference to the colonies: "But in order to enable parliament to answer all . . . ends of provident and beneficent superintendance, her powers must be boundless." This even included the power of taxation, but only "as an instrument of empire, and not as a means of supply" (*Parliamentary History*, XVII, 1267).

course of the seventeenth and eighteenth centuries. Indeed, it is impossible for students of the history of this period to accept at face value the earlier tactical position taken by colonials that, while Parliament could not legally tax colonials, it had power to regulate their trade and other business activities. Prohibition is an essential feature of regulation. Yet for Parliament to have prohibited the North American colonial trade with the foreign West Indies, even in time of peace—as was demanded of Parliament in 1752 by the Jamaica planters—would surely have presented an issue at least as threatening to the continued unity of the Empire as that of colonial taxation, if not more so. This would have been especially true in those colonies more particularly dependent upon this trade for the livelihood of hundreds, perhaps even thousands, of people. In other words, even the legal right of Parliament to regulate their business activities, one may rest assured, would have been frankly acknowledged by colonials in the 1760's and 1770's only under very narrowly circumscribed conditions—those, for example, that did not cut across the vested interests of powerful colonial groups.

Again, in seeking the causes for the break with the mother country, it is not particularly helpful to accept at face value the contention of colonials in the late 1760's and early 1770's that harmony would reign once again within the Empire were the government of Great Britain to return to the system of controls that existed before the late war with France. For this would be to deny one of the most fundamental of all facts in the life of states and other politically organized entities—that of growth and change in circumstance and attitude. A mature people cannot, nor would they if they could, wear the clothes of their childhood. Yet from 1764 to 1774, during the period of colonial agitation and growing resistance to the mother country's program for reorganizing the Empire, there is a striking uniformity in the utterances of Americans on the point that the old colonial system, under which they had grown from weakness to strength and from poverty to prosperity, was a good, rather than a bad one. In other words, there was a consistent harking back to "the good old days" of the first half of the century. Nevertheless, in 1776, although the searing indictment of tyranny embodied in the Declaration of Independence was aimed chiefly at the government of George III, many of the instances of tyrannical oppression listed might have applied equally to previous reigns—as, for instance, the reference to "a long train of abuses and usurpations pursuing invariably the same

Object . . . to reduce them [the inhabitants of the colonies] under absolute Despotism. . . ." Thus the promulgators of the Declaration did not stress the attempts on the part of Parliament to secure an American revenue as the chief source of disaffection, but rather listed a long series and wide variety of what they considered to be acts of oppression, in the enumeration of which the taxation of Americans without their consent was, surprisingly enough, given only the most casual mention.

But let no one accuse those responsible for the Declaration of Independence of insincerity or hypocrisy. They certainly believed what they asserted—whether they were right or wrong in their apprehensions—and they spoke to all mankind as the representatives of mature communities no longer willing to be held in the leading strings of their parent. Consistent with this attitude, the language employed was not that of dutiful or even refractory children, but of adults setting forth their rights in a manner best calculated to appeal to world opinion.

The position of colonials in 1776 was well anticipated in the "List of Infringements and Violations of Rights" of colonials attributed to the home government as published by the Boston town meeting of 1772 and broadcast by its committee of correspondence.[6] Although this action of the Boston town meeting was dealt with in Chapter II of this volume, it is well to reiterate the substance of the grievances there quoted. For the list of infringements declared: "The British Parliament have assumed the Powers of Legislation for the Colonists in all Cases whatsoever, without obtaining the Consent of the Inhabitants . . ." It went on to enumerate as specific unconstitutional measures of Parliament the assumption of power to raise a revenue in the colonies without their consent; to appoint customs officers to superintend the collection of these revenues in contravention of colonial charter rights; to invest these officers with absolute and arbitrary powers "entirely destructive to that Security which we have a right to enjoy"; to introduce fleets and armies to support these officers and maintain standing armies in time of peace without consent of the people; to commit the unconstitutionally laid revenue to the "management of Persons arbitrarily appointed and supported by an armed Force quartered in a free City" and for the support of

---

[6] See *The Votes and Proceedings of the Freeholders and other Inhabitants of the Town of Boston, in Town Meeting Assembled* . . . (Boston, [1772]); see also the detailed discussion on this subject in Chap. 2 of this volume.

the Governor, Lieutenant Governor, and judiciary, normally dependent upon the General Assembly for their salaries. Moreover, the indictments of the unconstitutional actions of the government of Great Britain were not limited to measures for raising a revenue, for objections were also made to the Crown instructions to the Governor whereby the Council was "made meerly a ministerial Engine" and the General Assembly adjourned and prorogued at will, which resulted in the Governor's refusal of local taxation to support the government and his allocation of Castle William to billet troops; in this connection reference was also made to the evils of the New York Quartering Act. In addition to the complaints against the extension of the powers of the vice-admiralty courts, as depriving colonials of the right of trial by jury, objection was taken to the statute by which colonials could be taken to England for trial, as in the case of the saboteurs of the *Gaspee*. Nor did the list fail to mention colonial fears of the establishment of an American episcopate or their protests against the alteration of boundaries by decision of the King and Council which resulted in their "Right of Soil" being affected by the pretensions of the Governors and the ministers "to grant in Consequence of a Mandamus." Also under attack were those acts that restrained colonials from erecting slitting mills, manufacturing hats, and transporting wool across water.[7] Thus, by 1772 the system of British regulation was almost as bitterly attacked as were the British measures to secure a revenue in America.

The widespread approval of the Boston resolves by other towns in Massachusetts Bay was indicative of the fact that this province no longer fitted into the pattern of colonial dependence that for 150 years had characterized its status. Furthermore, what was true of this colony was—largely as the result of its leadership—to become equally true of the other older colonies by 1774. Is it therefore any wonder that Governor Thomas Hutchinson should maintain before the Massachusetts Bay Assembly at the beginning of 1773 that no distinction could be drawn between parliamentary supremacy and the total independence of the colonies?[8] Is it surprising, either, that the House of Representatives should answer him: "If there can be no such Line, the Consequence is, either that the Colonies are Vassals

---

[7] *Ibid.*

[8] For Hutchinson's address to the General Court on January 6, 1773, see *Journal of the House of Representatives* (Boston, 1772–3), pp. 138–43. See also Chap. 2 of this volume.

of the Parliament, or, that both are totally Independent,"[9] and that the leaders of the colony from that time onward should leave no doubt as to the decisions they had made when presented by such alternatives? In other words, the real issue was no longer merely one of objection to American taxation by Parliament but something very much broader—although it is true that in formal pronouncements by colonials, political strategy dictated that the issues continue to be stated in the more restrictive terms. This is an important point to be kept in mind. In essence there was evident by 1773 a division of opinion within the Empire as to the nature of its constitution, with American leaders insisting on an idealistic and theoretical interpretation of what the constitution ought properly to be, rather than dealing in the practical terms of what it was functionally in its day-by-day application. Indeed, by the close of 1773 the British leaders in the Ministry and in Parliament were in no doubt as to the gravity of the challenge they had to face in order to defend the integrity of the constitution in operation. For letters, pamphlets, and newspapers continued to arrive from America showing not only the drift of colonial thought but the breakdown of legally constituted authority in the face of active resistance by great masses of people and of intimidation of those who sporadically ventured openly to defend the British government.

The news of the destruction of the East India Company tea in Boston Harbour was first published in the English press on January 20, 1774.[10] Three days later Sir Francis Bernard, writing from Aylesbury to John Pownall, Secretary to the Board of Trade and Under-Secretary of State for the Colonies, enclosed a letter dated Boston, December 16, 1773, from an unidentified person but "firm in the interests of government," who gave an account of the incident and expressed the view that it was unlikely that there would be "a general and open rebellion if the government should pursue coercive measures, but it may be feared when a firm union between the Colonies may be completed."[11] This observation was to prove correct.

---

[9] *The Speeches of His Excellency Governor Hutchinson, to the General Assembly . . . with the Answers . . .* (Boston, 1773), pp. 33–58.

[10] See *London Evening Post,* January 20, 1774. For a valuable study of the English press during the period under consideration see F. J. Hinkhouse: *The Preliminaries of the American Revolution as seen in the English Press, 1763–1775* (New York, 1926), especially Chap. 8, "Tea and the Punishment of Boston."

[11] For an extract of the above letter see the *Manuscripts of the Earl of Dartmouth, Vol. II, American Papers, Historical Manuscripts Commission, Fourteenth Report, Appendix,* Part X, 191, cited hereafter as *Dartmouth Manuscripts.*

The Earl of Dartmouth, Secretary of State for the Colonies, was meanwhile marshalling all available evidence having to do with resistance to the Tea Act in North America—evidence which had been reaching him since December, from the colonial governors, correspondents in America, such as Joseph Reed, and principally from the East India Company.[12] He also, apparently, determined to consult with his under-secretaries and others with American connections, such as the two former Massachusetts Bay Governors Thomas Pownall and Sir Francis Bernard.[13] Thus Dartmouth was well prepared for the meeting of the Cabinet Council held late in January 1774 at which (according to Lord North) he proposed "punishing

---

[12] *Ibid.*, II, 182–4 and 193–4, and *Calendar of Home Office Papers of the Reign of George III, 1773–1775* . . . (ed. R. A. Roberts, London, 1899), pp. 117–19, 164–8, 171–7; see also *Life and Correspondence of Joseph Reed* (2 vols., Philadelphia, 1847), I, and *American Archives*, 4th ser., I, *passim*.

[13] For example, as to the origin of the Boston Port Bill, William Knox, who in 1774 was second Under-Secretary of State for the Colonies, wrote: "The Bill for shutting up the Port of Boston, passed the last session, was the step proposed by [John] Pownall to have been taken, I was for an alteration in the Council; Lord Dartmouth went with me, but neither of us wished to make any further alterations in the Charter" (*The Manuscripts of Captain H. V. Knox* [ed. Mrs. S. C. Lomas, 1909], *Historical Manuscripts Commission, Report on* . . . *Various Collections*, VI, 257). For the influence of Pownall, then first Under-Secretary of State in the American Department and Secretary to the Board of Trade, upon Dartmouth and in the formulation of colonial policy before and during 1774, see F. B. Wickwire: "John Pownall and British Colonial Policy," *William and Mary Quarterly*, 3rd ser., XX, 543–54, especially pp. 549–53.

For the influence of his brother Thomas upon the administration and members of Parliament, on the basis that as one-time colonial Governor he had first-hand knowledge of the problems (as he had demonstrated in his book *Administration of the Colonies*, first published in 1764, and in its fourth edition in 1774 along with the appearance of the second volume), see J. A. Schutz: *Thomas Pownall: British Defender of American Liberty* (Glendale, Calif., 1951), pp. 183n, 232–6; see also *History of Parliament: House of Commons, 1754–1790* (eds. Sir Lewis Namier and John Brooke, 3 vols., London and New York, 1964), III, 317. It may also be noted that former Governor Sir Francis Bernard published in London the second edition of his *Select Letters on the Trade and Government of America, and the Principles of Law and Polity applied to the American Colonies* in 1774. Like Pownall, Bernard was torn between duty and loyalty as a Crown official and his sympathies toward the people he had governed, whose trade problems he had clearly grasped, however inept he may have been in interpreting American political aspirations. Whether Bernard was indeed responsible, as claimed by William Knox (*Historical Manuscripts Commission, Various Collections*, VI, 257), for having "infused the opinion into Lord North" that the jury system of the Bay colony should be altered and its town meetings prohibited, depends upon the accuracy of Knox's memory at a date later than the event. The question may also be raised as to whether Bernard's manuscripts on the "State of Disorders" and "Narrative" of events in Massachusetts Bay from 1766 to 1774 (Barrington-Bernard Correspondence . . . [Cambridge, Mass., 1912], Appendices III and IV) were prepared for use of the Ministry or members of Parliament in connection with the passage of the Coercive Acts.

the Town of Boston by removing the Custom House from thence & holding the assembly for the future in another place . . . as a measure that could be taken immediately by the sole power of the Crown."[14] As for the King's chief minister, Lord North, it is not clear what preparative steps he took to meet the American crisis or with whom he consulted in addition to the King, but it is certain that George III paid at least some heed to General Gage, whose advice on February 4 "as to the mode of compelling Boston to submit to whatever may be thought necessary" he wished North to take into consideration.[15] It was on the same day the King saw Gage, however, that the Cabinet Council agreed to "recommend to the King that the Governor remove to some place in the province least likely to be influenced by Boston," and determined to secure the opinions of Attorney General Edward Thurlow and Solicitor General Alexander Wedderburn as to "whether the late proceedings [in Boston] amount to high treason."[16] The following day consideration was given to the eventual measures to be taken in case the law officers found that there was sufficient ground "to institute a criminal proceeding against any of the persons concerned in the late outrages committed in Boston."[17] On February 11 the chief law officers reported that in their opinion "the acts and proceedings do amount to the crime of high treason," and on that same date Dartmouth inquired of them what powers "might be granted to the Commissioners under the Great Seal who should be appointed to make inquisition of the treasons committed in Massachusetts Bay."[18] The next day, while Dartmouth on the one hand was writing to the wealthy merchant John Thornton that he would be thought mad at this juncture "if he were to say a word of repealing the tea Duty now," John Pownall was sending precedents to the law officers "respecting the establishment of Courts of Oyer

---

[14] North to the King, January [29], 1774. *Correspondence of King George the Third* (Fortescue), III, 55; see also *Dartmouth Manuscripts*, II, 192, which shows that Dartmouth secured on January 31 and the first week in February a list of returns of New York militia headed "Royalist Militia" (*ibid.*, II, 192–3 and 195–6).

[15] *Correspondence of George III* (Fortescue), III, 59.

[16] Cabinet Minute, February 4, 1774, *Dartmouth Manuscripts*, II, 195. For Dartmouth's transmittal to the law officers on February 5, 1774, of "a narrative of facts relating to some transactions at Boston . . . with two questions thereupon for their consideration and answer," and his reminders to them on the 8th "of the necessity of some speedy decision . . ." and again on the 10th, see *Calendar of Home Office Papers, George III, 1773–1775*, pp. 178–9 and 181.

[17] Cabinet Minute, February 5, 1774, *Dartmouth Manuscripts*, II, 195–6.

[18] *Calendar of Home Office Papers, George III, 1773–1775*, p. 182.

and Terminer distinct from those established by the charter and laws of that Colony" (Virginia in 1717).[19] In other words, investigation was patently under way within the American Department to determine how far the government could go in measures to bring Massachusetts Bay back to a position of dutiful submission and whether such measures ought to be punitive, coercive, or simply preventive of a future recurrence of such recalcitrant behavior as the resistance to the Tea Act. However, it seems equally evident that no one in the Ministry—neither Lord North nor Dartmouth—was willing to deal with the London colonial agents for advice or for accounts of grievances submitted by the colonies they represented.[20]

Early in February, Lieutenant General Gage, Commander-in-Chief of the British Forces in North America, who was now in London, was interviewed by the King to determine his willingness to go to Massachusetts Bay and take over the executive function there in addition to his high military office. The General, however, was totally deceived in his estimation of the degree of determination of the Bay colony people to submit no longer to control by the government of Great Britain. For he assured the King on this occasion that "they will be Lyons, whilst we are Lambs but if we take the resolute part they will undoubtedly prove very meek." His opinion was that, if four regiments were sent to Boston, it would be sufficient "to prevent any disturbance."[21] The King and North, apparently well satisfied with Gage's assurances, took steps on April 7 to have him commissioned Governor-in-Chief of Massachusetts Bay.[22]

---

[19] *Ibid.*, p. 183, and *Dartmouth Manuscripts*, II, 197.

[20] See in this connection the paper delivered before the Colonial Society of Massachusetts by M. G. Kammen, "The Colonial Agents, English Politics, and the American Revolution," revised and printed in *William and Mary Quarterly*, 3rd ser., XXII, 244–63. In his study, which will form part of a larger study (much-anticipated by this writer), Dr. Kammen stresses the view that after the high-water mark of the effectiveness of the London agencies in 1765–6, in connection with the Stamp Act crisis, there was a steady decline of their influence, chiefly as the result of the instability in English politics, especially during "the seven years of confusion," as Sir Lewis Namier described the period between 1763 and 1770.

[21] The King to Lord North, February 4, 1774, *Correspondence of George III* (Fortescue), III, 59.

[22] Gage's commission of April 7, 1774, naming him "Captain-general and governor-in-chief," was simply a memorandum directing him to follow the revised copy of the Hutchinson commission of April 13, 1770, on which the alterations were written in red ink for Gage's guidance. For this commission see P.R.O., C.O. 5:765, pp. 96–113, and for the memorandum see *ibid.*, p. 294; for Gage's instructions, dated April 5, 1774, see C.O. 5:205, pp. 427–61. For Gage's additional commission as Vice-Admiral of April 5, see Adm. Reg. Mun. Bks., 10, f. 155.

On February 16 Dartmouth received a bill of indemnity for charges amounting to some £9,660 from the East India Company for its loss of tea.[23] On that same day the Cabinet reached the decision that two guard ships should be added to the squadron at Boston under command of Rear Admiral Montagu. At the same time—that is, from the 15th to the 18th—Dartmouth interviewed some of the witnesses of the events at Boston and called them to appear before the Privy Council on the 19th.[24] At this meeting, after hearing the depositions, the Cabinet decided:

> "In case a warrant is issued to arrest persons guilty of treason at Boston to recommend the King to send out a person conversant in the law to assist in its execution. Advices received from America, with the proceedings of the Privy Council thereupon to be laid before the Houses of Parliament. Permission to be gained to bring in the Boston Port Bill and a bill to alter the constitution of Massachusetts Bay."[25]

It would appear, however, that between this meeting of the Cabinet and the one held nine days later the Attorney General and the Solicitor General came to the conclusion that the government was not justified on the basis of the depositions in issuing the proposed warrants for treason. Thus, the Cabinet Council on February 28 was forced to come to the conclusion that the whole matter should be laid before Parliament.[26] Here then, in brief, is the background of the proceedings that led to the passage of the so-called "Coercive Acts."

Parliament had been prorogued on July 1, 1773, and by a series of prorogations did not meet again to transact business until January 13 of the following year. Although the press was filled with news of defiance of the government, as manifested in the chief seaports of

---

[23] *Calendar of Home Office Papers, George III, 1773–1775*, p. 184.

[24] *Ibid.* In this connection see "Dr. Williamson's Examination before the King's Council in London," Massachusetts Historical Society *Collections*, 4th ser., IV, 386–9.

[25] For the Cabinet Minutes of February 16 and 19, 1774, see *Dartmouth Manuscripts*, II, 198; see also *Acts of the Privy Council, Col. Ser., 1766–1783*, pp. 391–2.

[26] *Ibid.;* see also the Cabinet Minute for February 28, 1774, *Dartmouth Manuscripts*, II, 199, wherein Dartmouth recorded in his own hand: "As the charge of high treason cannot be maintained against any individuals on the ground of the depositions taken at the Council Board . . . ," it was agreed to lay all the papers before Parliament, "to address the King with assurances of support [and the] Boston Port Bill to be brought in and a bill for supporting the declaratory act of the 6th of this reign." For Under-Secretary of State Knox's version of why the law officers would not approve the warrants for treason, see *Historical Manuscripts Commission, Report on Various Collections*, VI, 270. For an interesting analysis of the events leading up to the passage of the Coercive Acts see J. M. Sosin: "The Massachusetts Act of 1774: Coercive or Preventive?" *Huntington Library Quarterly*, XXVI, 235–52.

the North American colonies, it was not until March 7 that the King at last sent a message to Parliament concerning "the violent and outrageous Proceedings at the Town and Port of Boston," actions that were "subversive of the Constitution thereof. . . ." In laying the whole matter before the two Houses the King asked the members to empower him to take such measures as would put a stop to the present disorders and requested them to consider what further regulations might be needed "for better securing the Execution of the Laws, and the just Dependance of the Colonies upon the Crown and Parliament of Great Britain."[27] Thereupon Lord North addressed the House of Commons, stressing the dangerous situation in the colonies;[28] he then produced some 109 documents throwing light on the proceedings of the East India Company and the conduct of American colonials in reaction to the Tea Act.[29] At this juncture Edmund Burke arose and moved that certain parts of the King's speeches to Parliament in 1768, 1769, and 1770 be read. This was approved and the following excerpts were reiterated: On November 8, 1768, His Majesty's address had referred to "Acts of Violence and of Resistance to the Law" in one of the colonies, "the Capital Town of which Colony, appears . . . to be in a State of Disobedience to all Law and Government," such as "manifest a Disposition to throw off their Dependance on Great Britain";[30] in his speech of May 9, 1769, he had asked Parliament for its hearty support in order to "defeat the Designs of the Factious and Seditious" in every part of "My Dominions";[31] finally, on November 13, 1770, the King had noted that while the people in most of the colonies had given up their combinations against the commerce of Great Britain, yet in some parts of Massachusetts Bay "very unwarrantable Practices are still carried on, and My good Subjects oppressed by the same lawless Violence which has too long prevailed in the Province."[32]

With the above expressions of the King's views before them,

---

[27] *Parliamentary History*, XVII, 1159.

[28] For this address see Peter Force: *American Archives*, 4th ser., I, 222–4

[29] *Journals of the House of Commons*, XXXIV, 541–3; *Parliamentary History*, XVII, 1160. For Charles Garth's summary of the action taken in Parliament during the passage of the various measures affecting the colonies brought before it during the spring of 1774, see his letters for March 15, 31, April 20, 30, and May 12, 1774, Garth Correspondence (Mss), South Carolina Commons House of Assembly Committee of Correspondence and London Agent Letterbook, 1766–1775, pp. 165–71, South Carolina Archives, cited hereafter as Garth Correspondence, 1766–1775 (Mss).

[30] *Journals of the House of Commons*, XXXII, 21.

[31] *Ibid.*, XXXII, 453.

[32] *Ibid.*, XXXIII, 3–4.

the way was prepared for the members of Parliament to proceed to the task of making obedient subjects out of the inhabitants of that colony considered to be the most disobedient in America, Massachusetts Bay. On the 14th of March 1774 a petition was presented to the House by William Bollan, acting in his capacity of London agent for the Council of the Bay province. It began by dealing briefly with the history of the colonization of North America by those who, when leaving England, were persuaded that they carried with them all their "public Liberties" and who, together with those who followed them, by their labours had "raised the King's *American* Empire out of a dreary and dangerous Wilderness" to such a height "that of late Years it hath given Employment unto Two Thirds of the British Shipping, with a comfortable Support to no small Part of the inhabitants of *Great Britain*, and great Addition to the Dignity and Strength of its Naval Empire. . . ." In defence of "their invaluable Rights," the document continued, permission was requested for Bollan to appear before the House in support of the Council's petition. But, after being read, the petition was tabled by vote of the House.[33] Instead, the House agreed that leave be granted to bring in a bill for the immediate removal of the customs officers from the town of Boston and, concurrently, to discontinue the landing and loading of goods at that port.[34] On the 18th a bill to that effect was presented by Lord North, read and ordered to be read a second time. This was done on March 21; on the 25th, with the addition of a number of amendments, the bill passed its third reading without a division[35] and was sent to the

---

[33] *Ibid.*, XXXIV, 561.

[34] *Ibid.* In this connection it may be noted that the Ministry apparently at first had the idea that the custom house could be removed from Boston upon the King's authority alone. On February 10 the Earl of Dartmouth asked the opinions of the Attorney General and the Solicitor General if this could be done. They replied the following day that the Lord's Commissioners of His Majesty's Treasury "may appoint the Custom-House in such parts of the Province as they think most convenient for the purpose." In reply to Dartmouth's second query—whether, after the removal of the present custom house from Boston, any places within the harbour could be established for legal importation or exportation—they answered: "The Trade of all other places where it is not thought necessary to appoint Custom-Houses must resort to the Custom-Houses which the Treasury shall think fit to appoint for Clearances" (P.R.O., C.O. 5:247, pp. 192–3).

[35] It was on March 25 that a petition, framed by Arthur Lee of Virginia and signed by Benjamin Franklin, as well as by several other "Natives of North America," was brought before the House of Commons and read. It declared that the bill was a violation of the "Rights of natural Justice" which would "sink deep in the minds of their Countrymen, and tend to alienate their Affections from this Country." The petition was rejected by a vote of 170 to 40. See *Journals of the House of*

House of Lords, where it passed *nemine dissentiente* on the 30th.[36]

The opposition to the bill as it progressed through Parliament had been much stronger in the House of Commons than in the House of Lords. In a speech on March 25 Edmund Burke declared: "I never knew any thing that has given me a more heart-felt sorrow than the present measure." Further along in his address he castigated the Governor (without naming him) for not exercising his authority and calling on the military to prevent riotous actions. "The fault of this governor ought not to be the means of punishment for the innocent." William Dowdeswell—who had been Chancellor of the Exchequer in a former administration and was a member of the Rockingham group, as was Burke—in the conviction that Parliament was "going to do very great mischief," asked: "Why will you punish Boston alone? Did not other towns send your tea back to England, and refuse the landing?" Rose Fuller, a member for Rye with West India planter interests, thought that before the bill was passed Boston should be given the chance to pay a fine. Colonel Barré, who had opposed the Stamp Act, insisted that a fine was a tax and he would oppose it. In fact, before the debate ended, he stated that as the bill stood "he could not help giving his hearty affirmative. . . ." But former Governor Johnstone of West Florida warned "that the effect of the present Bill must be productive of a General Confederation, to resist the power of this country."[37] Although the Earl of Chatham did not participate in the debate in the House of Lords, he voiced his opinion in reply to extensive information provided to him by

---

Commons, XXXIV, 595–6; Franklin to Thomas Cushing, April 2, 1774, *Writings of Benjamin Franklin* (Smyth), VI, 224; Lord North to the King, [March 25, 1774], *Correspondence of George III* (Fortescue), III, 85.

The May 23 edition of the *Boston Gazette* contained extracts from a number of letters written from London to people in New York and Philadelphia, in one of which the passing of the Boston Port Act was described as follows: "About a fortnight ago an Act of Parliament of the most extraordinary Kind, to shut up the port of Boston, was passed . . . being smuggled through the House, in 17 days only from its introduction. The Evidence before the Privy Council was suppressed, the agents refused a hearing at the bar, and no member for Boston or America in either House." This letter went on to state that a body of merchants trading to Boston and America waited on Lord North with a request that a petition might be heard against the bill but was informed that the bill had become a law. In view of the fact that the law gave the King constitutional power to suspend the Act in case the tea that was destroyed was paid for, the merchants then "offered Lord North £19,000 as a security to the India Company to pay for the tea if the suspension of the Act could be procured." But the offers were refused.

[36] For the changes in the Boston Port Bill agreed to on March 24, and its final passage, see *Journals of the House of Commons,* XXXIV, 596, 612, 615.

[37] *Parliamentary History,* XVII, 1168–9; *American Archives,* 4th ser., I, 35–61.

Shelburne.[38] He felt that the destruction of the tea was "certainly criminal," but that, before any coercive measures could be called just, Boston ought to have a formal opportunity to make reparation.[39] According to Shelburne, during the debates in the House of Lords Camden "met the question fully," but opinion divided on whether the crisis in Boston was properly "commotion" or "open rebellion," with a degree of disregard being displayed toward both Dartmouth and North. On the other hand, Lord Mansfield, speaking to the bill, alleged clearly that the violence against the tea ships "was the last overt act of high treason." The upshot of the debate was the passage of the Port Bill in that House, but not before it had become clear to Shelburne that the administration was temporizing on whether it would advocate repeal of the Tea Act. In his estimation Dartmouth, however, "appeared to stop after declaring the proposed alteration of the charter; but Lord Suffolk declared very plainly that other very determined measures should be offered." It was at this time that Shelburne urged Chatham to come to London, on the basis that his presence was "absolutely necessary in many views, and desirable in all."[40]

On March 31 the Boston Port Bill received the royal assent. The Act stated that in view of the "dangerous commotions and insurrections" in Boston, the commerce of His Majesty's subjects could not be safely carried on there; it then provided that after June 1, 1774, it would be unlawful for any person to unload or load any vessel or boat within the harbour on pain of forfeiture of both goods and vessel. Section 8 of the act read: "That whenever it shall be made to appear to his Majesty, in his Privy Council, that peace and obedience to the laws shall be so far restored in the said town of Boston, that the trade of Great Britain may be safely carried on there, and his Majesty's customs duly collected, . . . it shall and may be lawful for his Majesty, by Proclamation, or Order in Council," to reopen the harbour, appoint officers of the customs there, and for persons to load and unload goods, provided that these goods are loaded or unloaded at places so designated by His Majesty.[41] While there was no mention in the Act of a substitute for the port of Boston for the

---

[38] See Shelburne to Chatham, February 3, 27, March 15, and April 4, 1774, *Pitt Correspondence*, IV, 322–9, 334–6, 339–41.

[39] Chatham to Shelburne, March 20, 1774, *ibid.*, IV, 336–7.

[40] Shelburne to Chatham, April 4, 1774, *ibid.*, IV, 339–41.

[41] *Journals of the House of Commons*, XXXIV, 615. The Act (14 Geo. III, c. 19) carries the title "An Act to discontinue, in such Manner, and for such Time as are

vast commerce of Massachusetts Bay with the outside world, in the course of the debate in the House of Commons Lord North had informed the members that the custom house would be established at the town of Marblehead, close to Salem.[42]

But the Boston Port Act was not to stand alone. The Ministry felt that other steps must be taken in order that Massachusetts Bay might conform properly to the pattern of a loyal dependency in relation to the Crown and government of Great Britain. Therefore on March 28 the committee of the whole House of Commons reported that leave should be given to bring in a bill for the better regulation of the province's government.[43]

It will be recalled that as a part corporate, part royal colony, under the charter granted by William and Mary in 1691, Massachusetts Bay had a hybrid government. Whereas in other royal colonies the members of the Governor's Council were appointed under the sign manual of the King from nominations sent to the Crown and were therefore subject to suspension or dismissal, in Massachusetts Bay Council members were elected annually by the General Court, with only the right of veto vested in the Governor. In all royal colonies the Council was expected to strengthen the executive arm and aid in the delicate task of harmonizing the policies of the central government of the Empire with the local aspirations of the inhabitants. But in the Bay colony the Council had become a tool in the hands of the majority of members of the House of Representatives—themselves elected by freemen of the province—a tool used to frustrate and nullify the Governor's efforts to carry out his royal instructions. It was doubtless reasoned by Lord North and his advisers that if the first charter of the colony of 1628/9 could be annulled by the Crown in 1684 for what seemed to be good reason, Parliament—which had taken over the great prerogatives of the Crown as the result of the Revolution of 1688—could alter the charter of 1691, especially since this charter had been supplemented by an explanatory charter issued in 1725 (which, from the point of view of the majority of the House of Representatives, limited their choice of a Speaker).[44]

therein mentioned, the landing and discharging, lading, or shipping, of Goods, Wares, and Merchandise, at the Town, and within the Harbour of Boston, in the Province of Massachuset's Bay, in North America" (*Statutes at Large,* VIII, 341).

[42] *Parliamentary History,* XVII, 1171.

[43] *Journals of the House of Commons,* XXXIV, 601.

[44] Under date of February 19, 1774, there is a Cabinet Minute among the papers of Lord Dartmouth showing that permission was to be gained to bring in a bill "to alter the constitution of Massachusetts Bay" (*Dartmouth Manuscripts,* II, 198).

A bill to effect the alteration of the provincial constitution, presented on April 15, 1774, was read and ordered to be printed. On the 22nd it had its second reading and, on May 2, came up for the third reading. The House divided over the motion, passing it in the affirmative, 239 to 64. It was then sent to the House of Lords, which returned it on May 12 with amendments which were accepted by the Commons. On the 20th it received the royal approval.[45]

The preamble of the act revising the government of Massachusetts Bay referred to the provision made in the charter of 1691 for the election of the Governor's Council each year by the General Court "newly chosen" and to the fact that this method of filling the Council had tended "to weaken the attachment of his Majesty's well-disposed subjects . . . to his Majesty's government, and to encourage the ill-disposed among them to proceed even to acts of direct resistance to, and defiance of, his Majesty's authority." It was then enacted that after August 1 the Council should be composed of members appointed by the King with the advice of his Privy Council, in harmony with "the appointment of counsellors in . . . other colonies in America, the governors whereof are appointed by commission under the great seal of Great Britain," with the provision that the number so chosen should not exceed thirty-six or be less than twelve.[46] It was further enacted that after July 1 the Governor was to appoint, under the seal of the province, all judges of courts, the attorney general and all provosts, marshals, justices of the peace, as well as sheriffs. Further, to remedy the abuses resulting from meetings of townships —which, it was stated, had been diverted from their original purpose

[45] *Journals of the House of Commons*, XXXIV, 601, 649, 670, 685, 696–7, 742, 749–50, 776. King George, writing to Lord North on July 1, relates a conversation that he had with Thomas Hutchinson, who had now given up his post of Governor. Hutchinson took the position that "the Boston Port Bill was the only wise effectual method that could have been suggested for bringing them [the people of Boston] to a speedy submission, and that the Change in the Legislature will be the means of establishing some Government in that Province which till now has been a Scene of Anarchy" (*Correspondence of George III* [Fortescue], III, 116).

[46] With reference to the alteration of the Council of Massachusetts Bay, Thomas Hutchinson, writing to his son, Thomas, Jr., from London on July 6, 1774, made the following comment: "A Person in Administration informed me that he had a doubt of the expediency of the Act . . . for changing the Council and that he had mentioned my doubts and also produced my letters upon the subject, both in Lord Hillsborough's time [as Secretary of the Colonies] and since, but the Result of the Council in the affairs of the Tea [that is, the position taken by the Council of the province] was so exceptionable to the rest of the King's servants that it was to no purpose to oppose the measure. I warned the Council [of the province] of the Consequence . . . and, after the Tea was destroyed I knew it would enrage the Powers here against the Council more than all they had done before" (Hutchinson Family Correspondence, Egerton Manuscripts, 2659:82–3, British Museum).

and had instead passed "many dangerous and unwarrantable re-solves"—it was provided that after August 1 no town meeting should be held without written leave of the Governor, except the annual meeting for the choice of town officers and the election of repre-sentatives to the General Court, at which meetings no other matter should be treated except as approved by the Governor. An additional clause, aimed at doing away with the "many evil practices" that tend "to pervert the free and impartial administration of justice," provided that after September 1 the jurors of all courts, superior and inferior, should no longer be elected by the freeholders but were to be sum-moned and returned by the sheriffs, who were therefore to receive all writs for the return of jurors. Furthermore, in order to facilitate the choice of properly qualified jurors by the sheriffs, lists of people with their titles and qualifications were to be drawn up by the constables for delivery to the sheriffs each fall, after which they were to be displayed to the public and ultimately passed on by the justices of the peace at their general sessions. Finally, in case a sufficient number of jurors did not appear for duty, the court was authorized to issue a writ to the sheriff requiring him to summon other qualified persons to fill up the panels, with the provision that anyone so summoned who refused to serve should be fined no more than £10 or less than twenty shillings.[47]

Hand in hand with the Bill for Better Regulating the Government of Massachusetts Bay went another, destined for application exclu-sively within this province—the Bill for the Impartial Administration of Justice. Leave to bring in this bill was granted by the House of Commons on April 15; it was presented and read on April 21, on which date it was also ordered to be printed. On the 25th it was committed after its second reading. Amended on May 4, the bill had its third reading on May 6, when, after further amendment, it was passed by a majority of 127 to 24 and sent to the House of Lords. On the 19th the approval of the Lords was signified and the following day it received the royal assent.[48] The statute is entitled: "An Act for

---

[47] 14 Geo. III, c. 45, "An Act for the better regulating the Government of the Province of the Massachusset's Bay, in New England," *Statutes at Large*, VIII, 349.

[48] *Journals of the House of Commons*, XXXIV, 650, 667, 677, 702, 712, 771, 776. Writing to the King on the evening of May 4, Lord North had the following to say respecting the bill: "There was a debate of some hours today about a clause for taking away the appeal for death [that is, appeal for conviction on a capital offence] from the Colony of the Massachusetts Bay, but that regulation being alter'd to a direction for trying all such appeals either in the other Colonies or in G[t] Britain, the opposition was dropt" (*Correspondence of George III* [Fortescue], III, 103.

the impartial Administration of Justice in the Cases of Persons questioned for any Acts done by them in the Execution of the Law, or for the Suppression of Riots and Tumults, in the Province of the Massachuset's Bay, in New England."[49] Its preamble stated:

> ". . . an attempt hath lately been made to throw off the authority of the Parliament of Great Britain over the said Province, and an actual and avowed resistance, by open force, to the execution of certain Acts of Parliament, hath been suffered to take place, uncontrolled and unpunished, in defiance of his Majesty's Authority, and to the utter subversion of all lawful Government; and whereas . . . neither the Magistrates acting in support of the laws, nor any of his Majesty's subjects aiding and assisting them therein . . . should be discouraged from the proper discharge of their duty, by an apprehension, that in case of their being questioned for any acts done therein, they may be . . . brought to trial . . . before persons who do not acknowledge the validity of the laws, . . . or the authority of the Magistrate in the support of whom, such acts had been done."[50]

In view of this, it was provided that in the event an indictment were issued within the province against a person for any capital offence and it should be found on the oath of the Governor that the act was committed by a person in the execution of the duty assigned to his office or by any person acting under the direction of any magistrate or officer of the revenue, and should it further appear to the satisfaction of the Governor that a fair trial of such person could not be held within the province, he might, with the advice and consent of the Council, direct that the trial of the indicted person should take place "in some other of his Majesty's Colonies, or in Great Britain." Pursuant to this decision the Governor could then either order the accused under proper custody to be sent to the place appointed for the trial or admit such person to bail, with sufficient securities for his personal appearance at the designated place and time. Finally, in order to prevent a failure of justice for want of evidence, the Governor was authorized to bind in recognizance for their personal appearances all witnesses called by either the prosecutor or the accused and to provide a reasonable sum for each witness, who would ac-

---

[49] It is cited as 14 Geo. III, c. 39; see *Statutes at Large* (Eyre and Strahan), VIII, 347, which gives only the title of the act. For the statute in full see *Statutes at Large* (Pickering), XXX, 367–71; see also *American Archives*, 4th ser., I, 129–32.

[50] *Ibid.*, I, 129–30.

cordingly be furnished with a certificate redeemable out of the customs revenue. The Act was to continue for three years.[51]

Here then were the two statutes that placed the Massachusetts
Bay Assembly under severe restrictions, and that—together with the
Boston Port Act—were designed to bring to a test the issue as to
whether it was possible to reduce the inhabitants of the colony to
obedience to the sovereign power of the government of Great Britain.
Both bills were passed by huge majorities, as has been shown, and
both became law on May 20, 1774. There is every indication, moreover, that in taking this action the members thought they were obeying a popular mandate of the people of Great Britain,[52] who felt the
time had come to bring to terms this most recalcitrant colony, dominated, as it was believed to be, by Boston mobs and their sympathizers. The opposition in Commons, while eloquent, proved ineffective. When Dowdeswell on April 30 offered a petition on behalf of
William Bollan, acting as agent for the Council of Massachusetts
Bay, the petition was rejected—as had been three previous petitions
submitted by the agent—on the grounds that the Council had no
right to appoint such an agent.[53] Nor did a petition against the bill

---

[51] The Declaration of Independence viewed the purpose of this statute as being
"For protecting them [those acting in the name of the King] by a mock trial from
punishment, for any murder they should commit on the Inhabitants of these States."
Thomas Hutchinson, in commenting on this, stated: "To try men before a biassed
and pre-determined Jury would be *a mock trial*. To prevent this, the Act of Parliament, complained of, was passed. . . . Indeed, the removal of trials for the sake
of unprejudiced disinterested Juries, is altogether consistent with the spirit of our
laws, and the practice of courts [in England] in changing the venue from one county
to another." See *Thomas Hutchinson's Strictures upon the Declaration of the Congress
at Philadelphia; In a Letter to a Noble Lord* (*Old South Leaflets*, No. 227, ed.
Malcolm Freiberg, Boston, 1958), p. 21.

[52] That such a popular mandate was not evident in the English press but that
there was a division of opinion with no preponderance on either side is the argument
of F. J. Hinkhouse: *op. cit.*, pp. 160–70. For the view that the country gentry "silently
acquiesced in governmental policies," and initially gave encouragement to the ministers
to pursue coercive measures, as a matter of self-interest, while influential and radical
Londoners opposed such action but the merchant group in general did not, see Dora
Mae Clark: *British Opinion and the American Revolution* (New Haven, 1930), 133–4,
166–7, 227–30.

[53] In reporting the above action to South Carolina, London agent Charles Garth
wrote on April 30, 1774: "We have had a few Divisions in the House, and when
had, the Minorities have appeared so small as to discourage Divisions upon this
subject; indeed the Voice of the Nation in general seems at present to go with [the]
Administration in their Measures respecting the Massachusetts Bay." See Garth
Correspondence, 1766–1775 (mss.) p. 171. For London agent Bollan's repeated
attempts to be heard in petition, which were denied by both the Commons and
the Lords, see *Annual Register, 1774*, pp. 65–6 and 71, *American Archives*, 4th ser.,
I, 35–6, 46, 60, 79–80, 92–3, and *Last Journals of Horace Walpole during the Reign
of George III* (ed. A. F. Steuart, 2 vols., London, 1910), I, 344. For Bollan's reports

that was brought before the House by Sir George Savile[54] on May 2
—one of several presented on behalf of Americans living in England[55]—give any reassurance that, without some drastic and firmly
applied changes in the administration of the province, it would be
possible for the government of Great Britain to continue exercising
any control over Massachusetts Bay or over any of the other North
American colonies. For the petition stated that should the two bills
be passed and carried into execution they would be "fatal to the
rights, liberties, and peace of all America." It also affirmed that the
Bill Regulating the Government of Massachusetts Bay would tend
to "deprive a whole province, without any form of trial, of its chartered rights, solemnly secured to it by mutual compact between the
crown and the people" and that proceedings of the House in planning
this measure were "totally unconstitutional." The petition further
maintained that this bill, taken with

> "the appointment and removal of judges, at the pleasure of the
> governor, with salaries payable by the crown, puts the property,
> liberty and life of the subject . . . in his power [by] a system of judicial
> tyranny deliberately at this day imposed upon them. . . . of the same
> unexampled and alarming nature is the Bill, which, under the title
> of a more impartial administration of justice . . . empowers the
> governor to withdraw offenders from justice in the said province, . . .
> and, in effect, subjecting that colony to military execution . . . such
> as no free people can long endure. . . . [Indeed] the dispensing
> power which this bill intends to give to the governor, advanced as
> he is already above the law, . . . must constitute him an absolute
> tyrant. . . ."

The petitioners then voiced the wish that it were possible for them
to "perceive any difference between the most abject slavery, and
such entire subjection to a legislature, in the constitution of which
they have not a single voice, nor the least influence," but held that

---

to the committee of the Massachusetts Bay Council of March and April 1774 on his
abortive attempts to petition both Houses of Parliament see *American Archives*, 4th
ser., I, 225–35. For the reaction in the press against the refusal of the Commons to
hear Bollan see F. J. Hinkhouse: *op. cit.*, pp. 166–7.

[54] Sir George Savile, a highly respected member of Parliament representing Yorkshire, in protesting on April 22 the Bill for Regulating the Government of Massachusetts Bay, characterized it as "a most extraordinary exertion of legislative power"
(*Parliamentary History*, XVII, 1277).

[55] On March 25 and 28 and May 11, petitions from native Americans residing in
London were read and tabled; nor were petitions from them to the King on March 31
and May 19 any more effective. See *American Archives*, 4th ser., I, 46–8, 58–9,
60–1, 92, 96.

they must regard "the giving their property by their own consent alone, as the unalienable right, of the Subject, and the last sacred bulwark of constitutional liberty. . . ." They therefore prayed the House "not to attempt reducing them to a state of slavery, which the English principles of liberty they inherit from their mother country will render worse than death. . . ."[56]

In other words, the petitioners laid down the doctrine that it was "totally unconstitutional" for Parliament—which claimed ultimate sovereign authority within the Empire, a claim fully acknowledged by the King as a person and by the Crown as an institution—to change the form of a colonial government based upon a charter that had come into existence, so they asserted, as the result of a "mutual compact between the crown and the people" of that colony, in this case Massachusetts Bay. To do so, they charged, and at the same time seek to guarantee the safety of those in the colony who might be charged with carrying out any measures passed by Parliament regardless of colonial objections to them, would reduce the inhabitants of the colony to "the most abject Slavery." Indeed, nothing could better illustrate the fundamental difference in point of view, on the one hand, of the petitioners—who undoubtedly reflected the opinions of the popular leaders of Massachusetts Bay—and, on the other hand, of the ministers and their supporters in Parliament, who seem to have had in mind solely the curbing of what they considered to be a spirit of liberty and freedom that had grown out of all bounds compatible with loyalty to the mother country and its government. It is therefore not surprising that the petition, after being read, was left to lie in neglect on the table.[57]

A further explanation for the ineffectiveness of this petition may be found in William Bollan's report to the Council of Massachusetts Bay:[58]

"I had considerable expectation that the honorable India merchants would assist and strengthen your defence; afterwards that the manufacturers in the principal towns, who, according to my information, were alarmed, and stirring, would make their opposition to the Bill for shutting up the port; but all failed, even the London merchants

---

[56] *Parliamentary History,* XVII, 1297–1300; *American Archives* 4th ser., I, 81–3.
[57] *Ibid.*
[58] Bollan to a committee of the Council of Massachusetts Bay, undated, but by internal evidence written some time after the passage of the Boston Port Bill, *American Archives,* 4th ser., I, 234–5.

declining their opposition to it. . . .[59] so that no other Petition but my own was presented, save a petition of several natives of North America, which was presented to both Houses, admitted, and ordered to lie upon the table. The number of persons who signed the Petition to the House of Commons was seventeen; and the petitioners to the Lords were twenty-nine; this Petition was well drawn; but a noble Lord, who was your faithful and active friend from first to last, told me on these different occasions that this Petition had hurt the cause, by reason of the small number of petitioners, considering how numerous the natives of North America, residing in this metropolis, were, whence those Lords who contended for the Bill drew this prejudicial argument, 'that the voice of the country was plainly against you.' "

But it must not be supposed that the bills were permitted to pass in Parliament without the most serious debate or without an awareness of the current state of events in Massachusetts Bay, in so far as light could be thrown upon the situation by making available to the members a great number of official and unofficial papers. In proposing the bill for remodeling the government of the province, Lord North stated on March 28, among other things, that the purpose was to provide an executive power wanting in the colony's constitution and in so doing to "purge that constitution of all its crudities, and give a degree of strength and spirit to its civil magistracy. . . ."[60] He was strongly supported by Lord George Germain, who claimed that he desired "to bring the constitution of America as similar to our own as possible."[61]

The former Governor of Massachusetts Bay Thomas Pownall, on the other hand, gave high praise to Americans as a "conscientious, good, religious, peaceable set of people," adding that "there was not in all his Majesty's dominions a more respectable set of persons existing."[62] In the debates of April 15 on the government bill, Pownall

---

[59] That the British merchants failed to speak out against the use of coercive measures, despite the threat to their trade implicit in them, may be attributed both to their waning influence upon a government that had become more imperialist than mercantilist after 1763 and to their feeling that petitions had lost the power to influence the administration. See in this connection Dora Mae Clark: op. cit., pp. 75 and 229. For Franklin's view that "the violent destruction of the Tea seems to have united all Parties against our Province," that the petitions of the native Americans in London could have no other effect than to show their sentiments, and that the government was taking great pains to quiet the fears of the British manufacturers, see Franklin's Writings (Smyth), VI, 223–5. Nevertheless, Franklin joined the other native Americans in their petitions. See in this connection W. L. Sachse: The Colonial American in Britain (Madison, Wisc., 1956), pp. 186–9.

[60] For Lord North's speech see Parliamentary History, XVII, 1192–3.

[61] Ibid., XVII, 1194–7.

[62] Ibid., XVII, 1197.

also gave an intimate and sympathetic analysis of the workings of the Massachusetts Bay constitution at both the provincial and the local level, based upon his personal knowledge, and urged that before any changes in the governmental structure were made, the laws directly relating to this government be placed before the House.[63] Nevertheless, in a major speech at a still later stage of debate on April 22, while disclosing that the Governor of the province had power to act without the Council in emergencies—thus indicating that Hutchinson had not utilized all the power given him to support the laws—Pownall called the Council's failure to support the Governor not only "highly blameable" but "inexcusable." But the colony, he declared prophetically, would not stand alone; the people of America were prepared for resistance.

> "As soon as intelligence of these affairs reach them, they will judge it necessary to communicate with each other. . . . They will hold a conference—and to what these committees, thus met in congress, will grow up, I will not say."[64]

Speaking for the government, Lord North had made his position clear early in the debate. He did not consider the regulation of the government of Massachusetts Bay by altering its charter to be a revocation of the charter. The regulatory step, he stated, was a matter of absolute necessity. He then asked:

> ". . . will this country sit still, when they see the colony proceeding against your own subjects, tarring and feathering your servants; denying your laws and authority; refusing every direction and advice which you send? . . . Gentlemen say, let the colony come to your bar and be heard in their defence; though it is not likely that they will come, when they deny your authority in every instance."[65]

It should be emphasized that by this date London agent Bollan had failed in the several attempts to be heard at the bar of the House of Commons in defence of his petition on colonial charter rights previously mentioned, and Dowdeswell had not yet attempted to take up the cudgels for him. However, in the same debate, that is, on April 22, concerning the bill to regulate the Bay colony's government, Sir George Savile found the measure to be "a very doubtful and dangerous one" on the grounds that "Chartered rights have, at

---

[63] *Ibid.*, XVII, 1199.
[64] *Ibid.*, XVII, 1282–6.
[65] *Ibid.*, XVII, 1280.

all times, when attempted to be altered, or taken away, occasioned much bloodshed and strife. . . ." Welbore Ellis, rising to reply, saw chartered rights as "by no means those sacred things which never can or ought to be altered," but considered them "vested in the crown, as a prerogative, for the good of the people at large. . . ." Countering Ellis, General Conway held that the consequence of the bill would "be very important and dangerous"; he saw the "charter of Boston" [that is, of Massachusetts Bay] as representing "the charter of all America," and felt that Parliament could not interfere with charter rights "without hearing the parties" concerned, adding: "I think there is no harm, upon this occasion, in stretching a point; and I would rather hear Mr. Bollan as an agent of America (though he is a little irregular in his appointment) sooner than leave it to be said, that this Bill passed without it."[66]

In the final debate on the Bill for Regulating the Government of Massachusetts Bay, Colonel Barré, who had supported the Boston Port Bill, felt that the new bill was a fateful measure. Of it he said on May 2: "The question now before us is, whether we will chuse to bring over the affections of all our colonies by lenient measures, or wage war with them?" Again, he questioned "What security the rest of the colonies will have, that upon the least pretence of disobedience, you will not take away the assembly from the next of them that is refractory." Here he denounced the House for not receiving agent Bollan's petition concerning the colony's charter rights. In concluding his address he added that he saw nothing in the measure before them "but inhumanity, injustice, and wickedness. . . ." At this point, although it was apparently quite late at night, Burke felt forced to "protest against this Bill, because you refuse to hear the parties aggrieved . . . It has been asserted that the nation is not alarmed, that no petitions of discontent are received. How can persons complain, when sufficient time is not given them to know what you are about?" Urging repeal of "the Act which gave rise to this disturbance," he added: "If you govern America at all, . . . it must be by an army . . . and I am of opinion, they never will consent without force being used [and] Such remedies as the foregoing [force] will create disturbances that can never be quieted."[67]

Lord North replied to Burke and also answered an earlier charge that the bill would deprive people of their natural rights:

[66] Ibid., XVII, 1277–9.
[67] Ibid., XVII, 1305–6, 1314–15.

"Let me ask, of what natural right, whether that of smuggling, or of throwing tea overboard? Or of another natural right, which is not paying their debts? But surely this [the bill for regulating the government] does not destroy any of their civil rights? You have given them a civil magistrate and a council, which they had not before; you have given the innocent man a fair trial in some colony or other; and if he cannot get a fair trial in that country, the whole being in . . . opposition to the laws of the mother country, then, in that case, and in that case only, he must be sent to Great Britain. . . . We are now to establish our authority, or give it up entirely. . . ."[68]

But, turning away from North's summary of the crux of the matter, Sir George Savile had the final word when he concluded the debate by announcing briefly, but firmly: "I hold this to be a principle of justice, that a charter which conveys a sacred right, ought not to be taken away without hearing the parties, which has not been done. . . ."[69]

When on April 15 Lord North had asked "that leave be given to bring in a Bill for the impartial administration of justice," he proposed it "in the cases of persons questioned for any acts done by them in the execution of the laws, or for the suppression of the riots and tumults in the province of Massachusets Bay." He gave as its design to "effectually secure the province of Massachuset's Bay from future disturbances" by ensuring that anyone attempting to enforce the laws passed by Parliament designed to bind the inhabitants of the colony, should receive "a fair and impartial trial." Arguing that since the jury system in the colonies was not equal to that of Great Britain, he claimed that the bill should empower the colonial Governor to send an offender back to England to be tried at the Court of King's Bench in cases where "he cannot have such fair and impartial trial in any of the colonies," with the expenses of such trial to be paid out of the customs in the mother country. "We must consider, that every thing that we have that is valuable to us is now at stake; and the question is very shortly this: Whether they shall continue the subjects of Great Britain or not?"[70] Colonel Barré immediately rose to oppose the bill, declaring that "to stigmatize a whole people as persecutors of innocence, and men incapable of doing justice" was "so glaring; so unprecedented . . . ; so unwarranted . . . ; so big with misery and oppression to that country and with danger

---

[68] *Ibid.*, XVII, 1315–16.
[69] *Ibid.*
[70] *Ibid.*, XVII, 1199–1201.

to this—that the first blush of it is sufficient to alarm and rouse me to opposition." Before closing his address he said:

"When I stand up as an advocate for America, I feel myself the firmest friend of this country [Great Britain]. . . . Alienate your colonies, and you will subvert the foundation of your riches and your strength. Let the banners of rebellion be once spread to America, and you are an undone people."[71]

On April 21, in the second debate on the Bill for the Impartial Administration of Justice, John Sawbridge (who had helped John Wilkes regain political stature in 1768) declared, on the first reading of the Bill, that its true intent was to "enslave America; and the same Minister who means to enslave them, would, if he had an opportunity, enslave England; . . . but I sincerely hope the Americans will not admit of the execution of these destructive Bills, but nobly refuse them; if they do not they are the most abject slaves that ever the earth produced, and nothing that the ministry can do is base enough for them."[72]

In the last debate on the Bill, on May 6, Sawbridge again upheld the opposition view; Colonel Barré adding his final protest, predicted that the people of America would "receive these regulations as edicts from an arbitrary government." But Henry Cavendish[73] concluded for the government: "I am very glad to hear that there is a majority in this House for these measures; but am much better pleased that the country in general approve of them in as high a degree."[74]

When the bills were sent up to the House of Lords the debates proceeded apace, but were not officially recorded.[75] However, it is known that London agent Bollan—contrary to the action taken in the Commons, although equally to no avail—was permitted to present his petition and defend it at the bar before the Lords.[76] During the hearings on May 11 on the Bill for Regulating the Government of Massachusetts Bay the chamber was closed even to members of

---

[71] *Ibid.*, XVII, 1201–6.

[72] *Ibid.*, XVII, 1274.

[73] For the parliamentary biography of Henry Cavendish, which reveals that he "supported the Administration's punitive measures," although he was still reckoned as a member of the opposition in 1774 and was not returned for Lostwithiel in the election of that year, see *History of Parliament: The House of Commons, 1754–1790*, II, 201–3.

[74] *Parliamentary History*, XVII, 1318–20.

[75] *Ibid.*, XVII, 1320–1.

[76] For London agent Bollan's report of the event see *American Archives*, 4th ser., I, 60, 231, 233–4.

the House of Commons. Nevertheless, it was reported that there was strong but ineffectual opposition to both of the bills that related to Massachusetts Bay in general. Upon the third reading of the bill for reorganizing the government, we are told,

> "The lords in opposition cried out against a bill altering the constitution of a colony without having so much as the charter containing the constitution . . . laid before them. That the bill had also altered the courts and the mode of judicial proceedings in the colony, without an offer of the slightest evidence to prove any one of the inconveniencies which were stated in general terms in the preamble, as arising from the present mode of trial in the province. . . . [In contrast] the ministerial lords denied that the process [the bill] was of a penal nature; they insisted that it was beneficial and remedial, and a great improvement of their constitution, as it brought it nearer to the English model. This again was denied by the Lords of the minority, who said that the taking away of franchises granted by charters, had ever been considered as penal, and all proceedings for that purpose conducted criminally [that is, as a proceeding that followed the commission of a crime, and therefore one judicial in nature]."

Finally, they declared that "a council holding their places at the pleasure of the crown did not resemble the house of lords; nor approach in any thing to the perfection of the British constitution." Nevertheless, at the end of the debate, the bill was passed by a vote of 92 to 20.[77] As a matter of record, ten minority peers signed a formal protest which, under seven headings, presented their dissenting views in much the same form as outlined above. As the opposition lords were headed by the Marquess of Rockingham and his intimate advisers, the Dukes of Richmond and Portland, their stand must be understood in the light of the fact that it was the Rockingham administration which had brought about the passage in 1766 of the Declaratory Act affirming the supremacy of the Crown and Parliament over the colonies, with power to bind them "in all cases whatsoever."[78] Their position of opposition to the government seeking to implement that very act was therefore a delicate one. The seventh article of their dissent reads in part as follows:

---

[77] *Annual Register, 1774,* Chap. 7; see also *American Archives,* 4th ser., I, 93*n*.

[78] 6 Geo. III, c. 12, "An Act for the better securing the Dependency of his Majesty's Dominions in America upon the Crown and Parliament of Great Britain," *Statutes at Large,* VII, 571.

"Because this Bill, and the other proceedings that accompany it are intended for the support of that unadvised scheme of taxing the Colonies in a manner new and unsuitable to their situation and constitutional circumstances. Parliament has asserted the authority of the Legislature of this Kingdom, supreme and unlimited over all members of the British Empire. But the legal extent of this authority furnishes no argument in favour of an unwarrantable use of it. The sense of the nation on the repeal of the Stamp Act was, that, in equity and sound policy, the taxation of the Colonies for the ordinary purposes of supply, ought to be forborn; and that this Kingdom ought to satisfy itself with the advantages . . . from a flourishing and increasing trade, and with the free grants of the American Assemblies. . . ."[79]

In this connection it should be reiterated that fundamentally the colonial opposition was directed not against the advisability or manner of the imposition of taxes by Parliament but against the declaration of that body's *right* to impose taxes, as enunciated in the Declaratory Act.

Upon the third reading of the Bill for the Impartial administration of Justice in the House of Lords—and after a debate, during which the Marquess of Rockingham made the principal opposition speech[80] —it was passed by a vote of 43 to 12. Again, eight peers associated with Rockingham signed a formal protest. This dissent would appear to summarize the objections voiced by the opposition peers in the debate on the Bill. They were opposed to it, they declared—citing the fair trial of Captain Preston[81]—since no contrary evidence had been presented to show that persons accused of capital crimes in the performance of their duty in the colony could not get a fair trial. Their dissent concluded that

"after the proscription of the port of Boston, the disfranchisement of the colony of Massachuset's Bay, and the variety of provisions . . . made in this session for new modelling the whole polity and judicature of that province, this Bill is a humiliating confession of the weakness and inefficiency of all the proceedings of parliament. . . . The

---

[79] For the signed protest by the ten peers, see *American Archives*, 4th ser., I, 93–5, see also *Parliamentary History*, XVII, 1321–5. In this connection see also "A Speech intended to have been spoken on the Bill . . ." by the Bishop of St. Asaph, who voted against the bill in the House of Lords. Published in London in 1774, it is reprinted in *American Archives*, 4th ser., I, 97–104.

[80] *Ibid.*, XVII, 1350–1.

[81] See Volume XI of this series, Chap. 9, for a discussion of the so-called Boston Massacre and the trial following it.

Bill therefore amounts to a declaration, that the House knows no means of retaining the colonies in due obedience, but by an army rendered independent of the ordinary course of law, in the place where they are employed."[82]

During the action in Parliament on the two bills, an attempt was made to repeal the tea duty. Rose Fuller, Jamaica planter, so moved on April 19. His position was that the various regulations planned for Massachusetts Bay would be totally ineffective without the repeal of this act; he was sure such a step "would be productive of a great deal of good; and that it could not possibly do harm." While there were those who spoke against this motion and who affirmed that to repeal the Act would be to endanger forever the supremacy of Parliament, there were also some who favoured it. The debate was the occasion of one of the greatest of Edmund Burke's speeches. Supporting the motion, he said, in his own summary: "I have shewn . . . that in time of peace you flourished in commerce, and when war required it, had sufficient aid from the colonies, while you pursued your antient policy. . . . I have shewn that the revival of the system of taxation has produced the very worst effects; and that the partial repeal has produced not partial good, but universal evil."[83] However, when at length the question was put, there were but 49 in favour of it with 182 against. Doubtless the feeling of the majority was expressed by Solicitor General Wedderburn when he replied to Burke: "They [the colonials] consider all the Acts that restrain trade as illegal, and they want to treat with you upon an independent footing; but if you give up this tax, it is not here that you must stop, you will be required to give up much more, nay, to give up all."[84]

In the eyes of the administration a fourth measure seemed to be required in order to put the new system for Massachusetts Bay on a solid foundation. This was a "Bill for the better providing suitable Quarters for Officers and Soldiers in His Majesty's Service in North America," designed to clarify the point raised when regular troops were sent to Boston in 1768. At that time it had been contended that these troops should properly be quartered in the barracks at Castle

---

[82] For the protest and a list of those signing it see *Parliamentary History*, XVII, 1351–3.

[83] *Ibid.*, XVII, 1210–15 and 1215–69. Burke's speech is also reprinted in the *Gentleman's Magazine, 1774,* XLIV, 601–11. Of it the *Annual Register, 1774,* reported (p. 111): "On this occasion Mr. E. Burke distinguished himself in a masterly manner."

[84] *Parliamentary History*, XVII, 1269–70.

William, which was at a distance from the town. After the so-called Boston Massacre the regulars were removed to it. In view of what was held to be the wide-spread spirit of insurrection that had brought about the destruction of the tea, it was deemed essential to the safety, especially of the civilian ports under the Crown, to have the military arm close at hand. By a bill, introduced in the House of Commons on May 2,[85] which was to run until March 24, 1776— with general application to all the colonies but, by inference, specifically aimed at Massachusetts Bay—provision was made that where troops were quartered in barracks at too great a distance to be readily employed at places "where their presence may be necessary and required," then the rule would be in force that was already applicable to colonies not having barracks. In other words, it would be lawful for the Governor of a colony in need of troop support, in case quarters were not furnished to the incoming officers and soldiers within a period of twenty-four hours after a demand was made, to requisition and make fit for occupancy the necessary number of uninhabited houses, out-houses, barns, and other buildings, with a reasonable allowance to be paid for their use. The bill moved through the House of Commons without debate, as far as the records indicate. Amended by the committee of the whole House on May 5, it was, on the 6th, ordered engrossed and passed on the third reading without a division on the 9th, when it was sent up to the House of Lords.[86] There it moved through its first two readings without amendment and also apparently without debate, but on its third reading, on May 26, the ailing Earl of Chatham arose and gave a major address— directed not against the bill, but against the taxation of the colonies —in which he declared:

> ". . . this country had no right under heaven to tax America. It is contrary to all principles of justice and civil policy, which neither the exigencies of the state, nor even an acquiescence in the taxes could justify upon any occasion whatever."[87]

---

[85] Permission for the bill to be drawn by Lord Barrington and John Pownall was granted on April 29, 1774. See *Journals of the House of Commons*, XXXIV, 692, 695. It may be noted that the deliberations in Commons extended until two-thirty in the morning of May 3 (*ibid.*, XXXIV, 697).

[86] *Ibid.*, XXXIV, 705, 710, 714.

[87] *Parliamentary History*, XVII, 1353–6. Obviously only portions of the speeches made in Parliament appeared in printed form with accuracy—except for the Burke speech, which was clearly prepared for publication. The *Boston Evening-Post*, August 15, 1774, for example, printed a part of Chatham's speech which, unlike the version printed in *Parliamentary History*, heavily censured the people of Massachusetts Bay for their conduct, in line with his own statement made earlier in the year on the

The Quartering Act (14 George III, c. 54) was approved in the House of Lords by a vote of 57 to 16, and on June 2 received the royal assent by commissioners appointed by the King for that purpose.[88]

The last legislation relating to America passed by Parliament at this juncture was the Quebec Act. This statute provided for an appointed executive and legislative Council to act with the Governor, for extending the boundaries of the province to include the more western French-speaking settlements, for establishing French civil law, and finally for tolerating Catholicism. From the point of view of this writer, the Quebec Act cannot properly be viewed as one of the Coercive Acts.[89] Nevertheless, it was so regarded by most British

---

criminality of the destruction of the East India Company tea as an act of defiance against Parliament. In the excerpt of Chatham's speech published in Boston— whether as actually delivered or fabricated—he is quoted as saying: "I don't rest my Opinion of the People of Massachusetts, upon any one particular Action, their Tarring and Feathering this or that Man, or their throwing the Tea into the Sea. The whole Tenor of their Conduct, and their open and avowed Resolutions in their Assembly, manifests an evil and Rebellious Spirit against this Country; and therefore I think, that they ought to be brought to make a full and entire Submission. When this is done, we ought to treat them with Lenity; but not till they have made Submission. I know that these Declarations will be far from Popular in America; but I have already made the same out of this House, that I have now in it, Declarations, which I suppose will not prompt them to erect any more Statues of me." The *Boston Evening-Post* of August 22, 1774, gave a summary of the entire speech in which Chatham is said to have "condemned several parts of the late conduct of the Americans, particularly that of the Bostonians respecting the tea, which he said was contrary to all laws of policy [polity], civilization and humanity; but . . . he must reprobate the whole of government's acts relative to taxation; that this was his former opinion, and that he would maintain it till death." In referring to Chatham in a letter to Thomas Cushing on June 1, 1774, Franklin stated that he "delivered his Sentiments fully on the American Measures, blam'd us for destroying the Tea, and our Declarations of Independence on the Parliament; but condemn'd strongly the Measures taking here in consequence, and spoke honourably of our Province and People, & of their Conduct in the late War" (*Writings* [Smyth], VI, 232).

[88] *Parliamentary History*, XVII, 1356; see also *Journal of the House of Commons*, XXXIV, 789, 798. It may be noted that the Rockingham faction was notably absent at the time of the vote. See J. M. Sosin: *op. cit.*, p. 249.

[89] Professor Chester Martin's *Empire & Commonwealth: Studies in Governance and Self-government in Canada* (Oxford, 1929), Chap. 3, " 'New Subjects' in Quebec," and Professor W. P. M. Kennedy's *The Constitution of Canada, 1534–1937* (London, New York, and Toronto, 1938), Chap. 7, "The Quebec Act, 1774," present the most forceful arguments that the writer of this series has uncovered to justify classifying the Quebec Act as one of the Coercive Acts. The most convincing argument that the prime purpose of the Quebec Act was to meet the crying need for a government suited to the Canadian people is contained in Professor A. L. Burt's *The Old Province of Quebec* (Toronto and Minneapolis, 1933), Chap. 9, "The Quebec Act"; see also his highly objective yet critical essay on *Guy Carleton, Lord Dorchester, 1724–1808* (Canadian Historical Association *Historical Booklets*, No. 5 [1955], pp. 4–5). It may be noted that in the course of his analysis Professor Burt does not refer to the work of either of the above-mentioned scholars; although, in point of fact, his book represents an effective refutation of their theses.

colonials and also by some members of Parliament on the grounds not only that it would create a Catholic stronghold—something feared especially by the London radicals—but that it was an attempt to re-create a threat of containment of the colonials by powerful French Canadian and Indian forces on their frontiers. The Act was, however, rather the culmination of the efforts of both the British Ministry and of those directly responsible for the guidance of public affairs in the Province of Quebec to meet the complex problems of providing a suitable government for the new domain. But discussion of the factors that led to the passage of the Quebec Act and of general developments in Canada during the late 1760's and the 1770's must be reserved for a later chapter in Volume XIII of this series.

Here then we have the body of laws passed in the spring of 1774 that the Ministry and Parliament were persuaded would produce a happy return to good order in America and would firmly bind together Great Britain and the colonies. While the opposition to them was vocal enough, especially in the House of Commons, it was extraordinarily weak in the number of protagonists. This was due, it would appear, not so much to the King's support of these measures as to the fact that the generality of people in Great Britain strongly approved of them. Edmund Burke was undoubtedly correct when, writing as the London agent for the New York Assembly to its committee of correspondence on April 6, 1774, he declared: "The popular current, both within doors [of Parliament] and without, at present sets strongly against America. . . . Such is . . . the temper of Parliament and of the Nation at this Moment, which I thought it my Duty to lay before you without heightenings or without palliation."[90] Likewise, the Earl of Manchester, writing to the Marquess of Rockingham on April 20, warned that any opposition to the bill for altering the government of Massachusetts Bay might not meet with a favourable reception on the part of the public. "The high spirit of the people of England is certainly at the moment irritated against the outrages of the Bostonians; and the doctrine they now own of their absolute independency of this kingdom leads many moderate men to wish Government may succeed to reduce them within the bounds of law and order."[91] As Rose Fuller expressed it,

---

[90] *Correspondence of Edmund Burke*, (ed. T. W. Copeland *et al.*, 5 vols.+, Cambridge and Chicago, 1958–65+), II, *Correspondence, July 1768–June 1774* (ed. Lucy Sutherland, 1960), pp. 528–9.

[91] For this letter see *Memoirs of the Marquis of Rockingham*, II, 242.

at the time of the debates on the Port Bill: "We all agree that Bostonians ought to be punished, but we differ in the mode of it."[92] According to Dora Mae Clark: "The government had the support of the
country at large in its policy of coercion."[93] The landed gentry as a
whole were inclined to support the ministerial policy, persuaded
that the Coercive Acts would subdue America and thereby provide
relief to the British Treasury in funds that would reduce their taxes,
especially in the face of a threatened increase in land taxes. They
therefore succumbed to appeals from the government for the support
which their superior numbers and influence in Parliament could
readily produce. Futhermore, "the financial perils of 1772 and 1773
aroused an unwonted caution and circumspection in the merchants
who traded with America, and caused them to study and criticize
the conditions under which they did business with the colonies."
So that, while the "merchants and manufacturers were deeply impressed with the necessity of maintaining peace with America," it
was chiefly on the grounds of expediency. Thus, when they became
convinced that Americans wanted freedom of trade, they too were
inclined to support the policy of coercion.[94]

It is not without significance that while this legislation was going
through Parliament the only British petition presented to the House
was that of the Lord Mayor, Aldermen, and Commons of London
objecting to the Quebec Bill. A letter written from London on

---

[92] *Parliamentary History,* XVII, 1176–7.

[93] See Dora Mae Clark's *British Opinion . . . ,* p. 133. London agent Charles Garth,
reporting on the tenor of the Commons at the time of the passage of the Coercive
Acts, wrote: "Administration had the assistance of almost all the Country Gentlemen
present, Representatives of Counties" (Garth Correspondence, 1773–1775 [mss.],
p. 172). Shelburne, in his report of the action on the Boston Port Bill to Chatham of
April 4, 1774, wrote: "The landed property, except some of the most sensible, are,
as is natural, I believe, for violent measures. The interest of the commercial part
is very decidedly on the other side, and their passions are taking that turn. As to
parties and particular men, your Lordship's experience must suggest to you, how
far they are likely to hold together in such times" (*Pitt Correspondence,* IV, 341).

That American developments claimed priority attention in the affairs of the Empire
in 1774 is evident from the space devoted to the discussion of them in reports of
parliamentary proceedings and in the writing of contemporary historical chronicles,
as may be judged, for example, from the *Annual Register* and the *Gentleman's
Magazine* for that year. In the *Annual Register* (London, 1775, XVII, 43–78) the
greater part of "The History of Europe" is taken up with affairs centred on America,
as is "The Chronicle" and its "Appendix." In the *Gentleman's Magazine* (XLIV,
381–4, 437–40, 489, 516–19, 566–73, 627) we find a running account of the "Proceedings of the American Colonists, since the Passing of the Boston Port-Bill," and elsewhere (especially *ibid.,* pp. 413–16, 464, 514–16) we find additional discussion of
the constitutional issues involved in the dispute over the jurisdiction of Parliament.

[94] Dora M. Clark: *op. cit.,* pp. 68–76, 78–9, 116–18, 132–7, 165–9, 227–30.

May 12, which appeared in the *Boston Gazette* of July 11, 1774, throws light on why a proposal for a petition from the merchants was "totally defeated." For the leading merchants exporting to Boston who had the greatest stake in trade to the colony—that is, Hayley & Hopkins, Champion & Dickinson, Lane, Son & Fraser, and also the firm of Harrison—all refused to join or "be at all concerned in such a petition." The writer of the letter went on to state that these merchants, after refusing to petition, waited on Lord North, who assured them "that government was determined to proceed on a plan which was so settled that the Merchants in England would hereafter get their debts better paid, than they ever were before." In concluding his letter the writer stated: "I know every thing here written is the truth."

The position of the London radicals and the Rockingham Whigs was another thing. The former were moved in part by idealistic concepts of freedom and rights, and partly by their own concerns over domestic elections and parliamentary reforms—as demonstrated by the leadership of Alderman Sawbridge and other London aldermen and officials, including the two American-born sheriffs Stephen Sayre and William Lee. As for the Whigs, under Burke and Charles Fox they came out in favour of parliamentary supremacy at the same time that they opposed the application of it.[95]

Nor must the student be misled concerning British public opinion by certain articles appearing in the British press that denounced the policy of the Ministry toward America. It is well known that several Americans wrote for London newspapers and periodicals. For example, under the pseudonyms "Fabius," "A Fiddler," "A Friend of Military Government," and "A Freeholder of Old Sarum," Benjamin Franklin during the spring of 1774 contributed letters hostile to this legislation to Woodfall's London *Public Advertiser*.[96] Yet, in assessing British public opinion in the early part of 1774, there is evidence that, while the conduct of Bostonians was considered disgraceful by most people of Great Britain and while party politics were deeply involved in influencing the attitudes of people toward

[95] See G. H. Guttridge: *English Whiggism and the American Revolution* (University of California Publications in History, 28, Berkeley and Los Angeles, 1942), pp. 71–3. See also Volume XI in this series, Chap. 7.

[96] See V. W. Crane: *Benjamin Franklin's Letters to the Press, 1758–1775* (Chapel Hill, N.C., 1950), pp. 255–64. For various statements appearing in the press after the destruction of the tea in Boston Harbour see again F. J. Hinkhouse: *op. cit.*, pp. 160–81.

colonial policy, there was an attitude of forbearance in the press. This was not to last. As George Bancroft noted, it was the press that roused "the national pride, till the zeal of the English people for maintaining English supremacy [over British North America] became equal to the passions of the ministry."[97]

Such was the British setting for the momentous events to follow. Dartmouth's own résumé of the passage of the Coercive Acts denied that England wanted "to enslave America," and added:

> "What then, is the present case? The supreme legislature of the whole British Empire has laid a duty (no matter for the present whether it has or has not a right to do so, it is sufficient that we conceive it has) . . . the people of America, at Boston particularly, resist that authority and oppose the execution of the law in a manner clearly treasonable upon the principles of every government upon earth. The mother country very unwilling to proceed to extremities passes laws (indisputably within its power) for the punishment of the most flagrant offenders, for the reformation of abuses, and for the prevention of the like enormities for the future. The question then is, whether these laws are to be submitted to: if the people of America say no, they say in effect that they will no longer be a part of the British Empire; they change the whole ground of the controversy; they no longer contend that Parliament has not a right to exact a particular provision, they say that it has no right to consider them at all as within its jurisdiction."[98]

But this statement by Dartmouth was in reply to the efforts of Joseph Reed of Philadelphia to keep the King's minister informed as to the true sentiments of people within the colonies. In his letter of May 30, Reed had written to Dartmouth frankly announcing that he "could not admit the right of Parliament to tax America" and that he had been nominated by his fellow citizens to help draw up measures to prevent Parliament from attempting to exercise this right. At the same time he also advised, with equal candour, that "every Colony from Massachusetts to Virginia . . . have signified their resolutions to concur with each other in every measure to relieve Boston from the distresses the [Boston Port] Act will bring

---

[97] George Bancroft: *History of the United States* . . . (10 vols., Boston, 1834–74), VI, 511.

[98] Dartmouth to Joseph Reed, undated, *Dartmouth Manuscripts*, I, 355; see also W. B. Reed: *Life and Correspondence of Joseph Reed* . . . , I, 72–4, which gives the letter in full, dated July 11, 1774.

upon them."[99] Reed's letter could not have reached Dartmouth before the passage in June of the other bills which, when enacted, together with the Boston Port Bill, were to be called by the colonials the Intolerable Acts. Nor is it clear that Dartmouth, or any other member of the administration, was prepared to heed even the advice of those at hand in London who had an intimate personal knowledge of the American colonies, much less those civilians writing from America.[100]

---

[99] *Ibid.*, and *Dartmouth Manuscripts*, I, 351. Reed's unusual correspondence with Dartmouth began in December 1773, when he urged repeal of the Tea Act and gave a clear account of the arrival of the tea ships and "the rising spirit of the people" at Philadelphia, and continued into January 1775 until there was no possible hope of reconciliation. It was the result of the influence of Dennys De Berdt, merchant and London agent for Massachusetts Bay. Reed had met De Berdt's daughter while a student at the Middle Temple and had returned to London to marry her in 1770. While there he formed connections with other Americans such as Arthur Lee and Stephen Sayre. Upon his return to America he established connections with the Boston patriots he had met in 1769. His subsequent correspondence with them was an important link in an ever-widening chain of communications between the revolutionary leaders—one that stretched from Boston to South Carolina, and reached as far as London. See *ibid.*, I, *passim*, and W. B. Reed: *op. cit.*, I, 51–96. For the most recent biography of Reed see J. F. Roche: *Joseph Reed: A Moderate in the American Revolution* (Columbia Studies in the Social Sciences, No. 595, New York, 1957).

[100] The chief sources of information from the colonies from the fall of 1773 through the spring of 1774 upon which Dartmouth relied were the correspondence of Governor Hutchinson and that of Joseph Reed, with a few added letters from other colonial governors and military commanders, according to the evidence available in the *Dartmouth Manuscripts*, I, 339–53, *passim*. For Americans in the House of Commons and other members with a knowledge of American affairs and their influence during the critical period under consideration, see Sir Lewis B. Namier: *England in the Age of the American Revolution* (London, 1930), pp. 265–71; see also G. P. Judd: *Members of Parliament, 1734–1832* (New Haven, 1955), pp. 15–17, and Namier and Brooke's: *House of Commons, 1754–1790*, I, 159–62, II and III, *passim*.

CHAPTER V

Massachusetts Bay Resists

WHEN the Great and General Court of Massachusetts Bay reconvened in Boston on January 26, 1774, after its prorogation on May 26 of the preceding year, it was addressed by Governor Hutchinson, who was able to report the highly favourable financial position of the province. "There never has been a Time since the first Settlement of the Country," he declared, "when the Treasury has been in so good a State as it is now. I may congratulate the Province upon its being entirely free from Debt, the Tax of the last Year, with the Stock in the Treasury, being equal to all the Securities due from the Government and to the Charges of the current Year." He then suggested that a "moderate Duty on Spiritous Liquor" could provide the charges for the year ahead.[1] He might also have added how fortunate were the inhabitants in their prosperous situation by contrast to the people of Great Britain, still loaded down with an immense debt as a result of the nine years of war with France that had finally settled the fate of the North American continent after the outcome had hung in the balance for so many years. But this was not the mood of the moment.

To recapitulate certain points raised in Chapter III of this volume: When the tea which had been brought to Boston Harbour by the East India Company under sanction of a law passed by Parliament was thrown into the water in December of the preceding year, this action was apparently regarded in two ways by most of the people of the province. They saw it not only as a blow to the Company's plan to set up a monopoly in the sale of tea in America, but also as a gesture of defiance directed toward the government for its con-

---

[1] *Journal of the House of Representatives* (Boston, 1773–4), p. 103.

tinued efforts to levy an import duty on tea for revenue purposes—despite the fact that, from 1769 until the attempt to implement the act of 1773, most of the tea carried to Boston had been entered legally and had paid the duty levied under the Townshend Revenue Act. But it would be a mistake—a mistake still voiced by some in dealing with the causes of the American Revolution—to consider the issue of taxation by Parliament more than one of the issues that were to bring about a separation of the older North American colonies from the parent state. Certainly, in the minds of the popular leaders in Massachusetts Bay the paramount issue was the preservation of rights guaranteed by their charter, which they held were being denied. The unrepealed preamble of the Townshend Revenue Act of 1767 still remained on the statute books. This stated that a revenue should be raised in America "for making a more certain and adequate Provision for defraying the charge of the Administration of Justice, and the Support of Civil Government, in such Provinces where it shall be found necessary. . . ." Now the preamble was no longer merely a threat to some unnamed colony, but was being implemented and directly aimed at Massachusetts Bay, the most aggressive of the colonies, as a result of the decision of the government of Great Britain in 1772 to remove the Governor and the members of the Superior Court from dependence on the popularly elected General Assembly by granting them salaries out of the revenues drawn from America.

To leaders in the General Assembly the ministerial plan represented a breach in their charter so dangerous that it might be fatal. The Governor had already signified that he would accept a royal salary and would refuse one voted by the legislature. Were the justices of the superior court to do likewise and take their part in strictly enforcing the laws of Parliament that applied to the colonies, the character of the provincial government, it was felt, would be drastically altered. Therefore, the utmost pressure was brought to bear upon the justices. The least resolute, Edmund Trowbridge, yielded immediately, although on February 5, 1773, he had agreed to the Governor's demand not to accept any grant made by the Assembly after his salary "from the Crown may Commence."[2] On January 26, 1774, he signed a declaration stating: ". . . in Compliance

---

[2] Judge Trowbridge to Hutchinson, February 5, 1773, in reply to Hutchinson to Trowbridge of the same date, Hutchinson Correspondence, Massachusetts Archives, 25:553–4.

with the Resolve of the Honorable House of Representatives [of June 28, 1773], I do declare that I am determined still to receive the Grants of the General Assembly of this Province for my Services as a Justice of the Superior Court, without receiving any Grant from the Crown for the same Service."[3] This action was unanimously approved by the House on February 1;[4] the following day that body resolved that it was the duty of the remaining judges—Chief Justice Peter Oliver, Foster Hutchinson, Nathaniel Ropes, and William Cushing—also to declare explicitly on or before the 8th of the month whether they would receive grants from the Assembly "according to ancient and invariable Usage," or from the Crown.[5] On the 3rd Chief Justice Oliver signed a letter to the House referring to his services on the bench over a period of seventeen years, during which, he declared, he had "always endeavoured to act with that Fidelity required in so important a Character." He further stated that, although he had repeatedly sought to give up his post, by allowing himself to be persuaded to remain, he had suffered the loss of £3,000 sterling. When therefore His Majesty, without any application by Oliver, granted him a salary, as he did, in the words of the Justice, "to several others on the Continent in my station . . . I thought it my incumbent Duty . . . to take his Majesty's Grant. . . . With Respect to my not taking any future Grant from his Majesty; permit me to say, that without his Majesty's Leave, I dare not refuse it, lest I should incur a Censure from the best of Sovereigns."[6]

The House voted unanimously on February 8 that the Oliver reply was unsatisfactory. On that same day replies were read from Justices Foster Hutchinson and William Cushing that were voted satisfactory, as was the death-bed communication of Justice Ropes that he would continue to receive his salary from the Assembly.[7]

---

[3] Journal for February 1, 1774, *Journal of the House of Representatives* (Boston, 1773–4), p. 113.

[4] *Ibid.*

[5] *Ibid.*, pp. 117–18.

[6] *Ibid.*, pp. 133–5.

[7] *Ibid.*, pp. 136–9; see also *Letters and Diary of John Rowe, Boston Merchant, 1759 . . . 1779* (ed. Anne R. Cunningham, Boston, 1903), pp. 262–3. Chief Justice Oliver wrote in his memoirs of the events of 1774 that the judges, "hearing, sometime before, of his Majesty's gracious Intention of such a Grant, had agreed to accept of it; but when the Dog Star raged with such scorching Heat, four of them, who lived at and near that Focus of tarring & feathering, the town of *Boston,* flinched in the Day of Battle; they were so pelted with soothings one Day, & with Curses & Threatenings the Next, that they prudentially gave the Point up" (*Peter Oliver's Origin & Progress of the American Rebellion* [eds. Douglass Adair and J. A. Schutz,

In a step of the most unusual nature, the whole force of the House was now directed against the Chief Justice for obeying the request of the Crown to accept a salary not granted by the General Assembly. On the 11th the House passed a series of resolutions stating that Oliver's action tended "to the Perversion of Law and Justice," and that thereby he proved to be "an Enemy to the Constitution of this Province" and therefore "justly obnoxious to the good People. . . ." The representatives of the same good people thereupon resolved that his conduct had totally disqualified him from holding office and urged that he be removed. To that end they agreed that the House should remonstrate to the Governor and Council for Oliver's removal. These resolves were carried by a vote of 96 to 9. That same day a remonstrance was voted stating that, since "the said Peter Oliver, Esq., hath received the said Salary and Reward . . . unjustly and unconstitutionally levied and extorted from the Inhabitants of the American Colonies" and in so doing had acted "perversely and corruptly," he should no longer be suffered to act.[8] Governor Hutchinson's reply on the 15th made clear that, with certain stated exceptions, under the terms of the charter the Council was powerless to act in any other capacity than that of "advising and assisting." It further pointed out that since the King had directed warrants to be prepared for the payment of the other Supreme Court judges and had so notified the Governor, for him to comply with the request of the House to remove the Chief Justice for accepting a salary would be a display of "Contempt of his Royal Authority" as well as a breach of the trust placed in him under his royal commission. Nevertheless, Hutchinson assured the House that at the first opportunity he would transmit a copy of the remonstrance to the King and would subsequently conform to His Majesty's direction.[9] The next day the House sent a message to the Council concerning the Oliver case; it mentioned the Governor's refusal to act as requested and asked the Board to "act and determine as in their own Wisdom they shall think proper."[10] That same day the whole House

---

San Marino, Calif., 1961], p. 109; cited hereafter as *Peter Oliver's Origin of the Rebellion*). The royal warrant to Chief Justice Oliver, signed on August 6, 1772, providing a salary of £400 out of American duties, is given in full by O. M. Dickerson in his "Use Made of the Revenue from the Tax on Tea," *New England Quarterly*, XXXI, 239–40.

[8] *Journal of the House of Representatives* (Boston, 1773–4), pp. 146–50.

[9] *Ibid.*, p. 159. See also Hutchinson to Dartmouth, "Private," February 17, 1774, *Dartmouth Manuscripts*, I, 348–9.

[10] *Journal of the House of Representatives* (Boston, 1773–4), pp. 162–3.

waited upon the Governor with a petition to remove Oliver from office containing the following protest: ". . . your Excellency's determining on this Matter by yourself, would be to order and direct one of the most important Affairs of this Province without the Advice and Assistance of the Council, and contrary to the most evident Design of the Charter."[11] On the 21st of February, by a further set of resolutions, the House voted that it was no longer proper for the Chief Justice to act in the superior court, as it would "endanger the public Tranquility," and directed that a copy of this resolve be delivered to him.[12] The following day, in answer to the petition from the House, Hutchinson sent a long message setting forth his conception of the role of the Council and the responsibilities of the government under the charter. He also assured the House that as a "Servant of the King . . . I have received no Instructions nor any Significations of His Majesty's Pleasure, which are not perfectly consistent with your Charter." As to seeking the advice of the Council in the matter at issue, he stated: "If by taking their Advice you intend complying with it, though it should be contrary to . . . my Duty to the King, this would be giving up the Power of a Negative granted or reserved to me by the Charter. . . ." Before ending, Hutchinson said that if his judgment were erroneous, the House was free to make representation to the King, and could be sure of redress.[13]

The reply came on February 24, when articles of impeachment of the Chief Justice presented to the House were adopted. Oliver was charged with "High Crimes and Misdemeanors," by accepting a grant from the Crown, which would constitute "a continual Bribe in his judicial Proceedings, and expose him to a Violation of his Oath," an act by which "he hath betrayed the Corruption and Baseness of his Heart. . . ." Thereupon a committee of nine was appointed to appear before the Governor and Council and impeach him.[14] However, before the articles of impeachment were forwarded, a message from the Governor was delivered to the House informing the members that he had received leave to go to England on matters involving His Majesty's service and his own private affairs, and that he expected to avail himself of this leave at as early a date as would

[11] *Ibid.*, pp. 167–8.
[12] *Ibid.*, pp. 177–8.
[13] *Ibid.*, pp. 182–3.
[14] *Ibid.*, pp. 194–201.

be feasible. He therefore requested the House to dispose of the public business before it with all dispatch.[15]

Not to be deterred in its plan to impeach the Chief Justice, the House designated a committee to wait upon Hutchinson and ask him to be present in the chair when the articles of impeachment were presented to the Council. When Hutchinson requested that this—"a Matter of such Importance"—be reduced to writing, the House complied and the written request was placed before him. In his answer, delivered on the 26th, the Governor affirmed that he knew of no crimes and misdemeanors that were not cognizable in the courts of law of the province and was unaware that the Governor and Council had any concurrent jurisdiction with the courts in criminal cases under the charter whereby His Majesty's subjects could be deprived of trial by jury. He therefore stated that he esteemed the proposed step "to be unconstitutional" and that he could not "shew any Countenance to it." Still determined to press the articles, the House appointed a committee to go to the Council, read the articles to impeach Oliver, and ask that a time be appointed for hearing and determining the impeachment.[16] This the committee did at a Council meeting held without the Governor present—another highly unusual step. But the planned revolutionary action to unseat Oliver was not to succeed.

On March 1 the House took into consideration Hutchinson's opinion on the unconstitutionality of the proposed impeachment and decided to adopt another procedure. It simply dropped out the term "impeachment"and used the phrase "Articles of high Crimes and Misdemeanors" in the case against the Chief Justice. The case was then presented to the Governor and Council with the request that they order Oliver to appear before them to answer the charges and "be brought to a Hearing and Trial thereon."[17] Parenthetically, it should also be pointed out that on this same day the House voted to increase the compensation of the four judges who had agreed to receive their pay from the province. Then on March 7 a message to the Governor was voted in which the House submitted arguments against his position that it was unconstitutional for the Governor and Council to try criminal offences. It ended with the statement:

---

[15] *Ibid.*, p. 202. For the background of the Governor's request for leave see Chap. 2 of this volume; see also *Dartmouth Manuscripts*, I, 338.

[16] *Journal of the House of Representatives* (Boston, 1773–4), pp. 205–6.

[17] *Ibid.*, pp. 211–16.

"We assure ourselves, that were the nature of our grievances fully understood by our Sovereign, we should soon have reason to rejoice in the redress of them. But, if we must still be exposed to the continual false representation of persons who get themselves advanced to places of honour and profit by means of such false representations, and when we complain we cannot even be heard, we have yet the pleasure of contemplating, that posterity for whom we are now struggling will do us justice, by abhoring the memory of those men 'who owe their greatness to their country's ruin.' "[18]

The session was now nearing its close. On March 9—after giving his approval to various bills that had been laid before him, and having disapproved the salary voted to Benjamin Franklin as the London agent of the House of Representatives—the Governor prorogued the General Assembly. But before doing so he warned the two houses that "as some of your Votes, Resolves, and other Proceedings . . . strike directly at the Honour and Authority of the King and of Parliament I may not neglect bearing publick Testimony against them, and making Use of the Powers vested in me by the Constitution to prevent you from proceeding any farther in the same way."[19]

The revolutionary significance of the episode involving the attempts of the House to impeach Chief Justice Oliver and to remove the Governor did not escape the Governor, who wrote of it: "The

---

[18] *Ibid.*, pp. 232–6.

[19] *Ibid.*, p. 243. Hutchinson, in his *History of the Colony and Province of Massachusetts-Bay* (ed. L. S. Mayo, 3 vols., Cambridge, Mass., 1936), III, 317–26, gives a very full account of the efforts to remove the Chief Justice from the bench; see also his letters to Dartmouth, February 17 and March 9, 1774, *Dartmouth Manuscripts*, I, 348–9 and 350. It may be noted that the March 9 letter reports the destruction of tea from another ship "of persons disguised like Indians." Oliver, in his deeply emotional *Origin of the Rebellion,* writes (p. 111): "The Assembly, finding that the chief Justice did not go to *Boston* [to participate in a meeting of the Superior Court], to have his Brains beat out by their Rabble, they attacked him in a new Quarter, where he happened to be Invulnerable. They ordered the Records of the supreme Court to be laid before them, hoping to find some Malfeazance in his Office; but they were disappointed . . . At last, finding that they were pushed to Extremity, they sprung a Mine which involved theirselves in the intended Ruin of him. They drew up an Impeachment of him, as Inimical to his Country in taking the Kings Grant, but at the same Time they did him the Honor of joining his Majesty with him in the Impeachment, as offering a Bribe to him, which he received. This was such an Insult to Majesty, that the Governor could not let it pass unnoticed, & accordingly closed the Matter against them." The Chief Justice then referred to subsequent attempts to destroy him by assassination and concluded this episode by writing: "It was a little odd, that they should pursue him with such unremitting Vengeance when it is considered, that they had but just finished their Laugh at his bretheren, for being such Cowards as to quit their Hold of the King's Grants to them."

course of law was now wholly stopped. . . . All legislative, as well as executive power was gone. . . ."[20]

The feelings of hatred borne by the people of Boston against British officials, especially the customs officers, had been demonstrated earlier in 1774 when one of these officers, John Malcom, apparently carried away with rage at some insult in the midst of an altercation with a citizen of the town, drew his sword and wounded the man. Instead of proceeding against Malcom according to due process of law, the mob dragged him through the streets in a sled and then tarred and feathered him; later he was placed in a cart and carried to the famous Liberty Tree. When he refused to renounce his commission in the customs, he was taken to the gallows and threatened with hanging. After he persisted in refusing to accede to the demands of the crowd, they "then basted him for some time with the rope's end, and threatened to cut his ears off, and on this he complied and they brought him home."[21]

The solicitude of the House of Representatives—now firmly under radical leadership—for the provincial supply of powder, tends to show that, shortly after the display of defiance to the British government by the destruction of the tea, plans were being secretly laid in Massachusetts Bay for armed resistance. On February 1, a committee made up entirely of provincial military officers was ordered to wait upon Hutchinson with an address complaining that at the last ses-

---

[20] *History*, III, 326; see also Hutchinson to Dartmouth, February 17, 1774, *Dartmouth Manuscripts*, I, 348–9.

[21] For a rather detailed account of the Malcom episode see *Boston Evening-Post*, January 31, 1774. John Rowe, a prominent citizen of Boston and a keen observer of contemporary events, commented in his diary that possibly 1,200 people were on hand at the time of the incident, and then added: "This was looked upon by me & every Sober man as an act of outrageous Violence & when several of the Inhabitants applyed to a particular Justice to Exert his Authority & suppress & they would support him in the execution of his Duty, he Refused" (*Letters and Diary of John Rowe*, p. 261). In fact, there seemed to have been some sober second thoughts on the part of radicals respecting the treatment of Malcom. At least the January 31 edition of the *Boston Evening-Post* published the following notice as having been posted "in divers Parts of the Town": "Friends and Fellow Citizens! This is to Certify, that the modern Punishment lately inflicted on the ignoble John Malcom, was not done by our Order:—We reserve that Method for bringing Villains of greater Consequence to a Sense of their Guilt and Infamy. Joice, jun. (Chairman of the Committee for Tarring & Feathering)." For the most complete study of Malcom's career and the documents of the events leading up to and surrounding the episode of January 1774—including the graphic *Massachusetts Spy* account of January 27, 1774, Malcom's own report, and Hutchinson's letter to Dartmouth on the subject, not to mention the several cartoons that resulted from the affair—see F. W. C. Hersey: "Tar and Feathers: The Adventures of Captain John Malcom," Colonial Society of Massachusetts *Transactions*, XXXIV, 429–73.

sions, "being apprehensive that the Province Stock of Powder was then deficient," they had sought an appraisal of the amount on hand, but that the Governor had not complied with this request. In the address, the House restated its apprehensions that the stock of powder was "very deficient," and once more requested him, with due regard "to his Majesty's Service, and the Safety of this Province," to furnish a return of the powder in the magazines. To this, Hutchinson made a reply on the 4th, in which he dealt with the frugal use of the powder during the past year and stated that he believed—doubtless in an attempt to reassure the House that he was involved in no sinister move against the people—the present supply was "much greater than that of any other Colony," adding "if you chuse to keep the Stock intire, or to make an Addition, I shall not disapprove of it."[22]

By March the inhabitants of the province were engaging in military exercises under officers of their own choosing, "hinting the occasion there might soon be for employing their arms in defence of their liberties." Now thoroughly discouraged, Hutchinson hoped that by the time the General Assembly was prorogued he would be able to depart for England to lay the problems of the province before the King and his ministers.[23] But the death on March 3, 1774, of Lieutenant Governor Andrew Oliver forced a delay.[24]

Meanwhile, in London, plans were being conceived for relieving the civilian Governor of an impossible burden in view of the Ministry's preparations to have Parliament pass certain measures to bring the colony back to its duty. These punitive, coercive, and preventive

---

[22] *Journal of the House of Representatives* (Boston, 1773–4), pp. 113–14 and 131.

[23] Hutchinson stated in his *History* (III, 327) that he "wished for a temporary relief at least, from so heavy a burden as that of being at the head of a government, all the other parts whereof were united against an authority which he was bound to acknowledge, and, as far as was in his power, to uphold." Yet he calculated that it would not be less than three to four months before the appointment by the Crown of a new Lieutenant Governor would become effective and permit him to leave, and added that, "in the mean time, anarchy must be daily increasing." His loss of popularity in Boston was highlighted when—on March 5 in connection with the commemoration of the so-called Boston Massacre—effigies of the Governor and Chief Justice were exhibited "in derision" before the public without protest. *Ibid.*, III, 327–8.

[24] For an account of the funeral of Lieutenant Governor Oliver on March 8, 1774, and the fanfare attendant upon it—which states among other things that "Thro' some misunderstanding or Blunder the Gentlemen of the Councill did not attend this Funerall & very few of the House of Representatives"—see the *Letters and Diary of John Rowe*, pp. 264–5. It may be assumed that, like Governor Hutchinson, the members of the Council and the Assembly friendly to Oliver were absent because of the dangerous mood of the populace, while those hostile to him would not grace his funeral with their presence.

measures—the Coercive Acts—have already been considered in the preceding chapter of this volume, as has the appointment of a military Governor, General Gage, to replace Hutchinson.

In many ways the choice of Gage as Governor of Massachusetts Bay seemed to be a happy one. He had been in America almost twenty years. When acting as Governor of the conquered town and district of Montreal from October 1760 to the latter part of 1763, he had earned due popularity among the Canadians for the mildness of his rule;[25] further, during his long sojourn on the continent he had won many friends. In fact, his wife was the daughter of a prominent American, Peter Kemble of New Jersey, which made his children half American. In the role of successor to Amherst as Commander-in-Chief, with headquarters in New York, he had, moreover, shown caution and wisdom in the exercise of his military office and in his relations with the civilian authorities, especially during the Stamp Act crisis. It is perhaps not surprising, therefore, that when General Gage landed at the Long Wharf on May 17 for his formal reception at Boston,[26] he was welcomed with great ceremony by the Council, representatives of the Assembly, and local military units, which escorted him to the Council chamber. There his commission was read and he took the oath of office. The new Governor immediately issued a proclamation continuing office-holders in their places. This was followed by an elegant entertainment at Faneuil Hall.[27] But there was one conspicuous absence during the ceremonies attending Gage's formal installation—the Governor he was replacing was not present.

Unwilling to risk the rage of the people, Thomas Hutchinson remained in retirement until he finally sailed for England on June 1 and what was to be permanent exile from his native land, which he had—as measured by all rational standards—served with real distinction over a long period of years. Nevertheless, he was not permitted to depart without some measure of compensation; for he carried with him testimonials of appreciation from twenty-four attorneys and barristers. On May 28 they had signed an address signifying their "sincere Respect and Esteem" for his "inviolable

---

[25] "A milder and more beneficent rule . . . Montreal had never known. . . . His strong sense of justice and fair play, his caution, and his good humor won public acclaim" (J. R. Alden: *General Gage in America* [Baton Rouge, La., 1948], p. 58).

[26] General Gage had reached Castle William on May 13, after a rapid voyage of only twenty-eight days in H.M.S. *Lively* (*ibid.*, pp. 203–4).

[27] *Boston Evening-Post*, May 23, 1774.

Attachment to the real interests of your native Country"; that same day 123 Boston merchants and traders in another signed address praised his "wise, zealous and faithful Administration" during the five years of his incumbency; in like manner an address from thirty-three citizens of Marblehead assured him of their "entire Approbation" of his public conduct during his governorship.[28]

The news of the passing of the Boston Port Act had reached the Massachusetts Bay metropolis only three days before General Gage's arrival. For, when the *Harmony,* Captain Shayler, arrived from London on May 10 it brought what was described by the merchant John Rowe as "the Severest Act ever Penned against the Town of Boston."[29] The May 16 edition of the *Boston Evening-Post* described it as "The Act of Parliament For Blockading the Harbour of Boston."[30] On the 13th, at a town meeting, it was designated "the late *Edict* of a British Parliament for Blocking up the Harbor of Boston, & annihilating the Trade of this Town," and a committee, headed by Samuel Adams, was appointed to consider what line of action should be taken. To avoid any delay, the meeting voted that messengers be sent "with all possible Speed" not only to the other towns of the province but also to the other colonies, with the proposal that if the other colonies would agree with Massachusetts Bay to stop all trade to and from Great Britain "till the Act for Blocking up this Harbor be repealed, the same will prove the Salvation of North America & her Liberties."[31] At the next town meeting, on the

---

[28] For these addresses as well as one from the Anglican clergy, which was unsigned, see *Boston Evening-Post,* May 30 and June 6, 1774. The June 6 edition of this paper also carried a repudiation of the favourable addresses of the Boston and Marblehead merchants and traders for a person who had been branded by both branches of the General Assembly "as an inveterate Enemy to the Liberties of the Province." In the *Boston Gazette* of May 30 a writer signing himself "A.B." deplored the address of the Anglican clergy to a "disgraced and execrated *Traitor*." In fact, some of the signers of the addresses were forced to recant.

[29] *Letters and Diary of John Rowe,* p. 269.

[30] For a legalistic analysis of the Port Act, with a step-by-step refutation of certain of its clauses, see Josiah Quincy, Jr.,: *Observations on . . . the Boston Port Bill; With Thoughts on Civil Society and Standing Armies* (Boston, 1774). Quincy, it will be recalled, was co-defender with Adams of the British soldiers after the Boston Massacre. In 1773 he travelled for his health to Charleston, South Carolina, and on his return by land observed the political tendencies in other colonies and the men behind them—for example, Dickinson and Joseph Reed with whom he later corresponded. He was the member of the inner circle of Boston patriots chosen in 1774 to go to London to present the colonial point of view to government officials there and to bring back certain reports. See Josiah Quincy [III]: *Memoir of the Life of Josiah Quincy Jun. of Massachusetts* (Boston, 1825), containing correspondence, journals, and a reprinting of *Observations*.

[31] *Boston Town Records, 1770–1777* (Boston, 1887), pp. 173–4.

18th, a committee of five appointed to confer with the towns of Salem and Marblehead reported that the selectmen of these towns were disposed to support Boston "in the present Struggle for our invaded Rights." This gathering went on to record that "the Impolicy, Injustice, Inhumanity, & Cruelty, of the Act . . . exceed all our Powers of Expression & Conception . . ." Especially was this so in view of the fact that "the Trade of the Town of Boston has been an essential Link in that vast Chain of Commerce, which . . . has raised . . . the British Empire, to that Height of Opulence, Power, Pride & Splendor, at which it now stands."[32]

Boston was still under conditions of stress and excitement over the Port Act when the General Assembly met on May 25 and again elected Samuel Adams Clerk of the House of Representatives and Thomas Cushing Speaker. The House thereupon voted for the twenty-eight members of the Council. When the list was submitted to the Governor the following day, he refused to confirm the choice of thirteen of the men, among whom were James Bowdoin, John Adams, John Winthrop, and William Phillips.[33] In taking this action Gage was, of course, acting on the instructions dated April 9 he had received from Dartmouth (along with the commission appointing him captain general and Governor-in-Chief of Massachusetts Bay), amplifying the measures to be taken to implement the Boston Port Act. These instructions authorized Gage to meet immediately upon his arrival with the civilian and military authorities to see what steps should be taken to prepare for putting the Act into execution; to take all precaution to avoid force, but to use it if necessary; to remove the seat of government to Salem; to take every possible step for punishing the ringleaders in the criminal acts against the tea ships, but "to desist from prosecution" if the temper of the people was such that this step could not produce a conviction and might only "be Triumph to the Faction, and disgraceful to Government" and, finally, to negative the choice of any members elected to the Council "upon whose Attachment to the Constitution no Reliance can be had in any case

---

[32] *Ibid.,* pp. 174–5. For similar action by the town of Newburyport, as early as May 12, see B. W. Labaree: *Patriots and Partisans: The Merchants of Newburyport, 1764–1815* (Harvard Historical *Studies,* LXXIII, Cambridge, Mass., 1962), pp. 30–1.

[33] *Journal of the House of Representatives* (Boston, 1774), pp. 3–7. In reporting his action to the Earl of Dartmouth, Gage stated that three of the thirteen councillors he vetoed were "of the Old Council who drew up the Report of the Committee of Council on the 27th Nov' last and the rest either Committee-Men for Correspondence, or such Persons as I could not approve" (Gage to Dartmouth, May 30, 1774, *Gage Correspondence,* I, 355–6).

where the Sovereignty of the King in His Parliament is in question. . . ."[34]

In addressing the Assembly, Gage pointed out that by the King's particular commands he was from June 1 onward to meet the General Court at Salem "until His Majesty shall have signified his Royal Will and Pleasure for holding it again at *Boston*."[35] Then, on May 28, hoping to forestall the efforts of the House to hurry through its business in order to avoid going to Salem,[36] he adjourned the Assembly. This led the House, when it reconvened at Salem[37] on June 7, to appoint a committee, which presented a series of resolves the following day protesting the removal of the General Court "merely in Obedience to an Instruction," from "its ancient Seat the Court-House in *Boston*." These were entered in the journal. On June 9, in formal answer to that part of the Governor's opening speech having to do with the King's commands for the removal of the seat of government to Salem, the members declared: "We are intirely at a Loss for the Cause of this Command. . . ." They also stressed "their Loyalty to their Sovereign, their Affection for the parent Country, as well as their invincible Attachment to their just rights and Liberties."[38]

At this very time, however, on the basis of advance word of the passage through Parliament of the two new Coercive Acts,[39] the Boston Committee of Correspondence had gone into action. Meeting on June 2, the committee appointed Dr. Joseph Warren, along with

---

[34] *Ibid.*, II, 158–62.

[35] *Journal of the House of Representatives* (Boston, 1774), p. 8.

[36] *Gage Correspondence*, I, 356.

[37] *Journal of the House of Representatives* (Boston, 1774), p. 15.

[38] *Ibid.*, pp. 17–21.

[39] See Franklin to Cushing, April 2, 16, and June 1, 1774, Franklin's *Writings* (Smyth), VI, 224–6, 228–30, 231. Both the Act for Regulating the Government of Massachusetts Bay and that for the Impartial Administration of Justice were signed by the King on May 20, 1774, as has been discussed in full in the preceding chapter of this volume, but neither had been received by the Governor at this juncture. That full details of the provisions of these statutes were available to Bostonians, however, and were viewed by them as "glaring evidence of a fixed plan of the British administration to bring the whole continent into the most humiliating bondage," is attested by the letter sent to the other towns by the Boston Committee of Correspondence on June 8, 1774. See *Early American Imprints, 1639–1800* (ed. C. K. Shipton, Readex Microprint, American Antiquarian Society, Evans No. 13157). See also, in this connection, *Votes and Proceedings of the Town of Boston, June 17, 1774* (Boston, 1774, *ibid.*, Evans No. 13159) and another letter from the Boston Committee of Correspondence of July 26, 1774 (*ibid.*, Evans No. 13160), stating: "Two acts of Parliament altering the course of justice, and annihilating our once free constitution of government are every day expected."

Dr. Benjamin Church and Joseph Greenleaf, as a subcommittee to draw up a circular letter to go to every town in the province proposing a "Solemn League and Covenant" neither to import, export, nor consume British goods and to prepare the agreement itself for the individual signature of as many as possible of the merchants and consumers in the colony. With the letter and covenant, as drafted by Warren, approved on the 6th, the same subcommittee was reappointed to forward copies of the documents to the several towns "in a private way." It was also voted that Warren and Greenleaf be a subcommittee to prepare a letter to forward to the committees of correspondence of New York, Philadelphia, Rhode Island, and Connecticut. All of this was done as quietly as possible in order to permit time for a coordinated response to come in from the outlying towns.[40]

The House of Representatives, in the meantime, proceeded with its regular business until June 17, when the committee appointed on the 7th to examine the state of the province was ready to report. After the galleries had been cleared and the doors closed, the Speaker reported the committee's findings. These were: that the unhappy differences between Great Britain and the colonies necessitated a meeting of committees from the several colonies on the continent to consult upon "the Miseries to which they are and must be reduced by the Operation of certain Acts of Parliament respecting America," and thereby come to a determination upon "wise and proper Measures . . . for the Recovery and Establishment of their just Rights and Liberties. . . ." A resolve to that effect was then passed, as was the plan to appoint a committee of five for the purpose of conferring with similar committees to be appointed by other colonies and to meet either in Philadelphia or at some other suitable place. Further, to defer the expenses of this committee—since the Council had agreed to meet them by appropriation, but the Governor had refused his assent to this plan—it was voted to recommend that each town or district pay directly to its respective committee whatever proportion of £500 should be agreeable to its assessment list.[41] In a concomitant resolution the House also recommended that colonials everywhere come to the aid of the suffering people of

---

[40] "Boston Committee of Correspondence Minutes, 1772–1774," 9:763–4, New York Public Library.

[41] *Ibid.*, pp. 22–47. According to the *Boston Gazette* of June 20, the vote on the resolve was carried 129 to 12.

Boston and its near neighbour, Charlestown, by means of dona-tions.[42] When the Governor got word of the activities in which the House was engaged, he sent the Secretary to the court house to dissolve the Assembly. But the doors remained locked until the members had finished their business.[43]

Also in June, in the face of the manifest determination of the government of Great Britain to reduce the province to obedience and in view of the arrival in Boston of the 4th and 43rd regiments together with contingents of other regular forces, some of the con-servatively inclined people, especially certain merchants, finally took a stand. They came out openly in opposition to the activities of the Boston Committee of Correspondence, which they were persuaded would, if successful, lead to but one result—a general rebellion of the older American colonies. Taking the position, therefore, that the only way to save the town from ruin was to comply with the terms of the Boston Port Act, they were ready to make compensation for the destroyed tea.[44] On June 8 an address to Governor Gage had been offered by 127 merchants and other inhabitants in which they referred to his "known ability, steadiness, and moderation," which caused them the less to regret the departure of Thomas Hutchinson, "whose wise and faithful administration hath given us the most entire satisfaction." In it they referred to a proposal to make restitu-tion to the East India Company for damage caused "by the outrage of rash and inconsiderate men, [which] we look upon to be quite equitable," and expressed the hope that as soon as compensation had been made His Excellency would make favourable representation to His Majesty in Council to restore the town to his royal favour.[45] The conservatives took exception especially to the committee's ac-tion of June 8 in circularizing every town in the province with a letter enclosing the Solemn League and Covenant. For the signer of

---

[42] When this proposition reached the other colonies, it brought a hearty response. It is of interest to note that the little town of Glastonbury in central Connecticut was the first to open the subscription for the relief of the people of Boston, closely followed by Windham in eastern Connecticut, which donated a flock of sheep. For letters from the various towns on the continent that voted aid see "Correspondence, in 1774 and 1775, between a Committee of the Town of Boston and Contributors of Donations for the Relief of the Sufferers by the Boston Port Bill" covering the years 1774–75, Massachusetts Historical Society *Collections*, 4th ser., IV, 1–278.

[43] Gage to Dartmouth, June 26, 1774, *Gage Correspondence*, I, 357.

[44] Gage to Dartmouth, July 5, 1774, *ibid.*, I, 358; *Letters and Diary of John Rowe*, pp. 276–7.

[45] For this address see *American Archives*, 4th ser., I, 398–9; see also *Boston Evening-Post*, June 13, 1774.

this document pledged not to purchase after October 1 any article imported from Great Britain as well as to forgo all commercial intercourse with that country and to cease all connections with anyone who refused to sign it. Further, the boycott was to continue "until the harbour of Boston shall be opened, and our charter rights restored." Only by this procedure, the covenant affirmed, could the people be saved from a choice between "the horrours of slavery, or the carnage and desolation of a civil war."[46]

The Boston Committee of Correspondence was, in truth, working in secrecy.[47] It delayed as long as possible submitting to the ratification of a town meeting its bold plan to weld the continent into united action to oppose all commercial intercourse with Great Britain until Parliament should repeal the legislation directed against Boston. When the request was made in the town meeting of June 17 for a statement of the committee's activities, Dr. Joseph Warren, acting as spokesman, replied that the members "thought it best to defer making Report, till they had heard from the other Governments."[48] But by the 27th of June knowledge of the committee's assumption of authority to put its plan for a Solemn League and Covenant into effect had aroused so much opposition that the town meeting held on that day demanded that the committee lay before the assemblage all letters it had written to "other Towns and Governments since the Receipt of the [Boston] Port Bill.[49] When this was agreed to, the meeting adjourned to Old South Meeting House to accommodate the crowd that had gathered. Upon the reading of the Solemn League and Covenant and some letters, a motion was made "for censuring & annihilating the Committee of Correspond-

---

[46] For a copy of the Boston circular letter and of the covenant see Peter Force: *American Archives*, 4th ser., I, 397–8; see also Albert Matthews: "The Solemn League and Covenant," Colonial Society of Massachusetts *Transactions*, XVIII, 103–22, and John Cary: *Joseph Warren, Physician, Politician, Patriot* (Urbana, Ill., 1961), pp. 139–46.

[47] When the Boston Committee of Correspondence had been organized formally on November 2, 1772, with the designation by the town meeting of twenty-one people to compose it, the range of its responsibilities was "to state the Rights of the Colonists and of this Province in particular . . . to communicate and publish the same to the several Towns in this Province and to the World as the sense of this Town . . . ," but each member was bound in honour not to divulge any part of the proceedings, except that which the committee as a whole should judge proper to make public. See *Boston Town Records, 1770–1777*, pp. 92–3; see also minute of November 3, 1772, "Boston Committee of Correspondence Minutes," 1772–1774 (Ms), 1:1–2, Manuscript Division, New York Public Library.

[48] *Boston Town Records, 1770–1777*, p. 176.

[49] *Ibid.*, p. 177.

ence." After some discussion, as the hour grew late, it was agreed to adjourn the meeting to the following morning.[50] When the meeting reassembled, a lengthy and heated debate ensued over the motion of censure, but at the vote it was defeated "by a great Majority." A counter-motion was immediately made and passed to approve "the honest Zeal of the Comittee . . . & desire that they would persevere with their usual Activity & Firmness. . . ."[51]

As a reply to the above action of the town meeting, 129 of those openly opposed to the work of the committee promptly signed their names to a set of resolutions dated June 29 that were subsequently given wide circulation in the press. These resolves described the committee's Solemn League and Covenant—submitted "without the Consent or Knowledge of the Town, and recommended to the people of the Country"—as a document "of a most dangerous Nature and Tendency." They further protested the action of the town meeting in approving "the illegal Proceedings of the said Committee."[52] On that same date, the Governor issued a proclamation warning the people not to sign the Solemn League and Covenant and stigmatized the communication to the towns that accompanied it as "a scandalous, traitorous, and seditious Letter." In it he also commanded all "Magistrates to secure for trial all those who would presume to publish or to sign it."[53] That this proclamation undoubtedly had some restraining effect is indicated by the fact that out of over 200 towns qualified, either singly or jointly, to participate in electing representatives to the General Assembly, only some 15 had secured signers to the Covenant before the meeting of the Continental Congress in the fall of 1774.[54]

Strong support of Boston, and of what were held to be colonial rights, was nevertheless being generated outside Massachusetts Bay

---

[50] That the discussion on June 27 was heated can be inferred from the fact that the radical *Boston Gazette*, July 4, 1774, commented: "Nothing could equal the virulent Abuse offered to the Committee of Correspondence last Monday, but the Calmness those Gentlemen discovered under it; the foul Language used with unlimited Freedom by their Accusers is not to be palliated as being hastily uttered in the warmth of Debate, for it had been committed to Writing in a cool House, and was read in the meeting."

[51] *Boston Town Records, 1770–1777*, pp. 177–8. John Rowe noted that the majority in favour of the committee was four to one; see his *Letters and Diary*, pp. 276–7.

[52] See *Boston Evening-Post*, July 4, 1774. For other protests see the same edition of this paper.

[53] For the proclamation see *ibid.*

[54] John Cary: *op. cit.*, p. 142, and R. E. Brown: Middle-Class Democracy . . . (Ithaca, N.Y., 1955), pp. 74–7.

as well as throughout that province. For it was at this juncture that the intercolonial system of committees of correspondence went into active operation.[55] Responding to the appeal from Massachusetts Bay to come to the succour of Boston, and to their own inflamed indignation over the Boston Port Act, and subsequently the other Coercive Acts, the individual colonies passed resolves and formed special committees. These steps were chiefly the result of action taken in town meetings, county conventions, and other general meetings of inhabitants beyond the scope of the legally constituted lower houses of legislature—as will be developed in the next chapter of this volume. Even more important, most of the colonies also responded favourably to the call for a Continental Congress, which came first from Virginia—as will be emphasized in Chapter VII, which deals with that subject. But the impetus for this unity of action undoubtedly stemmed from the correspondence between such outstanding colonial leaders as Samuel Adams and Joseph Warren of Massachusetts Bay and Richard Henry Lee of Virginia, who had long had at heart the concept of the intercolonial committees of correspondence and other joint endeavours to protect "the constitutional liberty of and rights of all North America."[56] In this, they not only were sparked by many admonitions from the London agents as to the impact a united colonial front could have upon the Ministry,[57]

---

[55] For a discussion of the establishment of the intercolonial committees of correspondence at the instigation of the Virginia House of Burgesses on March 12, 1773, at the time of the *Gaspee* crisis, see Chap. 1 of this volume. For an indication of the volume of the exchange of communications between the various intercolonial committees of correspondence, see *Journals of the House of Burgesses, 1773–1776*, pp. 133–59; see also *Rhode Island Colonial Records*, VII, 287–302; this correspondence also shows the degree and nature of the material help sent from other colonies to relieve the sufferings of the people of Boston.

[56] Richard Henry Lee to Samuel Adams, June 23, 1774, *Letters of Richard Henry Lee*, I, 111–13, see also same to same, April 24 and May 8, 1774, *ibid.*, I, 106 and 110.

[57] *Ibid.*, I, 109, in which Richard Henry Lee quotes a letter from London urging colonial unity, doubtless from one of his brothers there, probably Arthur. See also Arthur Lee to Richard Henry Lee, March 18, 1774, in the latter's *Life of Arthur Lee, LL.D.* (2 vols., Boston, 1829), I, 207–9, also printed in *American Archives*, 4th ser., I, 228–9. In this connection, it should also be borne in mind that Franklin and Arthur Lee as London agents of Massachusetts Bay not only maintained a lively correspondence with Cushing and Adams, but in addition wrote privately to other colonial leaders. See Franklin's *Writings* (Smyth), VI, 224–6, 228–30, and *passim*, and *Life of Arthur Lee*, I and II, *passim*. These leaders, in turn, corresponded privately with others in several different colonies. See, for example, "Letters of Thomas Cushing, 1767–1775," Massachusetts Historical Society *Collections*, 4th ser., IV, 363–4, *American Archives*, 4th ser., I, 237–8, and Lee Papers, Harvard College Library. In this connection, Arthur Lee, before going to London, had attempted to establish relationships with leaders in Maryland, Philadelphia, and New York (*Life of Arthur Lee*, I, 244–5) and may well have been the "Gentleman in London" who addressed un-

but also sought the advice of the Americans in London and each other.[58] Nor was the home government unaware of "this dangerous and unwarrantable correspondence," as Dartmouth called it in a letter to Governor Gage early in June, speaking of specific letters from Franklin and Lee to "the Leaders of the Faction at Boston" and asking the General to obtain either the originals or copies so that they could be used as "the grounds of a proper Proceeding thereupon."[59] However, as the result of the interception of letters[60] such as these, the governments both in London and in Boston were aware that the colonists had been kept informed of the coercive measures being taken in Parliament.

Yet, by July 20 General Gage had not yet received the two Coercive Acts approved by the King on May 20 or the Quartering Act signed on June 2, although they were common knowledge in Boston and the general reaction described above had given the Governor little hope that they would meet with anything but the most outright opposition when officially promulgated.[61] When they finally reached him on August 6, accompanied by a lengthy letter from Dartmouth,[62] the Governor was made to realize that his last chance

---

named correspondents in Annapolis and New York in March and April 1774, urging a "general Congress" and a "United Continent of America" (*American Archives*, 4th ser., I, 230–1 and 241).

[58] See, for example, Cushing to Lee, October 28, 1773, *Life of Arthur Lee*, I, 239–41.

[59] See Dartmouth to Gage, "Separate and Secret," June 3, 1774, *Gage Correspondence*, II, 167, which lists a letter from Franklin dated July 7, 1773 (see Franklin's *Writings* [Smyth], VI, 81–5), and one from Lee dated December 25, 1773 (probably Lee to Adams, dated December 22 in *Life of Arthur Lee*, I, 238–40). See also Gage's reply to Dartmouth of August 25, 1774, that he could not obtain either originals or copies of the letters because "they are directed to the Speaker, who calls them private Letters, & after reading them to the House, he puts them in his Pocket as his own private Correspondence" (*Gage Correspondence*, I, 364).

[60] In this connection Franklin wrote to Cushing on April 16, 1774: "It is given out that Copies of several Letters of mine to you are sent over here to the Ministers, and that their Contents are treasonable, for which I should be prosecuted if Copies could be made Evidence" (Franklin's *Writings* [Smyth], VI, 229).

[61] Gage to Dartmouth, July 20 and August 27, 1774, *Gage Correspondence*, I, 361 and 365.

[62] Dartmouth to Gage, two letters, June 3, 1774, *ibid.*, II, 163–6 and 167. These letters, taken together with those cited in the preceding footnote, give some indication of the ordinary lapse of time in transatlantic correspondence and thus of the difficulties involved in maintaining communications that could be meaningful. For Dartmouth's first letter of June 3 shows that he had received accounts "of the public Proceedings [only] down to the 5th of April, at which time it does not appear that any Intelligence had been received in the Province of the Steps that were taking here [the passage of the Boston Port Bill and the continuing debates on the other coercive measures]," and the second letter mentions receiving word from Hutchinson "of so late a date as the 2ᵈ of May, at which time they had received at Boston an account of the Proceedings here down to the 15th of March, which I find had occasioned

for reconciliation was lost. For he had now to announce the appointment of the Council by the King—the mandamus Council which the Bostonians viewed as an intolerable threat to their charter rights—and the appointment on Hutchinson's recommendation of Thomas Oliver as Lieutenant Governor, something initially accepted with greater grace. The provisions of the Justice Act were for contingency measures that did not require immediate implementation, but Gage could not fail to be aware of the heated reaction that was being stirred up by them. Like Hutchinson, the General was a man of firm loyalty to the King and strict obedience to his duty and the orders of his superiors. Thus he dared not improvise any expedients to conciliate the colonists without recourse to the home government, and by the time he was forced to consider such steps, everything was against him. For the Coercive Acts only added fuel to the fires of resentment and protest kindled by the Boston Port Act.[63]

During the summer of 1774 the Boston town meeting now openly assumed new functions of local government. As a result of these gatherings, on July 19 a declaration was authorized to be drawn up, addressed "to Great Britain and all the world," setting forth the Massachusetts Bay grievances. Further, on July 26, the town meeting approved the establishment of a committee of safety. When Governor Gage finally intervened with orders prohibiting town meetings, pursuant to the provisions of the second of the Coercive Acts, the radical leaders—still headed by Samuel and John Adams, Warren, Quincy, and Hancock—sought out a means of evading this restriction.[64] The result was the series of county conventions which culminated in the one held in Suffolk County.

Preparations for the Suffolk County Convention occupied the minds of the Boston leaders throughout the month of August.[65] With

---

great alarm and apprehension, but had been attended with no other Consequence, so that I am willing to suppose that the people will quietly submit to the Correction their ill conduct has brought upon them. . . ." However, by the date of Dartmouth's writing, Hutchinson was on the high seas en route to England and Gage was faced squarely with the resistance of the province. Further, although by May 30 the new Governor had recommended to Dartmouth that he listen to "Mr. Hutchinson for many Particulars of the present Situation of this Town and Province, No Person is so capable to give you true Information, or to foresee the Consequences likely to Arise from all that is, or intended to be done" (ibid., I, 356), by September 2 Gage was forced to write "that the State, not of this Province only, but of the rest is greatly changed since Mr. Hutchinson left America" (ibid., I, 369).

[63] Gage to Dartmouth, August 27, 1774, ibid., I, 361–8.
[64] See Boston Town Records, 1770–1777, pp. 183 and 185.
[65] See "Boston Committee of Correspondence Minutes, 1772–1774," 9:777, New York Public Library.

the departure on the 10th of the two Adamses and the other delegates to the Continental Congress, the leadership devolved upon Joseph Warren. He not only kept in constant correspondence with Samuel Adams, now in Philadelphia, to advise him of the policies being formulated by the Boston Committee of Correspondence of which he was the head, but also planned the convention of the counties held at Faneuil Hall on August 26 to evolve plans for a provincial congress.[66] The county convention, likewise under the chairmanship of Warren, produced among other things a statement of the policies that later served to guide county congresses.[67] As to the policies themselves, they hinged primarily upon the argument of natural rights and colonial rights—rights which the people should be prepared to defend by force of arms, if necessary. Specifically, the convention sought a provincial congress in place of the legislature, a system of referees to substitute for the courts, and a refusal to submit to any officials acting under the authority of the Act for the Impartial Administration of Justice.[68] These were the ideas brought to Milton on September 9, when the Suffolk County Convention reconvened after the two preliminary meetings on August 16 and September 6, held respectively at Stoughton and Dedham. From them were to evolve the Suffolk Resolves as deliberated and agreed upon by more than seventy delegates appointed from nineteen towns within Suffolk County.[69] As the Resolves had their greatest influence when presented to the First Continental Congress, they will be examined in detail in a later chapter dealing with that subject. But that they were revolutionary in nature may be judged by their similarity to the later Declaration of Independence.

How close to open conflagration the situation was in Massachusetts Bay at this juncture may be gathered from an earlier incident that led indirectly to the Suffolk Resolves. When Salem called a town meeting for August 20 in defiance of the Governor's orders, Gage summoned the local committee of correspondence before him and declared the meeting unlawful. Faced with the town's reply that no law was being disobeyed, he ordered out troops, which loaded their muskets at the entrance of the town and advanced to within

[66] *Ibid.*, 9:783–5.

[67] For an illuminating discussion of these events, and the leadership of Joseph Warren throughout this period, see John Cary: *op. cit.*, pp. 149–51.

[68] "Boston Committee of Correspondence Minutes, 1772–1774," minutes for August 26–27, 9:783–5.

[69] *American Archives*, 4th ser., I, 776–9.

A view of Faneuil Hall by P. Hill.

(From *Massachusetts Magazine*, 1789, Massachusetts Historical Society)

A view of the Old State House by P. Hill.

one-eighth of a mile of the Town House. However, while the Governor was in conference with the committee, the town meeting had assembled and transacted all its business. When it then disbanded, the troops withdrew. But as a result of this flouting of authority, certain members of the committee of correspondence were arrested.[70] As a further result, within the following weeks Gage began to fortify Boston Neck. This action so outraged the people that it was the subject of heated debate at the Suffolk Convention and gave rise not only to one article of the Resolves but also to the naming by the Convention on September 9 of a special committee to wait upon the Governor and present a remonstrance against the fortifications.[71]

Equally alarming had been the reaction of the people earlier in August, when General Gage, pursuant to the instructions he had received on the 6th, appointed the members of the new Council.[72] This reaction became explicit with the Suffolk Resolves, which ordered the mandamus councillors either to resign before September 20 or to face charges of being "obstinate and incorrigible enemies to this country."[73]

How conservatives in Massachusetts Bay reacted to the denunciation of the government of Great Britain by patriots in that colony is indicated by a letter dated August 10, 1774, received by General Gage from a correspondent living in Hampshire County—apparently Israel Williams, judge of the court of common pleas, a close friend of Thomas Hutchinson, and a member of the provincial Council from 1761 to 1767. A portion of this letter reads as follows:

> "I sincerely congratulate your Excellency on your appointment & arrival to the Chief Seat of Government, & as heartily wish you may be the happy Instrument under God, of restoring peace, good order, & Subjection to Government now almost at an end. Never was a time when such numbers of wise & Good Men as well as others, were so infatuated, 'till the present; an enthusiastic Frenzy & surprising Madness obtains everywhere; nothing said in the coolest manner

---

[70] For the Salem town meeting of August 20, 1774, see *American Archives*, 4th ser., I, 730.

[71] See the 9th article of the Suffolk Resolves, *ibid.*, I, 777, and, for the remonstrance, *ibid.*, I, 779–80.

[72] See Gage to Dartmouth, August 25 (Secret) and 27, 1774, *Gage Correspondence*, I, 364–5. For a list of those who accepted appointments and those who refused, see Shelburne Papers, 66:345, Clements Library, Ann Arbor, Michigan; see also W. H. Whitmore: *Massachusetts Civil List for the Colonial and Provincial Periods, 1630–1774* . . . (Albany, 1870), p. 64.

[73] *American Archives*, 4th ser., I, 777.

avails, but rather irritates. Indeed, whoever proposes pacific Measures is considered as an Enemy to his Country & threatened with Ruin. . . . The fences of Law are broken down, & without your Excy's Aid, our Lives as well as our Property will be much endangered. . . . Every Measure proposed & pursued [by the popular leaders] seems to be with a view to insult Majesty & widen the Breach between this & the parent State, & even to dare the Vengeance of the supreme Authority of the British Empire in America . . ."[74]

But the conservative view did not prevail. By early September General Gage was deploring the harassment of the mandamus councillors, some of whom, for their safety, were obliged "to seek Protection amongst the Troops in Boston."[75]

Only the removal of the pressures brought to bear upon Massachusetts Bay to compel its obedience to the will of the government of Great Britain could now stem the revolutionary tide. The goal was the rescinding of the laws passed by Parliament which the patriot party had pronounced to be not merely objectionable but intolerable. Faced with the Massachusetts representation in the Continental Congress and with the inflammatory resolves that had been passed in the interim by many of the towns and counties within the colony, Governor Gage's only recourse was to issue a proclamation on September 28 cancelling writs for the election of representatives to the meeting of the General Assembly scheduled to be held at Salem on October 5.[76]

The revolutionary leaders determined to ignore the proclamation. On the date set for the meeting of the House of Representatives, a majority of previously elected members assembled at Salem; then, on the 7th of October, declaring Gage's proclamation to be "unconstitutional, unjust and disrespectful to the Province," they denied that the colony was "in a tumultuous and disordered state," and resolved that, since a legal General Assembly could not be held, they would turn themselves into a provincial congress.

Thus, the Massachusetts Bay Congress followed the pattern of the Continental Congress and, like it, met without legal standing

---

[74] Enclosed in Gage's letter of August 27, 1774, to Dartmouth, Shelburne Papers, 66:349.

[75] Gage to Dartmouth, September 2, 1774, *Gage Correspondence*, I, 369–70. For revealing accounts of the activities of the mandamus councillors (both those who were forced to resign their commissions and those who stood firm) see "Documents Relating to the Last Meetings of the Massachusetts Royal Council, 1774–1776," ed. Albert Matthews, Colonial Society of Massachusetts *Transactions*, XXXII, 460–504.

[76] For Gage's proclamation see *Boston Evening-Post*, October 3, 1774.

in the eyes of the government of Great Britain;[77] it was, furthermore, without sanction by any provision of the colony's charter. On October 11 John Hancock was elected President of the Congress and on October 13 this revolutionary body delivered a message to Governor Gage which spoke of the need for holding the Congress at this moment of crisis in order to focus the wisdom of the province on the problems of preventing "impending Ruin and providing for the public Safety." It further declared "your hostile Preparations . . . threatens to involve us in all the . . . Horrors of a Civil War; and, . . . [to the] Astonishment of all Mankind, . . . such Measures are pursued against a People whose Love of Order, Attachment to Britain, and Loyalty to their Prince, have ever been exemplary."

Gage quickly replied that he desired the Congress to give assurance to the people that he planned nothing hostile to Boston or the county and that his wish was to preserve peace and tranquility. As to the enforcement of the Boston Port Act, he stated that this belonged to other departments of the government and that there was redress through the law, should any steps warranted by the Act be taken. He added that the "Menances daily thrown out and the unusual, warlike Preparations, throughout the Country, made it an act of Duty in me to pursue the Measures I have taken. . . ." Finally, he declared: ". . . by your present assembling, you are yourselves subverting that Charter, and now acting in direct Violation of your own Constitution. It is my Duty therefore . . . to require you to desist from such illegal and unconstitutional Proceedings."[78]

After shifting temporarily to Concord, the Provincial Congress settled down at Cambridge, quite ignoring Gage's warning of the

[77] *Boston Evening-Post*, October 10, 1774. A proposal for holding a provincial congress had been incorporated in the Suffolk Resolves in September: at the same time, however, it had been provided that "due respect and submission" should be paid to the recommendations of the Continental Congress. At the Boston town meeting held on September 22 it was then voted—on the grounds that the conscientious discharge of their duty by the representatives to the General Assembly would undoubtedly bring about the dissolution of that body—that the members elected to it by Boston be instructed to join with members elected from elsewhere in "a General Provincial Congress, to act upon such Matters . . . most likely to preserve the Liberties of all America." Since two of the elected representatives—Thomas Cushing and Samuel Adams—were attending the Continental Congress, the town meeting chose Dr. Joseph Warren, Dr. Benjamin Church, and Nathaniel Appleton to join in the proceedings. See *Boston Town Records, 1770–1777*, pp. 191–2. For the important part played by Warren in planning the provincial congress see John Cary: *op. cit.*, pp. 163–5.

[78] For the message and Gage's replies see *Boston Evening-Post*, October 17 and 24, 1774.

illegality of their conduct. On October 21 a committee formed to report on the state of the province brought in a series of resolves directed against those who had accepted mandamus appointments by the Crown to be members of the Council. These were adopted. By the resolutions, the councillors were branded as "infamous Betrayers of their Country" whose names should be published "as Rebels against the States" that they might be "handed down to Posterity with the Infamy they deserve. . . ."[79] On the 24th a report of the committee on the defence and safety of the province was amended and approved. The estimate of the armaments required for the protection of the colony included two categories of field artillery, equipment for battering cannon and mortars, with twenty tons of grape and round shot, ten tons of bomb-shells, a thousand barrels of powder, and five thousand guns and bayonets; all this was at an estimated cost of £20,837. At the same time it was ordered that this decision be kept strictly secret until further orders of the Provincial Congress.[80] With this accomplished, on the 26th it was agreed to create a special committee of safety, to be composed of nine members, having responsibility for surveillance over the movements of any who might attempt to take hostile steps against the province and for alarming the people if necessary. If called upon, the militia was to take orders from this powerful committee, which was also given authority to supervise its state of readiness and to purchase without delay any armament needed.[81] The following day, John Hancock, Dr. Warren, and Dr. Church were selected as the three Boston members. These men, it would appear, thereafter guided its activities. A committee of five on military readiness was likewise selected. Moreover, a commanding officer of all provincial forces was commissioned in the person of Jedediah Preble, with Artemus Ward and Seth Pomroy named as second and third in command.[82] To round out the revolutionary provincial government, Henry Gardner was made receiver general of provincial revenues on the 28th in place of the provincial treasurer, Harrison Gray, who had opposed the plans of the radicals in a Boston town meeting. The Congress then resolved that all provincial taxes should thereafter be paid to the receiver general, and those officers who were accustomed to

---

[79] *Ibid.*, October 24, 1774.
[80] *American Archives*, 4th ser., I, 841–2.
[81] *Ibid.*, I, 843–5.
[82] *Ibid.*, I, 845.

collect them were called upon to do so promptly in view of the "unexpected and pressing demands of this Province."[83] In its final action, before adjourning on the 29th, the Congress recommended that all inhabitants perfect themselves in the military art; it also prepared a reply to Governor Gage's letter, accusing him of exerting himself "to execute the Acts made to subvert the Constitution of the Province" through his "connections with a Ministry inimical to the Province" and of being "surrounded by men of the worst political principles. . . ."[84]

Thus, by the fall of 1774, a great ground swell of resistance to British authority had formed in Massachusetts Bay. Even in the most distant counties, having little direct interest in overseas trade or in the restrictions that were throttling Boston, this was true. There as elsewhere the patriots gradually won over their Loyalist neighbours, friends, and relations.[85]

So that in early September Gage was reporting to the Secretary of State:

> ". . . Civil Government is near it's End, the Courts of Justice expiring one after another. . . . Precepts are issued for the Calling an Assembly . . . tho' uncertain whether the People will chuse Representatives, but we may be assured if chosen that they will not act with the New-Council . . . so that we shall shortly be without either Law, or legislative Power. . . . Nothing that is said at present can palliate; Conciliating, Moderation, Reasoning is over, Nothing can be done but by forceable Means. Tho' the People are not held in high Estimation by the Troops, yet they are numerous, worked up to a Fury, and not a Boston Rabble but the Freeholders and Farmers of the Country. A Check any where wou'd be fatal, and the first Stroke will decide a great deal."[86]

Ten days later he was writing of the anger of the people "at the Work throwing up at the Entrance of the Town," and of the "Country People . . . exercising in Arms in this Province, Connecticut, and Rhode Island. . . ." Within the next two weeks he was apparently

---

[83] *Ibid.*, I, 846–7.

[84] *Ibid.*, I, 849–50.

[85] For two valuable studies of the resistance movement in the counties of Worcester, Hampshire, and Berkshire, see L. N. Newcomer: *The Embattled Farmers. A Massachusetts Countryside in the American Revolution* (New York, 1953), which has an exhaustive bibliography, and R. J. Taylor: *Western Massachusetts in the Revolution* (Providence, R.I., 1954).

[86] Gage to Dartmouth, September 2, 1774, *Gage Correspondence*, I, 371.

toying with the idea of suspending "the Execution of the late Acts," but on the very day he wrote of this to Dartmouth he sent a second letter, saying:

> "We hear of Nothing but Extravagancies in some Part or other, and of military Preparations from this place to the Province of New York. . . . Upon a Rumor [that the troops were taking action against the people] . . . the whole Country was in Arms, and in Motion. . . . From present Appearances there is no Prospect of putting the late Acts in Force, but by first making a Conquest of the New-England Provinces. . . ."[87]

By the end of October the Governor of Massachusetts Bay—with no courts functioning, his mandamus Council impotent, and the remains of his government forced to remain in virtual imprisonment in Boston, behind the protection of troops—still held the hope that the Continental Congress would advise the payment for the tea as a step toward reconciliation, firm in the belief that the people of that colony would abide by any recommendations of the Congress. At the same time, he was realistically recommending that it would require a powerful force to subdue any outburst and expressing fears lest supplies be cut off from his troops.[88]

In the process of uniting the province to the pitch of open rebellion that had been reached, the press and the pulpit obviously played a role of extraordinary importance.[89] The chief spokesman for the Loyalists in the colony from early in the winter of 1774 to the spring of 1775 was the lawyer Daniel Leonard of Taunton. To the columns of the conservative *Massachusetts Gazette* he contributed a series of articles under the pseudonym "Massachusettensis."[90] In his writings Leonard stressed the stifling by the press of sentiments that were inconsistent with the radical viewpoint and the consequent loss of freedom of expression; he also denounced the development of an-

---

[87] Gage to Dartmouth, September 12 and 25, 1774, *ibid.*, I, 374, 375, 377.

[88] *Ibid.*, I, 374, 379, 380, 382–3.

[89] See Philip Davidson: *Propaganda and the American Revolution, 1763–1783* (Chapel Hill, N.C., 1941), and A. M. Schlesinger: *Prelude to Independence . . . 1764–1776* (New York, 1958).

[90] Leonard's articles were subsequently published in New York by James Rivington in a pamphlet entitled *The Origin of the American contest with Great-Britain, or the present political state of the Massachusetts-Bay in general, and the town of Boston in particular. Exhibiting the rise and progress of the disordered State of that country, in a series of weekly essays, published at Boston, under the signature of Massachusettensis. A native of New-England* (New York, 1775). For other loyalist efforts see Philip Davidson: *op. cit.*, Chaps. 14–16, and A. M. Schlesinger: *op. cit.*, *passim.*

archy in the affairs of the province. In his first essay, speaking as a lawyer, he warned those readers who had followed the lead of the agitators of their danger: "Should you be told that acts of high treason are flagrant through the country, that a great part of the province is in actual rebellion, would you believe it true?" He then enumerated the various acts committed by individuals which, under the law of treason, were capital offences. His argument was generally calm as he recounted the steps taken since 1764 to alienate by various means, including the spread of terror, the people from their loyalty to the government of Great Britain. However, when he approached the current scene of 1774, he wrote with deep emotion:

> "I saw the small seed of sedition, when it was implanted, it was, as a grain of mustard. I have watched the plant, until it has become a great tree, the vilest reptiles that crawl upon the earth, are concealed at the root, the foulest birds of the air rest upon its branches. I now would induce you to go to work immediately with axes and hatchets, and cut it down; for a two-fold reason, because it is a pest to society, and lest it be felled suddenly by a stronger arm and crush its thousands in the fall."[91]

The chief reply to "Massachusettensis" was made by John Adams after his return from the Continental Congress. Writing under the signature "Novanglus," his letters appeared in the extremely radical *Boston Gazette*; they were reprinted in London in an abridged version as the "History of the Dispute with America; from its Origin in 1754."[92] Adams argued that the whole dispute between Great Britain and the North American colonies turned on the fundamentals of colonial government. According to him, the King's chief minister pretends, and "Massachusettensis" supports the view,

> "that parliament is the only supreme, sovereign, absolute, and uncontrollable legislative over all the colonies; that, therefore, the minister and all his advocates will call resistance to acts of parliament by the name of treason and rebellion. But . . . they know that . . . parliament has no authority over them, excepting to regulate their trade, and this not by any principle of common law, but merely by the consent of the colonies . . . that, therefore, they [the patriots] have as good a right to charge . . . Massachusettensis, and the whole army

---

[91] *Ibid.*, pp. 4–6, 27.
[92] See John Almon's *Remembrancer,* for 1775.

[in Boston] to which he has fled for protection, with treason and rebellion. For, if parliament has not a legal authority to overturn their [that is, the Massachusetts Bay] constitution, and subject them to such acts as are lately passed, every man who accepts of any commission, and takes any steps to carry those acts into execution, is guilty of overt acts of treason and rebellion against his majesty, his royal crown and dignity, as much as if he should take [up] arms against his troops, or attempt his sacred life. . . . I would ask, by what law the parliament has authority over America? By the law of God, in the Old and New Testament, it has none; by the law of nature and nations, it has none; by the common law of England, it has none . . . by statute law it has none, for no statute was made before the settlement of the colonies for this purpose; and the declaratory act, made in 1766, was made without our consent, by a parliament which had no authority beyond the four seas."

Continuing, on the subject of the King and the Crown of England, Adams asserts: "Indeed, we owe no allegiance to any crown at all. We owe allegiance to the person of his majesty, King George III, whom God preserve." As to the powers enjoyed by the colonial assemblies, he finds, the colonial "houses of representatives have, and ought to exercise, every power of the house of commons." Indeed, since colonial "representation in parliament is impracticable, . . . we must have a representation in our supreme legislature here." He goes on to say that New England men derive their laws "not from parliament, not from common law, but from the law of nature, and the compact made with the king in our charters." It is true that the first charter was declared forfeited in an arbitrary reign, but "no American charter will ever be decreed forfeited again; or if any should, the decree will be regarded no more than a vote of the lower house of the Robinhood society. . . . We shall never more submit to decrees in chancery, or acts of parliament, annihilating charters, or abridging English liberties." Nevertheless, he concludes, the charge that "there are any who pant after 'independence' . . . is as great a slander upon the province as ever was committed to writing."[93] Here the writer—dealing frankly with the historic position of Massachusetts Bay in relation to the government of Great Britain—states that, previous to the beginning of the American crisis, the colony had submitted to decrees of chancery and the laws

---

[93] For the "Novanglus" letters see *Works of John Adams* (ed. C. F. Adams, 10 vols., Boston, 1850–6), IV, 1–177, with special reference to statements made on pp. 33, 37–8, 114, 117, 119, 122, 127–8, 131.

of Parliament and had upheld them as binding[94]—but now it could no longer do so, especially in so far as these affected the charter or limited American liberties.

Adams's position undoubtedly represented the attitude of other leaders in the colony, if not of the majority of the inhabitants in 1774.[95] In fact, when reflecting later upon the events of the years 1776 to 1775, he saw them as nothing less than revolutionary, and his comment was that "the revolution was complete in the minds of the [American] people . . . before the war commenced . . . on the 19th of April, 1775."[96]

---

[94] As evidence of the fundamental change in attitude of leading men in Massachusetts Bay by 1774 from that expressed in the midst of the Great War for the Empire, one need only repeat the resolution of the House of Representatives of 1758 stating: "The authority of all acts of parliament which concern the colonies, and extend to them, is ever acknowledged. . . . There is not a member of the general court, and we know no inhabitant within the bounds of the government, that ever questioned this authority" (Thomas Hutchinson: *The History of the Colony and Province of Massachusetts-Bay*, III, 47–8).

[95] In his fifth "Novanglus" letter, Adams asserted that as early as the mid-1760's nine-tenths of the people of the colony were "high whigs." See *Works* (C. F. Adams), IV, 73.

[96] *Ibid.*, X, 197.

CHAPTER VI

Other Colonies Prepare to Resist: New England and the Middle Colonies

W HAT proportion of the American people had become revolutionaries by 1774 will probably never be ascertained with accuracy. In times of great crisis, such as then obtained, great numbers of people were undoubtedly undecided and therefore uncommitted. Although they could not fail to be impressed by the realization that their fate depended upon the outcome of the bitter contest that was developing between those who sought to uphold the authority of the government of Great Britain and those who challenged that authority, some of them waited on the turn of events to see which side would emerge victorious. There were, nevertheless, two salient points which they could not ignore. It was clear toward the end of 1774 that the men who had come forward, openly prepared to resist by force of arms if need be, were often among the most prominent and well regarded in their respective communities and colonies; it was equally apparent that many of those who had ventured most openly to espouse the cause of Great Britain were being obliged either to disavow their loyalties or to flee their homes in order to escape the terroristic steps being directed against them. Yet there were still others who opposed the revolutionaries in 1774 but later joined their ranks. Such was the case of the Rev. Jeremy Belknap, pastor of the Congregational church in Dover, New Hampshire. When called upon to sign a solemn league and covenant to suspend all commercial intercourse with Great Britain, under the threat that refusal to do so would "evidence a Disposition enimical to or criminally negligent of the common safety,"[1] he refused to do so. On June 28, 1774, he presented his reasons at length. These embodied the central idea that

> "Tyranny in one shape is as odious to me as Tyranny in another. . . .
> Here is no Liberty of Conscience nor right of private judgment left
> to any person but all . . . must implicitly adopt & subscribe a Covenant
> drawn up by a few men without any lawful authority or else be
> stigmatized as Enemies to their Country. This is a species of Tyranny
> . . . as dangerous in its tendency as any acts of the British Parlia-
> ment . . . & the very first beginnings of such a spirit of lawless Imposi-
> tion & Restraint ought to be checked & discountenanced by every
> consistent Son of Liberty & every true friend to his Country."[2]

How the thirteen older North American colonies reacted to the
Coercive Acts and the trend toward united colonial action in defiance of the mother country in 1774 and 1775, can best be understood by a survey of their respective actions, which will form the
subject of this and the two chapters to follow.[3] Since the reaction
in Massachusetts Bay has been described in full in the previous
chapter, we will here consider the other New England and the
Middle colonies, moving from north to south.

New Hampshire

Among the colonies in 1774, New Hampshire, at least up to the
month of December, was held to be the most moderate in the
position assumed by its inhabitants on the issues that were to separate the Empire. For example, on June 25 a sloop arrived at Portsmouth loaded with tea. During the next few days the ship and cargo
were entered and twenty-seven chests of tea were placed in the
custom house. At a town meeting the people were informed of the

---

[1] This New Hampshire solemn league and covenant, drawn up by the Portsmouth
Committee of Correspondence, was patterned after the covenant of the town of Bos-
ton. For a copy of the New Hampshire document see the Massachusetts Historical
Society *Proceedings*, 2nd ser., II, 482–3.

[2] *Ibid.*, II, 484–5.

[3] For a view of each of the colonies at the middle of the eighteenth century see
Volumes II and III, revised, of this series; for their activities in the 1760's see Volume
X, which carries through the Stamp Act crisis, and Volume XI, which brings events
forward to the 1770's; see also the author's *The Coming of the Revolution, 1763–
1775* (New York and London, 1954), Chap. 9, "Old and New Northern Colonies,"
and Chap. 10, "Old and New Southern Colonies."

landing and a guard of freeholders was chosen to protect and defend the custom house until the consignee could reship the tea. Despite some efforts to assemble a group of radicals to obstruct the orderly procedure, the duty on the tea was publicly paid and the vessel and cargo set sail for Halifax on the 30th.[4] Nevertheless, New Hampshire gradually joined ranks with the other colonies. By July 21 the first provincial congress was held at Exeter; delegates to the Continental Congress were selected, money was voted for their expenses,[5] and a committee appointed to prepare their instructions. Moreover, when the heretofore popular Governor John Wentworth secretly managed to recruit carpenters to construct barracks for the British soldiers in Boston after the carpenters of that town had refused to do so, his action was denominated in the *New-Hampshire Gazette* as that of "an enemy . . . to the community."[6]

The incident that placed the popular leaders of New Hampshire in the front ranks of the revolutionaries, however, was the overwhelming on December 14 of the small garrison of Fort William and Mary, New Castle, located at the entrance of the harbour of Portsmouth. Although the commander of the fort, Captain John Cochran, put up the best possible defence against the attacking force of 400 men, he was wounded and temporarily placed in confinement. The King's colours were lowered at the fort, and a hundred barrels of the King's powder were seized by the marauders and carried off in boats. On the evening of the 15th, continuing their

---

[4] Governor John Wentworth to the Earl of Dartmouth, July 4, 1774, *New Hampshire Provincial Papers . . . Relating to the Province of New Hampshire, 1623–1800* (39 vols., eds. Nathaniel Bouton *et al.*, Concord, Manchester, and Nashua, 1867–1941), VII, 409–10. On September 8 another consignment of tea arrived—also, as in the case of the first shipment, directed to the agent of the East India Company, Edward Parry. Although Parry's home was stoned that night, the next day the magistrates took over and once again the consignee was permitted to reship the tea to Halifax. Wentworth to Dartmouth, September 13, 1774, *ibid.*, VII, 413–14.

[5] *Ibid.*, VII, 407–8 and 411–12.

[6] Wentworth to Dartmouth, November 15, 1774, *ibid.*, VII, 417–18, and *New-Hampshire Gazette, and Historical Chronicle*, October 28, 1774; see also Jeremy Belknap: *The History of New-Hampshire . . .* (3 vols., Boston, 1813), II, 287–8, L. S. Mayo: *John Wentworth, Governor of New Hampshire, 1767–1775* (Cambridge, Mass., 1921), pp. 138–9, and R. F. Upton: *Revolutionary New Hampshire . . .* (Hanover, N.H., 1963), Chap. 2. The last-named volume is especially good for its balanced treatment of events. It is of interest that the resolves inserted in the local paper denouncing the carpenters and those who had hired them to go to Boston, were signed by Hunking Wentworth, who, despite being the uncle of the Governor, was chairman of the Portsmouth committee of ways and means which drew up the resolutions. See Nathaniel Adams: *Annals of Portsmouth . . .* (Portsmouth, 1825), p. 246.

defiance of the government of Great Britain, the raiders returned to the fort and removed many of the King's cannon and some sixty muskets.[7] The Governor was helpless at the time to prevent this "insurrection." Yet, despite his growing unpopularity among the more radical inhabitants of the province and their open threats to his safety, with the coming of the new year fifty-five men banded together on January 17 to uphold law and order, to "defend and Protect Each other from Mobs[,] Riots or any unlawful attacks whatever, . . ." and to assume the special responsibility of guarding Wentworth. This protection continued until June 1775, when the Governor was obliged to seek refuge in the fort.[8]

Rhode Island

Little need be said with respect to Rhode Island and its support of the revolutionary cause.[9] While some voices in Newport, where the customs officers resided, were discreetly raised in favour of the policies of the King's government, their influence was of little avail in the face of the strength of the patriot group there and elsewhere in the colony. Within a week after news of the Boston Port Act had reached America, a town meeting held in Providence on May 17, 1774, resolved that an intercolonial congress be promoted "for establishing the firmest union." This has been called the first explicit movement in America for such a union.[10] The Newport town

[7] Governor Wentworth to General Gage, December 14 and 16, 1774, Captain Cochran to Governor Wentworth, December 14, 1774; see *New Hampshire Provincial Papers*, VII, 420–1 and 422, and Jeremy Belknap: *op. cit.*, III, Appendix, 328–31. See also Governor Wentworth's proclamation of December 26, 1774, *New Hampshire Provincial Papers*, VII, 423–4, and *New-Hampshire Gazette, and Historical Chronicle*, December 23, 1774, which fixes the number of powder barrels at 97. For an account of the disposition of the powder, see C. H. Bell: *History of the Town of Exeter* (Exeter, 1888); see also E. L. Page: "The King's Powder, 1774," *New England Quarterly*, XVIII, 83–92. It should be noted that on December 13 Paul Revere had arrived in Portsmouth from Boston with dispatches. Among the items of news he carried to the local committee of correspondence was word that Lord Dartmouth had sent a letter to all governors directing them to prevent the importation of munitions into the colonies, and the report that the inhabitants of Rhode Island had dispersed the artillery at Fort George, some of which had been purchased by that colony.

[8] See Kenneth Scott: "Tory Associators of Portsmouth," *William and Mary Quarterly*, 3rd ser., XVII, 507–15.

[9] For an account of the strong position of the radicals at the time of the *Gaspee* affair, see Chap. 1 of this volume.

[10] See *Rhode Island Colonial Records* (10 vols., ed. J. R. Bartlett, Providence, 1856–65), VII, 280, and S. G. Arnold: *History of the State of Rhode Island . . .* (2 vols., New York, 1859–60), II, 333–4.

meeting which followed on May 20 resulted in votes objecting to
"the injuries done to the town of Boston."[11] A letter from the committee of correspondence of the town of Westerly, sent to the Boston committee on May 19, seems to have expressed the attitude of
most of Rhode Islanders in its declaration that "This horrid attack
upon the town of *Boston*, we consider not as an attempt upon that
town singly, but upon the whole Continent." The hearty support
of the town was pledged for the measures taken.[12] So strong was
the revolutionary movement in this colony that the Assembly which
met in June[13] proceeded to endorse the Providence town-meeting
recommendations for calling a congress, and took steps to appoint
Stephen Hopkins and Samuel Ward as delegates[14]—thus again
taking the leadership in furthering the congress. However, the chief
emphasis of the colony during the major part of 1774 was on preparations for hostilities, with steps being taken for the reorganization
of the militia and the purchase of munitions of war.[15]

An additional action taken by Rhode Islanders in anticipation of
open resistance to Great Britain was the seizure and conveyance
to Providence of the armament at Fort George on Goat Island, consisting of the King's heavy artillery as well as the eighteen guns
belonging to the colony. When Captain Wallace of H.M.S. *Rose*
appeared at Newport on December 11 and learned that the fort had
been dismantled, he sought out Governor Joseph Wanton to inquire
the cause of this "extraordinary" step. According to Wallace, the
Governor "very frankly told me, they had done it to prevent their
falling into the hands of the King, or any of his servants; and that
they meant to make use of them, to defend themselves against any
power that shall offer to molest them."[16]

[11] See *Rhode Island Colonial Records*, VII, 281.

[12] Peter Force: *American Archives*, 4th ser., I, 336–7.

[13] For the action of the Assembly see *Rhode Island Colonial Records*, VII, 246–7.

[14] See W. E. Foster: *Stephen Hopkins, A Rhode Island Statesman . . .* , *Rhode
Island Historical Tracts*, No. 19 (2 vols., Providence, 1884), and William Gammell:
A Life of Samuel Ward in *The Library of American Biography*, 2nd ser., IX (ed.
Jared Sparks, Boston, 1846); see also the editor's introduction to *Correspondence of
Governor Samuel Ward, May 1775–March 1776* (ed. Bernhard Knollenberg, Provi-
dence, 1952).

[15] For the actions taken by the General Assembly in October for strengthening
the armed forces of the colony see *Rhode Island Colonial Records*, VII, 257–71;
see also D. S. Lovejoy: *Rhode Island Politics and the American Revolution, 1760–
1776* (Providence, 1958), pp. 173–9, and S. G. Arnold: *op. cit.*, II, 333–45.

[16] Extract of a letter from Captain Wallace to Vice-Admiral Graves, December 12,
1774, *Rhode Island Colonial Records*, VII, 306.

Connecticut

Connecticut was not so wholly committed to resistance to Great Britain as the other New England colonies in 1774. For example, about 1,000 people of Farmington assembled on May 19 at the liberty pole—upon hearing the news that the port of Boston had been blocked up—there resolved:

> "That the present Ministry, being instigated by the Devil, and led by their wicked and corrupt hearts, have a design to take away our liberties and properties, and to enslave us for ever. . . . That those pimps and parasites who dared to advise their master to such detestable measures, be held in utter abhorrence by . . . every American, and their names loaded with the curses of all succeeding generations."[17]

In contrast, the town of New Haven, when called upon by Boston to appoint a committee of correspondence, resolved to do so at a town meeting held on May 23, but the man placed as chairman of the committee was the ultra-conservative Joshua Chandler, who later became an uncompromising Loyalist. What is more, the town not only sent him to represent it in the General Assembly in 1774, but continued him in that post of trust until November 1775, when public sentiment finally compelled the town selectmen, of which he was one, to place him under house arrest.[18] Nevertheless, when the call came from Virginia to send delegates to the Continental Congress, even New Haven approved the step.

As for the Assembly, in May 1773 the House of Representatives had voted to set up a committee of correspondence. Thus it was able on June 3, 1774, by resolution to empower this committee to appoint deputies to the general congress of colonies.[19] The committee met at New London on July 13 and appointed five delegates, but three of them—including William Samuel Johnson, who had acted as London agent for the colony—declined to serve. As a result, it was only on August 3 at Hartford that the panel of delegates was fully made up.[20] The eastern part of the colony was, as had been true

---

[17] *American Archives,* 4th ser., I, 336.

[18] See L. H. Gipson: *Jared Ingersoll . . .* (New Haven, 1920), pp. 328–9.

[19] *Public Records of the Colony of Connecticut (1636–1776)* (eds. J. H. Trumbull and C. J. Hoadly, 15 vols., Hartford, 1850–90), XIV, 156, 324.

[20] *American Archives,* 4th ser., I, 554–5 and *n.*

in the past, greatly under the influence of Massachusetts Bay. It is therefore not surprising that the chief acts of terrorism took place there against those who expressed opinions unfavourable to the patriotic cause.[21] On the other hand, in western Connecticut, especially Fairfield County, the influence of the local Anglican clergy —who, as a group, were Loyalist in sentiment—was such that the patriotic cause lagged. Nevertheless, even in this area, once the Continental Congress had completed its task of committing the colonies to the Association, the towns gradually fell into line.[22]

New York

Turning to the Province of New York, it must be made clear that while in 1774 various towns, districts, and counties entered into resolutions bearing upon the crisis that confronted the Empire,[23] the citizens of the city of New York were the ones who carried the weight of making the decisions which largely determined the position taken by the colony as a whole. Also to be borne in mind is the internal situation in the province by 1774, which saw the Livingston and de Lancey political factions arrayed against each other, with the popular leaders lined up on the side of the Livingstons against the merchants who supported the aristocratic and conservative de Lanceys.[24]

---

[21] For such incidents as the treatment of the Rev. Samuel Peters of Hebron—who, as a Loyalist refugee, wrote and published in London his rather extraordinary *General History of Connecticut* (1781)—and the tarring and feathering at New London of a Captain Davis and at East Haddam of Dr. Beebe, another outspoken Loyalist, see *American Archives*, 4th ser., I, 711–12, 731–2, and 787. For Governor Gage's report to Dartmouth of how the Boston Committee of Correspondence had taken steps "to raise a flame . . . in the Colony of *Connecticut*," which was now abetting "popular rage . . . at the extremity of the Province," see *ibid.*, 4th ser., I, 741–3. For an excellent study of the struggle in Connecticut between conservatives and radicals see Oscar Zeichner: *Connecticut's Years of Controversy, 1750–1776* (Chapel Hill, N.C., 1949), Chaps. 9 and 10.

[22] *Ibid.*, pp. 180–7.

[23] For resolutions against the Coercive Acts entered into by inhabitants of Dutchess County (Poughkeepsie Precinct), Orange County (Orange Town), Queens County (Jamaica), Suffolk County (East Hampton, Huntington, and South Haven), Tryon County (Palatine District), Westchester County (Rye and the "borough town of Westchester"), see *American Archives,* 4th ser., I, 407, 420, 453, 506, 702–3, 726–7, 740–1, 1072–4. For Loyalist resolutions signed by 83 inhabitants of Rye, and those subscribed by five of the King's Justices and "a great number of the principal people" of the King's District, Albany County, see *ibid.*, I, 802–3, 1063.

[24] For the political struggles in New York during the period under consideration see C. L. Becker: *History of Political Parties in the Province of New York, 1760–1776*

After the temporary loss of political power by the radicals as a result of the failure of the non-importation movement in 1770, the popular leaders Isaac Sears, John Lamb, and Alexander McDougall were eager to make use of the crisis over the Coercive Acts to regain their political prestige.[25] On May 11 the ship *Sampson* arrived in New York, twenty-six days from London, bringing a copy of the *London Gazette* of April 5, in which was printed the Boston Port Act.[26] On the 16th, in consequence of this "very alarming News," a large body of city merchants met at the Exchange and, under the chairmanship of the wealthy Isaac Low (who later became a Loyalist), appointed a committee of fifty to carry the responsibility of corresponding with the other colonies on all matters of moment. On the 19th, in an address before a much more general meeting of people "of all Ranks"—including conservatives, moderates, and radicals—Low pleaded for reason in place of passion and asked those assembled to put aside "all little Party Distinctions, Feuds and Animosities."[27] And well he should, for the radicals had already set on foot a plan for a committee of twenty-five, most of whom leaned strongly toward the radical position.[28] By absorbing twenty-

(Madison, Wisc., 1909 and 1960). For a recent challenge to Becker, see M. M. Klein: "Democracy and Politics in Colonial New York," *New York History*, XL, 221–46. Two recent studies in this field, involving among other things residence requirements for seats in the Assembly as a partisan matter in which the Livingstons opposed the requirements, while the de Lanceys favoured them, are Roger Champagne: "Family Politics versus Constitutional Principles: The New York Assembly Elections of 1768 and 1769," *William and Mary Quarterly*, 3rd ser., XX, 57–79, and L. H. Leder: "The New York Elections of 1769: An Assault on Privilege," *Mississippi Valley Historical Review*, XLIX, 675–82. Another important study having to do with New York and the American Revolution is M. M. Klein's "Prelude to Revolution in New York: Jury Trials and Judicial Tenure," *William and Mary Quarterly*, 3rd ser., XVII, 439–62. The issue in the case of judicial tenure was between the Livingstons and Lieutenant Governor Colden, with the de Lanceys supporting the position taken by the Livingstons. An additional challenge to Becker is to be found in D. R. Gerlach's full-length study *Philip Schuyler and the American Revolution in New York, 1733–1777* (Lincoln, Neb., 1964).

[25] For a recent analysis of the radicals' attempt to use the Coercive Acts for local political purposes in New York, as revealed by Alexander McDougall's "Political memorandums relative to the Conduct of the Citizens on the Boston Port Bill" (Alexander McDougall Papers, Box 1, New-York Historical Society), see Roger Champagne: "New York and the Intolerable Acts, 1774," *New York Historical Society Quarterly*, XLV, 195–207.

[26] This was reprinted in the *New-York Gazette: and the Weekly Mercury*, May 16, 1774, cited hereafter as the *New-York Gazette*.

[27] For an account of the meetings of May 16 and 19, and a list of the committee of fifty-one, see *ibid.*, May 23, 1774.

[28] In the New-York Historical Society is a copy of a broadside issued by the radicals in favour of a committee of twenty-five with their names appended. For an excellent account of the formation of the committees see Note XIII, appended by editor

three of the members of this proposed committee and adding twenty-seven more, it had been possible for the factions on the 16th to agree upon the committee of fifty and the chairmanship of Low. At the meeting on the 19th the formation of such a committee was ratified, but with the addition of one more member.[29]

The first important task that confronted the committee of fifty-one was to answer the letters from Boston. On the 23rd a reply was agreed upon which lamented their "inability to relieve your anxiety by a decisive opinion." It suggested, nevertheless, that a solution might lie in a general congress of the colonies which should be assembled without delay.[30] At a meeting of the committee on June 29, one of the members, Alexander McDougall—a fiery agitator[31]— moved that five deputies be nominated to attend the Continental Congress and that their names be sent to the committee of mechanics for endorsement before seeking the approval of the freemen. After some debate, the committee voted that a decision on this point be postponed until July 4,[32] at which date the motion was defeated by a vote of 24 to 13. An additional abortive motion was made by Isaac Sears, an equally fiery agitator, that nominations for the five delegates should consist of conservatives Isaac Low and James Duane, Philip Livingston, a moderate tending toward the radical position, and radicals John Morin Scott and Alexander McDougall. However, the nominations ultimately went to Low, Duane, and Livingston, already named, to John Alsop, a friend of liberty but opposed to the independence of the colonies, and to John Jay, who later, as a member of the Continental Congress, was to support the Galloway proposal for a union of the colonies. The final action taken on July 4 was the

E. F. de Lancey to the *History of New York during the Revolutionary War* . . . (2 vols., New York, 1879, I, 428–48), written between 1783 and 1788 after he became an exile in England by Thomas Jones, a former justice of the Supreme Court of the Province of New York and a leading American Loyalist. In conjunction with the Jones *History*, the student is advised to use the pamphlet by H. P. Johnston: *Observations on Judge Jones' Loyalist History of the American Revolution. How Far is it an Authority?* (New York, 1880), which offers refutations of specific points.

[29] See C. L. Becker: *op. cit.* (1960 edn.), pp. 112–16, for an analysis of the political complexion of the committee of fifty-one; see also *New-York Historical Society Quarterly*, XLV, 196–7, in which Becker points to McDougall's "Political memorandums" to demonstrate that the committee of fifty-one, "instead of being a merchant-aristocratic counter to the radicals' Committee of Twenty-five, was itself the creation of the radicals who, only when the aristocrats had captured it . . . proposed their Committee of Twenty-five. . . ."

[30] For this letter see *American Archives*, 4th ser., I, 297–8.

[31] For Alexander McDougall's rise to prominence in 1769 see Volume XI in this series, Chap. 2.

[32] *American Archives*, 4th ser., I, 307.

decision to call a meeting of the inhabitants on the 7th to confirm these nominations or make alternative choices.[33]

Defeated in their objective, the radicals, by means of "an anonymous Advertisement," now called a meeting of inhabitants of the city to be held "in the Fields" on the 6th. Under the chairmanship of McDougall, this numerous gathering passed a series of resolutions which would commit the delegates to the Congress to work with the other colonies for a non-importation and non-exportation agreement that should remain in force until American rights and privileges had been secured.[34] The previous day, at Edward Bardin's tavern, a committee of mechanics had rejected two of the nominees for deputy to the Congress, Duane and Alsop, named by the committee of fifty-one, and substituted Leonard Lispenard and Alexander McDougall.[35] For this effort to take matters out of the hands of the committee of fifty-one, the radicals were rebuked when that committee met on the 7th. By a vote of 21 to 9 it disavowed the resolves of the 6th as "evidently calculated to throw an Odium on this Committee." It also agreed that the motion and act to repudiate the resolves should be printed in the press.[36] At the same time, to prevent a sharp division in the city, agreement was reached to appoint a committee to meet with a similar committee "from the Mechanics" on the 8th in order that a plan might be agreed upon whereby each ward of the city should be canvassed for the opinion of the taxpayers on representation in the Continental Congress. However, that same day, at a meeting that had been called at the Coffee House, the committee of fifty-one was in turn rebuked. For the inhabitants who assembled were influenced by the radicals to reject the resolves submitted by the committee. The following day, that is, the 8th, eleven of the most radical members of the committee resigned. Then, on the 19th, in response to an anonymous printed announcement, a second meeting of inhabitants was held at the Coffee House. At this meeting certain resolves were adopted and a new committee of fifteen was appointed to take the place of the committee of fifty-one. This committee, although weighted with radicals, also included such moderates as Low,

[33] *Ibid.*, I, 308–9.

[34] For these resolutions see *New-York Gazette*, July 11, 1774, and C. L. Becker: *op. cit.*, p. 123.

[35] See the "Advertisement" broadside of July 6, 1774, *Broadsides, etc., . . . relating to America, 1700–1840* (2 vols., New York, 1847), I, as cited by C. L. Becker *op. cit.*, p. 123n.

[36] For these proceedings see *New-York Gazette*, July 11, 1774.

Jay, Henry Remsen, and John Moore. Just as the radicals had resigned from the committee of fifty-one on the 8th, so on the 20th the four men just named—none of whom, it would appear, had been at the Coffee House on the 19th—resigned from the new committee. In doing so they made public as their reasons that the appointment of this new committee had been carried out without previous notice and was no part of the business for which the inhabitants had been assembled, that the meeting was irregular, and that it seemed to cast "an insidious reflection on the Committee of Correspondence" and therefore tended to divide the city into factions and parties.[37]

Out of this confusion order was achieved on July 25, when a proposal for selecting delegates to the Continental Congress was made and adopted by the committee of fifty-one. It recommended that an election be held in each ward of the city, to be supervised by aldermen, common councilmen, and vestrymen, as well as by two members of the committee of fifty-one and two from the committee of mechanics. The following day, a subcommittee of the committee of fifteen wrote to the five delegates named by the committee of fifty-one asking them to pledge that, if elected to go to the Continental Congress, they would use their utmost endeavours to secure a non-importation agreement. When a written reply was received from the five stating that "a general Non-Importation Agreement, faithfully observed, would prove the most efficacious means to procure a Redress of our Grievances," opposition disappeared. On the 27th the radicals gave their unanimous approval.[38] It is needless to add that the delegates from New York were in the conservative camp during the proceedings of the Congress. They and their conservative supporters in the province, especially the men of wealth, were doubtless fearful of the republican tendencies of such men as Isaac Sears, John Lamb, and Alexander McDougall.

Openly active as Loyalists at this juncture were Anglican clergymen[39] such as the Rev. Samuel Seabury, rector of the Church at West Chester, whose pamphlets published in New York in November and December of 1774—*The Congress Canvassed: or, an Examination into the Conduct of the Delegates, at their Grand Convention,*

---

[37] For the proceedings of the radicals on July 19 with their resolves and the letter of resignation of the four moderates from the new committee on the 20th see *New-York Gazette*, July 25, 1774.

[38] For the proceedings of July 25–27 see *ibid.*, August 1, 1774.

[39] For evidence of the willingness of some Episcopal clergymen to support a non-importation agreement see *New-York Historical Society Quarterly*, XLV, 203.

Held in Philadelphia, . . . followed by *Free Thoughts on The Proceedings of the Continental Congress, Held at Philadelphia, Sept. 5, 1774 . . .* and *A View of the Controversy between Great-Britain and her Colonies . . .* —tried to stem the tide against Great Britain. There was also Myles Cooper, President of King's College, whose *The American Querist: or, Some Questions Proposed Relative to The Present Disputes between Great Britain, and her American Colonies* was published in the fall of 1774, as was his *A Friendly Address to all Reasonable Americans . . .* , replies to which provoked the Rev. Thomas Bradbury Chandler to write *The Strictures on the Friendly Address Examined. . . .* Chandler, the rector of St. John's Church at Elizabethtown, New Jersey, also produced *What think ye of the Congress Now? . . .* (on the Galloway plan of union), both of his pamphlets appearing in New York in 1775. Finally, among the clergy must be counted that ardent Loyalist Charles Inglis of the Trinity Church of New York, who later became bishop of Nova Scotia.

In addition to the clergymen who openly and effectively supported the cause of loyalism within the province, there were prominent men like the great Indian Superintendent Sir William Johnson, whose family was entrenched in the Mohawk Valley. Although Sir William passed away on July 11, 1774, Johnson Hall remained a rallying point for supporters of the authority of the British government. Nor must we fail to mention the influence exerted by Loyalist publisher James Rivington or his *Gazetteer*—a colonial newspaper that, according to a statement made in its columns on October 13, 1774, was "constantly distributed thro' every colony of North-America" as well as in the West Indies and elsewhere in the English-speaking world. Nevertheless, once the Association was formed at the Continental Congress, it was to be rigidly enforced in New York. At least this was true in New York City, where on November 22, 1774, an election held at the City Hall set up a new committee, consisting of sixty members, to carry out the embargo against Great Britain. Yet the province remained a divided one in the course of the war that began in the spring of the following year.[40]

---

[40] The late Professor Becker's *History of Political Parties in the Province of New York, 1760–1776* still remains the best secondary source for the ramifications of the political developments during the period under consideration; see also A. C. Flick: *Loyalism in New York during the American Revolution* (Columbia University *Studies in History* XIV, No. 1, New York and London, 1901), Chaps. 1 and 2, W. C. Abbott: *New York in the American Revolution* (New York, 1929), Chaps. 5 and 6, and Virginia D. Harrington: *The New York Merchant on the Eve of the Revolution* (New York, 1935), Chap. 9. One extremely valuable source of information not used by any

New Jersey

The people of New Jersey, like those of New York, were divided in 1774 in their attitude toward measures that should be taken against Great Britain. The area that comprehended what had been the Province of East New Jersey—largely settled by the Dutch and people from New England—was much more active in supporting the cause of Massachusetts Bay than the western part of the province, which, as was the case when it had been the Province of West New Jersey, was dominated by the Quakers.[41] It is therefore not surprising that on June 11 a gathering of Essex County freeholders and other inhabitants, held at Newark, passed strong resolutions in support of Boston, favouring representation in the Continental Congress, and for the adoption of a general non-importation agreement. To promote these ends by means of a provincial convention, a committee of correspondence was appointed.[42] Among the members of this committee was William Livingston, who—before 1772, when he took up New Jersey residence at "Liberty Hall" in Essex County—had for many years been a very articulate critic of the British administration of the colonies in general and particularly as it affected the Province of New York.[43]

Writing to the Earl of Dartmouth about the Essex County meeting, Governor William Franklin took the position that although there was

of the above writers is *Historical Memoirs . . . 1763–1776 of William Smith . . .* (ed. W. H. W. Sabine, New York, 1956), especially pp. 156–256. These memoirs reveal how Smith, a leading Whig closely associated with Alexander McDougall, gradually moved away from the radicals. Like Galloway, he favoured an American parliament with ties to Great Britain, and when this could not be secured he, too, became a Loyalist. In this connection the student should read Dorothy R. Dillon: *The New York Triumvirate: A Study of the Legal and Political Careers of William Livingston, John Morin Scott, William Smith, Jr.* (New York, 1949), particularly Chap. 7.

For landlordism in Dutchess County and sectional differences within the county in 1774–5, see the first part of Staughton Lynd's "Who Should Rule at Home? Dutchess County, New York, in the American Revolution," *William and Mary Quarterly*, 3rd ser., XVIII, 330–7.

[41] For the respective orientations of East and West New Jersey at the middle of the eighteenth century see Volume III, revised, of this series, Chap. 6.

[42] For the Essex County resolves see *Pennsylvania Gazette*, June 29, 1774. As New Jersey did not have a newspaper an advertisement for the meeting was inserted in the *New-York Journal; or, the General Advertiser* issue of June 9.

[43] For the earlier activities of Livingston in company with radicals John Morin Scott and William Smith, Jr., the last-mentioned later to become a Loyalist, see Dorothy R. Dillon: *op. cit.*

a widespread desire on the part of leading New Jersey men to hold a general meeting of representatives from the various colonies, this did not alarm him since he felt the chief purpose of such a meeting would be "to fall upon Measures for accommodating the present Differences between the two Countries, and preventing the like in the future." In fact, according to the Governor, many of the friends of government in his province had come to the conclusion that an American congress, if properly authorized by the King and consisting of the Governors of the colonies together with some members of the respective colonial councils and assemblies, would be productive of much good to the British Empire in general, especially if there were also present "some Gentlemen of Abilities, Moderation and Candour from Great Britain commissioned by His Majesty for that Purpose."[44]

One may well stop to reflect on what might have been the consequences for the Empire had Governor Franklin's suggestion met with approval—even assuming that before such a gathering were called the Continental Congress had met and agreed upon a program of coercing the government of Great Britain to repeal the laws directed against Massachusetts Bay. Was it already too late to reach an accommodation? Were the advocates of measures that would lead inevitably to a war for the independence of the colonies firmly in control of the destinies of the colonies by the fall of 1774? Obviously, no clear answer can be given to these questions, but they point up the problems of colonial administration that faced the home government and the struggle for political equality that motivated American leaders. For—granted that there was no precedent for such a meeting, which would have meant treating dependent colonials as equals, and that any men acting on behalf of the British government would have had to have more than a Crown commission in order to commit Parliament—no harm surely could have resulted from a congress of this nature held in America and conceivably some fundamental plan of conciliation might have been the outcome of its deliberations. The time was ripe for some sort of dramatic move. Had a congress so conceived been able to be truly representative of all the factions, and with the advantages it offered of breaching distance and delay in communications by having some high British officials on the spot to observe the circumstances and the temper of the American people,

---

[44] Franklin to Dartmouth, June 28, 1774, *New Jersey Archives*, 1st ser., X, 464–5. Since the Governor wrote that the meeting was "on Saturday last," it would appear that his letter was dated on June 18 rather than on June 28.

it might have brought about a mutuality of ideas. But Dartmouth could not commit Parliament, and the tenor of that body, together with the attitude of the King and his close advisers in the middle of 1774, was not conducive to so startling an innovation for handling the unwieldy reins of imperial administration while remaining within the framework of existing constitutional practice.

On June 25 a well-attended meeting was held in Bergen County at which resolutions similar to those passed in Essex County were agreed upon;[45] they were followed on the 27th by resolves entered into by the inhabitants of Morris County,[46] on July 4, of Somerset County,[47] and on July 8 by those of Hunterdon County.[48] Even the counties in western New Jersey that had been lagging behind now responded. Certain people of Salem County on July 15 passed resolutions even more stirring than some of the resolves taken by the more eastern countries;[49] this was followed by the action taken in Gloucester County on July 18,[50] when county meetings were called for the election of delegates to the proposed Continental Congress. Other counties went on record with similar resolves; so that by July 21 it was possible to have a general meeting of county committees at New Brunswick, where seventy-two delegates gathered and remained in session for three days. Out of this meeting came the election of the five New Jersey delegates (including James Kinsey, the Quaker, and William Livingston) to the Continental Congress, the demand for a general non-importation and non-exportation agreement among the colonies, and a resolve "that the claim of the British Parliament (in which we neither are, nor can be represented) to make laws which shall be binding . . . 'in all cases whatsoever,' and particularly for imposing taxes . . . is unconstitutional and oppressive. . . ."[51]

Despite the various spirited resolves passed within the province, the New Jersey delegates to the Continental Congress took the moderate position. In fact, two of them—Kinsey and John DeHart—

---

[45] For these resolves see *New-York Gazette*, July 4, 1774.

[46] *Pennsylvania Gazette*, July 6, 1774.

[47] *New-York Gazette*, July 14, 1774.

[48] *Pennsylvania Gazette*, July 13, 1774.

[49] For example, the 4th resolve passed at the Salem meeting declared that the Iron Act (23 Geo. II, c. 29) was "an absolute infringement of the natural rights of the subject, and of an equal tendency [as the Boston Port Bill] to enslave America" (*Pennsylvania Journal*, July 20, 1774).

[50] For these resolves see *ibid.*

[51] For these resolves see *Pennsylvania Gazette*, July 27, 1774.

when elected to the Second Continental Congress, resigned from that body apparently because of the course it was taking.[52] Nevertheless, all the delegates gave their approval to the work of the Congress, including the agreement on the Association. When the New Jersey Assembly met at Perth Amboy on January 13, 1775, William Livingston, Elias Boudinot,[53] and John DeHart used their talents to persuade the members to approve this work. They succeeded in spite of the efforts of Kinsey to commit the Assembly instead to petition the King so that by royal instructions the Governors could consent to acts of the assemblies "to choose Delegates to meet in Congress (either in England or America) with such other Persons as his Majesty should please to appoint in Order to form some plan for accommodating Matters on a permanent & Constitutional Foundation. . . ."[54] The truth is that the province remained divided in sentiment on the proper course for the American people to pursue in facing the great issue now before them.

Pennsylvania

No colony offered a more delicate problem for the radicals, in their efforts to stir up the inhabitants to commitments of opposition to Great Britain, than did the Province of Pennsylvania in 1774. It was a haven for many pacifistic sects[55] which had no serious quarrel with the mother country over colonial policies, and whose members were grateful for the protection afforded within the Empire to live their lives freely according to their religious principles. They therefore were opposed to every proposal that would tend to alienate the inhabitants from obedience to the government of Great Britain. No one more fully realized this fact than did Charles Thomson, the Philadelphia politician and merchant, described by John Adams as

---

[52] See Governor Franklin to Dartmouth, January 5, 1776, *New Jersey Archives*, 1st ser., X, 676–8; see also D. L. Kemmerer: *Path to Freedom. The Struggle for Self-Government in Colonial New Jersey* (The Princeton History of New Jersey, III, Princeton and London, 1940).

[53] See G. A. Boyd: *Elias Boudinot, Patriot and Statesman, 1740–1821* (Princeton, 1952).

[54] Extract of a letter from Governor Franklin to Joseph Galloway, March 12, 1775, *New Jersey Archives*, 1st ser., X, 575–9.

[55] For a discussion of Pennsylvania at mid-century see Volume III, revised, of this series, Chap. 7.

"the Sam. Adams of Phyladelphia—the Life of the Cause of Liberty, they say."[56] In a long letter, written to William Henry Drayton of South Carolina, during the course of the War for American Independence, he told of the difficulties met by those in the province who favoured resistance to Great Britain after the passing of the Boston Port Bill.[57] In order to surmount these obstacles, according to Thomson, he and John Dickinson took account of the measures which should be pursued and which "were secretly concerted between them." They decided to call a mass meeting. But prior to this, in order to prevent the conservatives—particularly those of the Quaker persuasion who wished to limit the action of Pennsylvanians to a petition from the Assembly—from disrupting their plan, they called in Joseph Reed[58] and Thomas Mifflin. Gathering at Dickinson's home, the four agreed upon a plan of strategy for the meeting. The plan was that Reed should preside and speak first, to be followed by Mifflin and Thomson, who would advocate extreme measures, and then by Dickinson, who—with his great prestige, gained especially by his *Letters from a Pennsylvania Farmer*—would counsel more moderate steps than the other two, so as to prevent the conservatives from seceding from the meeting. At the same time Dickinson would also propose that a petition be sent to Governor Penn asking him to call a meeting of the Assembly.

Although the meeting held in the City Tavern long room at Philadelphia on May 20 was lively and turbulent,[59] the strategy adopted by the four worked. The meeting resulted in agreement to

---

[56] *The Adams Papers*, 1st ser., *Diary and Autobiography of John Adams* (eds. L. H. Butterfield *et al.*, 4 vols., Cambridge, Mass., 1961), II, 115; see also J. J. Zimmerman: "Charles Thomson, 'The Sam Adams of Philadelphia,'" *Mississippi Valley Historical Review*, XLV, 464–80.

[57] For this letter see *Pennsylvania Magazine of History and Biography*, II, 411–23.

[58] Reed also left an account of the steps taken to bring Pennsylvania in line with Massachusetts Bay. For his version, which conflicts somewhat with Thomson's, see the New-York Historical Society *Collections for 1878* (pp. xii and 269–73), which also publishes Thomson's account (pp. 274–8); see also J. F. Watson: *Annals of Philadelphia and Pennsylvania* (2 vols., Philadelphia, 1870), II, 325.

[59] According to Thomson, the "tumult and disorder was past description" (*Pennsylvania Magazine*, II, 415). Edward Tilghman, who had recently returned from study at Middle Temple, after attending the meeting, noted in a letter of May 26, 1774, to his father in Maryland that among those who spoke in opposition to the positions taken by Reed and Thomson was the Rev. William Smith. For an excerpt of the Tilghman letter see C. J. Stillé: *Life and Times of John Dickinson, 1732–1808* (Historical Society of Pennsylvania *Memoirs*, XIII, Philadelphia, 1891), pp. 107–8. For a study of the position taken by the conservative merchants of Philadelphia at this period see A. L. Jensen: *The Maritime Commerce of Colonial Philadelphia* (Madison, 1963), Chap. 13, "Armed Truce and Renewed Conflict, 1770–1774."

appoint a committee of nineteen, of which the four were to be members, which should wait upon the Governor to induce him to call the Assembly into session, should express the sympathy of the people of Philadelphia to the Bostonians for their plight, and, finally, should carry on a general correspondence with the other colonies.[60] Thomas Wharton,[61] writing to Thomas Walpole on May 31 about the meeting, stated:

> ". . . two persons very strenuously insisted that the city should enter into the proposals of nonexportation and nonimportation, and that we should aid and support the Bostonians in every respect. . . . Several persons who had never before met at any of their meetings thought it quite time to interpose, and not suffer those warm and violent men to carry measures as they pleased, attended that evening, among whom I was one, and we entered the lists and opposed their measures with so much resolution and firmness, that every step which appeared . . . to inflame was entirely set aside. . . ."[62]

But the major point was won.

The committee of nineteen met again on May 21 and addressed letters to other colonies. In the one sent to Boston the sense of the mass meeting was reported as being that "you are considered as now suffering in the general Cause"; and that the calling of "a general Congress of Deputies from the different Colonies, clearly to state what we conceive to be our Rights . . . we have Reason to think, would be most agreeable to the People of this Province, and the first Step that ought to be taken."[63] However, there was a feeling that further support of the plan for resistance was needed from the inhabitants of Philadelphia. It was therefore decided to call a meet-

---

[60] For accounts of the meeting, see *Pennsylvania Gazette,* May 25 and June 8, 1774. The names of the committee of nineteen together with the instructions are given in the edition of June 8.

[61] Thomas Wharton—not to be confused with his cousin Samuel Wharton, whose activities in connection with land company matters have been described in Volume XI of this series, Chap. 13—was to become president of the Supreme Executive Council of Pennsylvania in 1777.

[62] See "Letters of Thomas Wharton, of Philadelphia, 1773–1783," *Pennsylvania Magazine of History and Biography,* XXXIII, 336–9.

[63] For the letter to Boston, dated May 21, 1774, see *Pennsylvania Gazette,* June 8, 1774. According to Theodore Thayer (*Pennsylvania Politics and the Growth of Democracy, 1740–1776* [Harrisburg, 1953], p. 156), the letter was "said to have been written for the committee by the Rev. William Smith," Provost of the College of Philadelphia and a member of the committee of nineteen, and to have been "much too mild in tone to please the Radicals." Thayer gives as his source William Smith Notes and Papers, Vol. 9, Historical Society of Pennsylvania.

ing at the State House. "This," noted Thomson, "required great address [as] The Quakers had a aversion to town meetings, and always opposed them." However, arrangements were so managed that they gave their consent, but in order to satisfy both Quakers and other conservatives it was necessary for the designated speakers —the Rev. William Smith, a conservative, Joseph Reed, a moderate radical, and Charles Thomson, an extreme radical—to write down what they intended to say and submit these remarks to the prior scrutiny of the men chosen to chair the approaching meeting, Judge Thomas Willing of the Pennsylvania Supreme Court and John Dickinson. At a "very large and respectable Meeting of the Free-holders and Freemen of the City and County of Philadelphia" held on June 18 these gentlemen spoke as planned. Apparently only Smith's address was considered suitable for publication in the face of the powerful opposition within the province to any extreme measures. In his remarks, Smith emphasized points that would ap-peal to the Quakers—that nothing should be done in heat and passion and that the great task before them was to help in "closing that breach; and restoring that harmony from which, in our better days, Great-Britain and her Colonies derived mutual strength and glory . . ."[64]

But the resolves approved on June 18 were hardly in the spirit of the Smith address. The action of Parliament in closing the port of Boston was denounced as being unconstitutional and a congress of deputies from the North American colonies "for securing our rights and liberties . . . on a constitutional foundation" was urged. To achieve these ends and bring aid to Boston it was resolved that a committee of forty-three persons, named therewith, be appointed. It was this committee, made up of conservatives, moderates, and radicals, that was also empowered to appoint delegates to the proposed congress, thus by-passing the Assembly.[65]

When the first meeting of Philadelphians at the City Tavern on May 20 had authorized the committee of nineteen there appointed to ask the Governor to call the Assembly, a petition had been cir-culated and signed by "near nine hundred respectable Freeholders in and near the City of Philadelphia." The sole purpose for calling the

---

[64] For Thomson's account of these events, which lists an additional "president" chosen for the meeting, the Quaker merchant Edward Pennington, see Stillé's biog-raphy of Dickinson, Historical Society of Pennsylvania *Memoirs*, XIII, 344. For Smith's address see *Pennsylvania Gazette*, June 22, 1774.

[65] See *ibid.* for the resolves of June 18, 1774.

Assembly, according to the petition, was to take into account the fact that the act closing the port of Boston and involving its inhabitants "in one common ruin" was designed "to compel the Americans to acknowledge the right of Parliament to impose taxes upon them at pleasure. . . ."[66] As a reply to the petition, the Governor and his Council on June 7 framed the following statement: "Upon all occasions when the peace, order and tranquillity of the Province require it, I shall be ready to convene the Assembly; but as that does not appear to me to be the case at present, I cannot think such a step would be expedient, or consistent with my duty."[67] However, later developments led him and the Council to alter their view. People in Chester and Northampton counties entered into resolutions in favour of a general congress of the colonies.[68] In other counties the inhabitants were also demanding support of the cause of Boston at various general meetings. In view of this trend, it now seemed wise to Governor Penn to head off the radicals by calling the Assembly, the majority of whose members were—as a result of the weighted system of election in the older counties—strongly conservative, being either Quaker or Anglican.[69] An added impetus for taking this step undoubtedly came from the action taken by the Philadelphia committee of forty-three in sending a circular letter to the various counties. This communication had called for a meeting of county committees of correspondence on July 15, at which time, the letter stated, the Speaker of the Assembly would call an informal meeting of the representatives as individuals "to take into their consideration our very alarming situation"; this was to be preparatory to a formal convention scheduled for the 18th of the month.[70]

At the session held on July 15 all eleven counties were represented, although out of the total of seventy-five deputies the new county of Bedford had but one and the even newer counties of Northumberland and Westmoreland but two each, as against thirty-four repre-

---

[66] For the above petition see *American Archives*, 4th ser., I, 391-2.

[67] For the reply see *ibid.*, I, 391, and *Pennsylvania Colonial Records*, X, 177.

[68] For the Chester County resolves of June 18 and the Northampton resolves of June 21 see *American Archives*, 4th ser. I, 428 and 435-6, and *Pennsylvania Gazette*, June 29, 1774.

[69] Theodore Thayer: *Israel Pemberton, King of the Quakers* (Philadelphia, 1943), p. 208.

[70] For this circular letter see *Pennsylvania Gazette*, July 6, 1774. It stated that the "Speaker of the Assembly, in a very obliging and ready manner, had agreed to comply with the request. . . ." It would seem that Joseph Galloway, the Speaker, had come to the conclusion that the presence of the Assembly representatives at the convention of the county committees would have a moderating effect.

senting the city and county of Philadelphia. However, agreement was reached that, in case of any difference of opinion, the vote should be by county. It is clear that the resolutions presented on that day had been carefully prepared in advance. Fourteen were agreed upon unanimously, including the 5th, stating that the passage of the Declaratory Act by Parliament was unconstitutional, and the 9th, calling for a general congress as absolutely necessary.[71] The 11th, passed by "a great majority," was an agreement to join the other colonies in non-importation and non-exportation agreements if the forthcoming Continental Congress were to judge this expedient; while the 12th, passed by "a majority," was to the effect that should Parliament enter upon new measures which in the eyes of the Congress might require further steps, beyond non-importation agreements, the inhabitants of Pennsylvania would join in such unspecified steps. The 14th, adopted unanimously, declared that the people of the province would cease all business relations with anyone who refused to carry out the general plan adopted by the Congress. The 16th, also adopted unanimously, was that a committee of eleven to represent the convention should prepare instructions "on the present situation of publick affairs" to the members of the Assembly and also request these legal representatives to appoint a proper number of persons to attend the projected Congress.[72] This represented an alteration in the plan adopted at the June 18 meeting, which had specified that the committee of correspondence of forty-three was to have the power to select deputies to the Congress. Joseph Galloway as Speaker of the Assembly, while agreeable to a meeting of deputies from the colonies, was bitterly opposed to such irregular procedure. In a letter written on June 28 to the Massachusetts Bay Committee of Correspondence, signed by himself and three other members of the Assembly as the "Committee of Correspondence," it was stated that the "great cause of *American* rights" should be left to the legally elected representatives of the people, as they alone were properly vested with the constitutional power of redressing grievances, and that to proceed in any other way until this approach had failed would

---

[71] Professor Theodore Thayer points out in his *Pennsylvania Politics* . . . (p. 159) that nearly all the delegates from the west were Whigs ready to support the plans of the Philadelphia radicals.

[72] For the membership of the convention and the resolves adopted by it, as well as the membership of the committee of eleven, of which John Dickinson was chairman, and the instructions that it drew up, see *Pennsylvania Gazette,* July 27, 1774.

be improper.[73] In the light of Galloway's entrenched position and his continued great influence within the province, even the more radical leaders of the resistance doubtless realized that it was best to depend upon the Assembly for the choice of the delegates to the Continental Congress and to satisfy themselves with preparing instructions to remind those so chosen of their duty in these perilous times.[74]

The outbreak of Indian hostilities in the Ohio Valley, described in Volume IX of this series—together with the probability that, unless the Assembly were summoned, the province would be represented in the approaching Continental Congress by those with revolutionary ideas and a revolutionary program—led Governor Penn to convene the Assembly on July 18. His message to the opening session was confined to the Indian troubles. But uppermost in the minds of the members was the crisis confronting the colonies. Thus, on July 22 a motion was passed that the calling of a congress of deputies of the colonies was an absolute necessity. On the same day they also voted that a committee of seven members of the Assembly, or any four of them, should represent the province as delegates. The committee of seven had as its leader Speaker Galloway; the other members were Samuel Rhoads and Charles Humphreys, both moderates, and Thomas Mifflin, John Morton, George Ross, and Edward Biddle, identified with the radicals. The following day a report of an Assembly committee appointed to draw up instructions for the deputies to the Congress was approved, as was a circular letter to the various colonies, both couched in the most moderate terms—thus completely ignoring the more radical instructions to the Assembly that the convention of county committees had framed.[75] Not only that, but the desire of the convention that John Dickinson, James Wilson, and Thomas Willing be among the delegates to the Congress was ignored, since they were not members of the Assembly.[76] However, it should be noted that in the Assembly election held in the fall of 1774, Dickinson was returned as a member from the County of Phil-

---

[73] For this letter see *American Archives*, 4th ser., I, 485–6; for a strong criticism of this letter, dated New York, July 14, but unsigned, see *ibid.*, p. 486n.

[74] See Ernest H. Baldwin: "Joseph Galloway, the Loyalist Politician," *Pennsylvania Magazine of History and Biography*, XXVI, 303–8.

[75] For the proceedings of the Assembly during the brief session of July 18–23, see *Votes of Assembly, Pennsylvania Archives*, 8th ser., VIII, 7085–7102; see also *American Archives*, 4th ser., I, 602–10.

[76] See the account sent by Charles Thomson to William Henry Drayton in the late 1770's, *Pennsylvania Magazine of History and Biography*, II, 418 and *n.*

adelphia, and was on October 15 unanimously chosen as an additional delegate to the Congress.[77] Also of interest was the unanimous choice as Speaker of a man aligned with the radicals, Edward Biddle of Berks County. Galloway, however, was elected to the House from Bucks County. The decline of conservative influence in the Assembly was now apparent as the province became increasingly caught up in the vortex of the revolutionary movement.[78]

The Three Lower Counties on the Delaware

The inhabitants of the Three Counties on the Delaware[79] had for a decade been largely under the leadership of three men of great influence: Thomas McKean of New Castle, who in 1773 had been Speaker of the Assembly, Attorney General George Read, also of New Castle, and Cæsar Rodney of Kent County, Speaker of the Assembly in 1774. These three men had been among the most active opponents of the Stamp Act in 1765, and in 1768 had composed the committee of correspondence which drew up the address to the King in condemnation of the Townshend legislation. After the news arrived of the closing of the port of Boston, two of them, Read and McKean, with John McKinly, all of New Castle County and constituting the committee of correspondence of the colony, wrote to the Virginia Committee of Correspondence on May 26. This letter stated: "We consider each Colony on this Continent as parts of the same Body, and an Attack on one to affect all." It advised that the people of Delaware would undoubtedly support a non-importation, non-exportation agreement and approve the idea of a general congress.[80] However, it was not until June 17 that a call was sent out—doubtless drawn up by the committee—for all freeholders of New Castle County eligible to vote for representatives to the Assembly to meet at the court house in the town of New Castle on June 29.[81] On that

---

[77] For a list of members elected to the Assembly in October 1774, see *Votes of the House of Representatives,* from December 29, 1773 (Philadelphia, 1774), p. 53, and *Pennsylvania Archives,* 8th ser., VIII, 7148 and 7152.

[78] For a standard account of developments in Pennsylvania during the year 1774 see C. H. Lincoln: *The Revolutionary Movement in Pennsylvania, 1760–1776* (Philadelphia, 1901), p. 159–88.

[79] For a view of the Delaware Counties in 1750, see Volume III, revised, of this series, Chap. 8.

[80] See *Journals of the Virginia House of Burgesses, 1773–1776,* p. 149.

[81] Postscript to the *Pennsylvania Gazette,* June 29, 1774.

date some 500 freeholders assembled and, under the chairmanship of McKean, passed resolutions not only denouncing the closing of the port of Boston and supporting the proposal for a Continental Congress, but for taking additional steps to see that the three Delaware counties would participate in the congress. Among those steps was a plan for a committee of correspondence of thirteen, appointed therewith, to request Speaker Rodney to call the several members of the Assembly—who were not to be convened in legal session until September 30—to meet informally at New Castle not later than August 1 in order to take into consideration the alarming situation in America and appoint deputies to the projected congress.[82] On July 11 the committee addressed such a letter to the Speaker at Dover.[83] While Rodney was heartily in favour of the plan, as he indicated in a letter to the New Castle committee, he also expressed the view that, in light of the complaint voiced by the people of Kent and Sussex counties that they had been ignored in making the decisions, it would be well to wait until at least the people of his own county had met and come to resolutions.[84] On July 20 over 700 people of Kent County gathered at Dover and, despite an expression of displeasure at the decisions taken without them, passed resolves similar to those of New Castle County.[85] With two of the three counties now behind him and without waiting for the results of the Sussex meeting, scheduled for a later date, Rodney invited the eighteen representatives of the Three Counties to appear on August 1.[86] At a

[82] See W. T. Read: *Life and Correspondence of George Read* (Philadelphia, 1870), pp. 88–9; see also *Pennsylvania Gazette*, July 6, 1774.

[83] *Letters to and from Cæsar Rodney, 1756–1784* (ed. G. H. Ryden, Philadelphia, 1933), pp. 38–9. The letter was enclosed with one by Read to the Speaker signed on July 13, which indicates that the Attorney General was apparently the most active person in New Castle County in promoting the participation of Delaware in the approaching congress. For Read to Rodney see *ibid.*, p. 40.

[84] Rodney to the New Castle committee, July 15, 1774, *ibid.*, p. 41.

[85] For the Kent County resolves see *Delaware History*, VI, 92–4. These are among the documents edited by Harold Hancock in his article on "Kent County Loyalists," in *ibid.*, VI, 3–24 and 92–139; see also W. T. Read: *op. cit.*, pp. 89–90, and Rodney to Read, July 21, 1774, *Letters to and from Rodney*, pp. 41–2.

[86] See Rodney's letter of July 21 to Representative Charles Ridgely of Kent County, *ibid.*, pp. 42–3. In his letter to Read of July 21, Rodney indicated that the people of Sussex County were reportedly so offended at being slighted that they were determined, when they met, to appoint their own deputy to the congress. This did not materialize. It may be noted, however, that Thomas Robinson, merchant, land-owner, and the most prominent citizen of Sussex County, was sought as a delegate to the Continental Congress, but refused the appointment. In fact, Robinson opposed sending any delegation from the Three Counties and subsequently became an active Loyalist. See Harold Hancock: "Thomas Robinson: Delaware's Most Prominent Loyalist," *Delaware History*, IV, 1–36.

meeting of Sussex County freeholders held at Lewes (Lewestown, Lewistown) on July 23, when the question was put as to whether or not they should concur in the decisions made by New Castle and Kent counties, Thomas McKean delivered one of the most extreme denunciations ever voiced of British policy toward the colonies.[87] Under his influence the Sussex men were persuaded to meet with those from the other two counties.[88]

On August 1, the legal representatives of the Three Counties, responding to Speaker Rodney's call, met at New Castle.[89] The following day they not only "unanimously appointed Cæsar Rodney, Thomas McKean, and George Read, Esquires, or any two of them, deputies for the said colony at the ensuing general Congress," but provided them with carefully framed instructions, likewise unanimously adopted. The instructions were revolutionary in character —going far beyond the question of taxation of Americans by Parliament.[90] So it was that the radicals carried through their program in the Three Lower Counties on the Delaware, entirely ignoring the attitude of numbers of people, especially in Kent and Sussex counties, opposed to the extreme position taken.[91]

---

[87] This address is printed in *American Archives*, 4th ser., I, 658–61, where it is simply stated that it was by a "gentleman [who] introduced the business of the Assembly . . ." but the date is given as July 28 instead of July 23, the date of the Lewes meeting and the Sussex County resolves as shown in *ibid.*, p. 665; see also *Pennsylvania Gazette*, August 3, 1774, and *Delaware History*, VI, 100–1.

[88] In a letter to Thomas Robinson of Sussex County, the members of the Kent County committee wrote on July 21: "We are sensible of the Unreasonableness and impropriety of the Conduct of the New Castle People on this Occasion, in undertaking to dictate to You and us a mode of Conduct"; nevertheless, they announced that lest "this necessary and most important Plan should be Frustrated, and our Government lose that Reputation which it heretofore deservedly got and Merited," they had advised a meeting of the Assembly at New Castle. The Sussex County committee of correspondence, with Thomas Robinson at the head, replied on July 23 that, while surprised that the New Castle gentlemen should undertake "a Business which ought to have had the joint concurrence of the whole Government," they were prepared to go along with the decision of the Kent County committee and to recommend that the Speaker summon the representatives to a meeting. For these letters see *ibid.*, VI, 97–9. The separate resolves of all three counties are likewise to be found in *American Archives*, 4th ser., I, 664–6.

[89] Six were present representing New Castle County and four each for Kent and Sussex counties; *ibid.*, I, 663.

[90] See *Pennsylvania Gazette*, August 10, 1774, and *Letters to and from Rodney*, pp. 43–5; see also *American Archives*, 4th ser., I, 666–8.

[91] See Harold Hancock: *The Delaware Loyalists* (Historical Society of Delaware Papers, new ser., No. 3, Wilmington, 1940); see also his "The New Castle County Loyalists," *Delaware History*, IV, 315–53.

CHAPTER VII

Other Colonies Prepare to Resist: Maryland and Virginia

THE most dynamic of the American colonies, outside of Massachusetts Bay, was Virginia. Each important step that it took in connection with the crisis that had arisen within the Old British Empire had a profound influence upon the colonies preparing to resist British policy, especially in the South. In most of its measures it was closely supported by the neighbouring colony of Maryland. But in some respects the Marylanders acted in advance of not only the other Southern colonies but even the Old Dominion. For example, late in 1774 the Maryland convention formulated plans for the mobilization of all the province's manpower and financial resources in preparation for full-scale military resistance. In this, it provided a pattern followed by Virginia early in 1775.[1]

The two colonies had other things in common. Among these were the planter debts owed in England, for the liquidation of which tobacco was annually sent to Great Britain. It therefore seems desirable to separate a consideration of these two colonies from that of either the more northern or the more southern ones.

Maryland

The people of the Province of Maryland were greatly divided in sentiment, not so much over the lack of wisdom displayed by the government of Great Britain in the measures taken to reduce Massachusetts Bay to a state of obedience in 1774, as over what degree and type of resistance colonials might be justified in taking against

---

[1] See *American Archives*, 4th ser., I, 1145–6, and II, 168–9, for Virginia's later steps toward a militia.

the home government. On May 19 the act of Parliament for closing the port of Boston was printed in the *Maryland Gazette*, published in Annapolis. On the 25th, at a meeting of some eighty inhabitants of that town, resolves were entered into in order to "preserve North America and her liberties" and for a non-importation, non-exportation agreement "on oath" on the part of all the colonies in opposition to the Boston Port Act, until the Act should be repealed. They further resolved that no suit in law be brought "for the recovery of any debt due from any inhabitant of this province to any inhabitant of Great-Britain, until the said act be repealed."[2] A committee of seven, among them Charles Carroll of Carrollton, was appointed to join with a similar committee for Baltimore and other parts of the province in order to "effect such association as will best secure American liberty."[3] The statement of these resolves having appeared in the local papers without signatures led to a public notice, dated May 26, calling upon the inhabitants "to suspend forming any judgment of the sentiments of this city on a subject of so momentous a concern."[4] The following day handbills were issued, summoning "All the citizens" of Annapolis to a meeting that afternoon at which the resolves that had been approved on the 25th were to be considered. Despite a division on the second and third resolves (pertaining to non-importation and non-exportation) and an unsuccessful motion to expunge the fourth (having to do with the recovery of debts), the resolutions were confirmed.[5] This led to a protest meet-

---

[2] For the resolutions see *Maryland Gazette*, May 26, 1774, and *American Archives* 4th ser., I, 351–3. A circular letter advocating an association had been received from Boston and had been acted upon on May 24 by a number of merchants and mechanics of Baltimore, according to the [Baltimore] *Maryland Journal*, May 28, 1774; see also C. A. Barker: *The Background of the Revolution in Maryland* (*Yale Historical Publications, Miscellany*, XXXVIII, New Haven, 1940), p. 370.

[3] For the meeting on the same day (May 25, 1774) at the Baltimore court house which resolved, among other things, upon an embargo on commerce with Great Britain, and to form a committee of correspondence to send out a circular letter to the other towns of Maryland seeking action in support of such an association, see J. T. Scharf: *History of Maryland* (3 vols., Baltimore, 1879), II, 144. This same work (Chap. 20) gives a full account of the events in Maryland leading up to the outbreak of hostilities, including the various resolutions taken throughout the province; it also tends to show that Baltimore took a strong lead for action in support of Boston. There the committee of seven wrote immediately to the Virginia Committee of Correspondence offering the proposal that "the Sense of the People [of Virginia] be taken at their Meetings on the following heads"—followed by the substance of the above Maryland resolves. See *Journals of the House of Burgesses, 1773–1776*, pp. 145–6.

[4] *Maryland Gazette*, June 2, 1774.

[5] *Ibid.* Daniel Dulany, III, later a Loyalist, wrote to Arthur Lee, in London, shortly after the meeting of the 27th, that he and about thirty others who were present

A tobacco wharf on the Chesapeake, from Charles Grignion's engraving of Francis Hayman's cartouche on the Fry and Jefferson "Map of Virginia and Maryland," London, 1751.

(Courtesy A. Pierce Middleton)

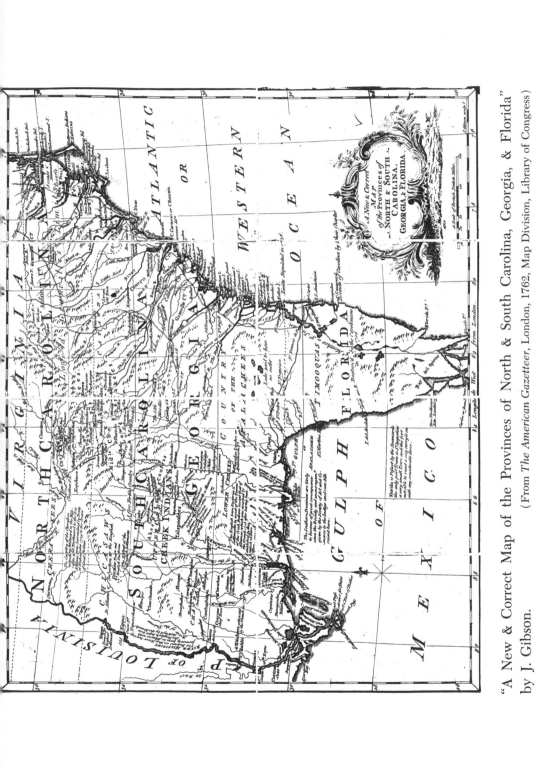

"A New & Correct Map of the Provinces of North & South Carolina, Georgia, & Florida"
by J. Gibson.

(From *The American Gazetteer*, London, 1762, Map Division, Library of Congress)

ing in the city on May 30, at which it was pointed out that during the meeting on the 27th only forty-seven inhabitants had approved the fourth resolution, while thirty-one had expressed their "explicit disapprobation." In the statement of dissent, those protesting declared that the resolution was "founded in treachery, and rashness, in as much as it is big with bankruptcy and ruin, to those inhabitants of Great-Britain, who, relying with unlimited security on our good faith and integrity, have made us masters of their fortunes; condemning them UNHEARD. . . ." They likewise declared that while the inhabitants of Great Britain would by this measure be "partially despoiled of every legal remedy to recover what is justly due to them, . . . our fortunes and persons are left at the mercy of domestic creditors, without a possibility of extricating ourselves, unless by a general convulsion. . . ." Finally, the protest pointed out that should such treatment be accorded to British creditors "our credit as a commercial people will expire under the wound. . . ." This protest was signed by 161 people.[6] Why there was not similar open objection to other resolves is revealed by William Eddis, the surveyor of customs at Annapolis. Writing on June 5 to a correspondent in England about the protest, he made the following interesting comment: "I need not mention, that it is *a particular resolution* against which

---

opposed the fourth resolve. "It seems to me," he stated, "to carry with it so much injustice and partiality, that I am afraid it will give a handle to our enemies to hurt the general cause. I would have agreed to it if it had extended to merchants in this country as well as foreign merchants" (*American Archives*, 4th ser., I, 354–5).

[6] For this protest with the list of the signers see *ibid.*, I, 353–4; see also *Maryland Gazette*, June 2, 1774, and *Annals of Annapolis* (ed. David Ridgely, Baltimore, 1841), pp. 152–5. The count of signers is 161, although Ridgely (*op. cit.*, p. 152) and William Eddis (*Letters from America, Historical and Descriptive; Comprising Occurrences from 1769 to 1777, Inclusive* [London, 1792], p. 162) both state that the protest was "signed by one hundred and thirty-five persons." Charles Carroll of Carrollton, later a signer of the Declaration of Independence, had opposed Daniel Dulany, Jr., over the issue of fees due to officers of the government—an issue that led the two to air their dispute in the columns of the *Maryland Gazette* during the first half of 1773 under the respective pseudonyms "First Citizen" and "Antilon." Writing to his father, also named Charles, in Annapolis on October 27, 1774, Carroll had the following comment to make about Dulany and the protesters: "It is certain all his connections, his admirers, & his own son were in the list of Protestors, & he himself declared that his son's signing the protest, was the same thing, as if he had signed it . . ." ("Extracts from the Carroll Papers," *Maryland Historical Magazine*, XVI, 40). Dulany had in 1765 become famous through the publication of his masterly *Considerations on the Propriety of Imposing Taxes in the British Colonies, For the Purpose of raising a REVENUE, by Act of Parliament.* In 1774 he was still occupying the office of provincial secretary and was on the Council but, as a Loyalist, he went into seclusion at the outbreak of hostilities in 1775. For an excellent study of Dulany see A. C. Land: *The Dulanys of Maryland* . . . (Baltimore, 1955), especially pp. 259–333.

the protest is levelled; the others [that is, the other resolves] being of too popular a nature to admit of opposition." He went on to note that the protesters were considered "by the more violent party, as actuated by sentiments inimical to the interests of America. . . . For my own part, I verily believe that the majority of the subscribers are influenced by motives which reflect the highest credit on their integrity. . . ."[7]

The attitude taken in other areas of the province was also expressed at this period. At Chestertown, Kent County, across the Chesapeake Bay from Annapolis, a meeting was held on May 18 at which strong resolves were entered into, among which was one that should anyone import tea while it carried a duty, he would be treated as an enemy of the American colonies. Likewise, at the Talbot County court house on May 24 it was agreed to support Boston in opposition to measures adopted against the colonials "by a weak or corrupt ministry to destroy their liberties, deprive them of their property, and rob them of their dearest birthright as Britons."[8] At Queenstown in Queen Anne's County on May 30 and at Baltimore on the following day, similar resolves were passed.[9] It may be noted that none of them embodied the Annapolis proposal respecting debts owed to the people of Great Britain. Nevertheless, among the resolves entered into by inhabitants of Harford County on June 11 was one that supported the idea, but with certain provisos to protect the British creditor when bad faith of the debtor was manifested. Again, on June 18, in Caroline County, one of the resolutions advocated the closing of the law courts in case of a non-importation agreement; and on the 20th in Frederick County it was likewise resolved that no suit for the recovery of any debt whatsoever be commenced whenever imports and exports should be stopped.[10]

"All America is in a flame! I hear strange language every day,"

---

[7] William Eddis: *op. cit.*, pp. 163–5.

[8] For the above resolves see *Maryland Gazette*, June 2, 1774.

[9] *Ibid.*, June 9, 1774. For the meeting in the Baltimore court house on May 31, which resulted in strong resolutions to join all others in ceasing commercial relations with Great Britain, as well as to call for both a provincial congress to be held at Annapolis and the sending of delegates to a continental congress, see *American Archives*, 4th ser., I, 366–7.

[10] *Maryland Gazette*, June 30, 1774. For earlier and subsequent resolutions adopted by Frederick County people, see J. T. Scharf: *op. cit.*, II, 151, 154, 164–5, 174, 181; see also his *History of Western Maryland* (2 vols., Philadelphia, 1882), I, 125–6.

declared William Eddis writing from Annapolis on May 28.[11] He was to hear more of this language. On June 22 a meeting of committees from the various counties gathered in a general convention at the provincial capital. It was continued to the 25th, when resolves supporting the idea of a general congress of the colonies for the redress of grievances were approved and five delegates were selected. On the issue of non-importation, the delegates were authorized, once at the congress, to approve importation of articles considered "*indispensably* necessary." The concept of a non-exportation agreement was accepted, but with the proviso that the non-export of tobacco "depend and take place only on a similar agreement by Virginia and North Carolina, and to commence at such time as may be agreed on" by the deputies of Maryland, Virginia, and North Carolina. Significantly, the idea of closing the courts to British creditors did not find a place among the resolves. With these resolutions approved, Maryland took an early lead in advocating an association and the sending of delegates to a continental congress, as it was later to do in forming a militia.[12]

Only one incident need be mentioned to show how, by October 1774, legal government had virtually abdicated in Maryland. On the 15th of the month the brig *Peggy Stewart*, Captain Jackson, arrived at Annapolis from London chiefly loaded with indentured servants but also carrying some goods, including seventeen packages of tea weighing 2,320 pounds consigned to the Annapolis firm of Thomas Charles Williams & Co. One of the owners of the vessel, Anthony Stewart, immediately paid the duty on the tea, although it was not yet unloaded. When the news spread that this forbidden article had arrived, four of the committee for Ann Arundel County considered the matter and decided that a public meeting should be called. It so happened that a number of people had come to the city from various parts of the province to attend the provincial court. They joined the meeting which gathered later that day in order to question the members of the firm importing the tea, the captain of the vessel, and the deputy collector of customs. After the questioning, it was voted unanimously that the tea should not be landed

---

[11] William Eddis: *op. cit.*, p. 158.

[12] For the above resolves see *Maryland Gazette,* June 30, 1774; see also *American Archives,* 4th ser., I, 438–40. For Maryland's preparations for military resistance see *ibid.,* I, 1031–3, 1059–61, 1140–4.

and that a committee, then appointed, should supervise the discharge of the balance of the cargo. On the 19th another mass meeting was held at which members of the Williams & Co. firm were examined, along with the owner of the brig, who now offered to destroy the tea. The committee was of the opinion that if this were done and "proper concession made," no further action should be taken, but the more radical elements felt that the offence was of so grave a nature that the brig itself should be destroyed. This, too, Stewart agreed to do. Notwithstanding, he and both Joseph and Charles Williams were required to sign a statement for publication in the local papers that they had "committed a most daring insult and act of the most pernicious tendency to the liberties of America," and to ask pardon of the public with the promise never again to "infringe any regulation formed by the people for the salvation of their rights." After signing this confession Stewart and the two members of Williams & Co. went on board the *Peggy Stewart* and, with her sails spread and her colours flying, set fire to the tea and, according to the *Maryland Gazette*, "in a few hours, the whole, together with the vessel, was consumed in the presence of a great number of spectators." Thus, Maryland emerges as a province that not only had a strong spirit of resistance, but also set the pace for its neighbouring colonies to the south.[13]

Virginia

The leading role played by the Virginia House of Burgesses in bringing about the gathering of the Continental Congress in 1774 has already been mentioned briefly in Chapter V, but the full account

[13] For the *Peggy Stewart* incident see *Maryland Gazette*, October 20, 1774; see also William Eddis: *op. cit.*, pp. 170–84, which gives certain documents not published in the *Gazette*. On December 30, Governor Robert Eden wrote from Maryland, apparently to Lord Dartmouth, that the spirit of resistance "against the Tea Act, or any mode of internal taxation, is as strong and universal here as ever . . ." (*American Archives*, 4th ser., I, 1076). This was borne out in July 1775. When the *Totness*, bound for Baltimore, ran aground on a shoal in the Chesapeake Bay and the rumour reached the associators that she carried forbidden goods, the ship was thereupon burned to the water's edge. See the account in the *Maryland Gazette*, July 20, 1774, which found nothing to criticize in such radical action. For the role of this newspaper as an important instrument of the patriot cause see D. C. Skaggs: "Editorial Policies of the *Maryland Gazette*, 1765–1783," *Maryland Historical Magazine*, LIX, 341–9. For an excellent brief statement of the relationship between Maryland and her sister colonies in the South at this period see J. R. Alden: *The South in the Revolution* (Baton Rouge, 1957), Chap. 10.

has been reserved for Chapter IX, which deals with the Congress. The Virginia legislators, as members of an élite group, constituted the most powerful force in the political life of the province because of their native talents, their education, and their great experience in public affairs.[14] What motivated each of them to take the position of resistance to British policy that he did can only be conjectured. Was it simply an attachment to certain concepts of government? Was it chiefly to serve some personal end, which the code of honour made him and his fellows reluctant to disclose?[15] Was it a combination of public interest and self-interest that motivated him?[16] Or was it—in addition to and beyond all rationalizations involving

---

[14] See J. P. Greene: "Foundations of Political Power in the Virginia House of Burgesses, 1720–1776," *William and Mary Quarterly*, 3rd ser., XVI, 485–506. For discussions of the colonial élite see the following earlier volumes of this series, II, revised, 42–7 and 125–6, especially footnotes 102 and 103, and X, 20–1 and 25–7; see also Ronald Syme: *Colonial Élites: Rome, Spain and the Americas* (London, 1958), pp. 50–6, and C. S. Sydnor: *Political Leadership in Eighteenth-Century Virginia* (Harmsworth Inaugural Lecture, Oxford, 1951) and *Gentlemen Freeholders* (Chapel Hill, N.C., 1952). For an older, colourful discourse upon individual Virginia leaders, see H. B. Grigsby: *The Virginia Convention of 1776* (Richmond, 1855); see also, in the same vein, P. A. Bruce: *The Virginia Plutarch* (2 vols., Chapel Hill, N.C., 1929), I. For a view of the revolutionary movement in Virginia as a popular one see T. J. Wertenbaker: *Give Me Liberty: The Struggle for Self-Government in Virginia* (Philadelphia, 1958).

[15] Reference is made here to the repudiation of the vast indebtedness, especially of the great tobacco planters, to British merchants. James Parker, writing from Norfolk, Virginia, on June 7, 1774, to Charles Steuart noted: "The nonpayment of debits is a favourite Subject & you may depend will be gone pretty generally into, & till our Courts are new modeled, or we have judges from home I never expect to See business regularly done. Generally speaking the more a man is in debit, the greater patriot he is, in short . . . Calling a man a patriot here is saying he is in bad Circumstances." Then, in a postscript written on June 13, Parker had this further comment to make: "Several of the County Courts have Stopt Sitting till the Boston Act is Repealed . . . there was some violent debates here about the association. George Mason, Pat. Henry, R. H. Lee & The Treasurer [Robert Carter Nicholas], as I am told, were for paying no Debts to Britain, no exportation or importation & no Courts here. Paul Carrington [a burgess representing Charlotte] was for Paying his debits & Exporting, in this he was joined by Carter Braxton [a burgess representing King William], Mr. E. Pendleton [a burgess representing Caroline], Thos. Nelson Jun. [a burgess representing York], & the Speaker [Peyton Randolph]." See Charles Steuart Papers, National Library of Scotland, microfilm copy in the Library of Colonial Williamsburg, Inc.

[16] Two of the most recent studies of this subject stress, as the factor which placed leading Virginians in the front rank of American patriots, their devotion to what they conceived to be certain constitutional rights, which Parliament was violating by actions involving the fate of all Americans, rather than selfish personal motivation. See T. W. Tate: "The Coming of the Revolution in Virginia: Britain's Challenge to Virginia's Ruling Class, 1763–1776," *William and Mary Quarterly*, 3rd ser., XIX, 323–43, and E. G. Evans: "Planter Indebtedness and the Coming of the Revolution in Virginia," *ibid.*, XIX, 511–33.

larger public or smaller personal considerations—the coming to
the surface of an intuitive feeling that Americans had reached a
state of maturity by 1774 which demanded recognition? For, were
not the intuitive feelings of enlightened colonials culminating in
the conviction that, no matter how valid might have been the
patriarchal scheme of government which had so long kept colonials
in utter political subordination during the infancy of the colonies,
this system was no longer adequate to meet the fundamental needs
of a dynamic, powerful, wealthy, politically experienced America,
and therefore was no longer a just system? There can be no doubt
that a mixture of these motivations operated in most of the Virginia
leaders to some degree; nor should this thought detract from a
recognition that out of this group came some of the greatest patriots
who gave form and shape to the new nation that was to emerge as
a result of their earlier efforts and was to thrive under their continued guidance.

The immediate task of the members of the House of Burgesses
—once they committed themselves to the idea of forming a united
colonial opposition capable of forcing the Ministry and Parliament
to retreat—was to gain the hearty support of their constituents in
the various counties. In this they were powerfully aided by the
local press in a manner characteristic of the support of the patriotic
cause manifested by newspapers in the other colonies.

Because the House of Burgesses on May 24, 1774, took the action
of appealing to the public for support of the sufferers in Boston,
Lord Dunmore dissolved the Assembly on May 26.[17] The following
day, however, a gathering of Virginia representatives at the Raleigh
Tavern became the historic meeting from which was to issue the
call for the First Continental Congress.[18] The *Virginia Gazette*
(Purdie and Dixon) published the full text of the Boston Port Act,
together with the text of the solemn agreement entered into at
the Raleigh Tavern on May 27 by eighty-nine members of the late
House.[19] This paper, as well as Clementina Rind's rival *Virginia*

---

[17] For the action of the House of Burgesses on May 24, and Dunmore's message
dissolving the House, see *Journals of the House of Burgesses, 1773–1776*, pp. 124
and 132.

[18] See Chap. 9 of this volume.

[19] The date-line of the *Virginia Gazette* is given as May 26, 1774, but it is clear
that its publication had been withheld until the following day, after results of the
meeting in the Apollo Room of the tavern had been made available.

Gazette, both printed at Williamsburg, continued the work of spreading the news of the developing crisis throughout the province and beyond.

The task of organizing Virginia for resistance, subsequent to the adoption of the agreement, now moved ahead.[20] At a meeting called at Williamsburg on May 30 by Peyton Randolph—late Speaker of the House of Burgesses and now "Moderator" of the Virginia Committee of Correspondence, composed of representatives from the late Assembly—it was decided that since so few members were present, a second meeting should be held on August 1 to bring together as many of the members of the late House of Burgesses as could attend for the purpose of coming to non-importation and non-exportation agreements directed against Great Britain "should the present odious Measures, so inimical to the just Rights and Liberty of America be pursued."[21] Other towns in Virginia also joined in passing appropriate resolves. At Fredericksburg in Spotsylvania County a gathering of inhabitants on June 1 agreed unanimously that Virginia should confirm every measure in support of Boston that the colonies in general would think expedient.[22] This sentiment was echoed by the Norfolk and Portsmouth committees of correspondence in letters sent to the Baltimore committee the following day.[23] On June 6, at a meeting of inhabitants of Prince William County at Dumfries, resolves in favour of non-importation and non-exportation were adopted and also, in protest against the passing of the other Coercive Acts, a resolve "that the Court[s] of Justice in this Colony ought to decline trying any civil Causes until the said Acts be repealed."[24] These resolves were followed by those of Frederick County on June 8, which were endorsed in toto as the senti-

---

[20] George Mason, commenting on the steps that the House of Burgesses could take at this time of crisis, wrote to Martin Cockburn on May 26: "Matters of that sort here are conducted and prepared with a great deal of privacy, and by very few members, of whom Patrick Henry is the principal" (Kate M. Rowland: *Life of George Mason, 1725–1792* [2 vols., New York, 1892], I, 168).

[21] *Virginia Gazette* (Purdie and Dixon), June 2, 1774; see also *American Archives,* 4th ser., I, 387.

[22] *Ibid.,* I, 373–4; see also, for the subscriptions and contributions made by various Virginia towns and counties to the Boston sufferers, *ibid.,* I, 517–18, 593, 787, II, 450, and *Virginia Gazette* (Purdie and Dixon), summer of 1774, *passim.* For relief to Boston provided by other colonies see Massachusetts Historical Society *Collections,* 4th ser., IV, 1–278.

[23] *American Archives,* 4th ser., I, 371.

[24] *Virginia Gazette* (Purdie and Dixon), June 16, 1774.

ments of the people of Dunmore County on June 16. Among them was the resolution that the act closing the port of Boston was not only "repugnant to the fundamental laws of natural justice, . . . but, also, a despotic exertion of unconstitutional power, calculated to enslave a free and loyal people."[25] In Westmoreland County, under the leadership of men like Richard Henry Lee, its representative in the House of Burgesses, one of the resolves passed stated that the lawyers of the county—so long as the contemplated colonial non-exportation agreement continued—should not "bring any writ for the Recovery of Debt, or push to a Conclusion any such Suit already brought. . . ."[26] Then came the resolves of Prince George County, the home of the eminent lawyer Richard Bland, who represented the county. Among them was the resolution "that the Dissolution of the General Assembly, by Order of the British Ministry, whenever they enter upon the Consideration of the Rights and Liberties of the Subject, . . . is an Evidence of the fixed Intention of the said Ministry to reduce the Colonies to a State of Slavery."[27] At a meeting held in Spotsylvania County on June 24, among the things resolved was "that we owe no Obedience to any Act of the British Parliament, that is, or shall be made, respecting the internal Police of this Colony, and that we will oppose any such Acts with our Lives and Fortunes."[28] A meeting of the county of Richmond on June 29 echoed the Westmoreland resolve respecting suits for the recovery of debts.[29] A similar position was also expressed in the resolves of Essex County on July 9.[30] The resolutions of the people of Middlesex County, entered into on July 15, were, however, much more conservative in tone than those of other Virginia counties. Although opposing taxation of the colonies, they accepted commercial regulation by Parliament "in Consequence of the Protection that is given to our Trade by the Superintendence of the Mother Country." Nor did they "approve the Conduct of the People of Boston in destroying the Tea belonging to the East India Company." To them the tax on tea was "a violent Infringement of one of the

---

[25] *American Archives*, 4th ser., I, 392 and 417–18; see also F. H. Hart: *The Valley of Virginia in the American Revolution, 1763–1789* (Chapel Hill, N.C., 1942), pp. 83–5.

[26] *American Archives*, 4th ser., I, 437–8; see also *Virginia Gazette* (Purdie and Dixon), June 30, 1774.

[27] *Ibid.*

[28] *Ibid.*, July 7, 1774.

[29] *Ibid.*

[30] *Ibid.*, July 21, 1774.

fundamental Privileges of loyal and free Subjects, yet we apprehend [that] Violence cannot justify Violence." Again, as to the adoption of a complete non-importation and non-exportation policy, they resolved that such a "Scheme is impracticable, and, were it no so, could be irreconcilable with every Principle of Justice and Honesty, injurious to the Commerce, and fatal to the Credit, of this Colony."[31]

Although most of the county resolves[32] favoured the embargo on importing non-essential goods from Great Britain, some, such as those of Prince George and Culpeper, made many exceptions of what were considered essentials.[33] A few of them did not mention non-exportation to Great Britain. The question here concerned the moral obligation of the Virginia planters to continue to ship their tobacco in order to keep faith with their creditors; for the planters of the chief Virginia staple, almost without exception, lived on credit which they repaid in tobacco shipments to the British merchants to whom they were indebted.[34] Some of the debts were for modest amounts, covering credit extended during the preceding season; others, including those of some of the great planters, were for huge sums, in many cases involving inherited debts that could not easily be paid by any means in sight and yet were even permitted to increase in some instances.[35] Thomas Jefferson, himself a debtor planter, made the following statement on the planter debts in retrospect (as cited in part in Volume X of this series):

[31] *Ibid.*

[32] For the resolves of some thirty Virginia counties from June 1 to July 28, 1774, see *American Archives*, 4th ser., I, 373 and *passim* to 643. See also D. J. Mays: *Edmund Pendleton, 1721–1803* (2 vols., Cambridge, Mass., 1952), I, 274–5.

[33] For the resolves of the inhabitants of Prince George and Culpeper counties, see *American Archives*, 4th ser., I, 493–5 and 522–3.

[34] In a recent study of the tobacco trade emphasizing the credit extended to the planter, the following comment is given: "This mercantile credit was a necessary ingredient for the growth and development of Virginia economy. Not only did the merchant finance the tobacco trade, but also by extending credit he financed every activity of the planter. The debts of the Virginia planter were the method by which the Virginia economy developed and expanded. They were also the method by which the planter himself participated in this growth and came to enjoy a higher standard of living. The importance of this aspect of debtor-creditor relationship has often been lost sight of because too much attention has been paid to the debit side of the ledger without any consideration of the credit side" (S. M. Rosenblatt: "The Significance of Credit in the Tobacco Consignment Trade: A Study of John Norton & Sons, 1768–1775," *William and Mary Quarterly*, 3rd ser., XIX, 383–99).

[35] See Volume X of this series, Chap. 8, "Virginia Private Debts and the Government of Great Britain," also published in *Virginia Magazine of History and Biography*, LXIX, 259–77; see also I. S. Harrell: *Loyalism in Virginia . . .* (Durham, N.C., 1926), pp. 24–9 and *passim*, E. G. Evans: *op. cit.*, and T. W. Tate: *op. cit., William and Mary Quarterly*, 3rd ser., XIX, 511–33 and 323–43, respectively.

"Virginia certainly owed two millions sterling to Great Britain at the conclusion of the war. Some have conjectured the debt as high as three millions. I think that state owed near as much as all the rest together. This is to be ascribed to peculiarities in the tobacco trade. The advantages made by the British merchants on the tobaccoes consigned to them were so enormous that they spared no means of increasing those consignments. A powerful engine for this purpose was the giving good prices and credit to the planter, till they got him more immersed in debt than he could pay without selling his lands or slaves. They then reduced the prices given for his tobacco so that let his shipments be ever so great, and his demand of necessaries ever so œconomical, they never permitted him to clear off his debt. These debts had become hereditary from father to son for many generations so that the planters were a species of property annexed to certain mercantile houses in London."[36]

Furthermore, as Professor Richard B. Sheridan has recently pointed out,[37] the British credit crisis of 1772[38] "was felt most acutely" in Virginia. For, as this writer emphasizes, to the accumulated burden of debt, the depressed price of tobacco, and the restrictions on credit as a result of the crisis, was added Virginia's problem over paper currency and counterfeiting which saw the province's treasury depleted by 1774, all of which "became a source of unrest which undermined the already strained relations with the mother country."[39]

Among those who had scruples about the propriety of stopping exports to Great Britain or the payment of debts was George Wash-

---

[36] "Additional Queries (of Jean Nicolas Démeunier) with Jefferson's Answers [Jan.–Feb. 1786]," *The Papers of Thomas Jefferson* (ed. J. P. Boyd *et al.*, 16 vols.+, Princeton, 1950–61+), X, 27.

[37] See R. B. Sheridan: "The British Credit Crisis of 1772 and the American Colonies," *Journal of Economic History*, XX, 161–86, perhaps the most detailed and thorough examination of debtor-creditor relationships in any study of Virginia private debts in connection with the coming of the Revolution.

[38] For the crisis, as seen in London in July 1772, see *John Norton & Sons: Merchants of London and Virginia* (ed. F. N. Mason, Richmond, 1937), p. 254 and *passim;* for the effects of the crisis, as felt in Virginia, see *The Letters of William Allason, Merchant of Falmouth, Virginia,* Richmond College *Historical Papers,* II, No. 1, p. 150. For a study of family relationships among the merchants of London and Virginia, see J. M. Price: "Who Was John Norton?" *William and Mary Quarterly,* 3rd ser., XIX, 400–7.

[39] R. B. Sheridan: *op. cit., Journal of Economic History,* XX, 175–9, in which Professor Sheridan cites the series of letters by Robert Carter Nicholas which appeared in Purdie and Dixon's *Virginia Gazette* in 1773, on the subject of private and public finance. For the problem of counterfeiting in Virginia see Kenneth Scott: *Counterfeiting in Colonial America* (New York, 1957), pp. 93, 103–4, 173, 210–11, 236–7, 262.

ington. Writing to Bryan Fairfax on July 4, he had expressed approval of non-importation, but had affirmed:

> "As to the withholding of our remittances [chiefly tobacco], that is another point, in which I own I have my doubts on several accounts, but principally on that of justice; for I think, whilst we are accusing others of injustice, we should be just ourselves; and how this can be, whilst we owe a considerable debt, and refuse payment of it to Great Britain, is to me inconceivable."[40]

Even Thomas Mason, brother of George Mason, although strongly opposed to submitting to "the authority of British Acts of Parliament in America,"[41] in the eighth of his series of articles written under the pseudonym "British American" (Rind's *Virginia Gazette*, July 21), warned those who wished to stop exports of the gravity of the step: "Common honesty requires that you should pay your debts, and if you refuse to do so, not only the persons injured but all mankind will . . . declare, that instead of bravely contending for your liberties, you are Knavishley endeavouring to cheat your creditors." This point of view was also stressed by "An American Cato" in the July 29 issue of Purdie and Dixon's *Virginia Gazette*:

> By stopping your Exports you will distress yourselves, without one good Consequence attending it. . . . It is alleged too, that you are considerably in debt to the British Nation. If that is the Case, let us not meanly take Advantage of the Times and give Room to our Enemies to say that we are a Set of Men void of publick Faith, who do not deserve the Freedom we are contending for. Policy, Justice, and a proper Regard to our national Character all forbid you to adopt this Plan."

Holding to the same view, Attorney General John Randolph affirmed in his anonymously published *Consideration of the Present State of Virginia* (1774) that to stop the exports required to settle debts owed in England "would fix an indelible Stain on the national Character of our Country. . . ."[42]

On the other hand, "A Contrite Debtor," also in the July 29 issue of the *Gazette*, referred to a manuscript written on "the present situation of our Affairs" which had stated that "the enormous Debt

---

[40] *Writings of George Washington* (39 vols., ed. J. C. Fitzpatrick, Washington, 1931–44), III, 229.

[41] Letter No. 4, *American Archives*, 4th ser., I, 418.

[42] See *Virginia and the Revolution, Two Pamphlets* (ed. E. G. Swem, New York, 1919), p. 32.

America owes to Foreigners is the only Tyrant which needs give her Alarm." Later, in the *Gazette* of August 18, he declared: "Let the great Gentlemen of the Land (i.e. *the great Debtors, the great Slavers, the great Parriers of Just Demands*) dare to appear simply in publick, and frugally in private. . . ." Another anonymous writer, signing himself "Experience," in the July 29 *Gazette*, sought to put at rest the qualms of conscience of those who realized "the necessary Consequences that a non-exportation would have upon their Debts due to the merchants of England. . . ." His stand was that above all considerations affecting "an *honest* Conscience" was the welfare of all America, which justifies non-exportation as well as non-importation "in Opposition to the Slavery intended by this Parliamentary Taxation. . . ." He also chided those who for conscience opposed non-exportation "because it tends, a While, to prevent the Payment of their Debts to the merchants at home, . . . I beg Leave to know why they have not then *religiously*, thus *conscientiously*, endeavoured to devote the Whole of their Exportation to the Discharge of their Debts, ever since so unhappily they became in Debt, as to prevent their doing as they please with their Property?" By the time this article appeared there was—as the Middlesex County resolutions of July 15 affirmed—a state of confusion in Virginia attributed to the dissolution of the Assembly, which left "the publick creditors unpaid; a stagnation of justice, by reason of the lapse of the Fee Bill; the Courts of Law occluded; every thing that is held sacred in civil society confounded; the just creditor deprived of property; and the dishonest debtor triumphant; these are the bitter fruits of the late dissolution."[43]

Yet the question must be raised with candour: Why was not the fee bill which lapsed on April 17, 1774, revised without delay when the General Assembly met on May 5? On May 10 the House of Burgesses resolved that it should be revived and the following day an appropriate bill was introduced; it passed two readings and was sent to committee, but apparently no further steps were taken to pass the bill before the dissolution of the Assembly on May 26.[44]

[43] Rind's *Virginia Gazette*, July 21, 1774, and *American Archives*, 4th ser., I, 551–2. Richard Henry Lee wrote on June 26, 1774, to his brother Arthur in London that the dissolution of the Assembly had left "the Country business unfinished, no fee bill passed, and the Courts of Justice consequently stopt" (*The Letters of Richard Henry Lee* [ed. J. C. Ballagh, 2 vols., New York, 1911], I, 114). On April 12, 1774, the "Act for the better regulating and collecting certain Officers Fees" (Hening: *Laws of Virginia*, VII, 244), passed in the nineteenth year of the reign of George II, lapsed.

[44] *Journals of the House of Burgesses, 1773–1776*, pp. 85, 90, 132.

The tarring and feathering of Customs Officer John Malcom, printed for Carington Bowles, London, October 12, 1774, the first of two such cartoons.

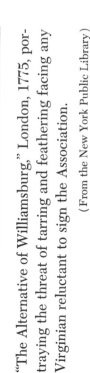

(From R. T. H. Halsey's The Boston Port Bill as Pictured by a Contemporary London Cartoonist, 1904, New York Public Library)

"The Alternative of Williamsburg," London, 1775, portraying the threat of tarring and feathering facing any Virginian reluctant to sign the Association.

(From the New York Public Library)

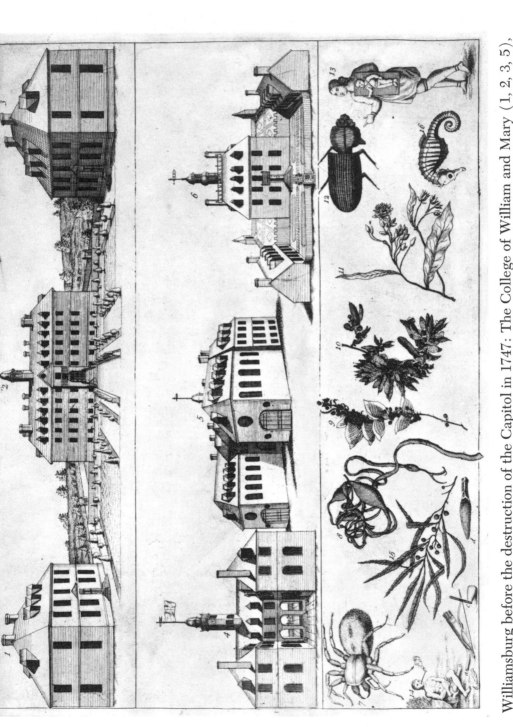

Williamsburg before the destruction of the Capitol in 1747: The College of William and Mary (1, 2, 3, 5), the Capitol (4), the Governor's Palace (6).

(From the Bodleian Plate, circa 1740, Colonial Williamsburg)

This raises the question whether the bill was held up for the purpose of preventing dissolution or as a threat to stop civil processes in which officers' fees played a part. Without attempting to give an answer, it may be stated that by June the courts for the trial of civil cases were ceasing to function, with "some justices declaring they would not grant attachments for debts due to British creditors and some clerks refusing to grant writs for the purpose."[45]

On August 1, with the courts closed for civil actions, many of those who had been elected to sit in the next House of Burgesses assembled in force at Williamsburg. It was for the guidance of these delegates that Jefferson, as will be emphasized in Chapter IX, drew up his *Summary View* . . . The convention continued its deliberations, with Peyton Randolph as moderator, until the 6th of the month. Before separating, the members drew up an "Association" that was destined to exercise great influence upon the proceedings of the Continental Congress. Among the articles adopted was the unanimous agreement that after November 1 there should be no further importations from Great Britain, the West Indies, or other places of any British goods, medicines excepted; also after that date there should be no importation of slaves. As for tea, "the detestable Instrument which laid the Foundation of the present Sufferings of our distressed Friends in the Town of Boston," the agreement continued, "We view it with Horrour; and therefore . . . we will not from this Day, either import Tea . . . or suffer even such of it as is now on Hand to be used in any of our Families." With respect to exports, the articles declared that unless American grievances were "redressed by August 10, 1775, that is a year hence, we will not after that day, . . . export Tobacco,[46] or any other Article whatever to

[45] D. J. Mays: *Edmund Pendleton, 1721–1803*, I, 273.

[46] For an analysis of the tobacco trade of the Upper James River naval district, which surpassed all others in the volume of tobacco exportation, see R. P. Thomson: "The Tobacco Export of the Upper James River Naval District, 1773–75," *William and Mary Quarterly*, 3rd ser., XVIII, 393–407. In this article the author uses the "manifest book" kept by the district naval officer to demonstrate that the resident British factors increasingly dominated the export market in the early 1770's, while the other Virginia merchant and planter shippers struggled with only a trifling balance of tobacco exports on a consignment basis. In his summary, Mr. Thomson raises the question: "To what extent did the Virginians make an honest effort to reduce their debts to their English creditors in 1775, after nonimportation had begun, but before the Continental nonexportation agreement took effect?" His answer is that the Virginia debtor exporters did not maintain the size of their tobacco consignments in that year but that "the large British firms whose agents obtained tobacco in Virginia got the lion's share of the valuable tobacco crop exported in 1775." What he does not make clear, however, is whether the great planters, who formerly had

Great Britain. . . ." Further, the breeding of sheep for wool was to be encouraged and, finally, merchants were not to take advantage of the scarcity of goods to raise prices. In order to enforce these resolves committees were to be chosen in each county and the associators were to agree not to have any dealing after November 1 with any merchants or traders who had not signed the association.[47]

Having adopted an association the convention now selected seven leading Virginians to attend the Congress[48] and presented them with instructions. These instructions stressed, among other things, that the source of the crisis in the relations between Great Britain and the colonies lay in the unconstitutional assumption by Parliament of the power "to bind America by their statutes, in all cases whatsoever," despite the fact "that British subjects in America are entitled to the same rights and privileges as their fellow-subjects in Britain." Of such unconstitutional character were "the several Acts of Parliament for raising a revenue in America; for the extending of the jurisdiction of the Courts of Admiralty; for seizing American subjects, and transporting them to Britain to be tried for crimes committed in America; and the several late oppressive Acts respecting . . . Massachusetts Bay." Moreover, that there should be

---

dominated the consignment export trade, were now selling their tobacco to the factors, rather than shipping it in payment of their debts.

For the contemporary view of a twenty-four-year-old Englishman, living in Alexandria, Virginia, in October 1775, that "the people in this Colony and the province of Maryland are in general greatly in debt to the Merchants in England, and think a revolt would pay all," see *The Journal of Nicholas Cresswell, 1774–1777* (New York, 1924), pp. 127–8.

[47] For the association see *Virginia Gazette* (Purdie and Dixon), November 3, 1774; see also *American Archives*, 4th ser., I, 686–90. Jefferson was very critical of the association as adopted. After listing its defects he noted: "Upon the whole we may truly say[:] We have left undone those things which we ought to have done. And we have done those things which we ought not to have done" (*Papers of Thomas Jefferson*, I, 143). "These Gentlemen from Virginia," John Adams noted in his diary on September 2, 1774, "appear to be the most spirited and consistent of any. Harrison said he would have come [to Philadelphia] on foot rather than not come. Bland said he would have gone, upon this Occasion, if it had been to Jericho" (*Adams Papers*, 1st ser. [Butterfield], II, 120).

[48] The delegates appointed were Peyton Randolph, Richard Henry Lee, George Washington, Patrick Henry, Richard Bland, Benjamin Harrison, and Edmund Pendleton—a group of men of exceptional ability. In writing to Charles Steuart of Glasgow on September 29, 1774, from Norfolk, James Parker noted that "the evil Sensably felt is the shutting up the Courts & nonpayment of debts. The stoping the Courts was certainly very convenient for Some of the Patriots; it prevented any difficulty in travelling to & from the Congress. Then [let] the Great R. H. L[e]e, P. H[enr]y, Old Spectacle B[lan]d, & B[enjami]n H[arriso]n Sell their Estates Pay their debits & I w^d not give my Old Brown Mare Matron for the Ball^n [balance] of the whole" (Steuart Papers, National Library of Scotland, microfilm in the Williamsburg, Inc., Library).

no grounds for insinuating that by the position they had taken the people of Virginia were seeking to repudiate their debts, the delegates were instructed to make clear to the Congress that the reason for postponing non-exportation until August 10, 1775, was the "earnest desire we have to make as quick and full payment as possible of our debts to Great Britain and to avoid the heavy injury that would arise to this country from an earlier adoption of the non-exportation plan. . . ." The final instruction was a thinly veiled threat that if Gage, Governor of Massachusetts Bay and Commander-in-Chief of His Majesty's Forces in America, should seek to enforce his "odious and illegal Proclamation" declaring it "treason" for the inhabitants of Massachusetts Bay "to assemble themselves to consider their grievances," it "must be considered as a plain and full declaration that this despotick viceroy will be bound by no law, . . . and, therefore, . . . will justify resistance and reprisal."[49] By these instructions the delegates to the Congress were authorized to place Virginia solidly behind Massachusetts Bay in denying the authority of Parliament to bind the colonials by statutes declared by the convention to be unconstitutional in nature.

---

[49] The instructions are printed in the *Virginia Gazette* (Rind) of August 11, 1774.

CHAPTER VIII

Other Colonies Prepare to Resist: The Carolinas and Georgia

ALTHOUGH the Carolinas and Georgia have been reserved for treatment apart from Maryland and Virginia, the influence that caused North Carolina to be the first of these colonies to take action came from the Old Dominion. The colonies of North and South Carolina had both recently experienced bitter sectional struggles between the older settled coastal areas and the newer settled backcountry over the issue of political equality (as has been discussed in detail in the preceding volume). In North Carolina the scars from this struggle were still visible by 1775, when former Regulators and Scottish Highlanders in the backcountry expressed loyalty to the mother country in addresses sent to Governor Martin. The province of Georgia, still dependent upon the financial aid voted each year by Parliament and threatened by Indian encroachments upon its backcountry which might require the help of British troops, was somewhat bewildered as to the position it should take in the American crisis—especially as it enjoyed the leadership of a popular Governor. Yet the influence of the Charleston radicals, combined with the growing strength of the Savannah radicals, ultimately persuaded the colony to cast in its lot with the other older American colonies.

North Carolina

In 1774 the Province of North Carolina was held to be in a state "of the greatest anarchy and confusion."[1] The wounds inflicted by

---

[1] John Pownall to Richard Jackson, April 22, 1774, P.R.O., C.O. 5:159, p. 133.

the uprising and crushing of the Regulators were still open and continued to divide the older and more settled eastern part of the province from the newer western counties, occupied chiefly by people from the northern provinces who had infiltrated the area, coming by way of the Valley Road of Virginia.[2] But the Assembly —still dominated by the eastern counties—which had maintained the most harmonious relations with Governor Tryon, was now arrayed against his successor, Josiah Martin, as the result of problems over currency, the provincial debt, fees in public office, the unsettled boundary dispute with South Carolina, and the so-called "Tryon Court Law."[3] What quickly became apparent was that Governor Martin, a former military man accustomed to giving and taking orders, felt far more bound by his commission and royal instructions[4] in dealing with the issues that arose—most of which were inherited from his predecessor—than by the will of the Assembly. This was especially true of the impasse over the Court Law which developed within a month after the opening of the General Assembly on January 25, 1773. The background of the matter stretched back into the 1760's with the enactment in 1766 of a comprehensive law for establishing courts of superior justice in six districts within the province, which included provisions regarding civil attachments.[5] This law had been amended in 1768, signed by Governor Tryon, and later reluctantly approved by the King in Council in the expectation that, upon its expiration at the end of five years, a new law would be enacted eliminating the objectionable features.[6] But the Assem-

---

[2] For the Regulator movement in North Carolina, see Volume XI in this series, Chap. 14.

[3] For the highlights of the problem over currency (which Martin solved by authorizing the issue of debenture notes), see *Colonial Records of North Carolina* (ed. W. L. Saunders, 10 vols., Raleigh, N.C., 1886–90), IX, 67–8, 76–7, 142, 193–4, 206–7, 260–1; for provincial debts, see *ibid.*, IX, 18, 77, 229–30, 275–6, and *passim;* for the boundary dispute, see *ibid.*, IX, 48–9, 91, 191–2, 211–12, 220, 276, 279–80, 299–300, 312, 562–4, and *passim;* (cited hereafter as *North Carolina Colonial Records*) see also M. L. Skaggs: *North Carolina Boundary Disputes Involving Her Southern Line* (Chapel Hill, N.C., 1941).

[4] For Martin's commission as Governor, dated December 21, 1770 (he began his administration on August 11, 1771), see C.O. 5:332, pp. 53–81; for his instructions of February 6, 1771, and additional instructions of February 7, see C.O. 5:326, pp. 4–122, and 5:203, pp. 407–72; see also *North Carolina Colonial Records*, VIII, 513–16.

[5] For this law, "An Act for dividing this Province into six several Districts . . . ," see *Laws 1715–1776, State Records of North Carolina*, XXIII, 688–703; for the clauses covering attachments see sections xxxvii–xliii of the Act.

[6] The amended law of 1768 does not appear in the printed colonial laws; however, Governor Tyron made clear in a letter to the Earl of Shelburne on March 7, 1768, the nature of the difference between it and the law of 1766. See *North Carolina*

bly, determined that no basic alteration in the earlier law should be made, on February 24, 1773, presented the Governor with a bill which Martin's instructions forbade him to approve.[7] For, on February 4, 1772, additional royal instructions had been issued to the Governor binding him not to sign any law that would place creditors living outside North Carolina at a disadvantage to those residing in the colony with respect to attachments on the property of a debtor who, although not a resident, owned property there.[8]

The Council, in the course of amending the bill providing for a new law of attachment sent up to it by the Assembly, introduced a clause to place limitations on attachments of the property of non-residents that would be in harmony with the laws and statutes of England "in like cases." When the bill was again received by the Council on February 27, 1773, the clause had been deleted; accordingly, a message was sent to the Assembly on March 1 complaining of this. On the 3rd, the reasons for this action were outlined to the Council by the Speaker of the Assembly. Because of the adamant stand of the Assembly, the Council and Governor gave way. On March 6, Governor Martin signed a bill containing the features considered objectionable by the government of Great Britain, but at least altered to limit the effective period of the act to but six months and with a suspending clause withholding the effective date until the Crown had taken action. It was then sent to the King in Council along with other acts.[9]

When the modified bill reached London, it evoked the disapproba-

---

Colonial Records, VII, 693–4. Richard Jackson, a member of Parliament and firm friend of the colonies—at least up to 1770—as well as of Lord Shelburne, had found "very material objections" to the law the Assembly favoured. See C.O. 5:159, p. 133. For Jackson's parliamentary record see Sir Lewis Namier and John Brooke: *The House of Commons, 1754–1790* (3 vols., London and New York, 1964), I, 669–72.

[7] *North Carolina Colonial Records,* IX, 533–5. For the leading role of Richard Caswell, Speaker of the House from 1770 to 1772, in presenting the bill to the Governor and in subsequent action on the court bill, see C. B. Alexander: "The Training of Richard Caswell," *North Carolina Historical Review,* XXIII, 13–31, especially pp. 29–31.

[8] For the Crown instructions to Martin and his acknowledgment of them, see *North Carolina Colonial Records,* IX, 235–6 and 292. For Martin's report to Lord Dartmouth of February 26, 1773, see *ibid.,* IX, 373–4, in which he states: "This indispensable conduct of mine turned the attention of the House of Assembly immediately to the instruction that had lain before it unnoticed (as it would seem) from the 29th of last month . . . , and I was yesterday informed, that there was a temperate but firm resolution in the majority of the House, rather to be without Courts of Justice, than conform to the direction of that Instruction."

[9] See *ibid.,* IX, 424, 427, 435–7, 446, 550–1, 558–60, 583, 586. For the Governor's letter of transmittal, explaining his action, see *ibid.,* IX, 624–32.

tion of the King in Council, according to the Earl of Dartmouth, who so advised the Governor, simultaneously instructing him to secure a better act.[10] Upon receiving word of the disapproval of the bill, Governor Martin again attempted to sway the Assembly from their firm position, but in vain. He was finally forced to conclude that the opposition to a law that would place all creditors on an equal basis came from "the interested views of a few individuals who have had the baseness to aim at the defeat of the powers of Government most conducive to the interest, peace and happiness of the community in order to serve their selfish purposes. . . ."[11]

By this time the Court Law of 1768 had lapsed. With no new act to authorize the holding of courts, justice in both civil and criminal cases was at a standstill. Under instructions from the King, who felt that he must exert his royal prerogative to prevent anarchy in the province, Martin commissioned judges of oyer and terminer,[12] but the Assembly refused to support these courts out of the public funds.[13] Nor could the members of the Assembly be induced to alter their position during either the December 1773 session or that of March 1774, in order to produce a court bill that the Governor could sign.[14] Thus North Carolina remained without courts of justice from March 6, 1773, until December 24, 1777, by which time its independence of the government of Great Britain had been fully asserted.[15]

---

[10] The King in Council not only objected to the features of the law relating to the attachment of property, but disapproved the clause that restrained a superior court from having any original jurisdiction over cases involving less than £50. See Dartmouth to Martin, August 4, 1773 (*ibid.*, IX, 680–3), in which he wrote: ". . . I am persuaded it must appear to every man of candour, that the mode of attachment insisted upon by the Assembly is . . . inconsistent with Justice. . . ."

[11] See Martin to Dartmouth, September 1, 1774, *ibid.*, IX, 1051.

[12] Governor Martin to the Assembly, December 4, 1773, *ibid.*, IX, 708.

[13] Resolves of the Assembly, December 7, 1773, *ibid.*, IX, 738; the Assembly to the Governor, December 9, 1773, *ibid.*, IX, 743.

[14] On December 21, 1773, the Assembly voted to appoint a committee to solicit the help of former Governor Tryon, then Governor of New York, to forward an address to the King seeking withdrawal of the royal instruction respecting courts and their powers. See *ibid.*, IX, 786–7. For the letter of the Assembly to Tryon and the address to the King signed by John Harvey, Speaker, see Dartmouth Manuscripts transcripts, E.R. 39:139, North Carolina State Archives, Raleigh, N.C. For a brief but excellent discussion of the North Carolina issue over the powers of the court respecting attachments, see J. P. Greene: *The Quest for Power. The Lower Houses of Assembly in the Southern Royal Colonies, 1689–1776* (Chapel Hill, N.C., 1963), pp. 420–4.

[15] It should be noted that in the March 1774 session there was a sharp division in the Assembly between the eastern "Whig" counties and the western "Regulator" counties over an attempt to solve the problem of the court bill by dividing it into three separate bills. All the western members but four favoured the effort at compromise; all the eastern members but three firmly opposed it. But the eastern

In view of the hopeless deadlock between the Governor, holding firmly to his instruction, and the equally adamant Assembly, Martin dissolved that body on March 30, 1774. Nor did he, according to his secretary, anticipate calling another until he could be assured it would be more co-operative.[16] To this challenge, John Harvey—the former Speaker and one of the most determined opponents of the King's representatives in North Carolina—replied: "then the people would convene one themselves."[17] The degree of alienation that had taken place between the colony and the mother country by this period was well expressed in April 1774 by William Hooper of Wilmington, a leader in the Assembly and later a signer of the Declaration of Independence. Writing on the 26th to young James Iredell, comptroller at the port at Edenton—who was also destined to play a role of great importance in the affairs of the new American nation[18]—he stated:

"With you I anticipate the important share which the Colonies must soon have in regulating the political balance. They are striding fast to independence, and ere long will build an empire upon the ruins of Great Britain; will adopt its constitution purged of its impurities, and from an experience of its defects will guard against those evils which have wasted its vigor and brought it to an untimely end."[19]

It was not until July 21, however, that the inhabitants of Wilmington and the surrounding country met under the chairmanship of Hooper

---

members easily out-voted the others. See *North Carolina Colonial Records*, IX, xxv. The *Virginia Gazette* (Purdie and Dixon) of April 15, 1773, printed the following unsigned statement: "The Right of attaching the Effects of Foreigners, or non-residents, is so essential to the Interests of this Province [North Carolina] that the People will not be easily prevailed upon to acquiesce with the Governor's Instruction depriving them of that Right." In his important essay "Making a Revolution: the North Carolina Whigs, 1765–1775," C. G. Sellers, Jr., comments upon the above statement: "Since the debts of Englishmen to North Carolinians could not have been extensive, it is impossible to credit the assembly leaders' justification of their reckless course on the ground that attachment was 'so essential to the Interest of this Province.' Actually, a heavy balance of debt went the other way, and the closing of the courts, ostensibly part of a campaign to help North Carolinians collect from their English debtors, in fact relieved indebted North Carolinians from the necessity of paying their English creditors" (*Studies in Southern History* [ed. J. C. Sitterson, Chapel Hill, N.C., 1957], p. 27).

[16] *North Carolina Colonial Records*, IX, 968.
[17] *Ibid.*
[18] For Iredell see G. T. McRee: *Life and Correspondence of James Iredell* (2 vols., New York, 1857–8).
[19] *North Carolina Colonial Records*, IX, 984–5. Memory can be very faulty. In his "Causes Leading up to the American Revolution, 1776" (manuscript in the

and resolved to send out circular letters to the freeholders of the other counties calling upon them to attend a meeting at the centrally located Johnston County court house on August 20. Resolves were also passed embodying expressions of sympathy for "our Sister Colony of the Massachusetts Bay for having exerted itself in defence of the constitutional Rights of America," and hearty approval was given to the proposal for holding a North American Continental Congress in Philadelphia.[20] With the sending out of the circular letters, other counties went into action. Apparently the first to respond was Mecklenburg County, with its resolves entered into on July 29.[21] At a sparsely attended meeting of freeholders in Rowan County, in the heart of Regulator country, the strongest possible support was given to the Wilmington proposal in a series of fiery resolutions which called on the colonies "to unite in an indissoluble Union and Association" against the measures of the government of

---

Library of the University of North Carolina), Iredell wrote (pp. 119–20): "I avoid the unhappy subject of the day, Independency. There was a time [illegible] lately within my recollection when neither myself nor any person I knew could hear the [illegible] but wish to war. I know it is a favorite argument against us, & that . . . this has been our aim since the beginning, and all other attempts [objectives?] were a cloak & disguise to this principal one. . . . But it is sufficient to say, our professions have been all to the contrary, we have never taken any one step which really indicated such a view, . . . and every Man in America knows that this is one of the most egregious *falsehoods* ever any People were duped with."

[20] For the Wilmington meeting, and a copy of the circular letter sent out by its committee of correspondence, see *North Carolina Colonial Records,* IX, 1016–18; see also C.O. 5:318.

[21] For the Mecklenburg County resolves see "An Interesting Colonial document" (ed. Archibald Henderson, *Virginia Magazine of History and Biography,* XXVIII, 54–7). These are not to be confused with the more famous and controversial Mecklenburg Resolves entered into in May 1775, which, according to Governor Martin, "surpass all the horrid and treasonable publications that the inflammatory spirits of this Continent have yet produced . . ." (Martin to Dartmouth, June 30, 1775, *North Carolina Colonial Records,* X, 48). A recent study designed to vindicate the authenticity of the Mecklenburg Declaration of Independence of May 20, 1775, is V. V. McNitt's *Chain of Error and the Mecklenburg Declarations of Independence. A New Study of Manuscripts: Their Use, Abuse, and Neglect* (Palmer, Mass. and New York, 1960); a review of this volume by H. T. Colbourn is in the July 1961 issue of the *American Historical Review,* LXVI, 1130–1. For the chief previous works relating to the controversy, see the following: G. W. Graham: *The Mecklenburg Declaration of Independence, May 20, 1775, and Lives of Its Signers* (New York and Washington, 1905); A. S. Salley, Jr.: *The True Mecklenburg "Declaration of Independence"* (Columbia, S.C., 1905), which denies the authenticity of the Mecklenburg County declaration; J. H. Moore: *Defence of the Mecklenburg Declaration of Independence . . .* (Raleigh, 1908); W. H. Hoyt: *The Mecklenburg Declaration of Independence: A Study of Evidence showing that the Alleged Early Declaration of Independence by Mecklenburg County, North Carolina, on May 20, 1775, is Spurious* (New York and London, 1907); A. S. Salley, Jr.: "The Mecklenburg Declaration: The Present Status of the

Great Britain.[22] Meanwhile, it was decided to hold the general convention not in Johnston County on August 20, as originally planned, but in the capital of the province, New Bern, on August 25.[23]

Upon receiving the news of these developments, Governor Martin called a meeting of the Council at which he reviewed the events and characterized the resolves as "derogatory to the dignity of His Majesty, and His Parliament." After seeking the advice of his councillors, he issued a proclamation on August 13 in which he enjoined "all and every His Majesty's Subjects, to forbear to attend at any such illegal meetings" as that planned for August 25 and called on the justices of the peace, sheriffs, and other officers to assist in preventing the proposed New Bern gathering.[24] But his proclamation went unheeded as freeholders in other counties took preparatory action.[25] When the day of the 25th arrived, Martin found that the arm of the legally constituted government of the province had been paralyzed. He sought the advice of his Council as to what should be done, but in the unanimous opinion of the councilmen there was no way to prevent the illegal gathering.[26] In fact, it had

---

Question," *American Historical Review* (1907), XIII, 16–43, which repudiates the findings of Graham and supports Hoyt's conclusion; Adelaide L. Fries: *The Mecklenburg Declaration of Independence, as Mentioned in Records of Wachovia* (Raleigh, 1907); and Archibald Henderson: *Cradle of Liberty; Historical Essays Concerning the Mecklenburg Declaration of Independence, Mecklenburg County, North Carolina, May 20, 1775* (Charlotte, 1955), composed of some thirty articles written from time to time to vindicate the Mecklenburg declaration. When the writer of this series was taking a course in historical methods, as a graduate student at Yale under Professor Max Farrand, the Mecklenburg Declaration of Independence of May 20, 1775, was held up as a classic example of an attempt to foist a fraud on the public; however, he has since been persuaded by the evidence to believe that a declaration of independence was made on May 20, 1775, at Charlotte, followed on May 31 by a series of resolves which, while not mentioning independence, were nevertheless outspoken in opposition to the government of Great Britain.

[22] For the Rowan County resolves of August 8, 1774, see *North Carolina Colonial Records*, IX, 1024–6. These resolves were entered into by but twenty-five freeholders. It is therefore difficult to determine what were the true sentiments of the majority of the inhabitants of the county. See J. S. Brawley: *The Rowan Story, 1753–1953, A Narrative History of Rowan County, North Carolina* (Salisbury, N.C., 1953), p. 63.

[23] See the letter to the freeholders of Craven County of August 9, 1774, *North Carolina Colonial Records*, IX, 1026–7.

[24] For the minutes of Council of August 12 and 13, 1774, and the proclamation, see *ibid.*, IX, 1028–30.

[25] For example, action was taken in Johnston County on August 12, the day before the proclamation, in Pitt and Granville counties on August 15, in Anson County on the 18th, and in Chowan and Halifax counties on the 22nd. See *ibid.*, IX, 1030–41.

[26] For the Council minute see *ibid.*, IX, 1041.

become clear by the summer of 1774 that North Carolina was offering allegiance to the King on the one hand but openly resisting Crown authority on the other.[27]

The first North Carolina provincial convention or congress, which met at New Bern, saw the gathering of seventy-one deputies selected from thirty counties and six towns.[28] The people chosen to attend were apparently those who would have represented their respective counties or towns in the Assembly, had it been called. With John Harvey[29] again acting as moderator, and ignoring the Governor at "Tryon's Palace," the meeting proceeded to take steps for setting up at least the beginnings of a *de facto* government. The members entered into certain resolutions, including an association not to import any slaves after November 1 or any goods coming from Great Britain or the West Indies after January 1, 1775, and after October 1, 1775, not to export any commodity to Great Britain "unless American Greivances are redressed." To enforce this association, it was voted that a committee of five associators be chosen from each county. It was also agreed to send three deputies to the Continental Congress.[30] One of the instructions given to them stated that they should "assert our rights to all the privileges of British subjects particularly that of paying no taxes or duties but with our own consent, and that the Legislature of this province, have the exclusive

---

[27] C. L. Raper: *North Carolina. A Study in English Colonial Government* (New York, 1904), p. 248.

[28] For some unexplained reason the counties of Edgecombe, Guilford, Hertford, Surry, and Wake were not represented at the convention; nor were the towns of Brunswick, Campbellton, (Cambeton, Cambleton, Cambelton), and Hillsborough. See *North Carolina Colonial Records*, IX, 1041–3. For the situation in Edgecombe County, complicated by the fact that it included all of the Granville district, see J. K. Turner and J. L. Bridgers, Jr.: *History of Edgecombe County, North Carolina* (Raleigh, 1920), Chap. 3.

[29] Apparently John Harvey continued as an active local leader after the provincial congress, for we find him signing a letter on September 20, 1774, on behalf of "the inhabitants of two or three Counties in the neighborhood of Edenton," announcing their donations to the Boston sufferers and enclosing a copy of the resolves taken by the provincial congress; see *North Carolina Historical Review*, IX, 303–4. For the acknowledgment of David Jeffries, for the Boston Committee of Donations, in which is given a vivid picture of Boston under siege in October 1774, see *ibid.*, IX, 304–6. In the Jeffries letter the North Carolina resolves are acknowledged as being "manly, spirited and noble."

[30] Among the delegates to the First Continental Congress was Richard Caswell, later to become first Governor of the state of North Carolina. For his activities, as they reflect those of the province in 1774–5, see C. B. Alexander: "Richard Caswell: Versatile Leader of the Revolution," *North Carolina Historical Review*, XXIII, 119–41.

power of making laws to regulate our internal Polity subject to his Majesty's disallowance." Thus, for all practical purposes, North Carolina declared its independence of Parliament.[31]

South Carolina

The revolutionary movement in South Carolina down to 1774 has already been treated in the preceding volume of this series,[32] with emphasis on the claim of the Commons House of Assembly to the exclusive right to appropriate funds and its denial that the Council of the province was a legislative body. Now the colony turned from its internal struggle for political equality to enter into political relations with the other North American colonies. Peyton Randolph, Speaker of the Virginia House of Burgesses, wrote to Rawlins Lowndes, Speaker of the South Carolina Commons House of Assembly, on March 19, 1773, enclosing the resolves of the Burgesses proposing an official intercolonial correspondence for the protection of "the ancient, legal, and constitutional Rights" of the colonies.[33] It was not until July 8, however, that Lowndes could bring this letter to the attention of the Assembly, which immediately gave hearty endorsement to the plan.[34] However, nothing beyond the appoint-

[31] For the proceedings of the first North Carolina provincial congress see *North Carolina Colonial Records*, IX, 1043–9. One thing that greatly disheartened Governor Martin was that members of the Council, who should have supported him in his position on the illegality of the New Bern convention, mixed with the delegates "and rather abetted and encouraged the measures that they had to me condemned" (Martin to Dartmouth, September 1, 1774, *ibid.*, IX, 1056). In determining the relative strength of the patriots and Loyalists of North Carolina, care must be taken to distinguish the Regulators and their sympathizers—most of whom were undoubtedly bitter against the low-country Whigs—from those who were actively "Tory" in sentiment. For the addresses of loyalty to the King from Rowan, Surry, Guilford, and Anson counties which were sent to Governor Martin early in 1775 see *ibid.*, IX, 1160–4. For a study of the strength or, rather weakness of the latter see I. S. Harrell: "North Carolina Loyalists," *North Carolina Historical Review*, III, 575–90; see also R. B. Morris: "Class Struggle and the American Revolution," *William and Mary Quarterly*, 3rd. ser., XIX, 15–16. For an excellent brief statement of the steps taken in the Carolinas and Georgia before the outbreak of hostilities, see J. R. Alden: *The South in the Revolution, 1763–1789* (Baton Rouge, 1957), Chap. 10, "Tea and Trumpets."

[32] See Volume XI, Chap. 15.

[33] Journal of the Commons House of Assembly of South Carolina (ms.), Vol. 39, Part II:25–7, South Carolina Archives Department, Columbia, S.C.; to be cited hereafter as Commons House Journals.

[34] See Lowndes to Randolph, July 9, 1773, concerning the resolves of the South Carolina Commons House of Assembly, *Journals of the House of Burgesses of Virginia, 1773–1776*, pp. 54–5.

ment of a special committee of nine, chosen from the general committee of correspondence, took place before the Assembly was adjourned until August.[35] Local affairs occupied the subsequent sessions, in the main, until, after further adjournments, the Assembly again met for business on March 1, 1774. But before this, when the news of the Boston Tea Party had arrived in January, a general meeting of the inhabitants had assembled in Charleston on the 20th, at which a large committee had been appointed to recommend to a subsequent general meeting every means necessary "to assert, preserve, and secure, the natural and constitutional Rights and Privileges of Britain American Freemen, against arbitrary and illegal encroachments." Also at this meeting strong resolves were entered into against the purchase and use of tea.[36] On March 8, Speaker Lowndes laid before the Commons House copies of letters received from various assemblies telling of the developing crisis within the Empire. He was ordered to send a reply to thank them for their support of American rights and to acquaint them with the particular grievances that the province lay under "in the Exercise of legal and Constitutional Rights of granting Aids to the Crown. And also of the assumed Power of the Council. . . ."[37] But thereafter the efforts of the Commons House were so directly concerned with the internal problems of the province that no further steps were taken in the field of intercolonial cooperation before the proroguing of the Assembly by Lieutenant Governor Bull on March 28 until May 3 and then by other prorogations to August 2.[38]

Although the Assembly was meanwhile chiefly concerned with the liquidation of the provincial debt in favour of a multitude of creditors, popular feeling against the government of Great Britain was also finding expression. On March 16 another general meeting of inhabitants took place at the Liberty Tree in Charleston. There the general committee appointed in January was authorized to carry out the resolves of the meeting, including the one on non-importation. The following day a great celebration occurred in Charleston to commemorate the date of the repeal of the Stamp Act. According to the account printed in the March 21 issue of the *South-Carolina Gazette*, this celebration was of such a nature as to convince every unprejudiced man that there were nowhere "more loyal Subjects, or

[35] Commons House Journal, 39, Part II:30.
[36] *South-Carolina Gazette,* January 24, 1774.
[37] Commons House Journal, 39, Part II:113.
[38] *Ibid.,* pp. 170–2.

a People more Desirous, or better disposed to live upon good Terms with the Mother Country, or that could more zealously support the just Claims and Expectations of [the British] Government, provided it would treat us as the English Constitution gives us a Right to expect, and not as Aliens, or illegitimate." The *Gazette,* up to the issue of April 18, 1774, featured news that was distinctly local in character, but from that date forward its columns were devoted chiefly to arousing the public to an awareness of the menace to American liberties implicit in the current actions of the British government. For example, there was the printing of inflammatory letters, such as the one by "Junius Americanus" (Arthur Lee) in the issue of June 6. This same number highlighted the leading part played by South Carolinians in England in protesting the closing of the port of Boston, by pointing out that among the twenty-nine Americans who signed a petition opposing the bill were eleven natives of the province.[39] The *Gazette* for June 13 was devoted almost exclusively to news of the revolutionary movement in other colonies, and the issue of June 20 contained an unusually bitter letter to the printer signed "A Carolinian," in which the writer stated that one purpose of the Boston Port Act was to make possible "the Support of a thousand more Bloodsuckers in America" and that the statute was enacted in spite of "the Sanctity of a most solemn Charter." The same number printed a call for a meeting of the inhabitants on July 6 at the Charleston Exchange, to consider letters received from the Northern colonies and also to decide what steps should be taken "in Union with the Inhabitants of all our Sister Colonies on this Continent." The following week there appeared an advertisement appealing for relief for the distressed people of Boston, which stated that any rice sent for that purpose to Christopher Gadsden's wharf would be handled and shipped to its destination without a farthing's charge; the same issue of the *Gazette* also contained a second letter by "A Carolinian" outlining a plan of economic pressure for the colonies to take that would bring Great Britain to terms.

By the time of the general meeting planned for July 6, the public had been thoroughly aroused. As a result, the gathering was the

---

[39] A. S. Salley, Jr., editor of the *South Carolina Historical and Genealogical Magazine* (IV, 32n), in publishing the letter written from Westminster by Henry Laurens, one of the signers, to his son John on March 25, 1774, points out that there were thirty signers of the petition, of whom sixteen were South Carolinians; see also, in this connection, W. L. Sachse: *The Colonial American in Britain* (Madison, 1956), pp. 180, 181, 183, 189.

largest that had taken place in Charleston up to that time.[40] Delegates, to the number of 104, came to it from every county or parish, except Granville County and the parishes of St. John in Colleton County and Christ Church.[41] But the non-delegates in attendance, chiefly mechanics and planters living in or about Charleston, apparently dominated the meeting, since everyone present was accorded an equal vote.[42] It may be noted that prior to this meeting the Charleston Chamber of Commerce had agreed to oppose any plan for embargoing Great Britain, and had determined to bind the South Carolina delegates to the proposed Continental Congress to stand against any non-importation and non-exportation measures. It is therefore not surprising that the resolves entered into after long debate[43] did not mention restrictions on commerce that would threaten the livelihood of the merchants,[44] or that, in enumerating the powers that the Congress itself might assume in defending American rights, it was specified that South Carolina would feel bound to submit only to those agreed upon by its deputies.[45] The choice of delegates thus became a matter of the highest importance, especially as a wide difference of opinion had developed during the meeting over the question of limiting their power. The merchants presented a slate, but in the voting the much more radically minded artisans and planters carried the day.[46] Their

---

[40] *South-Carolina Gazette*, July 11, 1774.

[41] John Drayton: *Memoirs of the American Revolution* . . . (2 vols., Charleston, 1821), I, 126, based on the manuscript left by William Henry Drayton; D. D. Wallace: *South Carolina. A Short History, 1520–1948* (Chapel Hill, N.C., 1951), p. 253; and Richard Walsh: *Charleston's Sons of Liberty* . . . (Columbia, 1959), p. 62.

[42] For an excellent account of the method of securing delegates for the July 1774 general gathering at Charleston, see W. A. Schaper: "Sectionalism and Representation in South Carolina," *Annual Report of the American Historical Association for the Year 1900* (2 vols., Washington, 1901), I, 357–9.

[43] For the Charleston resolves of July 6, 7, and 8, 1774, see *American Archives*, 4th ser., I, 525–7. The formation of the Charleston Chamber of Commerce in 1773 is discussed in Chap. 3 of this volume.

[44] See Drayton: *op. cit.*, I, 128–9, for pro and con arguments on the embargo plan.

[45] *Ibid.*, I, 130, in which Drayton points out that Rawlins Lowndes asserted at the gathering "that it was well known, the Northern Colonies in general, totally denied the superintending power of Parliament, a doctrine, which no one here admitted." In view of this difference of opinion, it was essential, Lowndes argued, to prevent the South Carolina delegates from being bound by the Congress to support views not held by the people. Therefore, the resolution that vested the deputies with power was so worded "that no vote in Congress could bind this Colony, but such as was agreeable to the opinion of our Deputies."

[46] In the election of the delegates to the Congress, held on July 7, "every free white person . . . entitled to vote" could cast a ballot, whether or not he was a formal deputy to the Charleston meeting. The announcement of the election results in the *South-Carolina Gazette* of July 11 listed the names of members of the Commons

choice included men with revolutionary views such as Christopher Gadsden[47] and Thomas Lynch, both of whom had represented South Carolina at the Stamp Act Congress in 1765.[48] Before adjourning on July 8, the Charleston general meeting assumed the authority to appoint a general committee of ninety-nine persons, empowering it not only to correspond with committees in other colonies but also to do anything "necessary for carrying the Resolutions of the General Meeting into execution." Thus, in the words of William Henry Drayton, it "virtually vested the Committee with unlimited powers, during their existence"[49]—powers that enabled it to become the *de facto* government of the province.

The manner of appointing delegates to represent South Carolina in the approaching congress—as was realized by leading men in the province—was highly irregular, since it ignored the Commons House of Assembly as the legally constituted organ for the expression of the popular will and also as the source of supply to finance the delegates. Preparations were therefore made to remedy this defect when the Commons House assembled on August 2. By private agreement the members gathered in the Commons chamber at an early-morning hour. Two of them then took a message to Lieutenant Governor Bull to inform him that they had assembled "agreeable to His Honor the Lieutenant Governor's Prorogation." Upon the return of the two members, the chairman of the Charleston gathering, Colonel George Gabriel Powell, who was also a member of the Assembly, reported on the work of that meeting—particularly the

House of Assembly who had voted, in order to show that the electors were not a mere gathering of the "Rabble." For an extended account of the Charleston meeting see *American Archives*, 4th ser., I, 531–4.

[47] Silas Deane, representing Connecticut at the Continental Congress, had the following to say about Gadsden after first meeting him in Philadelphia: "Mr. Gadsden leaves all New England Sons of Liberty far behind, for he is for taking up his firelock and marching direct to Boston; nay, he affirmed this morning, that were his wife and all his children in Boston, and they were there to perish by the sword, it would not alter his sentiment or proceeding for American Liberty. . . ." Deane to Mrs. Deane [September 7, 1774], *Letters of Members of the Continental Congress* (ed. E. C. Burnett, 8 vols., Washington, 1921–38), I, 18.

[48] Of the five delegates elected—Henry Middleton, John Rutledge, Thomas Lynch, Christopher Gadsden, and Edward Rutledge—the merchants were favourable to only the first two. Middleton was a lawyer who had inherited the great plantation "Middleton Place" near Charleston (still one of the show places in South Carolina). John Rutledge, like Middleton, had been a student at Middle Temple in London, but, unlike him, had concentrated on the law and built up a great practice in Charleston. In the First Continental Congress his position was a conservative one in contrast to views voiced by Lynch and Gadsden.

[49] Drayton: *op. cit.*, I, 131–2.

appointment of the five persons as "Deputies on the part and behalf of this Colony" to attend the Congress in Philadelphia for the purpose of securing a redress of colonial grievances by the repeal of acts by Parliament "which made an invidious distinction between His Majesty's Subjects in Great Britain and America." Powell thereupon proposed: "That this House do resolve to recognize, ratify and Confirm the said Appointments . . . and that this House do also Resolve to provide a Sum not exceeding One Thousand five hundred Pounds Sterling to defray the expense which the said Deputies will be at in the said Service." The members immediately resolved unanimously to approve the work of the general Charleston meeting and to guarantee to repay with interest any person who should advance the sum required by the deputies. While the Assembly was considering the next item of business—that of sending a message to the Lieutenant Governor relating to the defenceless condition of the settlers on the frontier—a message arrived from Bull summoning the members to the Council chamber. When they appeared, he immediately prorogued the General Assembly to September 6.[50]

By the procedure just described, the deputies of South Carolina were enabled to depart for the Continental Congress with the full sanction of the Assembly. They also undoubtedly carried with them Judge William Henry Drayton's pamphlet *A Letter from* FREEMAN *of South Carolina, to the Deputies of North-America, assembled in the High Court of Congress at Philadelphia*.[51] In it Drayton set down

[50] In his letter to the Earl of Dartmouth, dated August 3, Bull commented on the "perseverance, secrecy and unanimity" with which the Assembly "form and conduct their designs" (*American Archives*, 4th ser., I, 672). It should be noted that before transacting any business on September 6, the Assembly was again prorogued, this time to October 18. For the proceedings of the Commons House of Assembly on August 2 and September 6, 1774, see Commons House Journals, 39, Part II:173–4; see also David Ramsay: *The History of the Revolution of South-Carolina . . .* (2 vols., Trenton, N.J., 1785), I, 55–7. For two studies assessing the plagiarist aspects of Ramsay as a historian, see O. G. Libby: "Ramsay as a Plagiarist," *American Historical Review*, VII, 697–703, and E. D. Johnson: "David Ramsay: Historian or Plagiarist," *South Carolina Historical and Genealogical Magazine*, LVII, 189–98; for a defence of Ramsay see Page Smith: "David Ramsay and the Causes of the American Revolution," *William and Mary Quarterly*, 3rd ser., XVII, 51–77.

[51] The pamphlet was signed "FREEMAN, South-Carolina, Charles-Town, August 10, 1774"; see R. W. Gibbes: *Documentary History of the American Revolution . . . 1764–1776* (New York, 1855), pp. 11–39. For a recent penetrating study of Drayton, in which the authors point out the extent to which Drayton's thwarted ambitions seem to have influenced his change of sides from a loyal supporter of the royal government of South Carolina to a bitter opponent of it, see W. M. Dabney and Marion Dargan: *William Henry Drayton, and the American Revolution* (Albuquerque, N.M., 1962). For a brief note on Drayton's dismissal from the Council as a result of his "Freeman" pamphlet, see Volume XI in this series, Chap. 15.

a bill of rights denying the authority of Parliament to lay a tax on colonials or "in any shape to bind American freeholders of the British Crown, . . . because their consent is not signified in Parliament, by a representative of their own election." His position on the exercise of Crown powers in the colonies was that the King's prerogative "cannot of right, be more extensive in America, than it is by law limited in England." As to granting aid to the Crown by Americans and binding them by laws, this was to be done only upon the same basis as aids were granted and laws passed by Parliament. To this end there should be summoned "a High Court of Assembly of North America" by royal writs addressed to the two houses of assembly in every colony directing each of them to choose an equal number of representatives. The plan advocated by Drayton for setting up this High Court proposed limiting its powers to matters of "a general nature," with each colony "regulating her internal policy as heretofore, by her own internal legislature."

As a special postscript at this juncture, it is desirable to look ahead momentarily in order to examine certain actions of South Carolina during and after the First Continental Congress which point up one type of colonial rationalization with reference to debts. When the Continental Congress, working in committee, was dealing with plans for the Association to prohibit trade with Great Britain,[52] it found that the Virginia delegates wanted to postpone the embargo on the export of tobacco until the fall of 1776 and that the South Carolina delegates refused to support any measure that prevented the export of their province's rice and indigo. Concurrently, the Maryland and North Carolina delegates would not agree to prohibit their tobacco exports unless Virginia fell into line. When the Virginia delegates finally consented to stop all exports to Great Britain after September 10, 1775, the South Carolina delegation also capitulated to a limited degree, but only under duress. In fact, when the continental Association for non-importation and non-exportation had evolved to a point where the delegates were making signed commitments for their respective colonies, all the South Carolina representatives except Gadsden withdrew from the Congress.[53]

---

[52] On September 30 Congress resolved that after September 10, 1775, the exporting of commodities to Great Britain, Ireland, and the West Indies should cease. See *Journals of the Continental Congress*, I, 51–2. This was an outline of policy generally agreed upon, but was not binding on any colony that would not sign the Association.

[53] See F. W. Ryan, Jr.: "The Role of South Carolina in the First Continental Congress," *South Carolina Historical Magazine*, LX, 151–2.

Only when the proceedings had reached a point where the Congress was prepared, if need be, to exclude this colony from both the continental Association and the union of the colonies, did the South Carolina delegates capitulate to the extent of agreeing to cease the exportation of indigo. When these delegates were later criticized at the first meeting of the South Carolina Provincial Congress on January 11, 1775, for their refusal to yield on the point of rice,[54] they defended their action. John Rutledge pointed out that he and his fellow delegates from the colony had been prepared to agree to a total non-exportation of all commodities to all countries, but it had seemed unfair to them that the Northern colonies, with very little direct export to Great Britain but large exports elsewhere, should demand that South Carolina be ruined, since all its indigo and two-thirds of its rice went to the British Isles.[55] Nevertheless, an effort was made in the Provincial Congress to "recommend to our future Delegates, to offer on the Part of the Inhabitants of this Colony,

[54] The delegates from the other colonies introduced into the Association's agreement on non-exportation the clause "except rice to Europe." It was after this concession had been made that the Association was signed by all the delegates on October 20. Not all rice planters in South Carolina approved of this exemption in their favour. For example, in the *South-Carolina Gazette* of January 2, 1775, "A County Rice Planter" raised a series of queries having to do with what he felt was an unfair concession to South Carolina and suggested that the rice planters should patriotically refuse to avail themselves of this exemption from the general terms of the Association. It was at the January 11, 1775, meeting that the South Carolina Assembly's name was changed to "Provincial Congress."

[55] See *Journals of the Continental Congress*, I, 51–2; Drayton: *Memoirs*, I, 167–71 and 175–8; see also Edward McCrady: *The History of South Carolina under the Royal Government, 1719–1776* (New York and London, 1899), pp. 757–62 and 804–6. The reason why Virginia gave way on the export of tobacco, while South Carolina refused to concede on the matter of rice, doubtless lies in the fact that most of the tobacco shipped to Great Britain from the Old Dominion went by consignment to liquidate debts incurred by planters buying on credit, while the rice planters seem to have operated on a different economy, with their crops as a rule not mortgaged in advance of shipping. Thus the non-exportation of tobacco would affect chiefly the British creditors, but in the case of the non-exportation of rice, the planters themselves would suffer. It should be noted, however, that the Provincial Congress that met at Charleston in January 1775 followed the example of Virginia by resolving to close the courts to all cases involving debts, unless such action was opposed by the local committee of the parish or district in which the debtor resided; again, the court could act only where the debtor refused to renew his obligation or give reasonable security or where he was justly suspected of planning to defraud his creditor by leaving the province or other means. For this resolve and a series of other resolutions relating to it, see William Moultrie: *Memoirs of the American Revolution . . .* (2 vols., New York, 1802), I, 40–6. What part William Henry Drayton, deeply in debt to the royal Governor of East Florida, had in the passing of this resolve cannot be stated. At least he felt free enough from court proceedings to stop paying interest on the debt and eventually to repudiate it. In this connection see W. H. Dabney and Marion Dargon: *op. cit.*, pp. 45–7.

merely for the Advancement of the Common Cause, a Sacrifice of Every Advantage we might derive from the Words 'except Rice to Europe,'" but after heated debate the motion "barely was lost."[56]

Georgia

The Province of Georgia in 1774 was far from being the depressed, disheartened colony of twenty years earlier when John Reynolds, the first royal Governor, arrived in Savannah at the end of the Trusteeship.[57] It was now enjoying a degree of prosperity undreamed of during the earlier, precarious period of its existence. As late as 1760 the population comprised hardly more than 6,000 whites and 3,500 slaves,[58] but by 1772 there were some 18,000 white people employing 15,000 slaves. In 1761 the number of ships "entered and cleared in the whole province" was but 45;[59] in 1772, 217 vessels carried away the abundant exports of rice, indigo, tobacco, deer skins, lumber, staves, shingles, and other products of the land and forest, valued at £101,240 sterling, representing an average annual figure for a five-year period preceding 1773.[60] As an aid to this progress, Parliament had consistently lifted from the shoulders of the

[56] *South-Carolina Gazette*, January 23, 1775; see also Richard Walsh: *op. cit.*, pp. 65–6. It should be pointed out that on October 13, 1775, the Continental Congress resolved "That no rice be exported under the exception contained in the 4th Article of the Association from any of the United Colonies to Great Britain, Ireland . . . or any other European Island or Settlement within the British Dominions" (*Journals of the Continental Congress*, III, 292), thus placing rice under the same exportation restrictions as tobacco.

[57] For Georgia during the period of Trusteeship see Volume II, revised, of this series, Chap. 6, "An American Arcadia." For a recent important study of this province see T. R. Reese: *Colonial Georgia: A Study in British Imperial Policy in the Eighteenth Century* (Athens, Ga., 1963); unfortunately a copy was not available before the present volume went to the publisher.

[58] For Governor James Wright's report of November 18, 1766, covering the year 1760, see Shelburne Papers, 52:199–201, Clements Library.

[59] According to Wright's 1766 report (*ibid.*), "they loaded 42 sail vessels" in 1761.

[60] For these figures see Governor James Wright's "Answers to Queries," enclosed in his letter to the Earl of Dartmouth, December 20, 1773, C. O. 5:663; this report is also among the Public Record Office transcripts embodied in the Georgia Colonial Records (mss.), Vol. 38, Part I, Georgia Department of Archives and History, Atlanta. For other figures on the increase of exports and shipping from 1755 to 1770 inclusive, see B. M., King's Manuscripts, 197:72 (*ibid.*, Vol. 39), and P. S. Flippin: "Royal Government in Georgia, 1752–1776," *Georgia Historical Quarterly*, IX, 218–19 and 223n; see also Kenneth Coleman: *The American Revolution in Georgia 1763–1789* (Athens, 1958), pp. 11–12; Coleman, as does Flippin (p. 223n), gives the value of exports in 1773 as £121,677, but whether in terms of sterling or Georgia currency is not clear.

inhabitants a substantial part of the expense of maintaining their local government. For example, in 1767 the Assembly granted £1,343 colonial currency for this purpose, while Parliament granted just under £4,000 sterling.[61] Nor did the annual sums granted by Great Britain throughout the colonial period drop below £3,000 sterling.[62] In addition, until 1766, when the Cherokee and Creek Indians were quieted, the government at home had for years supported two troops of rangers for the protection of the province, at an annual cost of over £4,000 sterling.[63]

In fact, there is little doubt that during the period of royal government in Georgia, 1754 to 1776, the people of Great Britain contributed far more monetary support to the stability of the colony than did its inhabitants. This fact alone would undoubtedly help to explain the division of opinion among the people toward the mother country both at the time of the Stamp Act crisis in 1765[64] and in 1774. In addition, there was the continuing threat of Indian hostilities on the western frontier. In the spring of 1774—when some Georgians who went to settle on lands ceded by the Indians were "wantonly, and unprovokedly, attacked and Murdered by that inhuman and perfidious people, in open violation of the most solemn treaties"—the Commons House of Assembly made clear in an address to the King that the province was "yet very far from being able to Act against so numerous and dangerous an Enemy as the Indians without your Majesty's gracious support, . . . and [therefore] solicit your Majesty for such protection and Assistance as in your wisdom you may think sufficient . . . for our Security and Welfare."[65] Moreover, the colony of Georgia had, in the person of Sir James Wright, one of the most capable Governors that any American colony had enjoyed in the course of the eighteenth cen-

[61] See Governor Wright to the Earl of Shelburne, May 15, 1767, Shelburne Papers, 55:263–70, and the *Annual Register, 1767*, p. 218.

[62] For example, in voting the supplies for 1775, the sum of £3,086 was granted by Parliament for the support of the government of Georgia. See the *Annual Register, 1775*, p. 244.

[63] Wright to Shelburne, May 15, 1767, Shelburne Papers, 55:263–70. For the Cherokee and Creek hostilities see Volume IX in this series, Chap. IV, "The Cherokee War, 1759–1761," and pp. 220–4. See also General Gage to Shelburne, December 23, 1766, and February 20, 1767, *Gage Correspondence* (ed. C. E. Carter, 2 vols., New Haven, 1931, 1933), I, 115–16 and 120.

[64] For an interesting study of the Stamp Act crisis in Georgia see C. A. Ellefson's article in the *Georgia Historical Quarterly*, XLVI, 1–19.

[65] "The Humble Address of the Commons House of Assembly . . . ," March 7, 1774, *Colonial Records of Georgia* (ed. A. D. Candler, 26 vols., Atlanta, 1904–16), XV, 542–3.

tury, and one most devoted to the interests of the people.[66] Under these circumstances it undoubtedly seemed to many thoughtful Georgians in 1774 that to turn upon the King and Parliament was much like biting the hand that had fed them.

Nevertheless, Georgia could neither isolate nor insulate itself from North American colonial developments in the 1760's and 1770's. It had in the royal period come strongly under the influence of its neighbouring colony, South Carolina, especially in its parallel attempts to strengthen the power of the Commons House of Assembly. The chief point of departure in Georgia in the 1760's had been the pursuit of authority to make executive appointments—something which had virtually been achieved by 1770, except for the appointment of the public treasurer. However, Governor Wright foresaw in this development a threat to his appointive powers and, during his stay in England from 1771 to February 1773, had attempted to obtain a revision of this practice. As a result, he secured an additional instruction ordering him to withhold his assent to future laws involving "the appointment of any person or persons to any executive office or offices."[67] This additional instruction might well have become the basis for a serious dispute between the Governor and the Commons—similar to that which took place in South Carolina[68] —had it not been for three factors: the tact of Acting Governor James Habersham, the steps taken by the Governor to prorogue the Assembly upon his return from England, and the intervention of the revolutionary crisis.[69]

---

[66] In his Introduction to *The Revolutionary Records of the State of Georgia* (3 vols., Atlanta, 1908), the editor, A. D. Candler, wrote (I, 7) that "Georgia was the youngest, the most remote, the most sparsely populated, the poorest and, consequently, the least important of the thirteen [colonies]. She had not suffered as had other provinces from hostile legislation. . . . Her people, therefore, had but little to complain of, and much for which to be grateful. . . . Her Governor, Sir James Wright, was an able man, not unpopular with his people, for the province had prospered under his administration as it never had before. . . ." for the career of Wright in Georgia, see W. W. Abbot: *The Royal Governors of Georgia, 1754–1775* (Chapel Hill, N.C., 1959), pp. 84–183, Kenneth Coleman: *op. cit.*, pp. 3–4 *et seq.*, and by the same author the essay on Wright in *Georgians in Profile* . . . (ed. Horace Montgomery, Athens, 1958); see also *Historical Collections of Georgia* (ed. George White, New York, 1854); pp. 188–96, cited hereafter as White's *Historical Collections,* as distinguished from the Georgia Historical Society *Collections.*

[67] For the additional instruction of February 1 and 4, 1772, see P.R.O., C.O. 5:674, pp. 369–70, and C.O. 5:677, pp. 70–1.

[68] See Volume XI in this series, Chap. 15.

[69] For an excellent account of these developments see J. P. Greene: "The Georgia Commons House of Assembly and the Power of Appointment to Executive Offices, 1765–1775," *Georgia Historical Quarterly,* XLVI, 151–61; see also by the same author: *The Quest for Power,* pp. 248–9 and 429–33. For additional aspects

By 1762 Georgia had established its own provincial press and had appointed James Johnston its official printer. Johnston founded the *Georgia Gazette* the following year; it was a typical conservative colonial newspaper, which disseminated rather scanty news of the outside world, especially before the late spring of 1774.[70] But this could not be said of the *South-Carolina Gazette,* published by the Charleston radical Peter Timothy, which supplied Georgia readers with abundant news of political developments in the other colonies as well as in Great Britain. Moreover, by 1774 the colony possessed a hard core of radicals, all men of education, property, and influence—among them, Noble Wimberly Jones, politician, physician, and planter, and Savannah lawyers John Houstoun, Archibald Bulloch, and George Walton—who were determined that Georgia should no longer be a laggard in the cause of American freedom. Their opposition to British policy, at least in the case of the popular Dr. Jones, went back to the period of the Stamp Act.[71]

Doubtless as the result of the example set by the meetings of South Carolinians at Charleston on July 6–8, 1774, which were reported in the *Georgia Gazette* of July 13, notices were sent out on July 14 for a meeting to be held at Savannah on the 27th in order to take into consideration certain "late Acts of the British Parliament respecting the Town of Boston" and other acts.[72] When that day arrived, "a very Respectable number of freeholders and other inhabitants" met at the exchange (called also the Watch-House or Venue House) under the chairmanship of John Glen to consider

---

of the political struggle between the Governor and the emerging radical element in the Assembly, after 1766, see W. W. Abbot: *op. cit.,* Chaps. 6 and 7.

[70] See D. C. McMurtrie: "Pioneer Printing in Georgia," *Georgia Historical Quarterly,* XVI, 77–94. The *Gazette* was published continuously for thirteen years, except for a six-month period before the repeal of the Stamp Act. See also A. A. Lawrence: *James Johnston: Georgia's First Printer* (Savannah, 1956).

[71] Jones—whose father was the great landowner Noble Jones, proprietor of "Wormslow," one of the finest of Georgia estates, and a member of the Council—was unanimously chosen Speaker of the Commons House of Assembly in 1768 and remained in that position until, because of his very strong position on the Townshend Acts, his re-election was repeatedly vetoed by the Governor in 1771 and 1772 by order of the King. See *Colonial Records of Georgia,* XV, 7–8, 305–6, 320–3, 337–8. It may be noted in passing that when the Commons House felt obliged to give up Jones as Speaker in 1771, it selected his friend and close political associate Archibald Bulloch of Savannah, and in December 1772, when Jones resigned as Speaker the day following his election, it chose for that post another of Jones's close associates, William Young, likewise of Savannah, who still held the chair in 1774.

[72] For the notice of July 14, see *Georgia Gazette,* July 20 and September 7, 1774; see also *Revolutionary Records of Georgia,* I, 11.

letters and resolutions received from other colonies. A standing committee of thirty-one was named to draw up resolutions "as nearly similar to those of the northern colonies as the present State of the Province will admit," as well as to perform other duties.[73] However, after several gentlemen present objected to the immediate adoption of resolutions on the grounds that the inhabitants of the more distant parishes might not have had sufficient notification to be present, it was decided that appropriate resolves would be considered at a gathering to be held on August 10. The further decision was reached that the chairman should advise the various parishes and districts to send the same number of delegates to the next meeting as they had a right to send to the Assembly, giving these representatives full power to act in their behalf.[74] After passing a final motion that the resolves to be adopted on August 10 would be deemed representative of the sense of the province, the meeting adjourned.[75]

Five days before the proposed August gathering Governor Wright issued a proclamation forbidding the meeting on the grounds that it was "unconstitutional, illegal, and punishable by Law,"[76] but his action was ineffective.

It should be pointed out that by July the columns of the *Georgia Gazette*—despite the newspaper's official connections with the administration—had been opened to partisan discussion of the issues of the day. The issue for the 27th boasted a leading front-page article, "The Case Stated," having to do with a defence of the position taken by the Northern colonies in the dispute with Great Britain. In the same issue there also appeared a rousing appeal "To the Freemen of the Province of Georgia"—an effort to stir the great majority of Georgians from their passive attitude toward events involving all America. The next number of the paper contained a reply by "A True Friend to Georgia," pleading for sanity in judging

---

[73]See *Georgia Gazette*, August 3, 1774, which lists the thirty-one committee members. For variations in the names of these committee-men see Hugh McCall: *History of Georgia* . . . (2 vols., Savannah, 1816), II, 19; see also *Revolutionary Records of Georgia*, I, 12 and 13.

[74] John Glen, the chairman of the meeting, was a lawyer from Halifax and the parish of St. George. For his message of July 27, 1774, to the various parishes see *ibid.*, I, 12–13, *Georgia Gazette*, September 7, 1774, and White's *Historical Collections*, p. 44.

[75] For the proceedings of the July 27 meeting see *Georgia Gazette*, August 3, 1774.

[76] *Ibid.*, August 10, 1774; see also *Revolutionary Records of Georgia*, I, 14–15.

public measures. By quoting the exact words of the Act for the Impartial Administration of Justice, the writer demonstrated that the scope of this much-denounced statute was limited to Massachusetts Bay; he also showed that it applied only to those Crown officers whose duty of upholding the laws required them to act in such a way that, without the legislation, the ends of justice might be defeated. Again, on the very day of the August 10 meeting, the *Gazette* printed a letter signed "Mercurius" which took sharp issue with the author of "The Case Stated." Referring to the plight of Boston, the writer asserted that the question was not so much the old one of taxation, but that of "whether the Americans have a right to destroy private property with impunity." Had Boston been prepared to make reparation for the destruction of the tea, there would have been no legislation against either it or the Province of Massachusetts Bay. What the people of Georgia must keep in mind, the writer stressed, was that they had a powerful enemy, the Creeks, on their backs. People recently fled at the approach of the Indians; yet, no sooner had the panic subsided a little, "Mercurius" continued:

> "but we insult our best and only friend, from whom alone we can expect protection. *Carolina,* it is certain, will give us none. And it is in vain to expect it from the Northern Provinces. . . . Our entering into resolutions against the Government, in the present case, can answer no end but to injure our infant province, by provoking the Mother Country to desert us. Great Britain is our only dependence."

Concomitantly, the *Gazette* printed not only General Gage's June 30 proclamation of warning against signing the Solemn League and Covenant but also the protest made in the House of Lords on May 18 upon the third reading of the Act for the Impartial Administration of Justice.

Thus Georgians were fairly well informed when, "on Wednesday the 10th Day of August, 1774, at a General Meeting of the Inhabitants of the Province" assembled at Savannah "to consider the State of the Colonies in America," they entered into eight resolutions.[77] These resolves were moderate, on the whole, chiefly protesting the unconstitutionality of the parliamentary measures directed against Massachusetts Bay. No plans for an association were evolved, nor were any delegates appointed to the Continental Congress, despite

---

[77] *Georgia Gazette,* August 17, 1774.

the efforts of the people representing St. John's Parish.[78] This parish comprehended the towns of Midway and Sunbury. Its leading settlers were members of the Congregational communion and were closely knit within the so-called Society of Midway, which centred in the Congregational church they erected in that commonage.[79]

Ardently in sympathy with the aspirations of their fellow Congregationalists in Massachusetts Bay, the leaders of the parish of St. John, when rebuffed on August 10, according to the *Georgia Gazette,*

> "had a meeting last week at Midway, when they entered into resolutions differing from those published in last week's paper. We hear they are to meet again next Tuesday to chuse Deputies to attend at the approaching Congress: and that they have collected together about 170 barrels of rice and £50 in cash, to be sent to the poor in Boston."[80]

Held at Midway on August 30, the second meeting was apparently attended by representatives from three other parishes—St. Andrew, St. George, and St. David (the last-named located to the south of the Altamaha River). There, according to a report of the meeting, "they came to this further Resolution: 'That if the majority of the other Parishes would join with them, they would sent Deputies to join the General Congress, and faithfully and religiously abide by,

---

[78] See *American Archives,* 4th ser., I, 766–7, in which an unidentified person writing from St. John's Parish on September 2, 1774, explains the voting down of the motion to send deputies as the work of "a majority of numbers of gentlemen of Savannah, who were not properly constituted, and had no right to vote in the case."

[79] The history of this group in America goes back to the year 1630, when Dorchester, Massachusetts Bay, was settled by Puritans from southwestern England. Most of the original group of settlers removed to Connecticut five years later to establish the town of Windsor; then, in 1695, another Dorchester group accepted an invitation to settle on the Ashley River above Charleston, and there planted a town, likewise called Dorchester. But the land was not fertile and the settlers did not prosper. In 1752, when a generous grant of Georgia land was made to them, they formed the community of Midway. Some of these Congregationalists, still retaining their ties to the Midway church, removed to Sunbury, which by 1774 had become the second most thriving port in Georgia. See James Stacy: *History of the Midway Congregational Church, Liberty County, Georgia* (Newman, Ga., 1899) and Josephine D. Martin: "The Society of Midway," *Georgia Historical Quarterly,* XI, 321–9. For a history of Sunbury and the "Midway District" see *Georgia Historical Society Collections,* IV, 141–223; see also White's *Historical Collections,* pp. 513–31, for an account of "Liberty County" (which was formed in 1777 from the parishes of St. John, St. Andrew, and St. James) and Governor Wright's letter to the Earl of Dartmouth of April 24, 1775, describing the St. John's people as retaining "a strong tincture of Republican or Oliverian principles," and their radical actions in 1775 as those of "poor insignificant fanatics [who] no sooner entered into association, than they broke through it . . ." (*ibid.,* p. 523).

[80] See *Georgia Gazette,* August 24, 1774.

and conform to, such determinations and resolutions as should be there entered into, and come from thence recommended.' "[81] They also nominated a deputy, who would, "if the other Parishes agree, finally attend at the General Congress."[82] Another report of the meeting stated: "It is said Dr. Lyman Hall[83] was chosen to attend at the General Congress, but thinking himself not sufficiently authorized . . . having been appointed only by Deputies of St. John, St. Andrew, St. David and St. George, he declined."[84]

The Georgia records are neither detailed nor clear on precisely what took place at the August 10 meeting or at subsequent gatherings promoted by the leaders of St. John's Parish and others, but it is evident that Governor Wright was doing everything within his power to keep Georgia from being swept into the revolutionary movement. Whether it was through his efforts that the tide of protest swelled against the resolutions and other steps taken on the 10th can only be conjectured—since he undoubtedly exercised a great influence upon the official printer of the *Georgia Gazette* as well as upon men in influential places.[85] Yet the division between the people of the colony quickly became apparent at this juncture. This is especially evident in the colony's newspaper for the period.

The news, as reported in the *Gazette,* was mixed. On the one hand the paper printed accounts of the steps being taken in other colonies to enter into non-intercourse associations or, as in the case of Rhode Island, to proclaim "a day of fasting and prayer, on account of the dark aspect of our publick affairs," and on the other hand there appeared notices of the safe trans-shipment of tea on

---

[81] For the above extract of a letter from the parish of St. John, dated September 2, 1774, see *American Archives,* 4th ser., I, 766–7.

[82] See *ibid.,* which indicates that agreement of the parish of St. Andrew (lying north of the Altamaha and including the town of Darien) to the resolution came later.

[83] Hall, a native of Wallingford, Connecticut, was graduated from Yale, but after entering the Congregational ministry, deserted it for medicine. He decided to cast in his lot with the Dorchester, South Carolina, Congregationalists and when some of them founded the town of Sunbury he joined them, there built up a large practice, and became deeply involved in political affairs. No one in Georgia was a more ardent revolutionist than Hall, who later was seated in the Second Continental Congress and became a signer of the Declaration of Independence, as will be discussed in a subsequent chapter.

[84] *Georgia Gazette,* September 7, 1774.

[85] See White's *Historical Collections,* p. 47, which gives Hugh McCall as authority for stating that "the governor's influential friends" were instrumental in circulating throughout the province the petitions which resulted in the signed protests and other notices dissenting against the August 10 resolutions and other facets of the meeting.

July 1 in Portsmouth, New Hampshire, and, from New York on July 11, word of the Indians being stirred up by murders committed by Cresap and his associates on the Ohio.[86] Again, on August 31 the *Gazette* published an article by "Mercurius," followed by another by "Englishman," appealing for "Permanent Union and Harmony between Great-Britain and America"; it also printed the Boston Port Act in full at the Governor's request, but elsewhere gave accounts of fasting in Rhode Island, of the actions to appoint delegates to the Continental Congress in New Hampshire, Connecticut, and New York, and of South Carolina's gift of 205 tierces of rice to the Boston sufferers.

By September 7 the entire first page (and part of the last) of the *Georgia Gazette* was taken up with the Act for Better Regulating the Government of Massachusetts Bay.[87] In this same issue appeared the first of the public notices of protest and dissent coming in from the various parts of the colony. In it also certain inhabitants and freeholders of the town and district of Savannah,[88] who had met at the court house on August 30, sought to make clear that the August 10 gathering in no sense represented the real attitude of the people of Georgia, but was merely an unrepresentative, clandestine assemblage. The protest declared that "several districts and parishes, particularly St. Paul's, one of the most populous in the province [including the town of Augusta], sent no Deputies"; and, although two people "attended as Deputies from the parish of St. George,[89] yet upwards of 80 respectable Inhabitants of that parish sent down

---

[86] See *Georgia Gazette*, August 24, 1774.

[87] It may be noted that in August and September the *Gazette* repeatedly published the individual Coercive Acts in full, apparently "by order of His Excellency the Governor." See *ibid.*, August 31 and September 7, 14, 21, 1774.

[88] The 101 signers were led by James Habersham. Habersham, Savannah merchant, great landowner, and President of the Council—who had been Acting Governor in 1771 and 1772—was firmly loyal to the government of Great Britain. His family typifies the division of loyalties even in one family, for his three sons were as firmly committed to the patriotic cause; in fact, one of them, Joseph, was a member of the committee of thirty-one created on July 27 and later served on the Georgia committee of safety. See C. A. Ellefson: "James Habersham and Georgia Loyalism, 1764–1775," *Georgia Historical Quarterly*, XLIV, 359–80; see also the sketch of Habersham's life together with a large body of his correspondence in the Georgia Historical Society *Collections*, VI; also W. W. Abbott: *op. cit.*, pp. 156–8, and John Mebane: "Joseph Habersham in the Revolutionary War," *Georgia Historical Quarterly*, XLVII, 76–83.

[89] The parish of St. George adjoined St. Paul's to the southeast; it was the next most distant from the coast and therefore, like its neighbour, exposed to Indian attack.

their dissent; nor was the parish of Christ Church [which embraced the town of Savannah] represented at the meeting, unless the self-appointed Committee can be considered as their Representatives."[90] Those protesting further affirmed that the meeting had been a secluded one, held in a tavern behind locked doors, with only twenty-six persons present, yet it attempted to bind the whole province by the resolves adopted.[91]

Additional protests continued to appear in the colony's newspaper,[92] along with articles by "Mercurius," "Freeholder," "Agricola," and others,[93] and added evidence of the divided nature of Georgian opinion became apparent with a notice hidden among the advertisements in the *Gazette* announcing a solicitation for the relief of Boston, signed by nine gentlemen "willing to receive subscriptions and donations." By the time this notice was published for the third time,[94] the first page of the *Gazette* was taken up with reports of the meeting of the Continental Congress on September 17, and the

[90] *Georgia Gazette*, September 7, 1774.

[91] On September 17 the committee of thirty-one that had been appointed at the meeting on July 27, replied to the Savannah protesters. While this reply failed to answer the charges that the two most western and most exposed parishes—those of neighbouring well-populated St. Paul and St. George—were either not represented or were misrepresented, it asserted that the parish of Christ Church, including Savannah, was represented not only by the four members of the Commons House of Assembly, legally chosen, but by "two more for two places within the parish, and 12 other respectable inhabitants added to them. . . ." As to the charge that the doors of the tavern were closed for a considerable time, this the committee denied, although it admitted that "several Gentlemen [were] denied admittance," but only before the business meeting had begun, after which all persons were freely admitted, even several dissenters. See *ibid.*, September 21, 1774.

[92] For additional notices of protest and dissent see *Georgia Gazette*, September 21, 28, and October 12, 1774; see also *Revolutionary Records of Georgia*, I, 17–34, and White's *Historical Collections*, 48–9, 283–4, 412–13, 437–8, 603–6. Kenneth Coleman (*op. cit.*, pp. 42–3) indicates that the seven petitions he studied had 633 signatures. Hugh McCall (*op. cit.*, II, 24–5) points out that some of the signatures were of people who later became leaders of the revolutionary movement; he also reports a charge that the numbers of the subscribers exceeded the population of the parish whence the petitions originated and included names of men long dead. C. A. Ellefson ("Loyalists and Patriots in Georgia During the American Revolution," *The Historian*, XXIV, 347–56) gives a careful analysis of 535 signatures to these protests. He challenges some of the statements made by McCall, whom he classifies as a contemporary, and indicates that most of those who protested against the action of the meeting of August 10 remained true to their convictions.

[93] The degree of pamphleteering was apparently unusual enough to result in the following comment in the *Gazette* for September 7, 1774:
"Since Georgia now with writing is possess'd
I'll write as well as some, and do my best
To make as much waste paper as the rest." — "Anti Mercurius"

[94] *Ibid.*, September 14, 28, and October 19, 1774.

Suffolk Resolves, as laid before the Congress, appeared in full.[95] By this time, also, Governor Wright had become convinced that nothing could be done to heal permanently the breach between the mother country and her colonies without an effort "to settle the Line with respect to *Taxation* & by some new mode or Constitution [for the Empire]."[96] In fact, there was little that he or others holding office under the King could do even in Georgia, the weakest of the thirteen rebelling colonies, with no military force available. Proclamations were of no effect, he admitted, "and Prosecutions would only be Laughed at and no Grand Jury wou'd fine [find] a Bill of Indictment. . . ."[97]

In the final analysis, it was the people themselves who would decide the fate of the province. Their individual conception of their true interests would be the determining factor. Was protection of the frontier[98] by Great Britain more important in the minds of frontiersmen than joining with other colonials in denouncing British rule? Was the continued growth of commerce and the developing prosperity of the province of greater moment to the people of Savannah and other parts of the low country than an American union directed against Great Britain, which might have most adverse effects upon the merchants and the rice planters? Had the government of Great Britain acted as a tyrant or as a benefactor to the people of Georgia? Such questions must inevitably have been raised, and upon the answers each one gave rested his decision as to the role he would play as patriot, Loyalist, or neutral. So it was that the people of the parish of St. Andrew—chiefly Presbyterian Highlanders living in or about Darien, far removed from the western

---

[95] *Ibid.*, October 19, 1774. In the following week's issue appeared a notice to the printer "Signed by desire of the Committee of St. John's Parish, Lyman Hall, Chairman," which warned him that he should find room for more news from Boston and also requested him to print the reply to the dissent from St. Paul's Parish. Johnston published the communication in full, but footnoted it to suggest that he had been giving ample information on news from Massachusetts Bay and refused to be intimidated. Nevertheless, the front page of the following issue was devoted entirely to such news.

[96] Wright to the Earl of Dartmouth, August 24, 1774, Georgia Historical Society *Collections,* III, 180–2.

[97] *Ibid.*

[98] Although Governor Wright's successful efforts in securing important land cessions from the Creek and Cherokee Indians had been well received in the summer of 1773 (*Colonial Records of Georgia,* XVII, 707), new incidents on the frontier had by the beginning of 1774 again stirred up anxieties. See Governor Wright to Lord Dartmouth, January 4, 31, 1774, Georgia Colonial Records (Mss), Vol. 38, Part I, 161, 163–71.

hostile Indians—when adopting the continental Association early in January 1775, took their stand with the Congregationalists of St. John's Parish, with whom they were closely associated as near neighbours.[99] Not all the other parishes were so forward-looking. Nevertheless, the committee of a group of "Liberty People," as Governor Wright called them, proceeded with the plan for a provincial congress.

It was decided that the congress should assemble in Savannah on January 18, 1775, the same date that the Commons House of Assembly was to be in session.[100] Of the twelve parishes in Georgia, five were represented, but most conspicuously absent were representatives from St. John. However, delegates from this parish met as a committee at Savannah at the same time and, under the chairmanship of the redoubtable Dr. Hall, sought in an exchange of letters to commit the congress to come out firmly for support of the continental Association. In rebuffing this attempt to influence the proceedings, the congress stated: ". . . we apprehend every Delegate here, is accountable to his Constituents and his own conscience, for the opinion he gives at this time; and therefore, ought not to let any other man, or set of men, judge for him." The St. John people thereupon repudiated the congress as a body that did not represent the sentiments of the province and, before returning home, voted that they would not be bound by any of its resolves.[101] Nevertheless, the forty-five delegates to the congress on January 23 voted to send Noble Wimberly Jones, Archibald Bulloch, and John Houstoun to the next meeting of the Continental Congress; they also agreed upon some strong resolutions and an Association involving non-importation and non-exportation, but only such as seemed suited to the circumstances of the province and which, it may be noted, provided for the continued exportation of rice to Europe.[102]

But the structure of the provincial congress was weak. Not only was a majority of the parishes not represented in it, but out of the forty-five members who participated, apparently only six, including the three designated to attend the next Continental Congress, were

---

[99] For the resolves of St. Andrew's Parish, and of the "Darien Committee" of January 12, 1775, see *Revolutionary Records of Georgia*, I, 37–42.

[100] *Georgia Gazette*, January 25, 1775.

[101] For the exchange of letters between the two bodies see *Revolutionary Records of Georgia*, I, 54–6. For the proceedings of the St. John's Parish committee meetings see White's *Historical Collections*, pp. 521–2.

[102] For the articles of association, see *Revolutionary Records of Georgia*, I, 43–7.

members of the Georgia Commons House.[103] When the Assembly, meeting at the same time, did not find it possible to endorse the proceedings of the provincial congress before Governor Wright on February 10 put an end to the session,[104] the three men who were to have gone to Philadelphia refused to do so. Writing to the President of the Continental Congress on April 6, they stressed the divided sentiments of the people of the colony and, particularly, the opposition of the merchants of Savannah to any interruption of trade, and then asked: ". . . with what face could we have appeared for a Province whose inhabitants had refused to sacrifice the most trifling advantages to the public cause, and in whose behalf we did not think we could safely pledge ourselves for the execution of any one measure whatsoever?"[105] In fact, not until after the War for American Independence had begun was it possible for the leading patriots of Georgia, organized into a council for safety, to rally sufficient support to assemble a second congress. Then, on July 4, 1775, over a hundred delegates, representing all but two parishes, gathered in Savannah and continued sitting until the 15th. These delegates not only pledged to carry into effect all measures of the Continental Congress but elected five delegates to it.[106] Yet Georgia was to remain a colony divided in its loyalties. No one contributed more to the delay of the inhabitants in embracing the cause of revolution than Sir James Wright, who, as Governor from 1761, devoted himself to advancing the interests of the colony while remaining a faithful servant of the King.[107]

---

[103] See the interpretation of these events as presented by Kenneth Coleman: *op. cit.*, pp. 46–9, A. B. Saye: *A Constitutional History of Georgia, 1732–1945* (Athens, 1948), pp. 85–7, and the same author's chapter on the royal period in his *New Viewpoints on Georgia History* (Athens, 1948).

[104] For the action in the Assembly see *Revolutionary Records of Georgia*, I, 48–54.

[105] For this letter see White's *Historical Collections*, pp. 61–3. For a letter signed "N. Jones" of June 1, 1775, promising to send to Boston "a small contribution of sixty-three barrels of rice and one hundred and twenty-two pounds sterling, in specie," see *ibid.*, pp. 63–4.

[106] For the proceedings of the provincial congress and the address of the committee appointed by it see *ibid.*, pp. 65–85.

[107] See, for example, Wright's powerful address to the General Assembly on January 18, 1775, pleading with them to consider "the terrible consequences which may attend adopting resolutions and measures expressly contrary to law, and hostile to the mother country. . . . You may be advocates for liberty, so am I; but in a constitutional and legal way. You, gentlemen, are legislators, and let me entreat you to take care how you give a sanction to trample on law and government; and be assured it is an indispensable truth, that where there is no law there can be no liberty" (*ibid.*, pp. 50–1). For an account of Wright's final struggle with the "Liberty Boys," see W. W. Abbot: *op. cit.*, Chap. 8.

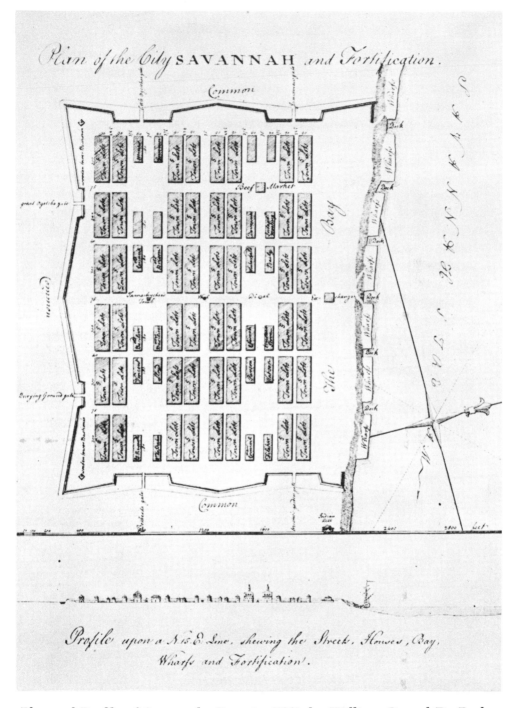

Plan and Profile of Savannah, Georgia, 1772, by William Gerard De Brahm, in the British Museum. (From the Map Division, Library of Congress)

A view of Carpenter's Hall, Philadelphia, seat of the First Continental Congress.

CHAPTER IX

The Gathering of the First Continental Congress

I N 1774 it was Virginia which once again took the initiative in giving form and shape to the idea that appeared to be springing up in many quarters—the idea that the colonies should take positive united action in support of Boston and in defence of American liberties. That the idea was not quite so spontaneously generated in the colonies may be judged from the letters written at this period by Arthur Lee of the famous Lee family of Virginia, who was living in London, and was, in addition to acting as London agent for Massachusetts Bay, active in London politics and the Bill of Rights Society from 1769 to the outbreak of war (as was his brother William).[1] For, at the time of advising Samuel Adams and other patriot leaders in Boston on the developments in Parliament, he urged upon them a "general, firm, permanent opposition . . . [as] the first object of American policy."[2] But Lee also wrote even more persuasively and strongly to his two brothers in Virginia, Richard Henry and Francis Lightfoot. As early as March 18, 1774, a letter addressed by Arthur to Richard Henry admonished him that if the colonies in general permitted the Boston Port Act to pass unnoticed and did not protest "the ruin of Boston . . . you may be attacked and destroyed, by piecemeal, *actum est*, every part will in its turn feel the vengeance which it would not unite to repel. . . ." He therefore advised "the colonies to break off all commercial intercourse with this country [Great Britain]."[3] By April he was writing a similar letter to his other brother in Virginia, giving it as his opinion that *"there ought to be a general congress of*

---

[1] R. H. Lee: *Life of Arthur Lee* . . . (2 vols., Boston, 1829), I, Chap. 1.
[2] Arthur Lee to Samuel Adams, December 22, 1773, *ibid.*, I, 239.
[3] *Ibid.*, I, 208–9; see also R. H. Lee: *Memoir of Richard Henry Lee* (2 vols., Philadelphia, 1825), I, 94, and *American Archives*, 4th ser., I, 228–9.

the colonies," and stressing the need to foster a non-importation association.[4] In addition "A Gentleman in London" was writing to unnamed correspondents in Annapolis and New York suggesting "a general Congress" of the colonies and a "United Continent of America."[5]

In an extract of a letter sent by a member of the Virginia House of Burgesses on May 20 to his correspondent in London, the writer stated:

> "Infinite astonishment, and equal resentment, has seized every one here on account of the war sent to Boston. It is the universal determination to stop the exportation of tobacco, pitch, tar, lumber etc., and to stop all importation from Britain while this act of hostility continues. . . . We see with concern, that this plan will be most extensively hurtful to our fellow-subjects in Britain; nor would we have adopted it, if Heaven had left us any other way to secure our liberty, and to prevent the total ruin of ourselves and our posterity to endless ages. . . . The plan proposed is extensive; it is wise, and I hope, under God, it will not fail of success."[6]

The "extensive" plan was none other than the appointment of deputies from the several colonies to meet annually in a general congress "to obtain the united Wisdom of the Whole, in every Case of General Concern."[7] It also contemplated, according to the writer of the letter, action of continental scope to bring economic pressure to bear on Great Britain to effect the repeal of the obnoxious coercive legislation.

On May 24 the House of Burgesses voted that June 1—the day when the Boston Port Act was to go into effect—be observed as a day of "Fasting, Humiliation, and Prayer," to implore divine interposition to avert the "destruction to our Civil rights, and the Evils of civil War . . . and that the Minds of his Majesty and his Parliament, may be inspired from above with Wisdom, Moderation, and Justice, to remove from the loyal People of America all cause of danger, from a continued pursuit of Measures, pregnant with their ruin."[8] With a

---

[4] Arthur to Francis Lightfoot Lee, April 2, 1774, *Life of Arthur Lee*, I, 37–40; see also *American Archives*, 4th ser., I, 237–8.

[5] *Ibid.*, I, 230–1 and 241. The "Gentleman in London" was undoubtedly Arthur Lee, who had by this time established connections with the patriot leaders in several colonies.

[6] See *ibid.*, I, 340.

[7] *Journals of the House of Burgesses, 1773–1776*, p. 138.

[8] *Ibid.*, p. 124. For the part played by Thomas Jefferson in the drafting of the

copy of this resolve in hand, the Governor on the 26th requested the members to attend him immediately at the Council chamber and, after announcing that the resolve was conceived "in such Terms as reflect highly upon his Majesty and the Parliament of Great Britain," dissolved the House.[9]

Meeting as individuals at the Raleigh Tavern the day after the dissolution of the Assembly, eighty-nine members of the late House entered into an association.[10] This compact described the Boston Port Act as "a most dangerous attempt to destroy the constitutional liberty and rights of all North America"; it agreed to forgo the use of tea until the grievances of America had been redressed, and to recommend that the Committee of Correspondence address the other colonial committees on the desirability of a general congress that would meet annually "to deliberate on those general measures which the united interests of America may from time to time require."[11] On May 28 the Committee of Correspondence sent out letters to the committees of most of the older North American colonies to sound them out on the desirability of a general congress. The responses were favourable to the idea.[12] On June 17 Speaker Thomas Cushing, at the direction of the Massachusetts Bay House of Representatives, proposed that the Congress be held in Philadelphia.[13] Charles Thomson, secretary of the Pennsylvania Committee of Correspondence, writing the following day, also suggested that city, as no regular troops were stationed to the south of it and few within its limits. So it was agreed.[14] As has been developed in the preceding four chap-

---

above resolve see *ibid.*, p. XV, and *The Papers of Thomas Jefferson, 1760–1776* (eds. J. P. Boyd *et al.*, 16 vols.+, Princeton, N.J., 1950–61+), I, 106n.

[9] *Journals of the House of Burgesses*, pp. xv–xvi and 132. It may be noted that in addition to the resolve for a fast, Richard Lee had prepared a set of seven strong resolutions of protest which the sudden dissolution of the Assembly prevented him from presenting. For these see *The Letters of Richard Henry Lee* (ed., J. C. Ballagh, 2 vols., New York, 1911), I, 115n; see also Lee's letter to Samuel Adams, June 23, 1774, and to his brother Arthur, June 26, 1774, *ibid* I, 111–18, and *Memoir of Richard Henry Lee*, I, 95–101, which includes Samuel Adam's reply.

[10] *Journals of the House of Burgesses, 1773–1776*, pp. xiii–xiv; see also *American Archives*, 4th ser., I, 350–1.

[11] For the association see *Papers of Thomas Jefferson*, I, 107–9. For even earlier demands for a continental congress see E. I. Miller: "The Virginia Committee of Correspondence, 1773–1775," *William and Mary Quarterly*, 1st ser., XXII, 109.

[12] For the "Minutes of the [Virginia] Committee of Correspondence, 1774," and the letters received in 1774 by this committee, see *Journals of the House of Burgesses, 1773–1776*, pp. 135–59.

[13] *Ibid.*, p. 156.

[14] *Ibid.*, p. 152.

ters, all the colonies with the exception of North Carolina[15] and Georgia[16]—either by vote of their popularly elected assemblies or by meeting of deputies elected for this purpose or by local ballot —chose delegates to meet on September 1 in Philadelphia.[17]

The First Continental Congress did not get down to work until September 5. On that date, after gathering at Smith's Tavern in Philadelphia, the delegates adjourned to Carpenter's Hall, which then became the seat of their deliberations. Peyton Randolph, former Speaker of the Virginia House of Burgesses, was elected President, and for Secretary the delegates chose Charles Thomson.[18] By agreement the proceedings of the Congress were to be kept secret, except for such information as it should jointly choose to issue. As to voting, after much discussion, the unit rule was adopted, with each colony represented having one vote.

As background to the Continental Congress, it should be pointed out that Thomas Jefferson, an elected member of the House of Burgesses from Albemarle County but not a delegate, drafted instructions to guide the Virginia delegates. Although not adopted by the Virginia convention, apparently because they were much too radical, when disseminated in printed form they were to prove a powerful force in shaping the thought of the times. Published in Williamsburg in August 1774, these proposed instructions appeared as *A Summary View of the Rights of British America. Set forth in some Resolutions Intended for the Inspection of the Present Delegates of the People of Virginia now in Convention.*[19] In this pamphlet Jefferson set forth (p. 8) the doctrine that "the exercise of a free trade with all parts of the world, possessed by American colonists, as of natural right,

---

[15] On August 25, 1774, a provincial convention was held at New Bern in North Carolina; on the 27th strong resolutions were passed against the acts of Parliament and three delegates were appointed to attend the Congress. But it was not until September 14 that two of the delegates put in an appearance, and not until the 17th that the third appeared. See *Journals of the Continental Congress* (eds. W. C. Ford *et al.*, 34 vols., Washington, D.C., 1904–37), I, 30–1. For the New Bern convention see Chap. 8 in this volume.

[16] For the failure of the August 10 meeting in Georgia to agree on sending delegates see *ibid.*; see also Kenneth Coleman: *The American Revolution in Georgia, 1763–1789* (Athens, 1958), pp. 42–3.

[17] For the credentials of the delegates, which disclose the manner of their choice, see *Journals of the Continental Congress*, I, 15–24.

[18] *The Adams Papers*, 1st ser., *Diary and Autobiography of John Adams* (eds. L. H. Butterfield *et al.*, 4 vols., Cambridge, Mass., 1961), II, 115. For the part of Charles Thomson as a leader of the revolutionary movement in Pennsylvania, see the article by J. J. Zimmerman cited earlier in this volume, Chap. 6, note 56.

[19] In connection with the *Summary View* see H. T. Colbourn: "Thomas Jefferson's Use of the Past," *William and Mary Quarterly*, 3rd ser., XV, 56–70.

and which no law of theirs had taken away and abridged, was . . . the object of unjust encroachment." Therefore, with respect to acts passed by Parliament since the seventeenth century, he wrote (p. 11): "The true ground on which we declare their acts void is, that the British parliament has no right to exercise authority over us." The long-term object of these usurpations of power on the part of the government of Great Britain was described as follows (p. 11): "Single acts of tyranny may be ascribed to the accidental opinion of the day but a series of oppressions, begun at a distinguished period, and pursued unalterably through every change of ministers, too plainly prove a deliberate and systematical plan of reducing us to slavery." Jefferson referred (p. 1) not to the rights of "colonies" but of "states." To him the governments of the American states were the equal of the government of Great Britain. In referring to the act of Parliament passed in 1767 suspending the sitting of the New York Assembly, he stated (p. 12): "One free and independent legislature hereby takes upon itself to suspend the powers of another, free and independent as itself, thus exhibiting a phenomenon unknown in nature, the creator and creature of its own power."

Had the delegates to the Continental Congress embraced Jefferson's thesis they would undoubtedly have issued a declaration setting forth at least the complete autonomy of the colonies on all matters of trade, and possibly a repudiation of the whole regulating system for trade and navigation as well as of those regulations of an internal nature, including the postal system, which Jefferson stigmatized (p. 13) as an example of "usurped power."[20]

On September 7 a grand committee on colonial rights, consisting of two delegates from each colony represented, was appointed by the Congress. John Adams, in harmony with the view of Jefferson, called the body "the Committee for States Rights." In studying the debates of this committee as summarized by Adams, it is difficult to determine radical from conservative. For example, Joseph Galloway, Speaker of the Pennsylvania Assembly, according to Adams, took a radical position in the debate on September 8 by stating:

"I have ever thought We might reduce our Rights to one. An Exemption from all Laws made by British Parliament, made since the

---

[20] For Julian P. Boyd's notes on the *Summary View* see *Papers of Thomas Jefferson*, I, Appendix, pp. 670–6; see also Professor T. P. Abernethy's edition of the document published by Scholars' Facsimiles & Reprints (New York, 1943).

Emigration of our Ancestors. It follows therefore that all the Acts of Parliament made since, are Violations of our Rights."[21]

Galloway, a conservative at heart, from the beginning of the formal activities of the Congress was disturbed by the close communication between the delegates from Massachusetts Bay and the two Southern colonies there represented.[22] Yet it was this spirit of alliance that was to prove to be of decisive importance in the outcome of the work of the Congress. Manifestations of such solidarity came early in the deliberations—for example, when Patrick Henry of Virginia declared:

"Government is dissolved. . . . Where are your Land marks? your Boundaries of Colonies. . . . The Distinctions between Virginians, Pennsylvanians, New Yorkers, and New Englanders, are no more. I and not a Virginian, but an American."[23]

Later on Christopher Gadsden of South Carolina, speaking of the colonies collectively, according to John Adams, was "violent against allowing to Parliament any Power of regulating Trade, or allowing that they have any Thing to do with Us."[24] This was obviously music to the ears of the Massachusetts Bay delegates.

While the deliberations of the Congress were progressing in committee on September 16, Paul Revere arrived from Boston, bringing

---

[21] The Adams Papers (Butterfield), 1st ser., II, 128–30.

[22] Galloway wanted the Congress to meet in the Assembly Room of the State House with its more conservative tradition rather than at Carpenter's Hall; he also was opposed to the selection of Charles Thomson as Secretary of the Congress, called by him one "of the most violent Sons of Liberty (so-called) in America." However, in writing to Governor Franklin of New Jersey, he asserted that these two decisions were made because the Virginians and Carolinians, at the instance of the Bostonians, voted in favour of them. See Galloway to Governor Franklin, September 5, 1774, New Jersey Archives, 1st ser., X, 477–8; see also Letters of Members of the Continental Congress (ed. E. C. Burnett, 8 vols., Washington, 1921–38), I, 9–10, which establishes Galloway as the author of this letter. As J. P. Boyd has himself made clear in his Anglo-American Union: Joseph Galloway's Plans to Preserve the British Empire, 1774–1788 (Philadelphia, 1941), pp. 35–6, it is difficult to reconcile all the versions of Galloway's statements.

[23] Adams Papers (Butterfield), 1st ser., II, 124–5.

[24] Ibid., II, 133. Gadsden, according to William Henry Drayton (Memoirs of the American Revolution . . . [ed. John Drayton, 2 vols., Charleston, 1821], I, 165), even proposed to the Congress that General Gage be "attacked and overcome in Boston, before the reinforcements could arrive," but this violent joint commitment was voted to be premature. The student should consult Letters of Members of the Continental Congress for a mine of information gleaned from the writings of members of the First Continental Congress.

with him the Resolves approved unanimously on the 9th by the Suffolk County Convention at Milton, as described in Chapter V of this volume. The Suffolk Resolves were revolutionary in character. The preamble declared:

> ". . . the Power, but not the Justice; the Vengeance, but not the Wisdom of Great-Britain . . . which scourged and exiled our fugitive parents from their native Shores, now pursues their guiltless Children with unrelenting Severity. . . . If a boundless Extent of Continent, swarming with Millions, will tamely submit to live, move and have their Being at the Arbitrary Will of a licentious Minister, they basely yield to voluntary Slavery, and future Generations shall load their Memories with incessant Execrations.—On the other Hand, if we arrest the Hand which would ransack our Pockets, if we disarm the Parricide who points the Dagger at our Bosoms, if we nobly defeat that fatal Edict which proclaims a Power to frame Laws for us in all cases whatsoever . . . Posterity will acknowledge the Virtue which preserved them free and happy. . . ."

Then came the Resolves, which may be summarized as follows: That "agreeable to [the] compact of the English Colonies in America," King George III was recognized as rightful sovereign; that it was nevertheless a duty owed to their God, their country, and posterity to defend the civil and religious rights for which many of the colonists' forefathers had died; that the late acts of Parliament were infractions of those rights and no obedience was due to them, "as the attempts of a wicked Adminisration to enslave America"; that the judges of the courts who held tenure other than by the charter and laws of the province were unconstitutional officers and no regard ought to be paid to them; that collectors of taxes were no longer to make payment to the appointed county treasurer "until the Civil Government of the Province is placed on a constitutional Foundation"; that Council members who had accepted office by virtue of a mandamus from the King and refused to resign their seats should be considered "obstinate and incorrigible Enemies to their Country"; that officers in the militia were to be elected in each town; that when individuals were apprehended "who have been conspicuous in contending for the violated Rights and Liberties of their Countrymen, . . . every Servant of the present tyrannical and unconstitutional Government" was to be seized and held until the persons so apprehended were set at liberty; that all commercial intercourse with Great Britain, Ireland, and the West Indies should cease until these rights were restored; that local manufactures were to be encouraged; that a provincial congress should be called; that the county would respect and submit to measures recommended by the Continental Congress; that riots should be discouraged; and finally, that should "our Enemies by any sudden Manœuvres, render it necessary to ask the Aid and Assistance of our Brethren in the Country," couriers were to be despatched to seek their help.[25]

The Suffolk Resolves came before the Continental Congress on September 17. In expressing the sympathetic feelings of the members for "the suffering of their countrymen in the Massachusetts-Bay, under the operation of the late unjust, cruel, and oppressive acts of the British Parliament," the delegates unanimously approved all the Resolves and commended "the wisdom and fortitude, with which opposition to these wicked ministerial measures has hitherto been conducted"; they also encouraged the people of Suffolk County to persevere in the same firm and temperate conduct.[26]

From the day of the reading of the Suffolk Resolves until September 28 the members were busily engaged in working out plans for placing restrictions on trade with Great Britain and in preparing a declaration of rights. On the 22nd they voted unanimously to request colonial merchants not to send any further orders for goods to Great Britain; on the 24th they further resolved that in dealing with the infringement of American rights the Congress would concern itself only with those acts of Parliament passed since 1763; then, on the 27th, on the motion of Richard Henry Lee, a resolution was passed setting the date of December 1 for an embargo on receiving any imports from Great Britain or Ireland or for the purchase or use by

---

[25] For the Resolves see *Boston Evening-Post*, September 19, 1774; see also *American Archives*, 4th ser., I, 776–9. For the part played by Dr. Joseph Warren in the framing of the Suffolk County Resolves see John Cary: *Joseph Warren* (Urbana, Ill., 1961), pp. 152–8; an article on this subject by M. P. Webster in the *New England Magazine*, new ser., XXVII, 353–72, is devoted to the background and the effect of the Resolves rather than to the Resolves themselves.

[26] *Journals of the Continental Congress*, I, 31–41. After the approval of the Suffolk Resolves, John Adams wrote in his diary: "This is one of the happiest Days of my Life. . . . This Day convinced me that America will support the Massachusetts or perish with her" (*Adams Papers* [Butterfield], 1st ser., II, 134–5). For other comments on the action of the Congress see *Letters of Members of the Continental Congress*, I, 33–6. In his *Historical and Political Reflections on the Rise and Progress of the American Rebellion*, which appeared in London in 1870, Joseph Galloway stated (p. 69): "By this treasonable vote the foundation of military resistance throughout America was effectually laid."

anyone in British North America of goods imported from these countries.[27]

With Congress thus committed, Joseph Galloway arose on the 28th and delivered a major address, in the course of which he proposed a plan of union that he hoped might make possible the restoration of harmony between Great Britain and the discontented colonies. What he actually said is difficult to determine, as more than one version of his speech has been recorded.[28] However, even taking into account the wide difference in point of view and lack of personal sympathy between John Adams and Galloway, it would seem that Adams's notes on the address correspond more closely to what Galloway actually said than the latter's version of his own speech as presented to the world years later when he was an exile in Great Britain.[29]

According to Adams—his notes, however, are so cryptic as to be liable to misinterpretation—Galloway thought that non-importation

---

[27] *Journals of the Continental Congress*, I, 41–3. For John Adams's notes on the debates that took place over non-importation see *Adams Papers* (Butterfield), 1st ser., II, 137–40. For certain aspects of disagreement over non-exportation, especially among the Virginia and South Carolina delegates, see the preceding chapters of this volume.

[28] For the version of the Galloway speech embodied in his *Political Reflections* of 1780 (pp. 70–81) see *Journals of the Continental Congress*, I, 43–8; for the version given by John Adams, see his notes of September 28, 1774, *Adams Papers* (Butterfield), 1st ser., II, 141–2. For a careful, critical analysis of both these versions see J. P. Boyd: *Anglo-American Union* . . . , pp. 35–6. In this connection the student should examine Galloway's *Arguments on Both Sides in the Dispute between Great-Britain and her Colonies. In which those in Favor of the Power of Parliament to bind the Colonies are stated and answered, and the Rights of the Colonists explained and asserted on new and just Principles. By a Sincere Friend to both Countries.* This was printed before the meeting of the Continental Congress but not published. Galloway sent a copy of it confidentially to Governor William Franklin of New Jersey. The Governor, writing to the Earl of Dartmouth on September 6, enclosed his copy with the explanation that its author had prepared the treatise in order to put the delegates in a proper frame of mind to accept the plan of union about to be proposed to the Congress. At this juncture Galloway apparently had the idea of committing Congress to petition for representation in Parliament. At least Governor Franklin's letter to Dartmouth has the following comment on the Galloway plan: "The principle Part of his Plan is, as I am told, the making an Application for Leave to send Representatives from each Colony in America to the Parliament in Great Britain . . ." (Franklin to Dartmouth, September 6, 1774, *New Jersey Archives*, 1st ser., X, 473–5; for *Arguments on Both Sides*, see *ibid.*, X, 478–92; for the original letter and pamphlet see P.R.O., C.O. 5:195). If this was indeed Galloway's original idea—and his close connection with Governor Franklin would lead one to believe that it was—he was to alter his plan fundamentally to match more nearly the temper of the majority of the delegates.

[29] The accuracy of Adams's summarization of the Galloway speech is especially evident in the end section dealing with the political union, as compared with Galloway's version published in his *Political Reflections* in 1780.

would not relieve Boston in time and that non-exportation would fatally weaken America by involvement "in another Struggle which I fear is too near." Galloway held the British position to be that "Without some Supream Legislature, some common Arbiter, you are not . . . part of the State," whereas the position of American extremists was: "As We are not within the Circle of the Supream Jurisdiction of the Parliament, We are independent States [and] The Law of Great Britain dont bind us in any Case whatsoever." Yet, in the last war, when "America was in the greatest Danger of Destruction," there had been a lack of union among the colonies despite the danger of their situation. As a result the mother country had acted. "Requisitions came . . . A No. of the Colonies gave most extensively and liberally, other[s] gave nothing, or late." Consequently the parent state was obliged to carry these "Delinquencies," and this burden "gave Occasion to the Stamp Act. America with the greatest Reason and Justice" complained of it. Nevertheless, in a crisis such as the late war, Galloway contended,

> "We want the Aid and Assistance and Protection of the Arm of our Mother Country. [But] Protection and Allegiance are reciprocal Duties. Can We lay claim to the Money and Protection of G. Britain upon any [other] Principles of Honour or Conscience? Can we wish to become Aliens to the Mother State? We must come upon Terms with G. Britain. Some Gentlemen are not for Negotiation. I wish I could hear some Reason against it."[30]

After delivering the above challenge, Galloway presented his plan of union—a plan which he thought had the greatest chance of winning the approval of Congress. The concept in itself was revolutionary, since it implied a fundamental reorganization of the constitution of the Empire by a repudiation of the Declaratory Act that the Marquess of Rockingham and his supporters, standing among the chief friends of America, had persuaded Parliament to adopt at the time of the repeal of the Stamp Act. The plan may be summarized as follows:

For the administration of the general affairs of America a legislature should be established to include all the older colonies. Under this government each colony was to retain its constitution and the powers of regulating its own internal polity "in all cases what[so]ever."

---

[30] *Adams Papers* (Butterfield), 1st ser., II, 141–2.

The central American government was to be administered "by a President General, to be appointed by the King, and a grand Council, to be chosen by the Representatives of the people of the several colonies, in their respective assemblies, once in every three years." The Grand Council was to meet for the first time as soon as convenient at the call of the President General and thereafter sit for business at least once a year; it would not only choose its own Speaker but enjoy all the rights, liberties, and privileges of the House of Commons of Great Britain. The President General would hold office during the pleasure of the King, his assent would be required to all acts of the Council, and he would also be responsible for carrying such acts into execution. The powers of the President General and the Grand Council would include "all the general polity and affairs of the colonies" in which Great Britain and any colony were concerned, "as well civil and criminal as commercial." This American government would be "an inferior and distinct branch of the British legislature . . . for the aforesaid general purposes. . . ." General regulations relating to America might originate either in Parliament or in the Grand Council and would then be transmitted to the other body for its approbation or dissent. Thus the approval of both would be "requisite to the validity of all such general acts or statutes," except that in time of war all bills of the Grand Council approved by the President General granting aid to the Crown would be valid without the assent of Parliament.[31]

Rising to second Galloway's motion, James Duane of New York stressed, among other points, that his colony desired Congress "to lay a Plan for a lasting Accommodation with G. Britain." To effect this, he was willing to limit the power of the proposed American government. "Justice requires we should expressly ceed to Parliament the Right of regulating trade," Duane concluded, adding: "In the Congress of 1754 which consisted of the greatest and best Men in the

---

[31] *Journals of the Continental Congress,* I, 49–51; see also J. P. Boyd: *Anglo-American Union* . . . , Appendix I, pp. 112–14. Writing from Philadelphia on July 5 to his brother Samuel in England, Thomas Wharton referred to the approaching meeting of the Continental Congress and then stated: ". . . I dare say thou'll join with me in believing it would be happy could our parent state assist us in thus establishing a Constitutional Union betwixt her and us, she appointing a supreme magistrate to reside on this continent, who, with a fixed number from each House of Assembly should form an upper legislature to control the general affairs of this continent, and who would be a proper check to the forward or ambitious views of any one colony" ("Letters of Thomas Wharton, 1773–1783," *Pennsylvania Magazine of History and Biography,* XXX, 436). This proposal, of course, goes back to Benjamin Franklin's Plan of Union of 1754.

Colonies, this was considered as indispensable. . . . A civil War with America, would involve a national Bankruptcy." In the discussion that followed, Richard Henry Lee of Virginia asserted that, since the proposed plan would make changes in the colonial legislatures, he would not agree to it without consulting his constituents. But John Jay of New York approved it and, apparently in reply to Lee, asked: "Does this Plan give up any one Liberty—or interfere with any one Right?" Patrick Henry of Virginia also opposed the plan, on the grounds that to free Americans "from a corrupt House of Commons" would throw them "into the Arms of an American Legislature that may be bribed by that Nation which avows . . . that Bribery is a Part of her System of Government." He then recommended that before "We are obliged to pay Taxes as they do, let us be as free as they. Let us have our Trade open with all the world." In contrast to the Virginia delegates, young Edward Rutledge of South Carolina, more moderate than his congressional colleagues from that province, declared: "I think the Plan may be freed from almost every objection, I think it almost a perfect plan."[32] In spite of this support and Galloway's efforts to answer the objections of Lee and Henry, the plan not only failed to win approval but was expunged from the original official record of the Congress.[33] Clearly the time had passed when such a union could be formed; for the revolutionary influence of the more powerful colonial leaders had too strong a hold on the American people by this date.

Was the plan of union a good one? Had the delegates to the Continental Congress accepted it, would it have been approved by the government of Great Britain? These questions inevitably arise, but they cannot easily be answered. The Earl of Dartmouth, then Secretary of State for the Colonies, in commenting on the plan in a letter to Lieutenant Governor Colden of New York, wrote: "The Idea of a Union upon some general constitutional Plan is certainly very just and I have no doubt of its' being yet attainable, thro' some channel of mutual consideration and discussion."[34] With respect to the approval by Parliament of acts passed by the proposed Grand Council and President General, it may be pointed out that under the existing

---

[32] For the discussion of the plan see *Adams Papers* (Butterfield), 1st ser., II, 142–4, and J. P. Boyd: *op. cit.*, pp. 32–8.

[33] See *Journals of the Continental Congress*, I, 43 and 51n; see also *Letters of Members of the Continental Congress*, I, 51–9.

[34] Dartmouth to Colden, January 7, 1775, *Letters and Papers of Cadwallader Colden*, VII, New-York Historical Society *Collections*, 1923, p. 260.

system all the colonies, except Connecticut, Rhode Island, and Maryland, were obliged to send their laws to Great Britain for approval by the King in Council and even these three colonies could have a law thrown out by appeal to the same authority. Thus the colonies were accustomed to checks on legislation. Moreover, the provision in Galloway's plan that would have obliged Parliament to seek the approval of the Grand Council on all statutes relating to American interests would doubtless have brought about a more accommodating attitude by Parliament toward American legislation, especially if there had been a recognition that the mother country was no longer dealing with dependent infant colonies. Assuming therefore that a desire had existed on both sides to reach a harmonious settlement of differences, no obstacle looms as too formidable to have stood in the way of implementing the plan—granted also that the colonial assemblies as well as Parliament had been disposed to work toward the end of creating a broader and higher legislative instrumentality to function in areas actually beyond the competence of the individual colony.

But the mood of the majority of the members of the Congress, after the approval of the Suffolk Resolves, was clearly not one of compromise. They probably reasoned that since Americans had compelled Parliament in 1766 to repeal the Stamp Act, and in 1769 most of the Townshend Revenue Act, by the strength and violence of their opposition, they could again force the issue and gain acceptance of their own interpretation of the scope of American rights, whether natural or charter rights. If not, they were prepared, but only as a last resort, to rebel and declare their independence. This was the view, at least, of Isaac Low, a delegate from New York, who, according to John Adams, defended "the just Rights of our Mother Country" in the course of the prolonged debate on the continental Association and stated: "We have too much Reason in this Congress, to suspect that Independency is aimed at."[35]

On September 30 the Congress made the next moves toward applying pressure on Great Britain to repeal the Coercive Acts. It resolved that unless American grievances were redressed by September 10, 1775, there should be no exportation of any commodities to Great Britain, Ireland, or the West Indies after that date. It also appointed a committee of five for bringing in a coordinated plan to enforce the non-importation, non-exportation, and non-consumption agree-

[35] *Adams Papers* (Butterfield), 1st ser., II, 148.

ments.[36] A further step of resistance to the government of Great Britain was sought at this period in order "to apprize the public of danger, and of the necessity of putting the colonies in a state of defence." This was Richard Henry Lee's proposal that "the Congress do most earnestly recommend to the several colonies, that a militia be forthwith appointed and well disciplined, and that it be well provided with ammunition and proper arms." But, according to a notation on the manuscript: "A majority had not the spirit to adopt it."[37] Instead, a motion was carried that a committee draw up an address to the King making clear that there was no need of parliamentary taxes in America to support the governments, administer justice, or defend the colonies, since the colonies were in a position to care for these needs and, in case of war, would readily grant supplies for any additional forces that might be necessary.[38] Further, on October 5, the committee selected to frame the address was instructed to assure His Majesty that if he were to abolish all laws and regulations relating to the colonies issued by the government of Great Britain since the close of the late war having to do with revenue, the courts of vice-admiralty, the trial of persons beyond the seas, and the extension of the limits of Canada, this would remove the grievances that these measures had occasioned and commerce with the mother country would be restored.[39]

On October 6 a letter reached the Congress at Philadelphia from the Boston Committee of Correspondence which dealt with the steps taken by Governor Gage to fortify the town and keep military supplies out of the hands of the inhabitants. It assured the delegates that if the Congress were to counsel Bostonians to quit the town, they would do so; if they were advised to stay, "they would not shrink from hardship and danger"; finally, the advice of the Congress was sought on how the colony should proceed without any courts in operation and with the General Assembly prevented from meeting by the Governor's proclamation of September 28, 1774.[40] Had Congress recommended the desertion of Boston, it would have meant but one thing—a determination to drive Gage and the regular troops from the town. But the majority of the members were cautious and looked to

---

[36] *Journals of the Continental Congress,* I, 51–3.
[37] *Ibid.,* I, 54n.
[38] *Ibid.,* I, 53–4.
[39] *Ibid.,* I, 54–5.
[40] *American Archives,* 4th ser., I, 809.

their commercial boycott against Great Britain to settle the matter short of war. As John Adams wrote to his friend William Tudor:

> "If it is a secret hope of many, as I suspect it is, that the Congress will advise to offensive measures, they will be mistaken. . . . They will not at this session, vote to raise men or money, or arms or ammunition. Their opinions are fixed against hostilities and ruptures, except they should become absolutely necessary; and this necessity they do not yet see."[41]

Nevertheless, it was resolved unanimously on October 10 that any person in Massachusetts Bay who would act under a commission granted by the King and based on the late act of Parliament regulating the government of that province, thus "violating the charter," ought to be held "in detestation and abhorrence by all good men . . . as the wicked tools of that despotism, which is preparing to destroy those rights, which God, nature, and compact, have given to America."[42] That same day Peyton Randolph, as President of the Congress, signed a letter addressed to Gage in the name of the delegates—appointed as "the guardians" of American "rights and liberties"—asking him to discontinue the fortification of Boston and to re-establish free communication between this town and the country.[43]

The Congress was now moving toward the culmination of its work. On October 14 it passed a series of resolutions—after much debate in committee and in the general Congress.[44] These resolutions enumerated a list of grievances and constituted a bill of rights for the colonists as "free and natural-born subjects." As such, they claimed the rights of representation and participation in their own legislative councils; rights of common law—especially trial by jury; constitutional and charter rights, as well as the right of assembly and

---

[41] Adams to Tudor, [October 7, 1774], *Letters of Members of the Continental Congress*, I, 65; see also Massachusetts Historical Society *Collections*, 2nd ser., VIII, 311–13. According to the *Memoirs* of William Henry Drayton (I, 165), after the Continental Congress had wound up its work, people began to regret that the delegates had not followed Gadsden's proposal to drive General Gage out of Boston. In point of fact, on October 10 it was unanimously resolved by the Congress that the desertion of Boston by its population would not only be too difficult but would have such consequences "as to require much deliberation before it is adopted" (*Journals of the Continental Congress*, I, 59).

[42] *Ibid.*, I, 60.

[43] *Ibid.*, I, 60–1.

[44] *Ibid.*, I, 63. Galloway states that "the Committee sat near three weeks." See *The Examination of Joseph Galloway, Esq., by a Committee of the House of Commons* (London, 1779), pp. 57 and 61.

petition. In voicing grievances over standing armies and mandamus councils, the resolutions claimed the right to independent legislatures whose powers could not be abridged without consent. Then followed a list of the acts of Parliament which infringed and violated the rights of the colonists[45] and therefore ought to be repealed or revised by "their fellow subjects in Great-Britain." Until such time as this was accomplished they unanimously resolved to enter into a non-importation, non-consumption, and non-exportation agreement or association," and to prepare an address to the people of Great Britain and "a loyal address to his Majesty."[46] Thus the resolutions struck squarely at the right of Great Britain to secure any revenue in America and even called into question the right of Parliament to have embodied revenue features in earlier statutes designed to regulate trade.

By the 20th of October, with the final touches placed upon the "Association," this formidable instrument was approved by the King's "most loyal subjects" to "redress their grievances, which threaten destruction to the lives, liberty, and property of his majesty's subjects in North America." For the enforcement of the Association, committees were to be chosen in every county, city, and town, with the added responsibility of publishing in the newspapers the names of those who did not conform, "that all such foes to the rights of British-America may be publicly known, and universally contemned, as the enemies of American liberty," and thereafter be boycotted. It was also proposed that the Association should be signed by as many people as possible as a first step. The members of the Continental Congress were the first to sign. Further, to gain the widest possible publicity, drafts of the Association were given to the press[47] and 120 copies were printed.

---

[45] The Coercive Acts, together with the Quebec Act, were denounced in the preamble as "impolitic, unjust, and cruel, as well as unconstitutional, and most dangerous and destructive of American rights" (*Journals of the Continental Congress*, I, 66).

[46] For the resolves see *Journals of the Continental Congress*, I, 63–73.

[47] For the Association with the signatures of the delegates, see *ibid.*, I, 75–80. Even Joseph Galloway attached his name to it. In his *Candid Examination of the Mutual Claims of Great Britain and the Colonies* (published by James Rivington, New York, 1775), Galloway explained (p. 52) that he had taken this action in hopes that something rational could be done to reconcile the unhappy differences, such as he had sought by means of his plan of union, and added: "the member proposing it [the plan of union] was weakly led to sign the non-importation agreement, although he had [in the Congress] uniformly opposed it; but in this he was disappointed." For the appearance of the Association agreement in newspapers see, for example, *Pennsylvania Gazette Postscript*, November 2, and *Massachusetts Spy Or Thomas's Boston Journal*, November 10, 1774.

The next day a very long and carefully framed address to the people of Great Britain was approved. This appeal began as follows: "When a Nation, led to greatness by the hand of Liberty, and possessed of all the glory that heroism, munificence, and humanity can bestow, descends to the ungrateful task of forging chains for her Friends and Children, and . . . turns advocate for Slavery and Oppression, there is reason to suspect she has either ceased to be virtuous, or been extremely negligent in the appointment of her rulers." It then repeated and enlarged upon "the ministerial plan for enslaving us," adding, on the subject of the Quebec Act: "Nor can we suppress our astonishment, that a British Parliament should ever consent to establish in that country a religion that has deluged your island in blood, and dispersed impiety, bigotry, persecution, murder and rebellion in every part of the world." Calling upon the traditional sense of justice of the English nation, the message pleaded: "Place us in the same situation that we were at the close of the last war, and our former harmony will be restored" and thus "save the violated rights of the whole empire from the devices of wicked Ministers and evil Counsellors. . . ."[48]

Also on October 21, the delegates approved a memorial to the inhabitants of the colonies represented in the Congress. Ably drafted by Richard Henry Lee, this paper gave a history of the measures adopted by Parliament after 1763 that, taken together, constituted a system "for subjugating these Colonies." The language of this document, it is interesting to note, is milder than the address to the people of Great Britain and would seem to testify to a realization on the part of the delegates that a greater degree of circumspection in the phrasing of the assertions made by the Congress was warranted if the proposals were to win the approval of the more literate and conservatively inclined people. In conclusion the memorial warned that "the most mournful events" might be in prospect and entreated the people to "implore the favour of almighty God . . . to take you into his gracious protection."[49]

One of the most delicate tasks confronting the Congress was the preparation of its address to the French-speaking, Roman Catholic inhabitants of the Province of Quebec. This address, approved on October 26, welcomed the former enemies, whom "the fortune of war, after a gallant and glorious resistance, had incorporated . . . with

---

[48] *Journals of the Continental Congress,* I, 81–90.
[49] For the memorial see *ibid.,* I, 90–101.

the body of English subjects. . . ." By it, these people were reminded of the royal proclamation of 1763 and the promises embodied in it "of the inestimable advantages of a free English constitution of government," and of how unimaginable it was then that succeeding British ministers would "so audaciously and cruelly abuse the royal authority, as to withhold from you the fruition of the irrevocable rights, to which you were thus justly entitled." Among the rights withheld, the address made clear, was that of electing representatives empowered to control money raised among the people, the right of trial by jury, the right of liberty of persons, the right of easy tenure of lands, and the right of freedom of the press. As to religious and other matters, the document questioned what the Quebec Act offered to Canadian Roman Catholics:

> "Liberty of conscience in your religion? No. God gave it to you; and the temporal powers with which you . . . are connected, firmly stipulated for your enjoyment of it. [In fact] a treacherous ingenuity has been exerted in drawing up the code lately offered you, . . . every sentence, beginning with a benevolent pretension, concludes with a destructive power. . . ."

The address thereupon appealed to Canadians to join with "your numerous and powerful neighbours . . . in our righteous contest." Nor should a difference in religion

> "prejudice you against a hearty amity with us. You know, that the transcendant nature of freedom elevates those, who unite in her cause, above all such low-minded infirmities. The Swiss Cantons furnish a memorable proof of this truth. Their union is composed of Roman Catholic and Protestant States, living in the utmost concord and peace with one another, and thereby enabled . . . to defy and defeat every tyrant that has invaded them."

As further evidence of such fraternal feeling, the Congress cited its resolution "That we should consider the violation of your rights, by the act [the Quebec Act] for altering the government of your province, a violation of our own. . . ."[50]

---

[50] *Ibid.*, I, 105–13. The letter to the Canadians was translated into French by Pierre Eugène du Simitière of Philadelphia, where it was published in 1774 by order of the Congress. It was also translated into German and published in Philadelphia (1774), and the English versions were printed in both Philadelphia and New York (1774). Of the 2,000 copies struck off, 300 were sent to Boston; *ibid.*, I, 122.

The final formal business of the Congress took place on October 26, when a petition to the King was adopted and signed by all the delegates.[51] Despite the care taken not to indict the King's ministers in this pronouncement, it presented a full catalogue of colonial grievances arising from measures passed by Parliament since 1763 and declared:

> "From this destructive system of colony administration adopted since the conclusion of the last war, have flowed those distresses, dangers, fears and jealousies, that overwhelm your majesty's dutiful colonists with affliction. . . . We ask but for peace, liberty, and safety. We wish not a diminution of the prerogative, nor do we solicit the grant of any new right in our favour. . . . We therefore most earnestly beseech your majesty, that your royal authority and interposition may be used for our relief; and that a gracious answer may be given to this petition."[52]

In sending this petition "under cover to Dr. Franklin directed to the above [London colonial] Agents" for presentation to the King—along with an address to the British people—Charles Thomson, Secretary for the Congress, had the following to say: "I hope administration will . . . be convinced that it is not a little faction, but the whole body of American freeholders from Nova Scotia to Georgia that now complain & apply for redress; and who, I am sure, will resist rather than submit." In closing he referred to those "who by their cursed schemes of policy are dragging friends & brothers into the horrors of civil war & involving their country in ruin."[53]

---

[51] Not all signed in person. See Letters of Members of the Continental Congress, I, lxiv. For John Dickinson's leading role in framing the appeal to the King see the illuminating article by Edwin Wolf 2nd: "The Authorship of the 1774 Address to the King Restudied," William and Mary Quarterly, 3rd ser., XXII, 189–224.

[52] Journals of the Continental Congress, I, 115–21.

[53] Ibid., I, 122–3. A covering letter dated October 26, 1774, over the signature of the then President of the Congress, Henry Middleton, but prepared by Richard Henry Lee, went to the following individual colonial agents: Paul Wentworth for New Hampshire, Benjamin Franklin for Massachusetts Bay, Pennsylvania, and New Jersey, William Bollan and Arthur Lee also for the Bay colony, Thomas Life for Connecticut, Edmund Burke for New York, and Charles Garth for South Carolina. This letter requested that the petition be made public through the press after its delivery to the King, and asked the agents to take "the most effectual care . . . as early as possible, to furnish the trading cities, & manufacturing towns, throughout the united Kingdom, with our memorial to the people of Great Britain." It also announced the proposal for a second congress, "but in the mean time" begged the agents "to transmit to the speakers of the several Assemblies the earliest information of the most authentic accounts . . . of all such conduct & designs of ministry, or parliament, as it may concern America to know" (ibid., I, 104–5).

With the immediate tasks that had faced them completed, the delegates to the First Continental Congress separated on October 26. But before doing so, they had resolved on the 22nd that a second congress should meet in Philadelphia on May 10 of the new year, "unless the redress of grievances, which we have desired, be obtained before that time." They also recommend "that all the colonies, in North-America, chuse deputies, as soon as possible, to attend such Congress."[54]

---

[54] *Ibid.*, I, 102 and 122.

CHAPTER X

A Crucial Decision

IT IS remarkable that of the men most responsible for British policy in 1774 none should have comprehended clearly the nature of the crisis that confronted the Empire. In a letter to his chief minister on September 11, 1774, the King stated his position clearly:

> "The dye is now cast, the Colonies must either submit or triumph; I do not wish to come to severer measures but we must not retreat; by coolness and an unremitted pursuit of the measures that have been adopted I trust they will come to submit. . . ."[1]

In view of the stand of His Majesty and the highly irregular measures being taken in the colonies, the opposition had gone along with the policy that punitive measures against the rebellious Province of Massachusetts Bay were necessary if Great Britain were to maintain its sovereignty over America. The chief opposition argument had been that the measures taken were too severe and that some efforts at conciliation were necessary if open conflict were to be avoided. But, in truth, the opposition remained divided and therefore unable to change the administration's American policy.[2]

With Chatham inactive, Shelburne—along with his followers Barré and John Dunning and a few others—was apparently undecided whether to negotiate with the Court party or to build a con-

---

[1] *Correspondence of George III* (Fortescue), III, 131.

[2] For a brief view of the situation in the House of Lords see A. S. Tuberville: *The House of Lords in the XVIIIth Century* (Oxford, 1927), pp. 356–61. For an excellent, concise analysis of the position of various members of the opposition in the House of Commons on the eve of the general election in the fall of 1774, see Sir Lewis Namier and John Brooke: *The House of Commons, 1754–1790* (3 vols., London and New York, 1964), I, 74–5.

stitutional faction with London political leaders, such as James Townsend, and disaffected radicals, such as Richard Oliver, John Sawbridge, and Robert Bernard, who had deserted the Wilkes connection and the Bill of Rights Society to form a Constitutional Society.[3] As to the Rockingham Whigs, they were handicapped in the Commons by Dowdeswell's illness and the fact that others, including Burke, were apparently ready to voice certain aspects of opposition to the government's American policy in the debates, but not to go on record in the same way with their votes; for they managed to absent themselves when the final action was taken on some of the Coercive Acts. As for Charles James Fox, chafing at his subordinate role in government at this period, he antagonized the King as much as he attracted most of his other contemporaries.[4] Thus, it was chiefly the radicals and independents who, once the Boston Port Act had been passed, opposed the measures for coercion.[5] In this connection, it is interesting to note that of the most influential Americans in London at this period—Benjamin Franklin and the Lee brothers, Arthur and William—Franklin, London agent for Massachusetts Bay, was closely associated not only with Shelburne and his group but also with the "Honest Whigs" and other liberal circles; while Arthur Lee, also a London agent for the Bay colony, was equally closely associated with the London radicals, as was William, who, along with another American, Stephen Sayre, served for a year as a sheriff of London as the result of the influence of Wilkes.[6] In this way there was a direct line of contact between those

[3] For the record in the House of Commons of the above-named men see *ibid.*, II, 50–4, 86, 367–8, III, 224, 410, 537–8. See also *Correspondence of Edmund Burke* (ed. T. W. Copeland *et al.*, 5 vols.+, Cambridge and Chicago, 1959–65+), II, *Correspondence, July 1768–June 1774* (ed. Lucy Sutherland, 1960), pp. 175, 182, 192, 410–11, 426–7, and George Rudé: *Wilkes and Liberty* . . . (Oxford, 1962), pp. 157, 165, 170.

[4] For the parliamentary careers of the above-mentioned Rockingham Whigs see *House of Commons, 1754–1790*, I, 75, II, 148–9, 334–5, 455–8. For the debates in Parliament over the passage of the Coercive Acts, see Chap. 4 of this volume. In this connection, for a most lucid analysis of the relationship of Wilkes to Rockingham and the opposition, see Lucy Sutherland: "The City of London in Eighteenth-Century Politics," *Essays Presented to Sir Lewis Namier* (eds. Richard Pares and A. J. P. Taylor, London, 1956), pp. 70–2. For Burke, see G. H. Guttridge: *English Whiggism, 1760–1783* (Berkeley and Los Angeles, 1942), pp. 73–6; see also *Correspondence of Edmund Burke* (Copeland), III, *Correspondence July 1774–June 1778* (ed. G. H. Guttridge, 1961), Introduction, pp. xi–xvii.

[5] *House of Commons, 1754–1790*, I, 75–7. For the minority list in the division of the House of Commons on the bill for the impartial administration of justice, see *Middlesex Journal*, May 7, 1774.

[6] For an important analysis of the role of the colonial students, merchants, and planters, as well as the more influential members of the American colony in London

of these circles who were in Parliament and the two men best informed on the views of the patriot leaders not only of Massachusetts Bay but of Virginia and other colonies. Yet neither this liaison nor the influence of other members of Parliament who had at one time or another been in America served to enlighten their colleagues as to the true nature of the American problem.[7] Nor was Thomas Hutchinson, now in London, able to change the course of events. Although he remained in close touch with various people in the province of which he had been Governor—including General Gage and Lieutenant Governor Thomas Oliver, as well as members of his own family—he also remained firmly attached to the administration in London and often consulted with Dartmouth and others. In this way, for example, he was able to undertake such steps as defending the action of Judge Oliver in resigning as President of the Council under duress of the mob. He was not, however, able to shed any clear light on the deeply rooted strength of the revolutionary movement in the land to which he was so devoted by ties of birth, both because his views reflected the situation as it was when he had left Massachusetts Bay and because they obviously reflected his own Loyalist sentiments.[8] Furthermore, Hutchinson was a thoroughly discredited man in the eyes of most of the Americans living in London. This was made amply clear when Josiah Quincy, Jr., arrived in the capital on November 17, 1774, as an agent of the Boston patriots.

In the course of Quincy's stay in London during the winter of 1774 and 1775, he had occasion to meet the native Americans living there, also the "friends of liberty," the men of the Honest Whig circle, and important government leaders. In his account of these meetings he emphasized the staunchness of Franklin as "a friend to America" and the villainy of Hutchinson, on the grounds that "Governor Hutchinson had repeatedly assured the ministry that a union of the colonies was utterly impracticable; that the people were greatly divided among themselves, in every colony; and that there could be no doubt, that all America would submit, and that they must, and

from the autumn of 1774 up to the outbreak of hostilities in 1775, see W. L. Sachse: *The Colonial American in Britain* (Madison, Wisc., 1956), pp. 178–90. See also, in this series, Volume XI, Chap. 7.

[7] For members of Parliament who had been army or naval officers in America see G. P. Judd, IV: *Members of Parliament, 1734–1832* (New Haven, 1955), pp. 16–17.

[8] See, for Oliver's forced resignation, *American Archives*, 4th ser., I, 763–6. For Hutchinson's activities at this period see *The Diary and Letters of his Excellency Thomas Hutchinson* (ed. P. O. Hutchinson, 2 vols., Boston, 1884), I, *passim*, cited hereafter as *Hutchinson's Diary;* for the visit of Welbore Ellis to him, at which he defended Oliver's actions, see *ibid.*, I, 320.

moreover would, soon." Such was the information that Quincy had from Inspector Jonathan Williams, Jr., of the Treasury—information that was confirmed by Franklin, with whom Williams lived. Thus, when Quincy was received by Lord North he made it plain that he considered the causes of most of the "political evils" to be "gross misrepresentation and falsehood." North's reply to this, as recorded by Quincy, was that "he did not doubt there had been much, but that very honest men frequently gave a wrong statement of matters through mistake, prejudice, prepossessions, and biases, of one kind or other." Quincy's subsequent interviews with Dartmouth, Pownall, and others only served to confirm the opinion "that all the measures against America were planned and pushed on by Bernard and Hutchinson."[9]

As for the members of the Commons with special experience and knowledge of the American colonies, the two most enlightened— apart from Isaac Barré in another category—were the former colonial Governors Thomas Pownall and George Johnstone. Pownall, successively Lieutenant Governor of New Jersey and Governor of Massachusetts Bay and brother of John Pownall, Secretary of the Board of Trade, had published in 1764 the first edition of his *The Administration of the Colonies*, which went through four other editions with revisions, the last of which appeared in two volumes in 1774. In 1768 he took the position he was to hold thereafter, that there must be an actual incorporation of all parts of the British dominions with the realm of Great Britain, by "extending the basis of its representative legislature to all the parts . . . so as to form . . . A GRAND MARINE DOMINION, CONSISTING OF OUR POSSESSIONS IN THE ATLANTIC, AND IN AMERICA, UNITED INTO A ONE EMPIRE, IN ONE CENTER, WHERE THE SEAT OF GOVERNMENT IS"—a position that found no support among colonials in 1774.[10] Similarly, George Johnstone, one-time Governor of West Florida and a bitter critic of the administration, was persuaded in 1775 that all the colonies desired was a "constitutional dependence on Great-Britain," such as had subsisted from their

---

[9] See Joseph Quincy, III: *Memoir of the Life of Josiah Quincy Jun. of Massachusetts* (Boston, 1825), pp. 228–342, especially, pp. 229, 233–6, 241–2. When, on November 24, 1774, Quincy recorded (p. 240) in his journal the gist of his hour-and-a-half conversation with Lord Dartmouth, he noted: "I was convinced that the American and British controversy would be much sooner, and much more equitably settled, if it were not for the malevolent influence of a certain Northern personage [Hutchinson] now in Great Britain." For an earlier reference to Quincy in connection with the Boston Port Bill see in this volume Chap. 5, note 30.

[10] *Administration of the Colonies* (4th edn., London, 1768), pp. 163–4.

beginning down to recent times, and that it was contrary to the constitution of Great Britain for Parliament to tax colonials who were not represented in that body and to take from them trial by jury and the right to a writ of *habeas corpus*. Once the colonies were secure in these rights, he argued, "they would immediately return to their duty and obedience."[11] But Johnstone was mistaken in his premise. Although Pownall was in general classed as a supporter of the administration, he thought of himself as an independent and claimed that he was unconnected with any party. Yet he appears to have wavered periodically as he became increasingly ineffective both in Parliament and in winning a government office.[12] Johnstone, too, seems to have veered back and forth in his connections, but was in the long run an independent voter and one of the few to oppose all the Coercive Acts, including the Boston Port bill.[13]

It is true that on April 19, 1774, in support of Rose Fuller's motion in the House of Commons for repeal of the tea duty, the great orator Edmund Burke made a powerful speech.[14] It stressed the futility of retaining the duty on tea and the impossibility of securing a revenue from the colonies by any other means of taxation. But the burden of his address was a defence of the navigation system, and he confidently assumed that, once the colonials were assured that the innovation—which had begun with the Sugar Act of 1764—of direct taxation for revenue was cast aside, the harmonious relations of the mother country with the colonies would be restored. Setting forth the power of Parliament to make laws of sufficient force and validity to bind the people of America "in all cases whatsoever," he made a powerful defence of the Declaratory Act, contending that there was nothing irreconcilable between the idea of the unlimited power of Parliament[15] and the enjoyment by the colonies of all their ancient privileges. He declared:

---

[11] See Johnstone's major speech in the House of Commons in 1775, *Parliamentary History*, XVIII, 740–57.

[12] *House of Commons, 1754–1790*, III, 316–18.

[13] *Ibid.*, II, 683–5.

[14] For Fuller's motion proposing that a time be set for the House to resolve itself into a committee to consider the repeal of the remaining parts of 7 Geo. III, c. 46, see *Parliamentary History*, XVII, 1210–11. For Burke's speech, which appeared in print later in 1774, see *ibid.*, XVII, 1215–69.

[15] Clearly Burke was under the influence of Blackstone's conception of the power and jurisdiction of Parliament, which was defined in the *Commentaries* in 1765 as, quoting Sir Edward Coke, "so transcendent and absolute, that it cannot be confined, either for causes or persons within any bounds." "And of this high court," Blackstone continues, "it may be truly said, . . . It hath sovereign and uncontrolable authority

"As all these provincial legislatures are only co-ordinate to each other, they ought all to be subordinate to her; else they can neither preserve mutual peace, nor hope for mutual justice, nor effectually afford mutual assistance. It is necessary to coerce the negligent [colony], to restrain the violent, and to aid the weak and deficient, by the over-ruling plenitude of her power. She is never to intrude into the place of the others, whilst they are equal to the common ends of their institution. But in order to enable parliament to answer all these ends of provident and beneficent superintendance, her powers must be boundless."

These powers would extend even to taxation on extraordinary occasions, he contended, illustrating in the following terms:

"We are engaged in war—the Secretary of State calls upon the colonies to contribute—some would do it, I think most would cheerfully furnish whatever is demanded—one or two, suppose, hang back, and easing themselves, let the stress of the draught lie on the others— surely it is proper, that some authority might legally say—'Tax yourselves for the common supply, or parliament will do it for you.' . . . But then this ought to be no ordinary power; nor ever used in the first instance. This is what I meant, when I have said at various times, that I consider the power of taxing in parliament as an instrument of empire, and not as a means of supply."[16]

Little did Burke realize, as he delivered his high-minded speech, the degree of conviction with which colonial leaders—men such as Franklin of Pennsylvania, Richard Henry Lee, Jefferson, and Madison of Virginia, Gadsden of South Carolina, Samuel Adams and Joseph Warren of Massachusetts Bay, and many others of local

---

in making, confirming, enlarging, restraining, abrogating, repealing, reviving, and expounding of laws, concerning matters of all possible denominations, ecclesiastical, or temporal, civil, military, maritime, or criminal: this being the place where that absolute despotic power, which must in all governments reside somewhere, is entrusted by the constitution of these kingdoms. . . ." Then, after refuting certain Lockeian theories, he concludes: "So long therefore as the English constitution lasts, we may venture to affirm, that the power of parliament is absolute and without control." See William Blackstone: *Commentaries on the Laws of England* (4 vols., 4th edn., Oxford, 1770), I, 160–2. For the concept that the American crisis was precipitated by toppling "into the mire of legalism, the last no less than the first refuge of the narrow-minded," when the issue "seemed in British eyes to whittle down to one of right. . . . legal rights at the expense of what was expedient," especially as under the influence of Blackstone, see John Ewing: "The Constitution and the Empire —From Bacon to Blackstone," in *Cambridge History of the British Empire,* Vol. I, *The Old Empire,* (New York and Cambridge, 1929), Chap. 21.

[16] *Parliamentary History,* XVII, 1266–7.

prominence in the colonies—had arrived at the conclusion that Parliament, in attempting to legislate for the colonies, had usurped powers that did not rightfully belong to it. Little did he realize how impossible it would be to restore the type of colonial dependence upon the mother country that had existed before the outbreak of the Great War for the Empire, especially in view of the disappearance after 1763 of threats to the security of British colonials in North America upon the withdrawal of French power from that continent. For among the vast implications of the outcome of the war was the intensification of the desire of colonials for complete freedom of movement—the urge to be no longer shackled by numerous and complex restraints laid down by those who neither represented them nor were obliged to endure these restrictions.

In fact, it was not Burke but one whom he classified among "this vermin of court reporters,"[17] Josiah Tucker, Doctor of Divinity and Dean of Gloucester, who perhaps saw most clearly the true nature of the crisis within the Empire. Early in 1774 Tucker, who had previously written a number of learned treatises having to do with commerce, taxes, war, and other matters of public interest,[18] published his *Four Tracts, together with Two Sermons on Political and Commercial Subjects*, among which, as "Tract IV," was his remarkable essay "The True Interest of Great-Britain set forth in Regard to the Colonies and the Only Means of Living in Peace and Harmony with them."[19] An independent thinker, Tucker held views which, at least at the time, met with the approval neither of the Court, the Ministry, and the majority in Parliament nor of the opposition in Parliament including Burke.[20] He held that it was the nature of all colonies, past

---

[17] *Ibid.*, XVII, 1253.

[18] See R. L. Schuyler: *Josiah Tucker. A Selection from His Economic and Political Writings . . .* (New York, 1931), Introduction. Tucker's writings are listed by Leslie Stephen in the *Dictionary of National Biography*, LVII, 282–4.

In the above connection the student should read the important article by C. F. Mullett: "English Imperial Thinking, 1764–1783," *Political Science Quarterly*, XLV, 548–79. In this study, Professor Mullett gives the views of many writers respecting the Empire and how to govern it, such as those of Soame Jenyns, William Knox, Joshua Steele, William Bollan, Thomas Pownall, Gervase Bushe, Francis Masères, Matthew Robinson, James Burgh, Granville Sharpe, Richard Price, Catherine Macaulay, John Cartwright, George Johnstone, and Adam Smith.

[19] For the Tucker essay, Tract IV, "The True Interest of Great-Britain," see R. L. Schuyler: *op. cit.*, pp. 333–69.

[20] It is of interest that while the Tucker volume was reviewed in the January, February, and March 1774 issues of the *Gentleman's Magazine* (XLIV, 29–30, 78–81, 126–9), no mention was made of Tract IV, doubtless because it dealt with ideas much too far removed from general opinion or approval to be given further circulation at that critical period.

and present, "to aspire after Independence, and to set up for themselves as soon as ever they find that they are able to subsist, without
being beholden to the Mother-Country. And if our Americans have
expressed themselves sooner on this Head than others have done,
or in a more direct and daring Manner, this ought not," he affirmed,
"to be imputed to any greater Malignity, or Ingratitude in them,
than in others, but to that bold free Constitution, which is the
Prerogative and Boast of us all [in the British Empire]." He then
continued his argument by pointing out:

> ". . . if the American Colonies belonging to France or Spain, have not
> yet set up for Independence, or thrown off the Masque so much as
> the English colonies have done,—what is this superior Reserve to be
> imputed to? Not to any greater filial Tenderness in them for their
> respective antient Parents than in others;—not to Motives of any
> national Gratitude, or of national Honour,—but because the Constitu-
> tion of each of these Parent States is much more arbitrary and despotic
> than the Constitution of Great-Britain; and therefore their respective
> Offsprings are awed by the Dread of Punishments from breaking
> forth into those Outrages which ours dare do with Impunity. Nay
> more, the very Colonies of France and Spain, though they have not
> yet thrown off their Allegiance, are nevertheless as forward as any in
> disobeying the Laws of their Mother-Countries, wherever they find
> an Interest in so doing. For the Truth of this Fact, I appeal to that
> prodigious clandestine Trade which they are continually carrying
> on with us, and with our Colonies, contrary to the express Prohibitions
> of France and Spain: And I appeal also to those very free Ports
> which the British Legislature itself hath lately opened [in the West
> Indies] for accommodating these smuggling Colonists to trade with
> the Subjects of Great-Britain, in Disobedience to the Injunction of
> their Mother-Countries."[21]

Thus, according to Dean Tucker, colonies cling to the parent country only as long as it is to their interest to do so or while they are too
weak to stand alone. He pointed out that the spirit of resisting regulations imposed on the English colonies by Parliament had appeared
even as early as the seventeenth century; therefore, "to frustrate all
Attempts of the Colonies either to throw off or evade the Power and
Jurisdiction of the Mother Country," Parliament in 1696 had by
statute (7 and 8 William III, c. 22, Par. 9) declared "That all Laws,
Bye-laws, Usages, or Customs at this Time, or which hereafter shall

21 See Tract IV (Tucker), R. L. Schuyler, *op. cit.*, pp. 338–9.

be . . . in Force or Practice, in any of the said Plantations . . . repugnant to this present Act, or to any other Law hereafter to be made in this Kingdom . . . are illegal, null, and void, to all Intents and Purposes whatsoever." But, he insisted, not until 1763, despite efforts on the part of colonials to evade the laws passed by Parliament, was there any ascertainable move to deny the authority of that body. In other words, to Tucker,

> "it was not the Stamp-Act which increased or heightened these ill Humours in the Colonists; rather, it was the Reduction of Canada, which called forth those Dispositions . . . which were ready to burst forth at the first Opportunity that should offer. For an undoubted Fact it is, that from the Moment in which Canada came into the Possession of the English, an End was put to the Sovereignty of the Mother-Country over her Colonies. They had then nothing to fear from a foreign Enemy. . . ."[22]

In face of the rebellious attitude manifested by colonials at the time that Tucker wrote, what possible solution to the problem should be sought? He made five proposals and argued the merits and demerits of each. The first was to permit things to go on as they had, under the supposition that the colonies might become more obedient "in Proportion as they are suffered to grow the more headstrong, and to feel their own Strength and Independence. . . ." This he rejected. The second was to "attempt to persuade the Colonies to send over a certain Number of Representatives to sit and vote in the British Parliaments. . . ."[23] He treated this possibility at great length, arriving at the conclusion that, far from restoring concord in the relations of the Americans and the British, such a legislative union would "tend to exasperate both Parties." The third proposal had to do with a resort to arms—should an offer of a legislative union get "the contemptuous Refusal of it by the Colonies" he was sure it would receive. Such a war would be waged to compel the Americans "to submit to the Authority and Jurisdiction of the supreme Council of the British Empire, the Parliament of Great-Britain." But he drew back from this solution with horror, not only "for all the Blood and Treasure

---

[22] *Ibid.*, pp. 337–8.

[23] *Ibid.*, pp. 340–55. For an earlier plan, attributed to Francis Masères, to create "commissioners of the Colonies of America" to sit in the House of Commons as members of Parliament from America and the West Indies, see *Consideration on the Expediency of Admitting Representatives from the American Colonies into the British House of Commons* (London, 1770).

which must be spilt on such an Occasion" but also for its baneful ultimate consequences. "Certainly, if ever the Inhabitants of that Country [America] should come (and they are almost come already) to be fully persuaded that the British Parliament hath no Right to make Laws either to tax or to govern them," then, even if they were conquered, "every Attempt towards throwing off this odious Yoke, would appear in their Eye, as so many noble Struggles for the Cause of Liberty." A fourth solution advanced was to recognize the future greatness of America and proceed to make Philadelphia, or New York, or some other city, an "American Imperial City," from which viceroys would be sent to govern Great Britain and Ireland. However, Tucker agreed that "there is not the least Probability, that this Country [England] should ever become a Province to North-America."[24]

Tucker's final proposal was "to separate entirely from the North-American Colonies, by declaring them to be a free and independent People, over whom we lay no Claim; and then . . . guarrantee this Freedom and Independence against all foreign Invaders whatever." He argued strongly in favour of this solution: "For if we neither can govern the Americans, nor be governed by them; if we can neither unite with them [in a legislative union], nor ought to subdue them; —what remains, but to part with them on as friendly Terms as we can?" Separation in the manner suggested, he affirmed, would not lessen the material advantages that Great Britain had enjoyed in the past but rather would greatly increase them. This would be true even with respect to trade with the former colonies. Despite all the benefits that would accrue from this idea of peaceful political separation, the writer concluded,

> "no Minister, as Things are now circumstanced, will dare to do so much Good to his Country; . . . And yet I have observed . . . that Measures evidently right will prevail at last: Therefore I make not the least Doubt but that a Separation from the northern [American] Colonies, and also another right Measure, viz. a complete Union and Incorporation with Ireland (however unpopular either of them may now appear) will both take Place within half a Century."[25]

---

[24] See Tract IV (Tucker), R. L. Schuyler, *op. cit.*, pp. 355–8.

[25] For the five proposals see *ibid.*, pp. 339–69. Lecky has the following comment on Tucker's essay: "Tucker, the Dean of Gloucester, a bitter Tory, but one of the best living writers on all questions of trade, maintained a theory which was then esteemed visionary and almost childish, but which will now be very differently regarded. He had no respect for the Americans; he dissected with unsparing severity

Here, surely, was a wise, well-informed man writing with prophetic insight. At the same time, Tucker could not escape a tone of bitterness in referring to the rebellious colonials, albeit inconsistently. For, according to his own theory of the destiny of colonies, in the course of time all would seek freedom from the parent state regardless of the behaviour of individual colonials. Yet he was right in his conviction that no minister of the King would dream of adopting his ideas for the peaceful separation of the colonies from the mother country and equally right that any suggestion to that end on the part of the government would arouse the thunder of Chatham, Burke, Rockingham, Charles James Fox, and others in opposition to the administration, as a betrayal of the Empire. In fact, the King, his Ministry, and their supporters both in and outside of Parliament, as well as those opposed to them, were alike the prisoners of certain fixed patterns of statecraft evolved during the past centuries. Not until the twentieth century was there to be a real revolution in the attitude of statesmen toward colonial dependencies; only then were Tucker's views, as expressed in "The True Interest of Great-Britain . . . ," to be broadly accepted by the government of Great Britain. Therefore, instead of a bold and courageous breaking with theories of empire wrapped up in the concepts of mercantilism of past ages, the government in 1774 proceeded along traditional lines of determining to apply force in order to bring colonials back to a state of obedience.[26]

---

the many weaknesses in their arguments, and the declamatory and rhetorical character of much of their patriotism; but he contended that matters had now come to such a point that the only real remedy was separation." Lecky then paraphrases Tucker as follows: "The Americans have refused to submit to the authority and legislation of the Supreme Legislature, or to bear their part in supporting the burden of that Empire. Let them, then, cease to be fellow-members of the Empire. Let them go their way to form their own destinies. Let England free herself from the cost, the responsibility, and the danger of defending them, retaining, like other nations, the right of connecting herself with them by treaties of commerce or of alliance" (W. E. H. Lecky: *A History of England in the Eighteenth Century* [8 vols., London, 1878–90], III, 388–9).

[26] Nevertheless, as F. J. Hinkhouse has pointed out in his *The Preliminaries of the American Revolution, as seen in the English Press, 1763–1775* (New York, 1926, pp. 114–15), the February 1774 issue of the *Monthly Review* noted that Tucker's idea of political separation had frequently occurred to others "who are daily convinced . . . that we can neither govern the Americans, nor be governed by them; that we can neither unite with them, nor ought to think of subduing them, and . . . that nothing remains but to part with them on as friendly terms as we can." He also cites the issue of March 15, 1774, of the radical *St. James's Chronicle,* in which a writer expressed the view that no other plan appeared to be "more generally approved of than Dr. Tucker's scheme"; while in the *Middlesex Journal and Evening Advertiser* of April 14, 1774, still another writer affirmed that "the soundest politicians are of opinion, that Dean Tucker's advice . . . is the wisest scheme ever yet proposed for accommodating

If the government of Great Britain were to continue to employ force to retain control of Boston and hold in awe the revolutionary elements of Massachusetts Bay and, simultaneously, to restore respect for the laws of Parliament throughout the colonies, it was vitally important to ascertain that the electorate in Great Britain was in sympathy with the coercive measures passed by Parliament and approved by the King during the spring of 1774. As a means of testing the sentiments of the nation, therefore, a proclamation was issued on September 30 dissolving the present Parliament and calling a new one to meet on November 29.[27] Defective as was the system of representation in the House of Commons, a new election seemed to be the only means available to determine the extent to which public opinion approved the current policy of the government. As Lord North put it: "Many good consequences will result from a sudden dissolution, but some seats in the H° of Commons will probably be lost by it."[28]

As had been anticipated, the county of Middlesex, which included

---

the present differences, and even strengthening the Mother Country." Yet, those who wrote in support of the Dean of Gloucester's proposal were apparently but isolated voices, as it were, crying in the wilderness.

[27] For the proclamation see Peter Force: *American Archives*, 4th ser., I, 810–11.

[28] North to the King, September 27, 1774, *Correspondence of George III* (Fortescue), III, 130–4. In reply, the King on that same date wrote: ". . . it will I trust prove a very salutary measure, and when that is the case I do not grudge a little additional trouble; and am thoroughly convinced that with temper, firmness and due activity [management of elections] that by degrees the hands of Government will be as strong as before the many untoward events that have of late years arisen" (*ibid.*).

It should be noted in this connection, however, that John Brooke, in his "Introductory Survey" to the new *History of Parliament* written in collaboration with Sir Lewis Namier (*The House of Commons, 1754–1790*, I, 74) raises a question as to North's reasons for deciding to dissolve Parliament. Brooke concludes that it was obviously better "to face the next stage of the American dispute with a new Parliament," rather than have a serious crisis develop in the middle of a general election, which normally would have taken place in 1775. He adds: "But there is nothing to suggest that North dissolved in order to obtain a vote of confidence from the electorate or to strengthen his majority. . . ." In this connection the Bristol merchant Richard Champion wrote to the Philadelphia firm of Willing and Morris in early October, as a postscript to his letter of September 30, 1774: "The Parliament is dissolved— the general Supposition for this unexpected Event is, the Minister dreads the News from America, & is fearful the People at home would be so inflamed as to elect a Parliament not answerable to his wishes. . . ." See *The American Correspondence of a Bristol Merchant, 1766–1776: Letters of Richard Champion* (ed. G. H. Guttridge, Berkeley, 1934), University of California *Publications in History*, XXII, 33. In his diary for November 20, 1774, Thomas Hutchinson recorded: "Lord North, to convince me of the determined design of Administration to do something effectual, said—'I will venture to tell you that Parliament was dissolved on this account—that we might, at the beginning of a Parliament take such measures as we could depend upon a Parliament to prosecute to effect' " (*Hutchinson's Diary*, I, 298).

London, elected as Lord Mayor and also to a seat in the House of Commons a man hostile to all the coercive legislation passed, John Wilkes. It was at this point that Wilkes took his seat without opposition, thus ending a memorable dispute which had seen him once expelled and repeatedly excluded from the House of Commons.[29] In other parts of England some of those who had sat in the last Parliament were not re-elected and their places were taken by new men.[30] However, as shall be noted in the course of this chapter, in the final analysis there was no major change in the position of the House toward support of the government, despite the fact that so many of the newspapers in England, including the provincial press, had pro-American leanings.[31] Broadly speaking, the leading merchants in most parts of England appeared to be opposed, at least during the latter part of 1774 and the early months of 1775, to the employment of punitive measures against the Americans, as was indicated by the many petitions to the government from the commercial interests during that period. On the other hand, the country gentlemen, as a body, were strongly committed to the idea of using any means required to restore loyalty in the colonies.[32] Radicals as well as members of the Society of Friends, whether radical or not, could be expected to oppose the government in any hostile action against the colonials, while those holding office in the gift of the

[29] See Volume XI in this series, Chap. 7. Before electing its four members to the House of Commons, the London livery called upon the candidates to agree to certain instructions. These included the vindication of "the injured rights of the freeholders of Middlesex" as well as "restoring to our fellow-subjects [in America] the essential right of taxation by Representatives of their own free election, and for repealing the universal excise [the Tea Act] which has lately been substituted in the Colonies instead of the laws of Customs; [and] for repealing the four late iniquitous Acts respecting America, . . ." (*Annual Register, 1774*, p. 152, and *American Archives*, 4th ser., I, 817).

[30] For Lord North on the election, see North to the King, September [30?], 1774, *Correspondence of George III* (Fortescue), III, 136–7. For an analysis of an important election see P. T. Underdown: "Henry Cruger and Edmund Burke: Colleagues and Rivals at the Bristol Election of 1774," *William and Mary Quarterly*, 3rd ser., XV, 14–34.

[31] See *House of Commons, 1754–1790*, I, 73–80. F. J. Hinkhouse's previously cited study of the English press during the period under consideration covers twelve provincial newspapers, as well as the chief ones in London. In searching the numerous election advertisements inserted in the press by candidates for seats in the House of Commons (p. 181) he fails to find one which took the stand that America should be punished.

[32] See Dora M. Clark: *British Opinion and the American Revolution* (New Haven, 1930), for a broad study covering the years 1763–83. See also, for example, *The American Correspondence of a Bristol Merchant, 1766–1776* pp. 2–4, 26, 30–3, 35, and *passim*.

Crown as well as seats in Parliament could usually be counted on to support the Ministry.[33]

Although the First Continental Congress had completed its work on October 26, Dartmouth did not receive reports of its proceedings until December 13.[34] Thus, when the new Parliament opened on November 29, 1774, only the government had any official intimations of the concerted action that had been taken by the colonies at the Philadelphia meeting.[35] In his speech to the two Houses, the King stated his concern that

> "a most daring Spirit of Resistance and Disobedience to the Law still unhappily prevails in the Province of the Massachusett's Bay. . . . These Proceedings have been countenanced and encouraged in other of My Colonies. . . ."

Declaring his determination that the Coercive Acts should be effectually carried out, he continued:

> "And, you may depend upon My firm and stedfast Resolution to withstand every Attempt to weaken or impair the supreme Authority of this Legislature over all the Dominions of My Crown; the Maintenance of which I consider as essential to the Dignity, the Safety, and the Welfare of the British Empire. . . ."

Then, appealing to the members of both Houses for their support, he recommended that they

> "proceed with Temper in your Deliberations, and with Unanimity in your Resolutions. Let My People, in every Part of My Dominions, be

---

[33] See *Parliamentary Papers of John Robinson, 1774–1784* (ed. W. T. Laprade, Royal Historical Society, London, 1922), Camden Third Series, XXXIII, Introduction, pp. 12–17. Here the editor gives an analysis of offices held by members of Parliament, with 70 peers and 170 members of the House of Commons holding office in 1774. For an analysis of the relationship between the landed society and the government see G. E. Mingay: *English Landed Society in the Eighteenth Century* (London and Toronto, 1963), Chap. 5, "The Landlords and Politics," especially pp. 111–17, 123, 263.

[34] *Hutchinson's Diary*, I, 323–4. It is of interest that Hutchinson recorded in his *Diary* on December 5, 1774 (*ibid.*, I, 313–14), that "no sort of intelligence [had] been received" from the Congress at Philadelphia, except an intimation that deputies would be sent to England, and that nothing had been heard from Boston for nine weeks.

[35] Dartmouth had undoubtedly received Gage's letters telling of action taken by the Congress up to August 27, September 25, and October 3, 1774 (*Gage Correspondence*, I, 367 and 377), as well as communications from other colonial Governors, as became evident when the American papers were laid before Parliament in January 1775, and especially from such informants as Joseph Reed. See, for example, Reed to Dartmouth, September 25, 1774, *Dartmouth Manuscripts*, I, 362–3.

taught by your Example to have a due Reverence for the Laws, and a just Sense of the Blessings, of Our excellent Constitution."[36]

When the usual address of thanks was moved in the House of Lords, the Duke of Richmond proposed an amendment desiring that His Majesty should make available "the accounts which have been received concerning the state of the colonies, that we may not proceed to the consideration of this most critical and important matter, but upon the fullest information. . . ." But the address giving the King unqualified support stood as first proposed.[37]

The first test of the attitude of the new House of Commons came similarly with the framing of the address in reply to the King's speech. An attempt was made to alter the original draft by substituting for the statement "Commons will use very Means in their Power to assist His Majesty in maintaining entire and inviolate the supreme Authority of this Legislature, over all the Dominions of His Crown," the statement "that our inviolable Duty and Respect to His Majesty, as well as our Situation in an immediate delegated Trust from His People, will not permit us to form any Opinion upon a Matter, which may . . . lead to Consequences of a still more alarming Nature, without the fullest and most satisfactory Information. . . ." On a division of the House this amendment was rejected by a vote of 73 in favour as against 264.[38] Nor were subsequent attempts in mid-December on

---

[36] *Journals of the House of Commons,* XXXV, 8.

[37] *Parliamentary History,* XVIII, 36–7. Among those who signed the dissenting protest were Camden, Richmond, and Rockingham. See *ibid.,* XVIII, 37–8.

[38] *Journals of the House of Commons,* XXXV, 8–9. By far the best accounts of the debates in Parliament covering the years 1774–5, outside of those in *Parliamentary History* and *Parliamentary Register,* are to be found in the *Annual Register, 1775,* a publication that had won the merited respect of the general public since its first appearance in 1759. These accounts are attributed to Burke, who founded the annual and contributed to it up to 1788; at least they presented his point of view and some portions are manifestly in the language employed in his writing. They are in consequence weighted in favour of the minority point of view, which was pro-American; nevertheless, they express with sufficient fidelity the arguments of the King's chief minister and the majority that supported him. In this connection it would be well to quote from a letter that Burke wrote on March 14, 1775, to James de Lancey of New York: "In my public letter [to the committee of correspondence at New York of the same date] I have stated the proceedings in Parliament as clearly and as shortly as I was able, not as I saw them, but as the leaders in them represented their own measures" (R. J. S. Hoffmann: *Edmund Burke, New York Agent* . . . [Philadelphia, 1956], p. 263). His public letter (*ibid.,* pp. 263–7) to New York outlining objectively and succinctly the plan of the Ministry is an example of the degree of detachment which Burke attained when required to give a candid and honest report of the opinions of his political opponents. For a first-rate list of sources for parliamentary debates see Appendix II, *House of Commons, 1754–1790,* I, 522–3. See also, in this connection, Volume XI in this series, Chap. 8, note 102.

the part of the opposition to insist upon being more fully informed on American affairs any more successful. Finally, on December 16, after Rose Fuller had challenged Lord North to state "if he had any information to lay before the House, or any measures to propose respecting America," the King's chief minister "confessed the very very great importance of the subject now mentioned . . . [but] said, it would require the utmost diligence and attention, as a matter of the greatest magnitude ever debated within those walls," and assured the House he would lay the information before it after the holidays.[39]

It is clear that even before this meeting of Parliament both the King and the Cabinet Council had become convinced that hostilities were now inevitable if the Empire were to remain intact. In the face of the waves of dispatches from America stressing the hostile attitude of colonials toward the British government and the warlike preparations being carried out, especially in the Northern colonies—the King had written to Lord North on November 18 acknowledging that "the New England Governments are in a State of Rebellion, blows must decide whether they are to be subject to this Country or independent. . . ."[40] Later that day, after his attention had been called to General Gage's suggestion concerning the expediency of suspending the implementation of the Coercive Acts "in order to be better prepared,"[41] the King again addressed Lord North, stating:

> ". . . his [Gage's] idea of Suspending the Acts appears to me the most absurd that can be suggested; the [American] People are ripe for mischief, upon which the Mother Country adopts suspending the measures She has thought necessary [;] this must suggest to the Colonies a fear . . . we must either master them or totally leave them

---

[39] *Parliamentary History*, XVIII, 55–68. It may be added that at the time the above issue arose in the House of Commons the reports on the results of the First Continental Congress had not yet been made public, having been received by the ministry only on December 13; they did not appear in the press until almost a week later, when they were widely publicized. See F. J. Hinkhouse: *op. cit.*, p. 182.

[40] *Correspondence of George III* (Fortescue), III, 153.

[41] Gage to Dartmouth, September 25, 1774, *Gage Correspondence*, I, 375, and Gage to Governor Hutchinson, July 12, 1774, cited in *ibid.*, note 4, as being in the Gage Mss although searches at the Clements Library and the Library of Congress have failed to bring this letter to light. The Earl of Suffolk, a member of the Cabinet Council and a Secretary of State, as was Dartmouth, wrote to the latter on November 22 that, in view of Gage's conduct, he was persuaded that the General should be superseded by one who would act with greater firmness. However, nothing was done. See *Dartmouth Manuscripts*, I, 370.

to themselves and treat them as Aliens; I do not by this mean . . . that I am for advice new measures; but I am for Supporting those already undertaken."[42]

However, almost a month later, after the proceedings of the First Continental Congress had been received by Dartmouth, the King approved a suggestion made by Lord North that various aids to the colonies—including bounties on colonial products and other beneficial regulations—should be suspended "towards bringing the Americans to their Duty." But he questioned the desirability of North's suggestion for sending royal commissioners to make an examination of their grievances, since this would look "so like the Mother Country being more affraid of the continuance of the dispute than the Colonies and I cannot think it likely to make them reasonable. . . ."[43]

Although the reluctance of Lord North to release any information on the state of the colonies was the subject of such dissent in Parliament that even a man as close to the government as Thomas Hutchinson wondered "at the strange silence upon American affairs,"[44] the explanation undoubtedly lies in the fact that the government had not yet completed its plan. Writing to his chief minister on December 18, the King stated:

"The sending a Major General to America will [be] very proper; but as a general plan is necessary to be formed for that Country would it not be right not to act by detail but have the whole digested before any step is taken . . . ?"[45]

At the same time Lord North submitted to His Majesty "a detail of the plan for carrying on a War in America, together with an idea of a Commission much approv'd by Lord Mansfield . . . the whole must

---

[42] *Correspondence of George III* (Fortescue), III, 154.

[43] The King to North, December 15, 1774, *ibid.*, III, 156. It may be added that at a Cabinet Council meeting on December 1, 1774, held to discuss the ominous news from Boston contained in Gage's dispatches, it was agreed that Lord Dartmouth should seek the advice of both the Attorney General and the Solicitor General "Whether the acts of the people of the Province of Massachusetts Bay therein stated are overt acts of treason and rebellion, and if they are, to direct them to prepare the draught of a proclamation requiring all persons who have been guilty of the same, except such as shall be therein excepted, to surrender themselves before a certain day, and to declare that such as shall not surrender themselves shall be treated as rebels and traitors" (*Dartmouth Manuscripts*, I, 371).

[44] See the entry for December 19, 1774, in *Hutchinson's Diary*, I, 329.

[45] *Correspondence of George III* (Fortescue), III, 157.

be consider'd as merely an object for deliberation & as quite imperfect."[46]

But when Parliament reconvened, the drastic steps being taken in the colonies could no longer be ignored.

---

[46] *Ibid.*, III, 158. This exchange of letters between the King and Lord North also makes clear that plans were well under way to replace Gage as Commander-in-Chief of the British Forces in America.

CHAPTER XI

Repudiation of Chatham's Plan of Conciliation

HE House of Commons reconvened on January 19, 1775. It was then that—at His Majesty's command and to satisfy the demands of the opposition—Lord North laid before the House of Commons 149 documents bearing on the American crisis. The two final documents presented were extracts of the votes and proceedings of the First Continental Congress and the petition of the Congress to the King, entitled "Petitions of sundry Persons, in behalf of themselves and the inhabitants of several of his Majesty's Colonies in America."[1]

---

[1] For the titles of the documents see *Journals of the House of Commons*, XXXV, 64–6; see also *American Archives*, 4th ser., I, 1489–93. Sixty-five of these papers as submitted to Parliament are printed in *Parliamentary History*, XVIII, 74–148; but the petition of the Continental Congress to the King is not included. As to this document, copies of which had gone to five London agents with a covering letter (see the preceding chapter of this volume), on December 19 Franklin sent notification to the others asking them to meet on the 20th at Waghorns' Coffee House to consider the "manner of presenting the Petition" (R. J. S. Hoffman: *Edmund Burke, New York Agent* . . . [Philadelphia, 1956], pp. 166–7). But only Arthur Lee and William Bollan were disposed to become involved with Franklin in this delicate matter. Edmund Burke, Thomas Life, and Paul Wentworth, agents respectively for the assemblies of New York, Connecticut, and New Hampshire, refused to take part in the enterprise, claiming they had received "no Instructions relating to it from their Constituents," while Charles Garth, agent for both Maryland and South Carolina, was out of town. See Franklin to Charles Thomson, February 5, 1775, *Writings of Benjamin Franklin* (Smyth), VI, 303; see also R. H. Lee: *Life of Arthur Lee* . . . (2 vols., Boston, 1829), I, 273–4. Wentworth, moreover, took the position that "the petition is an assertion of all their [the American] claims in a very high tone and with very offensive expressions" (*Dartmouth Manuscripts* I, 372). When this petition was handed to Dartmouth by Franklin, Lee, and Bollan for presentation to the King, the Earl was unwilling to do so before he had read it. Finding "nothing in it improper," he presented it to George III, who thereupon sent a verbal message through Dartmouth to the agents that the petition "contained Matters of such Importance, that, as soon as they met, he would lay it before his two Houses of Parliament" (Franklin to Thomson, February 5, 1775, *Writings of Benjamin Franklin* [Smyth], VI, 303–4). When Bollan, Franklin, and Lee attempted to be heard at the bar of the House of Commons in support of

In the House of Lords on January 20, after Lord Dartmouth had presented the American papers, the Earl of Chatham, long absent from this chamber, arose and, despite his physical infirmities, delivered one of his major addresses. It was both a denunciation of the Ministry and an encomium on the Americans.[2] The people of Massachusetts Bay had a right to resist, he declared, especially as, without a hearing to prove their guilt or innocence of the charge of criminality, they were proscribed as the result of vindictive decisions of the government. He denounced in particular the Declaratory Act, which "leaves you a right to take their money when you please." He was determined, unless fixed to a sick-bed, to see that America obtained "satisfaction for her injuries"; for he had a plan of reconciliation to propose at a later date that would be "solid, honourable, and lasting." For the present, and as a first step, he moved: "That an humble Address be presented to his Majesty . . . that immediate orders may be dispatched to General Gage for removing his Majesty's forces from the town of Boston, as soon as the rigour of the season, and other circumstances indispensable to the safety and accommodation of the said troops may render the same practicable."[3] In the debate that followed, Chatham was supported by the Earl of Shelburne, Lord Camden, and the Duke of Richmond; the Marquess of Rockingham, while taking exception to Chatham's denunciation of the Declaratory Act, also expressed himself in favour of the withdrawal

---

the petition on January 26, the question that the petition be brought up was defeated by a vote of 218 to 68. It is interesting to note, however, that the order of the day was read immediately thereafter and the House then resolved itself into a committee of the whole to consider the American papers. See *Journals of the House of Commons,* XXXV, 81, and *Parliamentary Register,* I, 114 and 124.

[2] Writing to Stephen Sayre from Hayes on December 24, 1774, with respect to the proceedings of the First Continental Congress, Chatham praised its "manly wisdom and calm resolution. . . . Very few are the things contained in their resolves, that I could wish had been otherwise" (*"Correspondence of William Pitt* . . . [eds. W. S. Taylor and J. H. Pringle, 4 vols., London, 1838–40], IV, 368).

[3] *Parliamentary History,* XVIII, 149–60. In a footnote (pp. 149–55) Hugh Boyd's version of Chatham's speech is given. Boyd, the essayist reputed by Almon and George Chalmers to be the author of the "Junius" letters, and gifted with a prodigious memory, wrote down the speech after its delivery. See also *Pitt Correspondence,* IV, 374–97, and Basil Williams: *The Life of William Pitt, Earl of Chatham* (2 vols., London and New York, 1913), II, 302–13. Josiah Quincy's *Memoir of the Life of Josiah Quincy Jun.* (Boston, 1825) also gives an account of the proceedings. But the most stirring report of Chatham's speech and the events surrounding it is to be found in a long letter written (but not sent) by Jonathan Williams, then in London visiting his great-uncle Benjamin Franklin. The manuscript letter, a holding of the Indiana University Library, is to be found printed as *Publications* No. 1 of that library, edited by Bernhard Knollenberg and entitled *Franklin, Jonathan Williams and William Pitt: A Letter of January 21, 1775* (Bloomington, Ind., 1949).

of the troops. However, according to the Earl of Suffolk, speaking for the government as a member of the Cabinet Council, Chatham was "mistaken, in almost every position he laid down"; coercive measures were adopted only after all conciliatory means had been exhausted. Lord Lyttelton, although holding no office, strongly supported the Declaratory Act and ridiculed "the absurd idea of an inactive right," as advanced by Rockingham and his followers, "when there was the most apparent and urgent necessity for exercising it." Although praising Chatham for his talents and past achievements, he censured him for applauding the Continental Congress, especially as "the whole of their deliberations and proceedings breathed the spirit of unconstitutional independency and open rebellion. . . . Now, therefore, was the time to assert the authority of Great Britain, for . . . every concession on our side would produce a new demand on theirs; and in the end, bring about that state of traitorous independency, at which it was too plain they were now aiming." Other lords spoke in the same vein. In the end the Chatham motion was rejected by a vote of 68 to 18.[4]

True to his word, on February 1 Chatham presented for the consideration of the peers a bill for "A Provisional Act for settling the Troubles in America, and for asserting the Supreme Legislative authority and superintending power of Great Britain over the Colonies."[5] The first of the eight clauses in the bill was a declaration "that the colonies of America have been, are, and of right ought to be dependent upon the imperial crown of Great Britain, and subordinate unto the British parliament," and that Parliament "hath, and of right ought to have, full power . . . to make laws . . . to bind the people of the British colonies in America, in all matters touching the general weal of the whole dominion of the imperial crown of Great Britain, and beyond the competency of the local representative of a distant colony," which would include laws regulating navigation and trade. The second—replying to the American position that to keep troops within a province without its consent was "against law"—stated that it was a prerogative of the Crown, with the consent of Parliament, to send an army to any of the British dominions, but that, to quiet groundless fears, it should be de-

---

[4] *Parliamentary History*, XVIII, 160–8.

[5] See *ibid.*, XVIII, 198–203. See also, in this connection, the recent study by H. G. Keller: "Pitt's Provisional Act for Settling the Troubles in America" (*Das Problem der Einheit des Britischen Reichs*), *Historische Zeitschrift*, No. 194/3 (Munich, 1963), pp. 599–645.

clared that no military force kept in a colony could "ever be lawfully employed to violate and destroy the just rights of the people." The third sought a declaration and enactment that no tax "for his Majesty's revenue, shall be . . . levied, from British freemen in America, without common consent, by act of the provincial assembly there, duly convened for that purpose." The fourth proposed to declare as lawful the projected second gathering of the Continental Congress on the 9th of May, in order that the delegates may take into consideration the giving "due recognition of the supreme legislative authority . . . of parliament over the colonies. . . ." The fifth provided that the delegates should be required "by the King's Majesty sitting in his parliament, to take into consideration . . . the making a free grant . . . of a certain perpetual revenue, subject to the disposition of the British parliament . . . to the alleviation of the national debt . . . in such honourable proportion as may seem meet and becoming from great and flourishing colonies towards a parent country labouring under the heaviest burdens, which, in no inconsiderable part, have been willingly taken upon ourselves and posterity, for the defence, extension, and prosperity of the colonies." To this great end it should be enacted that the Continental Congress should be empowered "to adjust and fix the proportions and quotas of . . . each province respectively, towards the general contributory supply," with the proviso that this authorization by Parliament was not to extend to the new provinces of East and West Florida, Georgia, Nova Scotia, St. John's (now Prince Edward Island), and Canada. An added proviso held that before such quotas were fixed, the delegates must be properly authorized by their respective provinces, and the colonial assemblies should, as an indispensable condition, recognize the supreme legislation of Parliament over the colonies. The sixth would declare that the powers of the vice-admiralty courts were to be restrained to "their ancient limits," that trial by jury in America should be restored, that no subject in America accused of a capital offence should be tried outside the colony where the alleged offence was committed, nor would it be lawful to send persons indicted for murder in one colony to another colony or to Great Britain for trial. The seventh would repeal all acts considered grievous by colonials, beginning with the Sugar Act of 1764 (4 George III, c. 15) and including the American Legal Tender Act (4 George III, c. 34), the act fixing American postal rates (5 George III, c. 25), the revised American import duties act of 1766 (6 George III,

c. 52), the act for setting up an American Board of Customs Commissioners (7 George III, c. 41), the act of 1767 providing duties for defraying the charges for administering justice and the support of civil government in America (7 George III, c. 46, already repealed, except for the preamble and the remaining duty on tea), the act of 1768 authorizing the Crown to erect district vice-admiralty courts (8 George III, c. 22), and the act of 1772 providing penalties for those who would set fire to or otherwise destroy His Majesty's dockyards, magazines, ships, ammunition, and stores (12 George III, c. 24). Moreover, all the acts passed in 1774 relating to America, including the Boston Port Act (14 George III, c. 19), the Act for the Impartial Administration of Justice in Massachusetts Bay (14 George III, c. 19), the Act for Better Regulating the Government in that province (14 George III, c. 45), the Quartering Act of that year (14 George III, c. 54), and the Quebec Act (14 George III, c. 83), were to be "suspended, and not to have effect or execution, from the date of this Act." Finally, it should be enacted that "his Majesty's judges in courts of law in the colonies of America, to be appointed with salaries by the crown, shall hold their offices and salaries as his Majesty's judges in England, *quamdiu se bene gesserint*," that is, during good behaviour, and that the colonies were to be entitled to all the privileges granted by their charters or constitutions.

Here then was Chatham's promised plan of reconciliation that would be "solid, honourable, and lasting." What did it imply? While it did not call for the formal repeal of the Declaratory Act (6 George III, c. 12)—so disliked by Chatham, but so esteemed as an essential constitutional principle by the Rockinghamites who had placed it on the statute books in 1768[6]—for all practical purposes it amounted to repeal, at least in so far as the power of Parliament to levy taxes on the colonials was concerned. All other legislation relating to America passed since 1763 that still stood on the statute books—except the Quartering Act of 1765—was also to be either

---

[6] Early in January 1775, Chatham called upon Rockingham and sought to persuade him that the Declaratory Act was "the cause of the revival of all the confusion" in American affairs; that there was a clear "line of distinction between the *no* right to tax and *the right* to restrain their trade" and that sooner or later in the session he would "move in the House [of Lords] for . . . reconsideration of that Declaratory Bill" in order to "take out the sting. . . ." Rockingham, however, refused to accept Chatham's point of view. See Rockingham to Burke, January 7 and 8, 1775, *Correspondence of Edmund Burke* (Copeland), III, *Correspondence, July 1774–June 1778* (ed. G. H. Guttridge, Cambridge and Chicago, 1961), pp. 90–3.

rescinded or suspended. Thus the colonies were to be given what they had demanded, a return to the conditions that had existed before 1763, with one exception. In view of the flourishing and prosperous situation of the colonies and the heavy burdens the mother country was carrying—to a great extent as the result of her sacrifices in protecting them and insuring their future in North America—they were expected to make a free but perpetual contribution to the payment of the national debt. But this manifestly lay in the future, until such time as the individual colony should authorize its representatives to a lawfully recognized Continental Congress to assume responsibility for fixing the quotas that each colony would contribute as "a free grant," without compulsion—an eventuality that might be postponed indefinitely should any colony or all the colonies plead inability to do so. It is true that all the older restraints on trade and navigation were to remain intact and that their enforcement would continue under the highly defective system of locally influenced customs officers and vice-admiralty courts; yet, this was to insure that there would be no repetition of events such as led to the burning of H.M. *Gaspee*. In other words, let the individual colonies, whether with tongue in cheek or not, recognize "the supreme legislature of Parliament" and they could rest assured that never again would that body attempt to interfere with what colonials considered to be their rights as Englishmen.

In its scope and implications the Chatham plan, for all practical purposes, made the colonies autonomous, although subordinate, states within the Empire; moreover, it recognized the legality of the union of the colonies in a Continental Congress and its authority to negotiate with the government of Great Britain. Thus, there would be a government within a government within a government, and all within the British Empire. The plan must also be taken to embody Chatham's proposal of January 20, that the army of occupation in Boston would be withdrawn. All this Chatham, the saviour of the Empire in the late war, would do—humiliating to Britain as many might think it—to save the Empire now face to face with disintegration.[7]

---

[7] According to Benjamin Franklin, himself versed in colonial matters, Lord Camden, versed in the law, and he were the only people consulted by Chatham before presenting his plan in the House of Lords on February 1, 1775. In this connection Franklin went to Hayes on January 27, and Chatham came to Craven Street on the 29th, when they two spent two hours in going over details of the plan. Franklin subsequently jotted down a number of points as questions that Americans would be apt to raise

Recommending the adoption of his plan, Chatham emphasized the urgency of the proposals and offered to act as a mediator between Great Britain and the colonies. In rejecting the charge that Americans were seeking independence, he added that if he should be persuaded "that they entertained the most distant intentions of throwing off the legislative supremacy and great constitutional superintending power and controul of the British legislature, he should be the . . . most zealous mover for securing and enforcing that power by every possible exertion . . ." He admitted that his plan might be defective and entreated the House to join in perfecting it before it was too late for measures of reconciliation.

While the Earl of Dartmouth, Secretary of State for the Colonies, seemed favourably disposed toward the Chatham plan and suggested that the proposals be brought up for further consideration, the Earl of Sandwich, First Lord of the Admiralty, bitterly attacked the proposals as nothing but a series of concessions, for "he was well assured America had already . . . the most traitorous and hostile intentions; . . . [and] it was clear the Americans were not disputing about words, but realities, it was to free themselves from the restrictions laid on their commerce, that was the principal motive for their present [dis]obedience."[8] He therefore moved that Chatham's plan

---

about the plan of reconciliation, and brought them to Chatham's attention at a four-hour meeting at Hayes on the 31st. He questioned whether, if the colonies were to recognize parliamentary supremacy, Parliament might not see fit to forbid further meetings of the Continental Congress. Again, he noted: "Laws should be secure as well as Charters," but the Privy Council would still retain its power to disapprove a law passed in America or to invalidate it on appeal. Further, the Continental Congress, not the government of Great Britain, should have the responsibility for both the defence of the frontier and the regulation of new settlements. The royal instructions respecting London agents, which required that the Assembly appoint these representatives with the consent of the Governor and the Council of the colony, should be withdrawn. Then, as to the right of the Crown to maintain British troops in America with the consent of Parliament, would not the people of Great Britain object if the King raised armies in America and quartered them in Great Britain? Or, might not the act of Parliament of 1765 for the quartering of troops in America (5 Geo. III, c. 33), which was not mentioned in the plan for repeal, "be made very burthensome to Colonies that are out of favour"? See the *Writings of Benjamin Franklin* (Smyth), VI, 363–8.

[8] According to Franklin's account of the debate, Sandwich declared "he could never believe it to be the Production of any British Peer . . . and turning his Face towards me, who was leaning on the Bar [of the House], said, he fancied he had in his Eye the Person who drew it up, one of the bitterest and most mischievous Enemies this Country had ever known." But Chatham took full responsibility for the plan, at the same time showering praise on Franklin as one "whom all Europe held in high Estimation for his Knowledge and Wisdom . . . ; who was an Honour, not to the English Nation only, but to Human Nature" (*ibid.*, VI, 368–70). For Franklin's further account of his efforts as a peace-maker, in collaboration with the eminent Quakers David Barclay and Dr. John Fothergill, as the result of which he produced his "Hints

be rejected. In the debate that followed the motion by Sandwich, Lord Camden was the only peer who declared he was prepared "to prove every leading proposition on which the Bill rests." The Duke of Manchester pleaded "that one sober view should be taken of the great question, before perhaps we blindly rushed into a scene of confusion and civil strife, the event of which is impossible to foresee." Both Shelburne and Richmond attacked the administration for mishandling the nation's affairs. On the other hand, Earl Gower condemned the plan in the severest terms, giving among other reasons that it "not only sanctified the traitorous proceeding of the congress already held, but further legalized it, by ordaining that another shall be held on the 9th of May next." The final vote on the motion to reject Chatham's plan was carried by 61 to 32[9]—a larger vote against the administration than any other taken in the House of Lords during the

---

for Conversation upon the Subject of Terms that might probably produce a durable Union Between Britain and the Colonies," see *ibid.*, VI, 318–99. These "Hints," which, through the offices of Barclay and Fothergill, apparently reached some of the highest dignitaries in the government to no avail, offered a seventeen-step plan thought to be essential for a complete reconciliation. For example, the tea destroyed in Boston Harbour should be paid for; the Tea Act repealed, as well as the coercive acts relating to Massachusetts Bay, the Quebec Act, and also all acts restraining manufacturing in the colonies. Again, "the Acts of Navigation [were] to be all reenacted in the colonies" in order to have validity, and all duties arising out of such acts for regulating trade to the colonies should be paid into the respective colonial treasuries, by locally appointed customs officers, with a naval officer appointed by the Crown to reside in each colony to see that such acts were observed. In view of "the monopoly Britain is to have of their commerce," no requisition for funds was to be made upon the colonies in time of peace, with Americans maintaining their own peace establishments. In time of war "on requisition made by the King, with the consent of Parliament," the colonies were to raise funds upon a basis stated in the plan that would have some relation to British war taxation; further, Castle William protecting the harbour of Boston should be restored to the keeping of Massachusetts Bay and no fortress should be built in any province without the consent of its legislature. With respect to judicial appointments, all colonial judges were to serve during good behaviour and be provided with permanent salaries paid by the Assemblies. The salaries of all Governors were likewise to be paid by the Assemblies. Further, the extension to the colonies of the Act of Henry VIII relating to treasons should be "formally disowned by Parliament" and all "powers of internal legislation in the colonies disclaimed by Parliament," with the admiralty courts in the colonies reduced to the same powers they had in England and acts for establishing them upon this basis re-enacted in America. See, in this connection, Betsy C. Corner and Dorothea W. Singer: "Dr. John Fothergill, Peacemaker," American Philosophical Society *Proceedings*, XC, 11–22. It was at the moment that these "Hints" were being circulated that the terms of the Continental Congress were received in London. For the revolutionary nature of the colonial demands for reconciliation, as expressed by the Continental Congress and reiterated by Franklin, see two articles by Herbert Osgood: "England and Her Colonies," *Political Science Quarterly*, II, 440–69, and "The American Revolution," *ibid.*, XIII, 41–59.

[9] *Parliamentary History*, XVIII, 203–16.

consideration of American affairs at this period and also a compliment to Chatham.

Had the administration brought wisdom and foresight to a general understanding of the state of affairs in America at the beginning of 1775, it would surely have grasped at Chatham's proposals, startling as they may have seemed. For the ministers would have recognized that the Chatham plan was based on realities, rather than on mere theories of imperial government, and would have attempted to implement it and come to the best possible terms with the Americans—assuming that colonials had not determined by that time to free themselves from the authority of Parliament and thus from the system of statutory controls that had bound their commerce and trade into a mercantalist system favouring the mother country. One thing was clear: a relationship of complete dependence upon the British Parliament was no longer applicable to the older North American colonies in view of the number of their inhabitants, their wealth, their political and economic maturity, their aspirations, and the strength and dangerous character of their discontent. Yet, it was equally clear that Great Britain had done well by the North American plantations. None of the colonies planted by any other Old World power had flourished like the American colonies; nor had any ever attained such strength and capacity for self-direction. But after 1763, it is true, the Empire exhibited at last the defects implicit in its virtues; the reasons have been set forth in earlier volumes of this series.

To do justice to the Ministry, it was not completely blind to the need for fundamental changes in the constitution of the Empire. This was apparent in a minute of the Cabinet Council meeting of January 21, 1775, which adopted the following resolution:

"Agreed, that an address be proposed to the two Houses of Parliament to declare that if the Colonies shall make sufficient and permanent provision for the support of the civil government and administration of justice and for the defence and protection of the said Colonies, and in time of war contribute extraordinary supplies, in a reasonable proportion to what is raised by Great Britain, we will in that case desist from the exercise of the power of taxation, except for commercial purposes only, and that whenever a proposition of this kind shall be made by any of the Colonies we will enter into the consideration of proper laws for that purpose, and in the meanwhile

to entreat his Majesty to take the most effectual methods to enforce
due obedience to the laws and authority of the supreme legislature
of Great Britain."[10]

But this resolution did not go far enough. It required that the individual colony take the initiative for assuming unclarified burdens
—which its inhabitants might feel incapable of bearing—and implied
that until this were done there would be no relaxation of government
efforts to reduce any recalcitrant colony to a state of obedience.

In fact, before presenting his proposal to the House of Commons
later in February, Lord North had, on the 2nd of that month, already
called upon the House to consider in committee the American disturbances. When introducing a motion at that time for a joint address
to the King on the subject of American affairs, the chief minister
stressed the efforts made on both sides of the Atlantic to stir up a
spirit of sedition among Americans. He also emphasized the heavy
financial burdens of supporting the Empire carried by the eight million people in Great Britain, who were obliged to pay £10,000,000
sterling in taxes each year—a per capita tax of twenty-five shillings,
or an average of fifty times as much as the three million Americans,
who paid a total tax of but £75,000 to support their governments,
which amounted to a per capita tax of only sixpence.[11]

The motion for the address stated that since a rebellion actually
existed in Massachusetts Bay and was countenanced by the people
of other colonies, His Majesty should "take the most effectual measures to enforce due obedience [in America] to the laws and authority of the supreme legislature" of Great Britain, and that only when
a colony should apply to Parliament "in a dutiful and constitutional
manner" would the two Houses be ready to pay attention to any real
colonial grievances. In the ensuing debate Charles James Fox moved
as an amendment that the measures heretofore taken by His
Majesty's servants had tended to widen rather than heal the unhappy differences "which have so long subsisted between Great
Britain and America." For his part, John Dunning, a stout defender

---

[10] *Dartmouth Manuscripts,* I, 372–3. See in this connection W. A. Brown: *Empire
or Independence: A Study in the Failure of Reconciliation, 1774–1783* (University,
La., 1941).

[11] North's calculations of the amount of taxes paid by the people on both sides
of the Atlantic manifestly did not take into account the many local levies. Were one
to assume that the margin of error was great enough to cut his ratio by one-half, the
difference in the burden carried by the two peoples was still very great, as has been
emphasized in earlier volumes of this series.

of the colonies, denied there was rebellion by any of them. On the other hand, Sir William Mayne, who doubtless voiced the sentiments of the majority, affirmed that if it were an act of treason for the colonies to embargo commerce between Great Britain and America, and if resisting "every act of the British legislature, and absolutely, in word and deed, denying the sovereignty of this country, if laying a strong hand on the revenues of America, if seizing his Majesty's forts, artillery, and ammunition, if exciting and stimulating, by every means, the whole subjects of America, to take arms and to resist the constitutional authority of Great Britain, are acts of treason, then are the Americans in a state of the most flagrant rebellion. . . ."[12]

The most notable reply to these charges against the colonials came in a long address by George Johnstone, who saw the actions of Americans flowing out of a right they held as sacred—that of the exclusive privilege of taxing themselves. "We are," he reasoned,

> "constantly stating the great obligation we have conferred on the colonies by our former behaviour towards them: if it was ever so good, we can claim no merit from hence in private or public concerns, to do injury in future. They do not complain of your former behaviour, but they say, you have altered this very system from whence you would now derive their submission."

In the final voting the Fox amendment was rejected by a vote of 105 in favour as against 288 opposed.[13]

In the debate on February 7 in the House of Lords over the motion for joining with the Commons in a joint address to the King, Lord Mansfield affirmed: "we were reduced to the alternative of adopting coercive measures, or of for ever relinquishing our claim of sovereignty or dominion over the colonies." Specifying the acts of Parliament complained of in the Continental Congress, he stated that every one of these acts was based upon the superintending power of Parliament which the Congress was not disposed to recognize. What was to be the return if all those acts were withdrawn? All they promised in return was "to consent to the Act of Navigation, while they were boldly contending for the repeal of every one Act almost which was to give that great constitutional law the least force or effect"; moreover, the colonies were actually in a state of rebellion,

---

[12] *Parliamentary History*, XVIII, 222–47.

[13] *Ibid.*, XVIII, 253–65. Johnstone, former Governor of West Florida, was named a member of the Carlisle Peace Commission in America in 1778, and later became a strong supporter of the administration's efforts to put down the American revolt.

and had denounced the Townshend Revenue Act of 1767 as the source of all the present trouble, he asserted. Lord Camden denied that the colonies were in rebellion, if "rebellion and treason meant the same thing"; as to the duty on tea, which he saw as the cause of the present "unhappy dispute," he "utterly disclaimed having the least hand in that measure." Reacting to this disavowal, the Duke of Grafton, who with Chatham was at the head of the administration in 1767, arose and heatedly turned upon Camden, accusing him of acting beneath the dignity of his exalted station in attempting to screen himself from the disagreeable consequences of the act which he had consented to as a member of the Cabinet Council and had acquiesced in as a member of the House of Lords; in fact, was not Camden, as Lord High Chancellor, the very person who had signified the royal approbation of it as a law? In the final voting, 104 lords approved the address to the King as against 29.[14] Thus, by the addresses of the two Houses, the King was assured of the full support of Parliament in any steps he might take to reduce the colonies to obedience.[15]

It may be well, at this juncture, to assess the effect upon England of the articles of Association adopted by the Continental Congress resolving not to import any merchandise from Great Britain or Ireland after December 1, 1774. For the American leaders had high hopes that this step would, as it had in 1766, bring the government of Great Britain to its knees.

On January 23 there was presented to the consideration of the House of Commons a petition from London in behalf of those concerned with the trade to North America. It emphasized the vast importance of this commerce as part of a system that also involved British commercial relations with continental Europe, India, and the British West Indies, and stressed the fact that there was owing to the merchants of London alone over £2,000,000 from North America. It also pointed out that a total stop was now put to all exports to the greatest part of the American continent, and that this not only menaced the public revenue but also threatened the petitioners with

---

[14] *Ibid.*, XVIII, 265–92. For two protests signed by 18 lords, including Camden and Rockingham—one of which objected to the address to the King as passed by the House of Lords and the other being against the refusal of the House to receive petitions from North American merchants before continuing their discussions—see *ibid.*, XVIII, 292–6.

[15] For the joint address, as voted, see *ibid.*, XVIII, 297–8; see also *Journals of the House of Commons*, XXXV, 99–100.

grievous distress and thousands of artificers and manufacturers with utter ruin. The petitioners therefore prayed that Parliament would immediately enter upon a full "Examination of that System of Commercial Policy, which was formerly adopted, and uniformly maintained, to the Happiness and Advantage of both Countries, and . . . apply such healing Remedies as can alone restore and establish the Commerce between Great Britain and her Colonies on a permanent Foundation; and that the Petitioners may be heard by themselves or Agents, in support of the said Petition."[16] As has been stressed, Lord North on the 19th had presented for the consideration of the House a large number of papers bearing directly upon the North American crisis and had moved that these be referred to a committee of the whole House. A motion was therefore made on the 23rd to have the London petition embodied with the American papers so as to come up for consideration with them and enable the petitioners or their agents to be present to support their position. There was undoubtedly a deep feeling in the Ministry as well as among a majority of the members of Parliament that the British merchants had by their petitions in 1766 exerted an undue and unfortunate influence upon Parliament in favour of the repeal of the Stamp Act, since by this concession parliamentary authority had been challenged by the Americans and the present crisis brought on. Apparently as a move to guard against a repetition of the use of such influence, the members approved an amendment that the petition be considered by a committee of the whole House without reference to the American papers.[17] A petition from the Merchant Venturers of Bristol followed. It expressed concern over "the many Thousands of miserable Objects, who, by the total Stop put to the Export Trade to America will be discharged . . . and must be reduced to great Distress . . ." and a wish for the return of "the former System of commercial Policy . . . [and] the Peace of this great Empire restored. . . ." This petition and a second one from Bristol—distinct from that presented by the Merchant Venturers—were also referred to a committee of the whole House after an attempt had failed to include them among the American papers.[18]

On January 25 a petition from Norwich—where the yearly value

---

[16] *Journals of the House of Commons*, XXXV, 71.

[17] The vote was actually on an amendment to the amendment and was lost by a vote of 197 to 81. *Ibid.*, XXXV, 71–2.

[18] *Ibid.*, XXXV, 72–3.

of its worsteds was placed at £1,500,000 and the industry gave employment to 80,000 people—sought relief, after pointing out the fearful "Consequences which must inevitably happen to the said City from the stoppage of the American Trade." This was also the refrain of a petition from Dudley in Worcestershire, a great centre for the production of nails. However, the inhabitants of one of the greatest centres for the production of iron ware, Birmingham, took a very dim view of the situation. Their petition voiced the apprehension "that any Relaxation in the Execution of the Laws respecting the Colonies of Great Britain will ultimately tend to the Injury of the Commerce of the said Town and Neighbourhood" and called upon the House "to support the Authority of the Laws of this Kingdom over all the Dominions of the Crown."[19] On the 26th the petition of merchants and manufacturers of Manchester, the leading producer of cotton goods in Great Britain, came before the House. It expressed alarm for the future, as did petitions from Wolverhampton, where the locksmith trade was concentrated, and from Liverpool; the latter stressed the immense debt owed to the British merchants by Americans, and the "dreadful Mischiefs" that must follow the stoppage of American trade.[20] On the 27th a counter-petition was presented from Birmingham, stating that whereas in the past thousands of people had found employment in producing articles for the American trade there was now stagnation in this trade. The petition therefore called for relief.[21] In the same vein was the petition that came before the House on the 31st from Newcastle in Staffordshire, "the principal Place in the Kingdom for Felt Hats," the bulk of which had been sold in America until the stoppage of trade. This, according

---

[19] For the above three petitions see *ibid.*, XXXV, 77–8. In an attack against the people of Birmingham for sending these petitions a writer in the *St. James Chronicle* of January 28, 1775, charged that "English Hollanders; or Birmingham Knaves" wished for an American war so that they could make arms for both sides and that they were already shipping arms to America by way of Holland and Germany. See also F. J. Hinkhouse: *Preliminaries of the American Revolution . . . English Press, 1763–1775* (New York, 1926), pp. 178–9.

[20] *Journals of the House of Commons*, XXXV, 80–1.

[21] *Ibid.*, XXXV, 82. In the House of Commons on January 31 Edmund Burke sought to institute an enquiry into the methods by which the first Birmingham petition was obtained. His motion to this effect was defeated by a vote of 85 to 37. It appeared from the evidence that the first petition was signed by inhabitants not directly concerned in producing for or selling to America and that the second petition came from those directly concerned in this trade. See *Parliamentary History*, XVIII, 195–8; see also Dora M. Clark: *British Opinion and the American Revolution* (New Haven, 1930), pp. 87–8.

to the petition, left these manufactured goods dead on the hands of producers, with payments suspended, work stopped, and the people left destitute by unemployment. On that day there was also received a combined petition from seven other towns in Staffordshire, concerned in the making of pottery, where the same unhappy effects of the stoppage of the export trade to North America were in evidence. Each of the petitions prayed for the reopening of commercial intercourse with America to alleviate these miseries.[22]

However, contrary to the Birmingham counter-petition of January 27, Leeds, in the West Riding of Yorkshire—supported by Wakefield, Halifax, Bradford, and other places located in the heart of the woollen industry of England—presented a petition on February 1 affirming that "the Preservation of the Commerce of this Country and its Colonies depends upon a due Obedience to the Laws of England." It therefore expressed fear "at the unwarrantable Proceedings now carrying on . . . in North America, in open Defiance of the Supreme Legislative Power of this Kingdom" and stated that there was great reason to believe attempts were being made to prey upon groundless fears in order to prevail upon the people of England to sign petitions to the House for the repeal of several acts of Parliament. In opposition to this, the signers were persuaded that "the best Security for all interested in the Trade to America" was to support such measures as were expedient for enforcing "a due Obedience to the British Legislature, and restoring Order and good Government in America." This Leeds petition was signed by the mayor, recorder, aldermen, and assistants of the borough. On the other hand, another from the same place, signed by merchants trading to the North American colonies, recounted that thousands of workers there were dependent upon the export trade to North America and that the merchants themselves had "very considerable Property in the Hands of the North Americans," for the safety of which they could not but be anxious; they therefore prayed for relief.[23] So did a petition that came before the House on February 8 from Nottingham, the county town of Nottinghamshire, where the production of hosiery for the American market was the means of livelihood of thousands of workers. With warehouses closed and the citizens faced with "Poverty, Distress, and Ruin," the petitioners

[22] *Journals of the House of Commons*, XXXV, 86.
[23] For the two Leeds petitions see *ibid.*, XXXV, 89–90.

could only look to Parliament to "find some temperate and honourable means of conciliating the Differences of the British Empire. . . ."[24]

Of all the petitions, that of February 15 from the Dorsetshire town of Bridport in southern England, was perhaps the most moving. It stated that the sole industry there was the manufacture of nets, lines, and canvas, all particularly designed for the needs of the North American fisheries, in connection with which thousands of labourers had been employed. But, "in Consequence of the Non-importation Agreements lately entered into in America," the petitioners declared, they could not expect "a Demand for a Shilling's Worth of Goods for those Parts" and therefore begged the House to take into consideration their distresses and the impending ruin of the labourers.[25] On that same day, certain of the towns in the West Riding of Yorkshire that had joined in the Leeds petition of February 1 to support the policy of the government toward the colonies, now begged the House to take steps to remove the causes of "the unhappy Differences subsisting between Great Britain and her American Colonies. . . ."[26] A petition offered on the 22nd from Whitehaven, the principal seaport of the county of Cumberland, also echoed the same idea, as did one from the merchants, linen drapers, and principal inhabitants of Belfast, Ireland. Also on that day a second petition was received from Nottingham signed by the aldermen, sheriff, and leading manufacturers and inhabitants. Unlike the first, it strongly supported the government and insisted that the earlier petitions signed in the town had greatly exaggerated the true situation of industry there. Finally, it expressed the conviction that "the Trade and Commerce of Great Britain with her Colonies cannot be effectually restored, and permanently secured, without a due and proper Submission and Obedience to the Laws and Government of this Kingdom."[27]

A petition from the Yorkshire cloth centre of Huddersfield, received on March 9, went even further than that from Nottingham by stressing not only that business was good, despite the difficulties arising from the conduct of the colonies, but also that the petitioners were prepared to suffer losses rather than to submit to the "unjust

---

[24] *Ibid.*, XXXV, 108.
[25] *Ibid.*, XXXV, 123.
[26] *Ibid.*, XXXV, 124.
[27] *Ibid.*, XXXV, 139–41.

and unlawful Demands" of the Americans, which if granted could only "make them more insolent and totally to overthrow the lawful Authority which the King and Parliament must have over all its Dominions. . . ."[28] The last of these petitions, submitted on March 15 from the clothiers of Trowbridge in Wiltshire, was perhaps the strongest of all in support of the government. Referring to the petition of the Continental Congress which had questioned the authority of Parliament to raise a revenue "in those Parts of His Majesty's Dominions," the Trowbridge petitioners took the position that such an exemption from sharing the burdens of the Empire "must occasion the People here being unequitably and too heavily burdened" as they had been in the past, with the result that to escape their burdens numbers of workers had already emigrated to America. These workers prayed that the House would ever maintain entire the supremacy of Parliament over the colonies and oblige them to bear "an equitable Share towards the honourable Support of that Government, and the Means of providing for the common Defence and Security of that Empire."[29]

All the petitions from the towns were automatically referred to the committee of the whole House to which the London and Bristol petitions had been referred. The first Birmingham petition vigorously supporting the government had been presented on January 25. When the committee of the whole House sat on the 27th to take into consideration the other petitions submitted earlier, it was informed by a representative of the London merchants that they now waived appearing before the special committee of the House appointed to hear these petitions, on the grounds that "the mode of examination is such as totally precluded them from answering the great public object" they had in mind.[30] Nor did petitioners from other towns press to be heard. Further, in light of the fact that— like the first Birmingham petition—a number of the others were strongly pro-government, the Ministry now felt less threatened by the pressure from the mercantile interest.

Thus, the anticipation of the colonial leaders that the non-importation Association would produce an effective economic pressure upon

---

[28] *Ibid.*, XXXV, 186.

[29] *Ibid.*, XXXV, 198–9.

[30] *Parliamentary History*, XVIII, 194. See also, in connection with the petition movement, E. C. Black: *The Association: British Extraparliamentary Political Organization, 1769–1793* (*Harvard Historical Monographs*, LIV, Cambridge, Mass., 1963).

the British government was not fulfilled; nor were the deep fore-bodings that many British manufacturers had expressed early in 1775. To the contrary, when Charles Irving made a tour that took him through a number of the leading manufacturing towns in 1775, not only did he find an absence of distress as a result of unemploy-ment,[31] but in most places in northern England business was boom-ing, and large improvements were being introduced. That Irving was correct seems to be indicated by the fact that in the West Riding of Yorkshire the production in 1775 of both broadcloths and narrow cloths exceeded that of 1774; likewise the total value of English exports in 1775, though somewhat lower than in the pre-ceding year, exceeded that of 1773.[32] His explanation of this was that "owing to the great consumption of our commodities on the Continent . . . the interruption of commerce with America has been little felt."[33] It should be added that when Great Britain found itself at war with the Thirteen Colonies, there was a greatly increased demand for many articles of military supply, such as armament, uniforms, and other equipment, all of which—taken together with the dawning industrial revolution—supported England's economy.

Meanwhile, in Parliament, leave was given in the House of Com-mons on February 10, on a motion by Lord North, to bring in a bill "to restrain the Trade and Commerce of the Province of Massa-chusetts Bay and New Hampshire, and Colonies of Connecticut and Rhode Island, and Providence Plantation, in North America, to Great Britain, Ireland and the British Islands in the West Indies; and to prohibit such Provinces and Colonies from carrying on any Fishing on the Banks of Newfoundland, or other Places therein to be mentioned, under certain Conditions, and for a Time to be limited."[34] Following this, action was taken on February 13 and 15, at the specific request of the Crown, for augmenting the sea and land forces, consistent with the government policy that the colonies

---

[31] For the Irving report submitted to John Pownall, Under-Secretary of State for the Colonies, September 28, 1775, see *Calendar of Home Office Papers of the Reign of George III, 1773–1775* (London, 1899), p. 416; the Bristol merchant Richard Champion also supports this evidence in a letter of March 6, 1775, to the Philadelphia trading house of Willing, Morris & Co.; for this see the *Letters of Richard Champion*, pp. 45–7 (cited in full in Chap. 10 of this volume, note 28); see also Dora M. Clark: *op. cit.*, pp. 107–8.

[32] See T. S. Ashton: *An Economic History of England: The 18th Century* (London, 1955), Appendix, Tables 11, 12, 14.

[33] *Calendar of Home Office Papers . . . 1773–1775*, p. 416.

[34] *Journals of the House of Commons*, XXXV, 112.

must be made to submit before their grievances should be heard or concessions made to them.[35]

Still hoping to avoid war, on February 20 Lord North rose in the committee of the whole House to present the previously mentioned conciliatory plan conceived by the Cabinet Council in January. This proposal, he said, was based upon the assumption that the issue between the Americans and Parliament was, as earlier stressed by the colonials, chiefly a matter of taxation. However, if the dispute now "goes to the whole of our authority," he stated, "we can enter into no negociation, we can meet no compromise." The minister therefore proposed that a resolution be drawn to the effect that when any of the colonies should proffer adequate provisions for the common defence, as well as for the support of its civil government—including the administration of justice—it would be proper, if approved by the King and Parliament, to forbear from levying any duty or tax upon this colony, except duties designed for the regulation of commerce, the net revenue of which would be credited to the complying colony.[36]

Thomas Pownall, one-time Governor of Massachusetts Bay, in supporting the resolution, declared: "I have always defended their rights, where I thought any infraction was made on them. . . ." Then, pointing to his publications as proof that he had never wavered in his principles or conduct, he added: ". . . when I see that the Americans are actually resisting that government that is derived from the crown, and by the authority of parliament; when I see them opposing rights which they [previously] always acknowledged, and for asserting which, I could produce the best authority . . . , I cannot but say, that it is become necessary that this country . . . should oppose its force to force; when that force is to be employed only in maintaining the laws and constitution of the empire." Before concluding his address, he sought to impress upon the members of the House that the system of colonial government must be altered in line with the present needs of Americans and said:

---

[35] For the legislation augmenting the forces see *ibid.*, XXXV, 110–11, 114–17, 124, 128, and *passim;* see also *Parliamentary History*, XVIII, 298, 305–13, 316–17.

[36] *Ibid.*, XVIII, 319–20. For the exact wording of the resolution, as read and approved on February 27, see *Journals of the House of Commons*, XXXV, 161. For a study of another attempt at reconciliation, along the lines proposed by Lord North, see H. A. Meistrich: "Lord Drummond and Reconciliation," New Jersey Historical Society *Proceedings*, LXXXI, 256–77.

". . . I wish the committee [of the whole House] would attend to what I am going to say, (for I know it to be true) that the country of America must, for the future, be governed under [new] regulations and forms; and a constitution that must be settled by compact. The relation between the two countries, must, in its future process, stand upon the compact; or this country must hold its dominion in the colonies by the tenure of a war, that will cost more than they are worth, and finally ruin both."

This was equally true of the regulation of colonial trade, Pownall asserted, which likewise must be settled by compact.[37]

In opposition to the Ministry, Charles James Fox, Colonel Barré, and Edmund Burke charged that North's offer of a conciliatory measure was an act of insidious cunning by which he was practising the art of divide and rule; all stressed the point that the plan would increase rather than lessen the disorders. Also speaking against it, David Hartley (a great friend of America and a close associate of Franklin, with whom he was to draw up the terms of the definitive treaty of peace in 1783) pointed out that before the Christmas holidays he had made a really conciliatory proposal, which was for the government "to make a free requisition to the colonies for a supply towards the expence of defending, protecting, and securing the colonies. The present motion [respecting the granting of supply by the colonies] is not free but compulsory; it is attended with menaces and threats. . . . To say, Give me as much money as I wish, till I say enough, or I will take it from you, and then to call such a proposition conciliatory for peace, is insult added to oppression." Although additional objections were voiced by other speakers, the resolution was approved in Commons without a division.[38]

What seemed to give force to the arguments of the opposition

---

[37] *Parliamentary History*, XVIII, 322–9. Pownall, at this juncture representing Minehead, a Somersetshire borough with its seat in the gift of Lord North (after having lost the election at Tregony), was doubtless aware that his support of the government's decision to use force, while pretending to be a friend of the colonies, left him open to serious reproaches of inconsistency. He later broke completely with the administration. For, on December 2, 1777, he urged the government to recognize that British sovereignty over the colonies was lost, never to be regained, and recommended that the best method of facing this fact, and of keeping the colonials from seeking a French alliance, was to enter into a treaty with them. See *Parliamentary History*, XVIII, 984–9, and XIX, 526–7. For an excellent study of Pownall see J. A. Schutz: *Thomas Pownall, British Defender of American Liberty* . . . (Glendale, Calif., 1951).

[38] *Parliamentary History*, XVIII, 329–58. For a study of Hartley as "an advocate of conciliation" see G. H. Guttridge: *David Hartley, M.P.* . . . (Berkeley, 1926), reprinted from University of California *Publications in History*, XIV, 231–340.

—in maintaining that the chief objective of the administration was not conciliation but rather compulsion to force the colonies to recognize the sovereign powers of Parliament—was that the motion for leave to bring in a bill for restraining the commerce of the New England colonies had been granted on February 10, as previously mentioned. In supporting the motion Lord North had declared "that as the Americans had refused to trade with this kingdom, it was but just that we should not suffer them to trade with any other nation," and that as the fisheries by undoubted right belonged to Great Britain, but as there was a rebellion in Massachusetts Bay, "it was just, therefore, to deprive that province of its fisheries." Further, the people in the other New England colonies, by acts that he specified, had also acted in a rebellious manner and therefore should be "included in the prohibition to fish and to trade."[39] This motion was approved but only after a debate during which the legal points of what constituted rebellion had been raised. In the course of the discussion, in which other opposition speakers took part, Burke had risen to the defence of New England on the grounds of the hardships that would be worked upon British manufacturers as well as the colonials.[40] On February 17, Lord North presented the New England Restraining Bill. It came up for its second reading on the 24th,[41] only three days before the ultimate approval of the minister's plan for conciliating the colonies.

The final action on the New England Restraining Bill came in March 1775. Upon a motion made on the 6th that the bill be engrossed, Rear Admiral Richard Lord Howe (who had succeeded to the title upon the death of his brother, George Augustine, a man much loved by Americans, killed in the Ticonderoga campaign in 1758) spoke on the necessity of the measure "as the only moderate means of bringing the disobedient provinces to a sense of their duty, without involving the empire in all the horrors of a civil war."

---

[39] Parliamentary History, XVIII, 298–300; see also American Archives, 4th ser., I, 1622–3. The motion limiting restraints to New England was predicated upon a conclusion, based on letters from America, that the attitude of the other older colonies differed from that prevalent in New England, where preparations for war were under way. As one writing to Governor Tryon from New York on October 5, 1774, put it: "The cloud to the eastward seems to thicken, and will, it is probable, break in thunder and lightning. Powder and arms in these ports [are] bought up and carried eastward" (Dartmouth Manuscripts, II, Appendix, Part X, 233–4).

[40] For the debate see Parliamentary History, XVIII, 300–5, and American Archives, I, 1623–6. Others who spoke out against the motion were John Dunning, Governor George Johnstone, and Sir George Savile.

[41] Journals of the House of Commons, XXXV, 129 and 152.

In reply, Charles James Fox declared the bill was "calculated to put an end to all that remained of the legislative authority of Great Britain over America"; he also emphasized the point that the crisis had been brought on by Parliament's abuse of its powers and maintained that the proposed measure was designed solely "to exasperate the colonies into open and direct rebellion," since by the bill "all means of acquiring a livelihood, or receiving provisions were cut off, no other alternative was left [to New England], but starving or rebellion." To Burke, the New England Restraining Bill was but the beginning of a tragedy that would be extended "till one by one parliament will ruin all its colonies, and root up all its commerce; until the statute book becomes nothing but a black and bloody roll of proscriptions, a frightful code of rigour and tyranny. . . ." Despite this and other denunciations of the measure, the vote to engross it was carried by 215 to 61.[42] On March 8, at the third reading of the bill, David Hartley offered an amendment: "That nothing in the Act shall extend to prohibit the importation into any . . . of the said provinces, of any fuel, meal, corn, flour, or victual, which shall be brought coastwise from any part of the continent of America." He emphasized the humanitarian grounds of the amendment and charged that the refusal of it

> "will be a declaration on your part, that you mean to bring famine upon them, to the utmost of your power. . . . destroying the North American fishery . . . will disable the provinces, under the prohibition, from the means of paying their debts to this country, . . . and . . . you will then turn accusers of the North Americans for not paying their debts, and you will add, according to the usual falsehoods towards the Americans, that they never intended to pay their debts. . . ."[43]

Governor Pownall, to refute the imputation of motivations of cruelty in the framing of the bill, reportedly declared:

> "As to the starving and famine, supposed as an effect which might follow from the operations of this Bill, it was a supposition too idle to combat. The colonies of New England were provision colonies, they were great grazing settlements . . . [and] they raised [at least] sufficient corn, rye, and barley for their subsistence. . . . He concluded by saying that he considered this Bill simply as a commercial regulation; as a temporary withholding of those indulgences which

[42] Parliamentary History, XVIII, 385–92.
[43] Ibid., XVIII, 393–5, and Journals of the House of Commons, XXXV, 182.

particular laws and connivance had given . . . so long as the colonies should think fit to prohibit the trade of Great Britain. . . ."

The Hartley amendment was rejected with only 58 yeas as against 188 noes.[44] The bill was then sent to the House of Lords.

The debate on the Restraining Bill was even sharper in the House of Lords than in the House of Commons. In a lengthy address, Lord Camden analyzed the proposed measure and, after reviewing various interpretations that had been placed upon it, argued:

"But my lords, the true character of the Bill is violent and hostile. My lords, it is a Bill of war; it draws the sword, and in its necessary consequences plunges the empire into civil and unnatural war. . . . But it has been observed and argued, that in this great question, trade is a secondary consideration . . . subordinate to the great discussions of polity. . . . We are then to understand . . . that to maintain a legislative power over America, . . . and for the reduction of the colonies to an unlimited obedience, all considerations of the benefits of trade . . . and of the ruinous michiefs of its loss, be they however certain and fatal, are to be suspended; that we are to contend through every hazard, and in neglect of every other [consideration], for this grand object, the establishment of supreme dominion. . . . I wish, my lords, to place the question on its proper basis. . . .

"To conquer a great continent of 1800 miles, containing three millions of people, all indissolubly united on the great Whig bottom of liberty and justice, seems an undertaking not to be rashly engaged in. . . . What are the 10,000 men you have just voted out to Boston? Merely to save general Gage from the disgrace and destruction of being sacked in his entrenchments. It is obvious, my lords, that you cannot furnish armies, or treasure, competent to the mighty purpose of subduing America . . . but whether France and Spain will be tame, inactive, spectators of your efforts and distractions, is well worthy the considerations of your lordships."

Despite the efforts of Camden and others to defeat the bill, when the House divided on March 16 on the second reading, it was carried by a vote of 104 to 29.[45] After passing its third reading the bill was sent back to the House of Commons with certain amendments, which, however, were not pressed by the lords when objected to by the Commons. On March 30 the bill received the royal assent.[46]

[44] Parliamentary History, XVIII, 398–400.
[45] Ibid., XVIII, 421–55.
[46] Journals of the House of Commons, XXXV, 220–1, 224–6, 231, 241.

By the provisions of the Restraining Act great restrictions were placed on the commerce of the New England colonies. The design, as indicated, was to limit their trade, under specified conditions, to operate solely with Great Britain, Ireland, and the British West Indies, thus rebuking the Association agreement made by the Continental Congress to ban such trade. Further, no New England ship was permitted to fish off the coasts or banks of Newfoundland "or any other part of the coast of North America"; any ship from the other colonies proceeding to the fisheries had to carry ownership certification from the governor of the colony from which the ship originated, while vessels from Great Britain, Ireland, the Channel Islands, and the Isle of Man were free to operate in the fisheries as in the past. The purpose of the Act was simply to restore obedience to the laws of Parliament by putting an end to the Association within the specified colonies; it was therefore provided that when any Governor was satisfied that trade or commerce had been restored between his colony and the mother country, he should so notify the customs and other trade-enforcement officers and then issue a proclamation lifting the restraints.[47]

As news continued to arrive that the inhabitants in other colonies south of New England were being equally zealous in promoting the continental Association, it seemed desirable to extend similar restraints to their trade. Therefore on March 9 Lord North begged leave of the House of Commons to bring in a bill for restraining the trade of New Jersey, Pennsylvania, Maryland, Virginia, and South Carolina.[48] Because all reports from New York seemed to indicate that it, of all the colonies, was the least favourably disposed toward the resolves of the Continental Congress,[49] while North Carolina and Georgia, among the older Southern colonies, were the least active in promoting revolutionary activities, these colonies were omitted from the bill. To David Hartley the measure was well intended to drive "the whole continent of America into despair"; with irony he added that it held "out no temptation to the moderate and less offending, and that is the sure way to restore peace and har-

---

[47] For the terms of 15 Geo. III, c. 10, see *Statutes at Large* (Pickering), XXXI, 4–11.

[48] It should be noted that the Three Lower Counties on the Delaware were not listed in the title of the Act, but by Clause 7 in order to enforce the restrictions on the other colonies named, the Delaware counties were virtually placed under the same restraints of trade.

[49] See Lieutenant Governor Colden's letters to the Earl of Dartmouth of December 7, 1774, January 4 and 21, and February 1, 1775, *New York Colonial Documents*, VIII, 512–14, 528–9, 530, 531–2.

mony, to recover our commerce, just on the verge of destruction, and reconcile them cordially to our government."[50] Nevertheless, leave to bring in a bill was granted.[51]

It was in the midst of the proceedings on the measure to apply pressure on the recalcitrant colonies that Edmund Burke rose in the House of Commons on March 22 and delivered his great plea for a true reconciliation of all differences, in a speech said to have taken three hours. Although Burke's oration may not have changed the votes of members, it apparently deeply impressed many of them. Writing to Richard Champion the evening after his brother spoke, Richard Burke commented:

> "From a Torrent of Members rushing from the house when he sat down, I could hear the loudest, the most unanimous and highest strains of applause. That such a performance even from him was never before heard in that house. . . . I found, that in the clear opinion of his hearers, there was more knowledge of the Subject, a greater compass of understanding, far more political wisdom, a clearer insight into the nature of Government in general, . . . that surpassed very far any thing they had ever expected to hear from any man."[52]

No one fresh from a study of the background of the crisis that confronted the Empire in the spring of 1775 who reads the Burke speech with the attention that it deserves, can fail to be struck by the humanity and nobility of Burke's outlook. This, combined with a certain quality of intellectual integrity displayed in the address, entitles it to a unique place among the political utterances of the eighteenth century. Indeed, in the judgment of the author of this series, it surpasses in these qualities the finest speeches of the other friends of America, including Chatham, Camden, and Charles James Fox. It is doubtless true that Burke's addresses have a more potent effect upon the reader than they did upon his listeners; whereas the contrary is undoubtedly true of Chatham's speeches. Henry Flood, writing to the Earl of Charlemont shortly after Burke had delivered his speech, makes the following comment:

> "Last Wednesday, Burke made a motion of conciliation towards America. . . . His performance was the best I have heard from him in the whole winter. He is always brilliant in an uncommon degree,

[50] *Parliamentary History*, XVIII, 411–12.
[51] *Journals of the House of Commons*, XXXV, 206.
[52] *Correspondence of Edmund Burke* (Copeland), III, 139–40.

and yet I believe it would be better he were less so. I don't mean to join with the cry which will always run against shining parts, when I say that I sincerely think it interrupts him so much in argument, that the house are never sensible that he argues as well as he does. [Charles James] Fox gives a strong proof of this, for he makes use of Burke's speech as a repertory, and by stating crabbedly two or three of those ideas which Burke has buried under flowers, he is thought almost always to have had more argument."[53]

In the course of his remarks, Burke drew a picture of the exceptional growth of the colonies, particularly in trade. Using the most reliable figures at his command, he pointed out that in 1704 the total value of English exports to the colonies and to Africa, which supplied them with slaves, amounted to £569,930, but that in 1772 it stood at £6,022,132 as compared with the whole export trade of England in 1704, which was £6,509,000. Further, at the beginning of the century the value of the trade to the colonies was but one-twelfth the total value of exports, whereas in 1772 it amounted to over one-third of the total. In the case of Pennsylvania, the exports in 1704 were valued at a mere £11,459, while in 1772 they had risen to £507,909—nearly fifty times as much. Burke went on to depict America as a land of abundance with vast surpluses of food supplies. He gave as the annual export figure for grain, including rice, for some years past as amounting to better than £1,000,000. In these wealthy colonies, he said, was a numerous population amounting to two million people, more or less, who were now to be ruled by force. But, he contended, "we have no sort of experience in favour of force as an instrument in the rule of our colonies. Their growth and their utility has been owing to methods altogether different." He then pointed out that love of liberty among Americans was their predominating feature. In fact, this "fierce spirit of liberty is stronger in the English colonies probably than in any other people of the earth; and this from a great variety of powerful causes." Next he enumerated and enlarged upon the six chief sources of this spirit in Americans: their descent from the freedom-loving English, their popular form of government, the quality of the Protestant religion in the older Northern colonies, the influence of slave-holding upon the manners and attitudes of people in the Southern colonies, the wide-spread education in the law in all the colonies, and, finally,

[53] *The Manuscripts and Correspondence of James, First Earl of Charlemont,* Vol. II, *Historical Manuscripts Commission, Thirteenth Report, Appendix,* Part VIII, 391.

the remoteness of the colonies from the parent country, with the consequent feeling of separateness. There were, he asserted, only three possible ways to deal with this spirit: first, to change it, if possible; second, to prosecute it as a criminal tendency; and, third, to accept it as a fact. In rejecting the first two alternatives, Burke presented his views on the Empire as "the aggregate of many states under one common head," with these subordinate parts, in the case of the British Empire, possessed of

"many local privileges and immunities. . . . But though every privilege is an exemption . . . from the ordinary exercise of the supreme authority, it is no denial of it. . . . [Therefore] I can scarcely conceive any thing more completely imprudent, than for the head of the empire to insist, that, if any privilege is pleaded against his will, or his acts, . . . his whole authority is denied; instantly to proclaim rebellion, to beat to arms, and to put the offending provinces under the ban. . . . Will it not teach them [the colonials] that the government, against which a claim of liberty is tantamount to high treason, is a government to which submission is equivalent to slavery?"

Burke thereupon proceeded to advocate that in dealing with the colonies the government "comply with the American spirit as necessary; or, if you please submit to it, as a necessary evil." Then, leading up to his own plan of conciliation, he declared to the House:

"I am resolved this day to have nothing at all to do with the question of the right of taxation. . . . The question with me is, not whether you have a right to render your people miserable, but whether it is not to your interest to make them happy. . . . My idea therefore, without considering whether we yield as matter of right, or grant as matter of favour, is *to admit the people of our colonies into an interest in the constitution. . . .*"

It is true, Burke continued, that the "more moderate among the opposers of parliamentary concession freely confess, that they hope no good from taxation; but they apprehend the colonists have further views; and if this point were conceded, they would instantly attack the trade-laws." This he disputed, stating that before one could judge whether the trade laws were, as asserted, the real cause of the quarrel, it would be necessary to put taxation by Parliament out of the question by a repeal of the revenue act. In place of it he advocated as equitable and just "a taxation of America by grant, and not by imposition." He then presented proposals for six resolves, explaining the implications of each: (1) that the fourteen colonies,[54] each with a separate government, have not had the privilege of sending members to Parliament; (2) that they have, nevertheless, been liable to pay taxes granted by Parliament, which have been prejudicial to subjects dwelling within them; (3) that, because of the distance of the colonies, no method had been devised for procuring a representative in Parliament; (4) that each of the fourteen colonies had an assembly with powers to raise taxes; (5) that these assemblies have "at sundry times freely granted several large subsidies and public aids for his Majesty's service, according to their abilities, when required thereto by letter from one of his Majesty's principal secretaries of state"; (6) that it had been found "that the manner of granting the said supplies and aids, by the said general assemblies, hath been more agreeable to the said colonies, and more beneficial, and conducive to the public service, than the mode of giving and granting aids in parliament, to be raised and paid in the said colonies." Here then, said Burke, was the heart of the matter: "whether you will chuse to abide by a profitable experience, or a mischievous theory. . . ."

Burke now proposed five more resolutions calling respectively for the total repeal of the Townshend Revenue Act of 1767, the Boston Port Act, the Act for the Impartial Administration of Justice in Massachusetts Bay, and the Act for the Better Regulating the Government of that province and for an amendment of the Act of 35 Henry VIII relating to the trial of treason. By a twelfth resolution, he moved that when a North American colony, by a duly confirmed act of assembly, had settled a salary on its superior court judges, these should hold office during good behaviour, and not be subject to removal by His Majesty, except on complaint of the Assembly or the Governor. A thirteenth resolution was that the courts of vice-admiralty in America be made more convenient for those who would sue in them and that the judges be provided with a more decent maintenance. In other words, he would retain these courts with their extended jurisdiction as "one of the capital securities of the Act of Navigation."

Before closing, Burke paid his respects to the plan of reconciliation presented by Lord North as a proposal "of a ransom by auction" —a plan that was "neither regular parliamentary taxation, nor

---

[54] There were, including Nova Scotia and West Florida, fifteen colonies with popular assemblies.

colony grant"; something that, if applied, "must be fatal in the end to our constitution," since Parliament could not settle the particular quota that each colony should pay to the common cause, and since under the plan some obedient colonies might be heavily taxed while the refractory ones remained unburdened. Furthermore, even if quotas could be fixed, this would not guarantee their payment. Non-payment of quotas would surely produce new quarrels or new laws, and the Empire would never know an hour's tranquillity. Comparing the minister's plan and his own, he observed: ". . . as I propose the peace and union of the colonies as the very foundation of my plan, it cannot accord with one whose foundation is perpetual discord. Compare the two. This I offer to give you is plain and simple. The other full of . . . intricate mazes."[55]

In summarizing his plan, Burke reiterated in concise form all thirteen of his resolutions.[56] After he had moved the adoption of the first of them—to wit, that the colonies were not represented in Parliament—a debate followed. Charles Jenkinson made the principal reply to Burke, with a defence of the position that Parliament had the exclusive right to make grants to the King. In doing so, he quoted the language of the famous English Declaration of Rights of 1688/9 that "Levying money for, or to the use of the crown, by pretence of prerogative, without grant of parliament . . . is illegal." To him, this restriction was as prudent as it was necessary. However, it was pointed out in the course of the debate that the practice of the colonial assemblies in voting supplies had been to grant them, in language at least, to the King. When the House divided on this resolution but 78 voted for it as against 270. The other resolves met with similar rejection.[57] They deserved a better fate. Could members of Parliament, including the King's chief minister, have peered into the future, they surely would not have dismissed Burke's resolutions out of hand. Yet, had Burke's plan been approved, it is not at all clear to what extent enforcement of the navigation and trade laws, which he advocated so strongly, could have been possible in view of the intensity of revolutionary sentiment in America by

[55] *Parliamentary History*, XVIII, 478–538.

[56] For Burke's resolutions, as summarized, see *ibid.*, XVIII, 536–8.

[57] Actually, when it came to the first four resolves and the last, the previous question was moved, so that the voting was on the latter motion; the other resolves were directly voted down. See *ibid.*, XVIII, 538–40. For an excellent summary of the debate of March 22 see *Annual Register, 1775*, pp. 108–10; see also *Parliamentary Register*, I, 363–9.

the spring of 1775—not to mention the actual outbreak of hostilities in Massachusetts Bay in April of that year. Nor is it clear that colonials would have been willing to see the courts of vice-admiralty —with their enlarged powers—function in America, although Burke saw this as a necessity to support the restrictions on trade.

Another valiant effort to rescue the Empire from division and war was attempted five days later by David Hartley in a lengthy major speech. Returning to the proposal he had made as early as December 13, 1774,[58] that whatever revenue was secured from the colonies should be by requisition, he sought to meet the objection raised in the House that Parliament alone could raise a revenue, since this could not be done constitutionally simply by the use of the royal prerogative. Hartley now embodied in his proposal that royal requisitions on the colonies be made by the authority and sanction of Parliament. Therewith, he presented the draft of a letter of requisition "drawn up after the manner of former requisitions to the colonies" but adapted "to the present circumstances." It was a letter of reconcilement, ignoring what had gone before and looking forward to the restoration of harmony and mutual confidence between the mother country and the colonies. Therefore, only a recognition of the principle of freely granting requisitions when made by the Crown was touched upon. His motion began with the words: "That an humble Address be presented to his Majesty, that he will be graciously pleased to give orders, that Letters of Requisition be written to the several . . . colonies and plantations in America to make provisions for the purposes of defending, protecting and securing the said colonies and plantations; and that his majesty will be pleased to order all such addresses as he shall receive, in answer to the aforesaid letters of requisition, to be laid before this House."[59] Embodied in the Hartley plan was the provision that ". . . the inestimable privilege of judging for themselves of the expediency, fixing the amount, and determining the application of the grants, would still be left in the assemblies."[60] What was said of the Burke proposal for conciliation may also be said of this one—it merited the most serious consideration before being rejected, as it was by the House, without even a division. Not that there was much hope that the colonies would have approved it, for the issue between the

---

[58] See *Parliamentary History,* XVIII, 58; see also *Parliamentary Register,* I, 374–91.
[59] *Parliamentary History,* XVIII, 552–71.
[60] *Annual Register,* 1775, p. 110.

two countries—and we may surely now speak of British North America as a country—was reaching the dramatic and dreaded test of war. Hartley subsequently presented three more motions. In view of the failure of Burke's proposal for the *repeal* of the three coercive statutes directed against Boston and Massachusetts Bay, he simply pressed for their *suspension,* but this step met with no greater success than had his principal motion.[61]

But, to return to the bill to restrain the trade of the colonies south of New England. On March 30, on its second reading in the House of Commons a debate followed in which Temple Luttrell, a speaker for the opposition, declared: "To force a tax upon your colonists, unrepresented, and universally dissentient, is acting in no better capacity than that of a banditti of robbers." The bill was then ordered to be engrossed. On April 5 it was brought up for its third reading, at which time the Marquis of Granby, a loyal supporter of Chatham, denounced it in the following terms:

> "In God's name, what language are you now holding out to America! Resign your property, divest yourselves of your privileges and free-dom, renounce every thing that can make life comfortable, or we will destroy your commerce, we will involve your country in all the miseries of famine; and if you express the sensations of men at such harsh treatment, we will then declare you in a state of rebellion, and put yourselves and your families, to fire and sword."

Nevertheless, the bill passed by a vote of 192 to 46,[62] was approved in the House of Lords, and on April 13 received the royal assent.[63]

As has been mentioned, the Province of New York was one of the three colonies exempted from the commercial restrictions of the Restraining Act. However, by the spring of 1775, its General Assembly sent a petition to the King, a memorial to the House of Lords, and a remonstrance to the House of Commons, all strongly supporting the stand of the more aggressive colonies. For example, the remonstrance, dated March 25, stressed the point that the only

---

[61] *Parliamentary History,* XVIII, 574. For the debate of March 27 see *Parliamentary Register,* I, 370–95.

[62] *Parliamentary History,* XVIII, 595–606, *Journals of the House of Commons,* XXXV, 221, 232, 240, 241, 251, 259; see also, for the debate, *Parliamentary Register,* I, 415–22.

[63] *Journals of the House of Commons,* XXXV, 306, 309. This act, listed as 15 Geo. III, c. 18, carries the title "An Act to restrain the Trade and Commerce of the Colonies of New Jersey, Pennsylvania, Maryland, Virginia, and South Carolina, to Great Britain, Ireland, and the British Islands in the West Indies, under certain Conditions and Limitations." See *Statutes at Large,* VIII, 431.

way to restore harmony between the mother country and the colonies was "by ascertaining the line of parliamentary authority, and American freedom, on just, equitable, and constitutional grounds"; it declared that American grievances had come about as the result of "the innovations which have been made in the constitutional mode of government since the close of the last war." Among the grievances was one objecting to Parliament's denial that the respective colonies had the exclusive right of self-taxation. The other grievances protested the revival and application to colonials of the statute of treason passed in the reign of Henry VIII, the extension of the jurisdiction of the American courts of vice-admiralty, the Quartering Act of 1767, the act of 1764 against making the bills of credit of a colony a legal tender, the extension of the boundary of the Province of Quebec by the Quebec Act of 1774, and that act's provision for tolerating the Roman Catholic religion. The remonstrance, while claiming certain "essential rights," denied that New York colonials entertained "the most distant desire of independence" and gave assurances that, on the contrary, they acknowledged "the parliament of Great Britain [to be] necessarily entitled to a supreme direction and government over the whole empire. . . ."[64]

Edmund Burke, as London agent of the New York Assembly, presented its remonstrance on May 15 and moved that it be brought up for consideration. Lord North immediately took exception to it. Although referring appreciatively to the good conduct of New York, he nevertheless took the position that no paper should be presented for the consideration of the House "which tended to call in question the unlimited rights of parliament" as set forth in the Declaratory Act. He therewith moved to amend Burke's motion so as to include the statement that the Assembly "claim to themselves rights derogatory to, and inconsistent with, the legislative authority of parliament, as declared by the said Act." Upon the approval of the amendment, the remonstrance was rejected.[65] Nor did the New York Assembly's memorial to the House of Lords (couched in language in some ways even less respectful of Parliament) meet with any better reception when presented on May 18 by the Duke of Manchester, a leading Rockinghamite.[66]

The introduction before Parliament of the New York Assembly's

[64] For the New York Assembly remonstrance to the House of Commons see *Parliamentary History*, XVIII, 650–5.

[65] *Ibid.*, XVIII, 643–50.

[66] For the memorial, and the debate upon it, see *ibid.*, XVIII, 684–92.

protests might well have served the useful purpose of demonstrating to that body that *no* colony would rally to the support of the government's coercive policy. However, it was clear by now that the generality of the members of Parliament were not disposed to listen objectively to any American grievances or petitions until colonials should give at least token indication of their willingness to abide by the supremacy of the laws of Great Britain and to acknowledge responsibility for a share in the support of the realm. Such was the impasse as that session of Parliament drew toward a close.

A final attempt to rebuke the government began in the House of Lords on May 17, when Lord Camden presented a petition from the Protestant settlers in the Province of Quebec, dated November 12, 1774, praying that the so-called Quebec Act should be either repealed or amended so that the inhabitants might enjoy those "constitutional rights, privileges, and franchises heretofore granted to all his Majesty's dutiful subjects." In his speech, Camden attacked every feature of the Act: the extension of the limits of the province, the establishment of "Popery" there, and the "civil despotism in which the inhabitants of that immensely extended province are to be perpetually bound, by being deprived of all share in the legislative power, and subjected in life, freedom, and property, to the arbitrary ordinances of a governor and council appointed by, and dependent on the crown." He then produced the draft of a bill to repeal the Act, which should take effect on May 1, 1776—thus giving time to provide a better plan of government for the province. In his reply to Camden, the Earl of Dartmouth referred to the gratitude expressed by some 100,000 French Canadians when news was received in Canada that the Quebec Act had restored to them "their ancient rights and privileges." He insisted that it would be unfair to render this numerous people "unhappy and miserable, purely to gratify the unreasonable request of two or three thousand persons, who wished for what was impracticable [a popular assembly] and looked upon themselves deprived of what they were actually in possession of." He thereupon moved the rejection of the bill. But the most effective rebuttal came from Lord Lyttelton, who held that the Quebec Act

> "was framed for the conquered subjects of France, consonant to the faith of treaties, and to the stipulations . . . of the solemn pact between Great Britain and France, convenanted for, and ratified by both nations at the conclusion of the war . . . I will go a step further . . .

and will uphold that the general principles and policy of this Canada Bill were founded in wisdom . . . they are principles, my lords, of toleration, unrestrained by prejudice, and unfettered by absurd and odious restrictions."

At the end of the debate the Dartmouth motion to reject the bill was upheld by a vote of 88 to 28.[67] Nor did Sir George Savile have any better success in the House of Commons on May 18 with his motion to repeal the Quebec Act, although Colonel Barré denounced the Act as a "monstrous production of tyranny, injustice, and arbitrary power" and Lord North asserted "that if the refractory colonies cannot be reduced to obedience by the present force [in America], he should think it a necessary measure to arm the Roman Catholics of Canada, and to employ them in that service." The vote on the motion to repeal was 86 in favour as against 174 opposed.[68]

At the conclusion of this session of Parliament on May 26, the Speaker of the House of Commons addressed the King when presenting the bills requiring the royal assent. Acknowledging the inordinate size of the money bills to provide for the service of 1775, especially in a period peace, he added:

"The unhappy differences in America, have been the chief cause of this expence; and I trust, that when the people of America see, in a proper light, the conduct of this country, they will learn to pay proper obedience to the laws; if, on the contrary, they should persist in their resolutions, and that the sword must be drawn, your faithful Commons will do every thing in their power to maintain and support the supremacy of this legislature."

In this speech proroguing Parliament, the King replied:

"You have maintained, with a firm and steady resolution, the rights of my crown and the authority of parliament, which I shall ever consider inseparable. You have protected and promoted the commercial interests of my kingdoms; and you have at the same time, given convincing proofs of your readiness (as far as the constitution will allow you) to gratify the wishes, and remove the apprehensions of my subjects in America; and I am persuaded, that the most salutary effects must in the end result from measures formed and conducted on such principles."[69]

---

[67] Ibid., XVIII, 655–76.
[68] Ibid., 676–84; see also Parliamentary Register, I, 479–86.
[69] Ibid., I, 487, Parliamentary History, XVIII, 693–4, and Journals of the House of Commons, XXXV, 395.

Anyone who examines carefully the reports of the debates in the two Houses of Parliament covering the proceedings of 1774 and the winter and spring of 1775, cannot fail to be impressed with the depth of feeling and conviction manifested by the speakers both for and against the administration. One cannot doubt the sincerity of men who pledged their wealth to maintain the unity of the Empire against a movement which, they were convinced, would mean a disruption of imperial unity if not halted. To charge that these men were but puppets who simply responded when the minister of the King pulled the strings, is as unfair to them—office-holders as many of them were—as it would be, for instance, to impugn the motives of members of the Congress of the United States when called upon by President Lincoln in 1861 to save the American Union from destruction. Further, it is to the credit of Parliament that every proposition designed to support British sovereignty throughout the Empire was submitted to the most searching analysis and criticism by the opposition.[70] Only after the proposed measures—their potential weaknesses, their possible unfairness to the resisting colonials, their latent dangers to the whole pattern of British constitutional government—had been dissected in debate were they finally approved by Parliament. Other important conclusions that emerged from these proceedings may well be recapitulated. It was conceded by the Ministry and the majority in both Houses of Parliament that the colonials had tangible and serious grievances which must and should be considered and acted upon, once their assemblies recognized the supremacy of Parliament as the final source of power within the Empire. The governmental authorities further agreed that, when a colony had taken steps to support the government of the Empire by such appropriations of funds as seemed reasonable to the home government, no further attempt would be made by Parliament to levy upon it, except for the purpose of regulating commerce. Thus, what was developing out of the discussions was the realization that the once weak and dependent North American colonies were now in reality mature commonwealths which must be given a new constitutional status within the Empire. What that status would be, however, was never

---

[70] For an important study of the three schools of thought which emerged in Great Britain in 1775 to debate the crucial issues of the American crisis, see R. W. Van Alstyne: "Parliamentary Supremacy versus Independence: Notes and Documents," *The Huntington Library Quarterly*, XXVI, 201–33.

to be determined, since the outbreak of hostilities in the War for American Independence intervened. For, given the delays in communications, both transatlantic[71] and intercolonial, and the strength of the patriot movement in America, now so powerful, it is not likely that the impatient colonists could have been convinced that a solution to meet their legitimate demands was being prepared. Nor is it profitable to bring hindsight to an examination of eighteenth-century Great Britain—whose own intellectual and philosophical concepts so largely inspired the emerging American nation—without keeping in mind that the deeply rooted social and political mores of the period inhibited its government from conceiving a solution that only a twentieth-century government would be ready to evolve.

[71] For a brief discussion of the time involved in transatlantic voyages see W. L. Sachse's *Colonial American in Britain* (Madison, Wisc., 1956), pp. 7-11.

CHAPTER XII

Open Rebellion

B Y THE beginning of 1775, the revolutionary movement had gathered so much impetus that there was no longer any doubt in the minds of Americans in general that a new order of things had arrived.

Although the First Continental Congress was dissolved on October 26, 1774,[1] the measures it had adopted were held by the patriots to be nothing less than the supreme law of the land, taking precedence over any measure or pronouncement of the individual colonial assemblies, not to mention the laws of Parliament relating to America.[2] Therefore, it was not surprising that the Association adopted by the Congress was entered into and enforced with a high degree of unanimity. Clearly a new nation was in the process of forming. As one writing from Salem, Massachusetts Bay, on December 20, 1774, put it: "Indeed the whole *United Colonies* are extremely active and zealous in the common cause, all nobly exerting themselves for carrying into execution the measures agreed upon by the late Continental Congress—excepting a few disappointed factious Tories . . ."[3] "The Proceedings of the Continental Congress astonish and terrify all considerate Men," wrote General Gage, and added that "tho' I am confident that many of their Resolves neither can nor will be observed, I fear they will be generaly received, as there does not appear to be Resolution and Strength enough amongst

---

[1] *Journals of the Continental Congress, 1774–1789*, I, 114.
[2] In this connection, see the article by C. P. Nettels: "The Origins of the Union and of the States" (Massachusetts Historical Society *Proceedings*, LXXII, 68–83), which describes the major role of the Continental Congress in creating the American Union after July 2, 1776, and in bringing into existence the member states.
[3] Peter Force: *American Archives*, 4th ser., I, 1053.

the most Sensible and moderate People in any of the Provinces, openly to reject them."[4] Nevertheless, some individuals did dissent from the resolves of the Congress, as might have been anticipated. Even in Massachusetts Bay, certain towns were more strongly under the influence of conservatives than others. For example, a well-attended town meeting, held on January 4, 1775, at Barnstable in the area of Cape Cod, agreed to appoint a committee of inspection (in harmony with the request of the Continental Congress), but the work of the committee was limited to inspecting imports and exports, thus ignoring the resolves of the Congress on consumption of prohibited items. Nor did the meeting agree to approve any of the resolves entered into by the Provincial Congress at Salem on November 23, 1774, for providing troops and money to defend the province.[5] Further, later in January in Marshfield, a coastal town lying south of Boston, some two hundred inhabitants, who had been "insulted and intimidated by the licentious spirit . . . prevalent amongst the lower ranks of people in the *Massachusetts* Government," applied to General Gage for military protection; as a result a contingent of a hundred regulars was sent to the town.[6]

But the action of the Worcester County convention on January 27, 1775, was far more characteristic of the attitude of the people of Massachusetts Bay and elsewhere. A covenant, drawn up for the signature of the people in the county, heartily approved the Association and agreed not only to uphold its every article and clause, but to treat as enemies those who would not do so.[7] For Gage was right, in the main, in his report of November 15, to the Secretary of State for the Colonies, especially in so far as his observations bore upon weakness of the Loyalists in Massachusetts Bay. In a long letter addressed to the members of the Provincial Congress of the colony,

---

[4] Gage to Dartmouth, November 15, 1774, *Gage Correspondence* (ed. C. E. Carter, 2 vols., New Haven, 1931, 1933), I, 384.

[5] *American Archives*, 4th ser., I, 1092–3.

[6] *Ibid.*, I, 1177–8; see also the Marshfield town-meeting resolves of February 20, 1775, repudiating the resolves of the Continental Congress and thanking General Gage and Admiral Thomas Graves for coming to the aid of the people, and the protest of sixty-four Marshfield inhabitants on the same date against the votes of the town meeting. *Ibid.*, I, 1249–50. The Marshfield town-meeting resolves appeared in the *Boston Evening-Post* of March 6, 1775; the protest by the inhabitants of Marshfield against these resolves was printed in the March 13 edition of this paper, together with the names of the signatories.

[7] For a copy of the proceedings of the convention see *Boston Evening-Post*, February 13, 1775.

an unnamed person writing from Boston on February 23 listed numerous acts of terrorism directed against "those people, who, from a sense of their duty to the King, and a reverence for his laws, have behaved quiet and peaceable; and for which reason they have . . . suffered such barbarous cruelties, insults, and indignities, besides the loss of their property by the hands of lawless mobs and riots, as would have been disgraceful even for savages to have committed."[8]

The second Provincial Congress of Massachusetts Bay assembled at Cambridge on February 1, 1775, and continued sitting until the 16th, when it adjourned to meet at Concord. There it continued its deliberations from March 22 until April 15.[9] Its members were chosen after the manner of selecting representatives to the former General Assembly. Most of the towns were represented; although, of the thirty-nine towns within Hampshire County entitled to representatives, nineteen did not respond.[10] From the day the Congress convened, events moved rapidly. John Hancock was again elected President. It was again voted that the proceedings be kept "an entire secret, unless special leave be first obtained for disclosing the same." At an early stage of the proceedings, the Congress chose John Hancock, Thomas Cushing, Samuel Adams, John Adams, and Robert Treat Paine to represent the colony at the coming gathering of "the American Congress" in May.[11] When attention was drawn to the activities of certain persons who had been employed to supply the King's troops in Boston with lumber, carts, and other necessaries, the Congress voted that all guilty of doing so should be held "in the highest detestation, and deemed inveterate enemies to America. . . ."[12] On February 7 approval was given to an address to the inhabitants, pointing out to them that when

"invaded by the Hand of Oppression, and trampled on by the merciless Feet of Tyranny, Resistance is so far from being criminal, that it becomes the christian . . . Duty of each Individual. . . . Though

---

[8] *American Archives*, 4th ser., I, 1260–3.

[9] For the "Proceedings of the Massachusetts Provincial Congress" see *American Archives*, 4th ser., I, 1323–66.

[10] *Ibid.*, I, 1325–6.

[11] *Ibid.*, I, 834, 842, 996, 997, 1328.

[12] *Ibid.*, I, 1330. For public notice warning individuals against supplying the troops see *Boston Evening-Post*, February 13, 1775.

we deprecate a Rupture with the Mother State, . . . unless you exhibit to your Enemies such a Firmness as shall convince them, that you are worthy of that Freedom your Ancestors fled here to enjoy, you have nothing to expect but the vilest and most abject Slavery."[13]

The proceedings of the Massachusetts Bay Provincial Congress disclose the care being given to prepare the militia and the so-called "Minute Men" for the eventual outbreak of hostilities and to provide for the collection of taxes so that the required armament could be secured. Later, additional steps were taken to prepare rules and regulations for the "Massachusetts Army" and "a General Court Martial" for enforcing them.[14]

In other words, by the spring of 1775 the regular government of Massachusetts Bay, as altered by the Coercive Acts, had been repudiated by a majority of the people in favour of a revolutionary, military government. The chief organ of the new regime was the Provincial Congress, with a committee of safety and a committee on the state of the province (later called the committee of supplies for the waging of war) acting as its most important executive instrumentalities.[15] By this time, all orders issued by the King, and all acts of Parliament passed from 1773 onward, were likewise repudiated as being violations of the rights of the people. Governor Gage's estimate of the situation referred to "the Phrenzy which had Seized the People," but he was convinced: "if a respectable Force is seen in the Field, the most obnoxious of the Leaders seized, and a Pardon proclaimed for all other's, that Government will come off Victorious. . . ."[16] What he was faced with was, in truth, a rebellion against the parent state. Yet, those promoting it still professed loyalty to King George III. In resolves passed by the Provincial Congress on March 16 setting aside a day of fasting and prayer, the people were asked among other things to implore God's blessing "upon all the British Empire, upon

[13] For this address as it appeared in the press see *ibid.*, February 20, 1775.

[14] For the fifty-three rules and regulations of the "Massachusetts Army" see *American Archives,* 4th ser., I, 1350–5.

[15] For the minutes of the Massachusetts Bay committee of safety, from November 2, 1774, to April 1, 1775, when it was voted: "That the Stores at Concord and elsewhere shall not be removed, without written orders from the Committee of Safety," see *ibid.*, I, 1365–70. The activities of the committee on the state of the province are set forth in the minutes of the Provincial Congress. See *ibid.*, I, 1328–66.

[16] Gage to Dartmouth, January 18, 1775, *Gage Correspondence,* I, 390; see also Bradley Chapin: "The American Revolution as Lese Majesty," *Pennsylvania Magazine,* LXXIX, 310–30.

George the Third our rightful King, and upon all the Royal Family."[17] Thus the rebellion was stated as being not against the King but against "the Ministry and Parliament," that is, the King's government. How different was to be the language employed in the Declaration of Independence in 1776 when it was charged that George III was the real author of all the evils that were disrupting the Empire!

But the real temper of the majority of delegates to the Provincial Congress must not be misinterpreted. It has been emphasized that the use of propaganda in the press to stir up the people was an important factor in fomenting rebellion.[18] There is also evidence to suppose that the more radical leaders planted false rumours as another powerful propaganda weapon. For example, General Gage, ever keeping a close eye on developments in North America, had the following explanation for the conduct of the patriots in support of the Congress:

> "The Fury into which People were thrown and which spread like an Infection from Town to Town and from Province to Province is hardly to be paralleled where no Oppression was actually felt, but they were stirred up by every Means that Art could invent; they were made to believe that their Religion was in Danger, their Lands to be taxed [by Parliament], and that the Troops were sent to enforce the Measures [of Parliament], and wantonly to Massacre the Inhabitants."[19]

The day before the resolves were adopted in favour of a day of fasting and prayer, reports were circulated in the Provincial Congress that large reinforcements of regular troops would soon arrive in the colony. The members therefore apprehended that "from the present Disposition of the British Ministry and Parliament, . . . sudden Distruction of this Colony in particular is intended." Whereupon it was resolved that "the great Law of Self-preservation, calls upon the Inhabitants of this Colony, immediately to prepare against every attempt that may be made to attack them by *Surprize*." To this end

---

[17] For the resolves of the Provincial Congress of February 16 for a day of fasting and prayer see *Boston Evening-Post*, February 20, 1775.

[18] In the above connection see A. M. Schlesinger: *Prelude to Independence, The Newspaper War on Great Britain, 1764–1776* (New York, 1958), and Philip Davidson: *Propaganda and the American Revolution, 1763–1783* (Chapel Hill, N.C., 1941).

[19] Gage to Dartmouth, February 17, 1775, *Gage Correspondence*, I, 392.

the militia and Minute Men were to spare neither time, pains, nor expense in perfecting themselves in military discipline, and people skilled in making fire-arms and bayonets were to be given every encouragement by the town.[20] Where such a report stemmed from is not clear, but, in view of the warning broadcast to the Bay colony inhabitants, there can be no doubt that the leaders of the Congress, acting on the theory that an attempt would soon be made by the British army to disrupt their plans for resistance by force, were convinced that the army of the colony, now under a regular staff, must be ready to fight when called upon. To hasten preparations, therefore, the committee of safety on February 21 voted unanimously that the committee of supplies should "purchase all kinds of War-like Stores, sufficient for an Army of fifteen thousand men to take the field."[21]

Gage was fully aware of what the committee of safety was doing under the cloak of secrecy within the Provincial Congress.[22] In line with his duty and responsibility, as both Governor of Massachusetts Bay and Commander-in-Chief of the British Forces in North America, he attempted to stop the build-up of armament designed to be used against his troops. When a false report reached him that eight brass field-pieces had been brought to Salem from Holland on February 26, he sent Lieutenant Colonel Alexander Leslie with 200 soldiers from the Castle William barracks on a secret expedition to seize the cannon. On the arrival of the British regulars in Salem, a multitude of people assembled in the town and began to make menacing gestures toward the soldiers. But the troops, having found none of the reported pieces, abandoned their fruitless mission without incident.[23]

Despite the gathering storm that was to break so soon, public affairs, even in Boston, moved along in the accustomed way. Such a marked figure as John Hancock, President of the Provincial Congress and chairman of the committee of safety, not only moved freely in and out of the town but was chosen moderator of a legally held town meeting on March 13. However, in view of the limitation placed

[20] For the publication of the resolves taken by the Provincial Congress on February 15 see Boston Evening-Post, February 20, 1775, and Massachusetts Spy, February 23, 1775. See also American Archives, 4th ser., I, 1340–1.

[21] Minute of the committee of safety, ibid., I, 1367.

[22] See Allen French: General Gage's Informers (Ann Arbor, 1932), Chap. 1 and passim, for intelligence received at this period.

[23] See Gage to Dartmouth, March 4, 1775, Gage Correspondence, I, 393–4, and the long account of the incident in the Boston Evening-Post, March 6, 1775.

by Parliament on town-meeting activities, there was little business beyond the selection of officers for the ensuing year, and Hancock was chosen as one of the seven selectmen.[24] He also, as President of the Congress, shortly afterward publicly warned the people through the press—still free to denounce the British government— that they continued to be "threatened by a powerful Army" gathered in Boston "with a professed Design of executing certain Acts of the British Parliament, calculated to destroy our invaluable Rights and Liberties, and the Government of this Colony as by Charter and Law established." He therefore called on them, in the name of the Congress, to put "this colony into a compleat State of Defence" and also to be prepared "to oppose with Firmness & Resolution, at the utmost Hazard," such designs.[25] General Gage was stating sober fact when, in referring to the state of the province on March 28, he affirmed that "Government is so totally unhinged, and the People so possessed with the Notions instilled into them, that all Authority is derived from them, that it may be doubted whether Government can ever revert again to its old Channel without some Convulsion."[26] The convulsion was to take place sooner than he thought.

Gage's mission, which was to bring about the enforcement of the acts of Parliament directed against Massachusetts Bay, was manifestly a failure. To recapitulate the sequence of disastrous events: He had arrived in Boston on May 13 of the preceding year with orders to transfer the seat of government to Salem. By August of that year he had been obliged to take up headquarters in Boston, where the army was concentrated. By September, members nominated by him for the mandamus Council, domiciled in various parts of the colony, had been obliged either to flee to Boston for safety or to resign their seats. Early in October the first Provincial Congress, in defiance of his dissolution of the General Court, had met in Salem in both public and secret session and had taken initial steps to organize a government in opposition to the established authority of King and Parliament. In November, at the second session of the

---

[24] The certified minutes of the meeting were printed in the *Boston Evening-Post* of March 20, 1775. However, one other item of business at this meeting made no attempt to disguise the degree of hostility caused by the presence of troops in the town and the navy in its harbour, when it was voted that the committee of correspondence of the town be directed to draw up an exact state of the behaviour of these forces in the town and carefully observe their conduct in the future. *Ibid.*, April 3, 1775.

[25] *Boston Evening-Post,* March 27, 1775.

[26] Gage to Dartmouth, March 28, 1775, *Gage Correspondence,* I, 394–5.

first Provincial Congress, also held at Salem, further steps were taken to perfect this irregular but popular government. By the time the second Congress had met in February, first at Cambridge and later at Concord, a revolutionary, military government had come into being, dedicated to the purpose of holding the British army within the confines of Boston. With the drilling of the militia, the organization of the Minute Men, and the collection of armament and other military supplies from all available sources, it became clear that this revolutionary government was seeking to make its warlike preparations so formidable that Gage would be persuaded of the hopelessness of attempting to employ his troops beyond the narrow bounds of Boston and would realize that any attempt to disrupt the province's preparations would mean an open fight. The General was fully aware of all these facts through the secret intelligence at his disposal.

On April 16 Gage received a long secret communication from his superior in England. This letter from the Earl of Dartmouth, while couched in most courteous language and expressing appreciation of his service, could scarcely have been construed by Gage as other than a stinging rebuke for his lack of action. Written and signed in January, it referred to the outrages that had been committed in the colony in 1774 by "a tumultuous Rabble, without any Appearance of general Concert; or without any Head to advise, or Leader to conduct that could render them formidable to a regular Force led forth in support of Law and Government, . . . conformable to the Spirit & Tenor of the King's Commands signified to you in my several Letters. . . ." The letter then announced that the large reinforcements on the way "will enable you to take a more active & determined part. . . ." Remarking on Gage's opinion, as expressed in October of the preceding year, that if an army of 20,000 were placed at his disposal, it would "in the end save Great Britain both Blood and Treasure,"[27] the Secretary of State replied: "I am unwilling to believe that matters are as yet come to that Issue." At the same time he informed the General that it was the opinion of the King's advisers, in which the King concurred, that "the first & essential step to be taken towards re-establishing Government, would be to arrest and imprison the principal actors & abettors in the Provincial Congress . . . (whose proceedings appear in every light to be acts of

---

[27] Gage to Dartmouth, October 30, 1774, *ibid.*, I, 383.

treason & rebellion). . . ." In doing so, Gage was advised, every means should "be devised to keep the Measure Secret until the moment of Execution." But, in leaving it up to Gage himself to decide whether such a step was practicable, Dartmouth considered the possibility that such action might be "a Signal for Hostilities, yet," he argued, "it will surely be better that the Conflict should be brought on, upon such ground, than in a riper state of Rebellion."[28]

When Gage received this letter, he recognized it as a command for action—directing that an end be put to any delay that would permit the rebellious colonials to increase their resistance to the King's law or his troops. But it was not against the popular rebel leaders who had long been within his reach, such as John Hancock, Samuel Adams, and Joseph Warren, that Gage elected to move. Rather he had already decided upon the destruction of one of the two principal depots of military supplies in the colony, choosing the one located at Concord—the meeting place of the Provincial Congress—because the other depot was at more distant Worcester. If the means of making war were destroyed, he reasoned, the fate of the promoters of rebellion could be decided later. By April 15, preparations were under way for a secret expedition to start for Concord on the night of the 18th.[29] But news of the expedition reached the patriots, although details were unknown.[30]

Under cover of darkness on the night of April 18 some 700 grenadiers and light infantry under command of Lieutenant Colonel Francis Smith and Major Thomas Pitcairn moved out of Boston and crossed the Charles River. Their orders were to destroy the military supplies at Concord, the exact location of which had been described by informers. Very early in the morning of the 19th an advanced detachment of regulars appeared at Lexington, where some 75 poorly accoutred Minute Men commanded by Captain John Parker had already assembled on the village green. The British officers ordered them to disperse. When they hesitated, the Redcoats

---

[28] Dartmouth to Gage, January 27, 1775, *ibid.*, II, 179–83.

[29] In this connection see J. R. Alden: "Why the March to Concord?," *American Historical Review*, XLIX, 446–54, and by the same author: *General Gage in America* (Baton Rouge, La., 1948), pp. 237–44.

[30] For the role played by Joseph Warren, Paul Revere, William Dawes, and Israel Bissell in spreading the alarm of the British expedition see John Cary: *Joseph Warren* . . . (Urbana, 1961), pp. 182–4, Esther Forbes: *Paul Revere & the World He Lived in* (Boston, 1942), pp. 251–64, and Allen French: *The First year of the American Revolution* (Boston and New York, 1934), pp. 22–4.

opened fire. The Minute Men quickly fled, leaving behind them on the green eight killed and ten wounded.[31]

Important as were the results of this skirmish in the history of the British Empire, the objective of the expedition was not to engage rebellious Americans in combat but to destroy their military supplies at Concord and then to return to Boston, hopefully without shedding blood. The troops therefore continued their march. But before they reached Concord most of the military stores there had been either secreted or removed by the patriots. Some barrels of flour were destroyed and a small quantity of military equipment was burnt by the British troops, but after spending two hours in this activity they had accomplished little of strategic importance. Suddenly, firing broke out near the bridge at the north end of the town. With the arrival of large reinforcements of Minute Men from nearby towns, the patriots had determined to force the British beyond the bridge, where some 300 light-infantrymen had been posted. The colonials did not disperse at the initial shots, but returned the fire with deadly accuracy. Forced to retreat from the bridge, the British detachment rejoined the main body of regulars, as did other parties which had been engaged in a futile attempt to uncover and destroy provincial war stores. Clearly, nothing more could be done to carry out their basic mission. The chief responsibility resting on Lieutenant Colonel Smith's shoulders now was to bring his soldiers safely back to Boston.

By the time orders were given to march it was midday. Meanwhile the whole countryside for miles around had been alerted and Minute Men, stirred up by the news of the Lexington engagement, had poured in from all directions, determined to wipe out the troops. From stone wall, from tree, from depression, from every possible cover, they now fired upon the retiring Redcoats. Although Smith did everything possible to protect the line of march—by the use of flank guards and other standard tactics—little could be done in

---

[31] Which side began the firing is not clear. It now appears that an American not attached to the body of the Minute Men fired first. For a detailed account of the Lexington skirmish see Harold Murdock: *Nineteenth of April, 1775* (Boston, 1925), Chap. 1, Allen French: *The Day of Concord and Lexington* (Boston, 1925) and also his *General Gage's Informers*, previously cited, and F. W. Coburn: *Fiction and Truth about the Battle on Lexington Common, April 19, 1775* (Lexington, Mass., 1918). For thirteen depositions of participants and witnesses of the dispersion of the Lexington Minute Men see *Journals of the Continental Congress, 1774–1789*, II, 28–36. For a British report see also "An Account of Lexington in the Rockingham Mss. at Sheffield," ed. J. E. Tyler, *William and Mary Quarterly*, 3rd ser., X, 99–107.

"The Battle of Lexington, April 19, 1775," by Amos Doolittle.

(Lexington Historical Society)

"The Engagement at the North Bridge in Concord," by Amos Doolittle.

the woody defiles of the road against an invisible enemy which continually harassed the retreating soldiers. Fortunately for the Redcoats, their commanding officer—realizing that the movement of his troops was known and that an alarm had been spread—had sent a request early that morning for reinforcements. In response, Gage ordered Lord Percy, an excellent soldier, to march to Smith's assistance with three regiments of infantry, two companies of marines, and two field-pieces.[32] This relief force left Boston about nine o'clock the morning of the 19th and, by two in the afternoon, within half a mile of Lexington, came in sight of Smith's harassed and all but demoralized expeditionary force, overburdened with wounded men. Forming a protective square about them with his fresh troops, Percy used his field-pieces to keep the provincials at a distance while the exhausted soldiers rested.

Then came the march back to Charlestown and Boston with a renewal of hostilities along the way. The fighting reached its highest pitch of intensity in the area of Cambridge. The large number of wounded impeded rapid movement, but at length the troops reached Charlestown. There, quiet finally reigned for the soldiers as night settled down and an additional relief force was sent to patrol the town and keep the enraged provincials at a distance.[33]

Such was the beginning of the actual fighting that culminated in independence for thirteen British colonies in America. From April 19, 1775, to the departure of the British army on March 17, 1776, Boston was a besieged town, for even nearby Charlestown was evacuated. From all parts of Massachusetts Bay came provincial contingents, soon followed by men from New Hampshire, Connecticut, and Rhode Island—only later did forces from the more southern colonies appear. But the responsibility for holding Gage and his army virtual prisoners within the town was to be shifted to the shoulders of the Continental Congress.

As was indicated in the opening of this chapter, the First Continental Congress, by establishing the continental Association, had become in the minds of patriotic colonials a governing force, if not

---

[32] From General Gage's account of the engagement, as sent to both Dartmouth and Barrington on April 22, 1775, the impression is gained that the General had anticipated the need for the relief force. See Gage Correspondence, I, 396–7, II, 673–4.

[33] For additional accounts of the expedition to Concord see the balance of the depositions to be found in Journals of the Continental Congress, II, 36–42; see also Richard Frothingham: History of the Siege of Boston, and of the Battles of Lexington, Concord, and Bunker Hill (Boston, 1872), pp. 60–84.

a government, superior to that of the government of Great Britain. The Second Congress was to create, in effect, a *de facto* government with authority not only superior to that of Great Britain but also to that of any individual colonial government. The cause was American liberty—not that of any one colony. Such liberty could be achieved, it was realized, only by the union of all the colonies in obedience to the instrumentality of the Continental Congress.

What did the term "American liberty" imply? Certainly, at the beginning of the contest, not independence from Great Britain or withdrawal from the Empire and the relinquishing of the manifold advantages that this connection had previously bestowed upon all colonials. No, most if not all Americans determined to resist by force of arms would undoubtedly have preferred to remain within the Empire, but only under certain conditions which would put an end to the excesses of authority wielded by the government of Great Britain. Moreover, they had a good deal of confidence—especially in view of the repeated concessions made by that government in the course of the 1760's—that these conditions would finally be met short of all-out war.

As to the specific conditions that were paramount in the eyes of Americans by 1775, freedom from taxation by Parliament, in any form, was but one of them, if the lists of grievances drawn up by the various provincial conventions, county conventions, and local gatherings of freeholders in 1774 may be given weight. The sources of some of these grievances against so-called abuses in the exercise of parliamentary authority reached back even before 1763 and related to such matters as the extension of the powers of the courts of vice-admiralty, the activities of royal revenue and customs officers, the discouragement of American manufacturers and restrictions on exports, and the circumvention of the will of the people by the device of royal instructions to Governors. The most authoritative list of grievances expressing the views of Americans is, of course, the catalogue embodied in the Declaration of Independence. Had guarantees been given that all of them would be remedied to the satisfaction of the colonial leaders, there might have come into existence within the Empire a virtually autonomous group of American states—for all practical purposes free from any effective control by Parliament and only nominally under the authority of the Crown. This could have come about, it would seem, only as a result of a concerted decision on the part of the King, the Ministry, and the majority in Parliament to appeal to the colonies for a statement of the exact terms under which their inhabitants would still care to be recognized as subjects of the King and a concomitant decision to accede to these terms. Yet, there is little doubt that to most Britons such a surrender to colonial "arrogance" would have been unthinkable. Constituting a national disgrace, it would in all probability have led to a demand for a general election in which the electorate could repudiate the Parliament that had agreed to the terms, or to an overturning of the Ministry that had shown such culpable weakness, or possibly even to a threat to the permanency of the British monarchy itself. For it must be borne in mind that the climate of opinion of Great Britain in the 1770's was a highly volatile one.

Since no such accommodation as mentioned above was forthcoming on the part of the British government, the Continental Congress gradually assumed increasing power. On May 10, 1775, as pre-arranged,[34] accredited delegates from each of the older colonies, except Georgia and Rhode Island, gathered in Philadelphia for the Second Continental Congress. On the 13th, however, Lyman Hall, representing the parish of St. John in Georgia, appeared and his credentials were approved (as were those of the three additional Georgia delegates when they arrived on September 13); then, on the 15th and 18th, Samuel Ward and Stephen Hopkins, respectively, took their seats as delegates from Rhode Island.[35] Thus all thirteen North American colonies were finally represented in the Congress.

After the presentation of credentials, the Congress turned to the consideration of a letter that Joseph Warren had written on May 3 at the request of the Massachusetts Bay Provincial Congress, of which he was Acting President. This message stressed the point that, "in support of the Cause of America," Massachusetts Bay had reached a critical and alarming state of affairs and now sought "direction and assistance" from the Continental Congress. It also conveyed the information that the local congress had resolved to raise 13,500 men, and had proposed to the other New England colonies that they should furnish men in like proportion, and begged leave to suggest "that raising a powerful Army, on the side of Amer-

---

[34] See, in this volume Chap. 9, note 53.

[35] *Journals of the Continental Congress, 1774–1789*, II, 11–12, 44–5, 50, 55, 192–3, 240–1.

ica, . . . [was] the only means left to stem the rapid Progress of a tyrannical Ministry." With such a force available, the message continued, there might be hopes of putting an end to "the inhuman Ravages of mercenary Troops in America and the wicked authors of our Miseries, brought to condign punishment, by the just Indignation of our Brethren in Great Britain." Accompanying the Warren letter were various papers bearing upon the British expedition to Concord, and upon the steps taken by the Provincial Congress to solve its fiscal problems.[36] While the letter and supporting documents were turned over to the consideration of the committee of the whole, the Congress on May 17 unanimously resolved to cut off all exportations to those British North American colonies which had not agreed to support the continental Association of 1774—including Georgia (with the exception of the parish of St. John), as well as Quebec, Nova Scotia, Newfoundland, and East and West Florida.

The following day came the report of the capture of the King's fort at Ticonderoga early on the morning of May 10 by a detachment of some veteran soldiers from Massachusetts Bay and twice as many so-called Green Mountain Boys led by Colonel Ethan Allen. According to an earlier estimate of Colonel Benedict Arnold—who arrived at the last minute to take command under orders from the committee of safety—the fort contained eighty pieces of heavy cannon, twenty brass guns, and about a dozen mortars.[37] This aggressive step put a new and serious face upon matters. Although the First Continental Congress had endorsed a purely defensive war, this was most decidedly an offensive action and could be comprehended within the category of acts of high treason. However, the event, together with the subsequent capture of Crown Point on May 11 and the seizure of the King's vessels of war on Lake Champlain, was defended as helping to frustrate a design formed by "the British Ministry of making a cruel invasion from the province of Quebec, . . . for the purpose of destroying our lives and liberties."

Congress voted on May 18 that the common and military stores be removed from Ticonderoga but that an exact inventory be made of the articles taken in order that they might be returned when

---

[36] For the Warren letter and documents see *ibid.*, II, 24–44.

[37] See Arnold to the Massachusetts Bay committee of safety, April 30, 1775, and letters from Allen and others to the Massachusetts Congress, relating to the capture of the fort and the disputed command, written on May 10 and 11, *American Archives*, 4th ser., II, 450, 556–60.

harmony was restored between Great Britain and the colonies.[38] On the 25th the Congress took an even more advanced position in assuming power. Instead of recommending to the New York Provincial Congress appropriate defensive action, it resolved that a post be immediately set up and fortified at or near King's Bridge on the Hudson, in order to avert the interruption of communication between the city of New York and the rest of the province; that batteries be erected at suitable places dominating both sides of the Hudson so as to prevent British vessels from ascending the river to harass the inhabitants; and, finally, "That the militia of New York be armed and trained and in constant readiness to act at a moments warning." For the rest, certain details of this plan for the security of the colony were to be left to the decision of the Provincial Congress.[39]

On May 20 the New Jersey House of Assembly voted to lay before the Congress the resolution adopted by the House of Commons on February 27 for settling the issue over taxation of the colonies, which provided that whenever a colony should make adequate provision for contributing its proportionate share to the common defence, and should provide for the support of civil government and administration of justice within its boundaries, all subject to the approval of the King and Parliament, no further tax would be levied upon it. The resolution, presented to the Congress on May 26, was immediately referred to the committee on the state of America. That Congress took a very dim view of this conciliatory offer is indicated by a resolve passed the same day, that the Provincial Congress of New York "persevere the more vigorously in preparing for their defence, as it is very uncertain whether the earnest endeavours of the Congress to accommodate the unhappy differences between G. Britain and the colonies by conciliatory Measures will be successful."[40] In line with this position, it was voted on the 27th that a committee—consisting of George Washington, Philip Schuyler, Thomas Mifflin, Silas Deane, Lewis Morris, and Samuel Adams —consider means of supplying the colonies with ammunition and

---

[38] *Journals of the Continental Congress*, II, 56.

[39] *Ibid.*, II, 59–60. On the day these resolves were entered into, James Duane, one of the New York delegates, had emphasized the highly exposed position of his colony and its vulnerability to control by the "Ministerial troops," who could thus "cut off the communication between the Eastern and Western provinces. . . ." He therefore urged that large armies be kept on foot, "one to defend the Massachusetts the other to secure New York" (*Letters of Members of the Continental Congress* [ed. E. C. Burnett, 8 vols., Washington, 1921–38], I, 98–101).

[40] *Journals of the Continental Congress*, II, 61–4.

military stores.[41] Then, on the 29th, a letter was approved "To the oppressed Inhabitants of Canada" which painted their condition in darkest colours and, referring to a previous letter addressed to them by the Congress on October 26, 1774,[42] called their attention to the idea that they, along with the inhabitants of all the other colonies, were involved in "the designs of an arbitrary Ministry, to extirpate the Rights and liberties of all America. . . ." The Canadians were also warned:

> "By the introduction of the present form of tyranny, you and your wives and your children are made slaves. You have nothing that you can call your own, and all the fruits of your labour and industry may be taken from you, whenever an avaritious governor and a rapacious council may incline to demand them. . . . We are informed you have already been called upon to waste your lives in a contest with us. . . . As our concern for your welfare entitles us to your friendship, we presume you will not, by doing us injury, reduce us to the disagreeable necessity of treating you as enemies. . . . We yet entertain hopes of your uniting with us in the defence of our common liberty . . . [so that] our sovereign . . . will at length . . . forbid a licentious Ministry any longer to riot in the ruins of the rights of Mankind."

It was simultaneously ordered that the letter be translated into French and a thousand copies be sent to Canada for distribution among the inhabitants.[43]

On May 30 a paper in the handwriting of Grey Cooper, a joint secretary of the Treasury, came before the Congress, presumably at the direction of Lord North. The chief minister desired it to be placed before the Continental Congress as presenting the government's views of the reconciliation resolution taken by the House of Commons on February 27. "It is earnestly hoped by all the real friends of the Americans," the paper stated, that the resolution be accepted by all the colonies having the least affection for their King and country. "These terms," it affirmed, "are honourable for Great Britain, and safe for the colonies . . . [and] will remove every

---

[41] *Ibid.*, II, 67. John Adams, writing to his wife Abigail on May 29, 1775, noted that "Coll. Washington appears at Congress in his Uniform and, by his great Experience and Abilities in military matters, is of much service to Us" (*The Adams Papers*, 2nd ser., *Adams Family Correspondence* [eds. L. H. Butterfield *et al.*, 2 vols., Cambridge, Mass., 1963], I, 207).

[42] See *Journals of the Continental Congress*, I, 105–13.

[43] *Ibid.*, II, 68–70.

grievance relative to taxation, and be the basis of a compact between the colonies, and the mother country." Beyond the terms of the resolution, it went on, no other conciliations could be made, for the "temper and spirit of the Nation are so much against [further] concessions, that if it were the intention of administration, they could not carry the Question." Therefore, it continued, let there be no misunderstanding: if these honourable terms were not accepted, the government was "united in opinion and determined to pursue the most effectual measures, and to use the whole force of the Kingdom . . . to reduce the rebellious and refractory provinces and colonies."[44] It is noteworthy that this document contained a phrase which demonstrated that the colonies were now given a new and important status in the eyes of the British government, for it read that the concessions offered would "be the basis of a compact between the colonies, and the mother country"—with all that was implied in the use of the word *compact*. But, manifestly, such a concession was no longer enough to satisfy the American patriots. It was therefore voted that the paper "lie on the table."

Granted that the Congress was in no mood to consider British concessions, how far was this governmental agency of the new American union prepared to go in breaking the constitutional connections between Great Britain and the colonies? In his "Autobiography" John Adams wrote that, by the time the Second Continental Congress had assembled, he had arrived at the conclusion: "We ought to recommend to the People of all the States to institute Governments for themselves, under their own Authority, and that, without Loss of Time. That We ought to declare the Colonies, free, Sovereign and independent States, and then to inform Great Britain We were willing to enter into Negotiations with them for the redress of all Grievances, and a restoration of Harmony between the two Countries, upon permanent Principles." At the same time he admitted that when "I had freely and explicitly laid open my Thoughts, on looking round the Assembly, I have seen horror, terror and detestation, strongly marked on the Counte-

---

[44] *Ibid.*, II, 72. Franklin, who was acquainted with Cooper and his handwriting, accepted the authenticity of the document (*ibid*). The North resolution (passed in the House of Commons on February 27, as indicated in the preceding chapter) provided that any colony making proper provisions for its proportionate share of the common defence, and for the support of civil government and the administration of Justice, would not have any taxes levied upon it by Parliament, except duties necessary for regulating commerce. See *Journals of the House of Commons*, XXXV, 161.

nances of some of the Members. . . ."[45] According to him, the chief
support for his ideas at the time came from the South Carolina
delegation, particularly from John Rutledge.[46]

It was on June 2 that the question of colonial constitutions was
raised; for on that date the Congress received an urgent communication from the Provincial Congress of Massachusetts Bay seeking
advice as to whether or not it should assume "the powers of civil
government, wch we think absolutely necessary for the Salvation of
our country and we shall readily submit to such a general plan as you
may direct for the colonies, or . . . establish such a form of government here, as shall not only most promote our advantage but the
union and interest of all America." The appeal went on to state that
as an army was "now collecting from different colonies . . . for the
general defence of the right of America, we w^{d} beg leave to suggest
. . . the propriety of y^{r} taking the regulation and general direction
of it. . . ."[47] The reply to this appeal was considered a matter of such
constitutional importance that a committee of five was elected by
ballot to frame it. Those selected were John Rutledge of South
Carolina, Thomas Johnson of Maryland, John Jay of New York,
James Wilson of Pennsylvania, and Richard Henry Lee of Virginia.
On June 9 the report of the committee was read and adopted. The
resolution taken was:

"that no obedience being due to the Act of parliament for altering
the charter of the Colony of Massachusetts bay, nor to a Governor, or
a lieutenant-Governor, who will not observe the directions of, but
endeavour to subvert that charter, the gov^{r}. and lieutenant-gov^{r}. of
that Colony are to be considered as absent, and these offices vacant;
and as there is no council there [for the Congress did not recognize
the presence in Boston of the Council appointed by the Crown], and
the inconveniences, arising from the suspension of the powers of
Government, are intollerable, . . . that, in order to conform, as near
as may be, to the spirit and substance of the charter, it be recommended to the provincial Convention, to write letters to the inhabitants of the several places, which are intituled to representation in
Assembly, requesting them to chuse such representatives, and that the
Assembly, when chosen, do elect counsellors; which assembly and

---

[45] *The Adams Papers,* 1st ser., *Diary and Autobiography of John Adams* (eds.
L. H. Butterfield *et al.,* 4 vols., Cambridge, Mass., 1961), III, 315.

[46] *Ibid.,* III, 316; for a biography of Rutledge see Richard Barry: *Mr. Rutledge of
South Carolina* (New York, 1942).

[47] *Journals of the Continental Congress,* II, 77-8.

council should exercise the powers of Government, until a Governor, of his Majesty's appointment, will consent to govern the colony according to its charter."[48]

Thus the decision of Congress for remodeling the Massachusetts Bay government was that the new government should adhere as closely as possible to its original charter form, while adopting a legal fiction that as the Governor and Lieutenant Governor were absent, the practice pursued in such a royal government as New York or proprietary government as Pennsylvania for dealing with the absence of the legally constituted executive should be generally followed.[49] The resolve taken to this effect on the Massachusetts Bay appeal was additional evidence of the assumption by the Continental Congress of the authority to determine the type of civil government a colony should enjoy—an authority which previously had been exercised only by the Crown of Great Britain.

However, no immediate reaction was forthcoming to the appeal that Congress should take over the responsibility of directing and maintaining the army that had surrounded Boston. Involved in such a decision was the question whether the war begun at Lexington and Concord was to be fought by individual colonies, each acting more or less independently, or by all the colonies in union, acting under orders issued by the Congress. If the decision were made in favour of the second alternative it would be to the incalculable advantage of Massachusetts Bay and its leaders, some of whom, if apprehended, were liable to be tried for high treason. If all the colonies were equally involved in hostilities against the King's forces the character of the rebellion would be changed. On June 14 Congress took a decisive step in this direction by voting that six companies of riflemen be raised in Pennsylvania, two in Maryland, and two in Virginia, and that as soon as their ranks were filled they

---

[48] *Ibid.*, II, 83–4.

[49] The rule was for the senior member of the Council to exercise limited executive powers during the absence of the Governor or Deputy Governor or Lieutenant Governor. While John Adams during the debate expressed himself in favour of preserving "the English Constitution in its Spirit and Substance, as far as the Circumstances of this Country required or would Admit," Samuel Adams inclined "to the most democratical forms, and even to a single Sovereign Assembly" (*Adams Papers* [Butterfield] 1st ser., III, 354). According to Thomas Cushing's letter to Joseph Hawley of June 10, a "motion was made in Congress that advice should be given to the *Present provincial Congress* to chuse Counsellors, but there being many objections to it, it was withdrawn" (*Letters of Members of the Continental Congress*, I, 118–19).

should march to join the army near Boston and there serve as light infantry under its commanding officer. Under the terms of the requisition, each volunteer was required to bind himself "as a soldier, in the American continental army" to obey its rules and regulations; in addition, the scale of his pay was fixed as that of a "continental soldier."[50]

The next logical step was taken the following day when it was voted that "a General be appointed to command all the continental forces, raised, or to be raised, for the defence of American liberty" and that $500.00 per month be allowed for his pay and expenses. Thereupon George Washington was unanimously chosen by ballot to this all-important post. In accepting the appointment Washington declared, without doubt in great sincerity, that he did not feel himself equal to the command with which he had been honoured; he also rejected the proposed salary in favour of keeping an exact account of his expenses, which, he doubted not, would be duly discharged when presented.[51] In the commission framed for him by "the delegates of the United Colonies . . ." Washington was to command the army raised or to be raised "for the Defence of American Liberty, and for repelling every hostile invasion thereof," and was to regulate his conduct "by the rules and discipline of war, . . . as herewith given you. . . ."[52] In line with this, it was voted that every officer in the continental army should receive a new commission at the hands of Washington to duplicate the one which he held under

---

[50] *Journals of the Continental Congress,* II, 89–90. A committee of five appointed to draw up the military rules and regulations governing the army consisted of George Washington of Virginia, Philip Schuyler of New York, Silas Deane of Connecticut, Thomas Cushing of Massachusetts Bay, and Joseph Hewes of North Carolina. On June 30 the committee's report was adopted. For the rules and regulations see *ibid.,* II, 111–22. It may be noted that Washington and Schuyler had accepted military appointments and had left the Congress to join the army at Cambridge before the adoption of the regulations.

[51] *Ibid.,* II, 91–2. In his "Autobiography," John Adams describes the events in Congress which led to his own proposal "that Congress would Adopt the Army at Cambridge and appoint a General," who should be George Washington, much to the consternation of John Hancock, whose friendship he thereby lost. For Adams's description of the lobbying of the "Southern Party" for a southern general to head the continental army, the division among the New England delegates on this subject, and the pretensions of Hancock to the compliment of being appointed Commander-in-Chief, whether he would have accepted or not, see *Adams Papers* (Butterfield), 1st ser., III, 321–3.

[52] The commission was approved by Congress on June 17, 1775; see *Journals of the Continental Congress,* II, 96. Instructions to Washington, consisting of but six articles, were approved by Congress on June 20; for these see *ibid.,* II, 100–1.

the authority of the revolutionary organization of his own colony.[53]

The plan of defensive military operations envisaged by the Congress comprehended the organization of two armies—one of 10,000 men to surround Boston, and the other of 5,000, to protect from invasion the Province of New York, because of its importance as a link in the route of communication by land between New England and the colonies south of it.[54] These forces were to be supported at the expense of the continental union and not by allocating to the individual colony proportionate charges of the military operations. As a result the Congress on June 22 came to the decision to take on another attribute of sovereign power when it voted that "a sum not exceeding two millions of Spanish milled dollars be emitted by the Congress in bills of Credit, for the defence of America"[55] and further that "the twelve confederated colonies be pledged for the redemption of the bills of credit, now directed to be emitted."[56]

Other major tasks also faced the Congress, now that it had taken upon itself full power to direct the course of the revolution. It must, among other things, inspire the continental soldiers already gathered about Boston, and those who would join them, to feel that they were committed to a great and sacred cause worthy of their utmost sacrifices. It must also seek to persuade the world at large of the justice of resorting to arms. Therefore "A Declaration . . . setting forth the Causes and Necessity of their taking up Arms," designed to achieve these goals, was issued on July 6, 1775.[57] The document, strongly

---

[53] *Ibid.,* II, 103.

[54] John Adams to Abigail Adams, June 10, 1775, *Adams Papers* (Butterfield), 2nd ser., I, 213–14; James Duane to the New York Provincial Congress, June 17, 1775, *American Archives,* 4th ser., II, 1016–17; and John Hancock to Joseph Warren, June 18, 1775, *Letters of Members of the Continental Congress,* I, 134.

[55] As is well known to all students of American colonial history, the specie with the greatest circulation throughout the British Colonies was the Spanish-milled dollar or so-called "piece of eight." Colonial bills of credit were customarily valued in terms of the Spanish dollar. Par value, based upon Queen Anne's proclamation as to the exchange value at which these bills were to be maintained, was six shillings of colonial bills of credit for a dollar. For a study of the colonial monetary system, see E. J. Ferguson: "Currency Finance: An Interpretation of Colonial Monetary Practices," *William and Mary Quarterly,* 3rd ser., X, 153–80.

[56] *Journals of the Continental Congress,* II, 103. In John Adams's letter to Elbridge Gerry of June 18 referring to the vote by Congress to issue two million dollars in bills of credit, he adds: "for the redemption of which, . . . twelve colonies have unanimously pledged themselves" (*Letters of Members of the Continental Congress,* I, 135.

[57] A committee of five, appointed by the Congress on June 23 to draw up the declaration, consisted of John Rutledge, William Livingston, Benjamin Franklin, John

worded, if not defiant, declared that although "Government was instituted to promote the Welfare of Mankind . . . the Legislature of Great-Britain . . . [had] attempted to effect their cruel and impolitic Purpose of enslaving these Colonies by Violence. . . ." In making known the justice of the colonial cause, the declaration offered an extended statement of the mounting injuries suffered by colonials during the past decade—the rejection of their appeals for redress, the barbarous treatment of the people of Massachusetts Bay, and the general threat of "Fire, Sword, and Famine" directed against all Americans who would not submit to tyranny. Then followed the announcement to the world:

> "Our cause is just. Our union is perfect. Our internal Resources are great, and, if necessary, foreign Assistance is undoubtedly attainable."

Following this veiled threat with a declaration of the unanimity of the colonials' determination "to die Freemen rather than to live Slaves," the document continued:

> "Lest this Declaration should disquiet the Minds of our Friends and Fellow-Subjects in any part of the Empire, we assure them that we mean not to dissolve that Union which has so long and so happily subsisted between us, and which we sincerely wish to see restored. Necessity has not yet driven us into that desperate Measure, or induced us to excite any other Nation to War against them. We have not raised Armies with ambitious Designs of separating from Great-Britain, and establishing Independent States. We fight not for Glory or for Conquest. We exhibit to Mankind the remarkable Spectacle

---

Jay, and Thomas Johnson. Rutledge apparently had already drafted such a statement— at least a declaration attributed to him was reported to the Congress the following day, but after some debate was postponed for later consideration. On the 26th it was again debated but, because of manifest dissatisfaction, was recommitted. It was at this point that John Dickinson and Thomas Jefferson (the latter having appeared as a delegate on the 21st with credentials from the Virginia convention) were added to the committee. How far the Rutledge draft was followed in framing the final draft of the declaration cannot be ascertained, since no copy of it exists. It is clear that Jefferson was called up to make a draft and that when Dickinson raised objections to it in committee, he was directed to try his hand at revising the declaration. For a careful analysis of the Jefferson and Dickinson drafts and the contribution of each to the final text see *The Papers of Thomas Jefferson* (eds. J. P. Boyd, *et al.*, 16 vols. +, Princeton, 1950–61 +), I, 187–219. It is apparent from this analysis that there was no contest between Jefferson, who favoured extreme measures, and Dickinson, who stood for reconciliation, but that the final text was rather a fusion of ideas. For the original publication of the declaration see *Journals of Congress*, I, 143–8 (Philadelphia, 1777, *Early American Imprints, 1639–1800* [ed. C. K. Shipton], Evans No. 15683). See also J. P. Boyd: "The Disputed Authorship of the Declaration on the Causes and Necessity of Taking up Arms, 1775," *Pennsylvania Magazine*, LXXIV, 51–73.

of a People attacked by unprovoked Enemies, without any imputation or even suspicion of Offence."[58]

By far the most important British reply to this declaration is to be found in a pamphlet entitled *The Rights of Great Britain Asserted against the Claims of America: Being an Answer to the Declaration of the General Congress.* It appeared anonymously in London in 1776, went through ten editions there and two in Philadelphia, and has been attributed to James Macpherson, Sir John Dalrymple, and Lord George Germain, among others. One thing is clear. The author of the pamphlet, whoever he was, was given every assistance by the Treasury and other governmental offices in compiling the various tables given in the body of the text and in the Appendix on the degree of financial support accorded to the colonies. In reply to the declaration that the colonists had established themselves in the New World "without any charge to the country from which they removed," a table is presented listing a total of £3,835,900 granted to the various colonies for the support of civil government and provincial forces in North America. A second, much more detailed table shows the extent of parliamentary reimbursement of the colonies for their expenses in the late war, amounting to £1,081,771, a figure included in the earlier table. A third table provides a partial account of bounties given on American commodities for the encouragement of colonial industry, which totalled £1,609,344. As to the taxation of the colonies—in reply to the stand of Congress that "Taxation and Representation are inseparable" and that American taxation was an innovation—it was asserted that while in their infancy and poverty the colonies were indulged, yet ever since the passing of the act of 12 Charles II, c. 4 the colonies were expected to contribute financial support to the Crown. This act stated that specific tonnage and poundage duties "shall be payable upon commodities not only imported into the realm of England, but also into the dominions thereunto belonging," thus including the colonies. Although, due to the limited commerce, these duties were not collected—as the expense of collection would have been too great—the principle, nevertheless, was thus laid down. By 25 Charles II, c. 7 all colonies exporting certain enumerated articles

---

[58] See *Papers of Thomas Jefferson* (Boyd), I, 213–18, which demonstrates by use of italics (not used above) the portions reflecting respectively the pen of either Dickinson or Jefferson; see also the parallel printing of Jefferson's first and second drafts in the *Journals of the Continental Congress,* II, 128–57.

were required to pay duties on them. Likewise, there was the statute of 9 Anne, c. 10, an act to establish a general post-office in North America, whereby the revenues from it could be used "for the Service of the War, and other her Majesty's occasions." Moreover, by 9 Anne c. 27, all goods taken in prize ships that were imported into America were to pay the same duties as if imported into Great Britain, with the exception of wine and brandy. By 2 George II, c. 7 all seamen on American ships were required to pay for the support of the Greenwich Hospital, whether serving on the high seas or "in any port, harbour, bay or creek, within any of the Colonies," and finally by 6 George II, c. 13, duties on rum, sugar, and molasses imported into America were to be paid. In reviewing this legislation the pamphlet stated that the power of Parliament to raise a revenue in the colonies "was never disputed" during this early period—much less the power of Parliament to regulate trade and the internal affairs of the colonies, which was also discussed. In dealing with the relations between Great Britain and the colonies after 1763, the writer said of Great Britain:

> "Her pity, her kindness, and affection, were lost upon the Americans. They advanced rapidly from claim to claim, and construed her forbearance into timidity. Each Act that was repealed furnished a subject for triumph, and not an object for gratitude. Each concession became the foundation of some new demand, till, at length, by assuming all to themselves by rebellion they left the Mother-Country nothing to bestow."[59]

The pamphlet shows how far apart were the views of patriotic Americans, on the one hand, and patriotic Englishmen on the other.

---

[59] *The Rights of Great Britain Asserted* . . . (10th edn., London, 1776), pp. 12–15, 27–40, 41–4, 94–5.

CHAPTER XIII

Failure of the
Olive Branch Petition

Two days after agreeing on "the Causes and Necessity of their taking up Arms," the members of the Congress signed a petition to the King, which became known as the "Olive Branch Petition." John Dickinson, who had such a petition very much at heart, was the author. He enjoyed great prestige throughout the colonies as one of the leading penmen of the revolutionary movement, especially in Pennsylvania, where powerful sentiment still prevailed against war with the mother country.[1] There is little doubt, nevertheless, that although the Congress agreed to send such a petition there was much latent opposition to it among the more radical members. John Adams, one of the signers, referred to it in his "Autobiography" as this "Measure of Imbecility" that "embarrassed every Exertion of Congress. . . ."[2] Couched in terms of deep loyalty to the King, it referred to the "mild and just government" that had previously prevailed whereby Great Britain and the colonies had become "the wonder and envy of other Nations" and had risen "to a power the most extraordinary the world had ever known." But all this, the petition continued, was being sacrificed by "your Majestys ministers" whose "delusive pretences, fruitless terrors, and unavailing severities" were directed against the people of the colonies by means of statutes and regulations, which had "filled their

---

[1] Charles Thomson, Secretary of the Continental Congress, writing later of the petition and of its effect upon the people of Pennsylvania, affirmed that, although it "was drawn up in the most submissive and unexceptionable terms, meeting with the same fate as others, . . . [it] had a powerful effect in suppressing opposition, preserving unanimity, and bringing the Province in a united body into the contest" (*Pennsylvania Magazine*, II, 423).
[2] *Adams Papers* (Butterfield), 1st ser., III, 321.

minds with the most painful fears and jealousies; and to their inexpressible astonishment [they] perceived the dangers of a foreign quarrel quickly succeeded by domestic dangers, in their judgment of a more dreadful kind." They, however, were attached "to your Majestys person, family and government with all the devotion that principle and affection can inspire" and as loyal subjects, therefore, besought the King "to direct some mode by which the united applications of your faithful colonists to the throne, . . . may be improved into a happy and permanent reconciliation. . . ."[3]

Did Dickinson really expect that the King would pay the slightest attention to a paper addressed to him by a rebellious body engaged in plans to wage war against his troops, and while deep hatred of his government was filling the pages of American newspapers? Could George III have been brought to believe that these professions of loyalty to him were sincere, and not a trap designed both to win over the American and British people and to dissuade him and the Ministry from pursuing their retaliatory plans?[4] Answers to these questions must remain mere speculation.

The petition was duly carried from Philadelphia to London by Richard Penn, and on August 21 a copy was sent by him and Arthur Lee to the Secretary for the Colonies, Lord Dartmouth, with an urgent request for an answer. They were finally informed that "as his majesty did not receive it on the throne, *no answer would be given*."[5] With this refusal at hand the two delivered copies of the petition to

---

[3] *Papers of Thomas Jefferson* (Boyd), I, 219–23. The calendar of the *Dartmouth Manuscripts,* II, carries the following notation: "Petition. Representing that the union between the mother country and the colonies has been broken by a system of statutes and regulations made by His Majesty's ministers and enforced by hostile measures, and beseeching him to interpose with his royal authority and influence to procure them relief from that system and to direct some mode by which the applications of his faithful colonists may be improved into a happy and permanent reconciliation" (*Historical Manuscripts Commission, Fourteenth Report,* Appendix, Part X, 358).

[4] Dickinson, writing to Arthur Lee in London later in July, has the following to say of the petition: "You will perhaps at first be surprised that we make no *claim*, and mention no *right*. . . . If administration be desirous of stopping the effusion of British blood, the opportunity is now offered to them by an unexceptionable petition, praying for an accommodation. If they reject this application with contempt, the more humble it is the more such treatment will confirm the minds of our countrymen to endure all the misfortunes that may attend the contest." The original of this Dickinson letter, in a mutilated form, is among the Arthur Lee Papers in the Harvard Library; see also R. H. Lee: *Life of Arthur Lee . . .* (2 vols., Boston, 1829), II, 312.

[5] Richard Penn and Arthur Lee to John Hancock, September 2, 1775, *ibid.,* I, 45. The words in italics were underlined in the letter; see also *Dartmouth Manuscripts,* II, 352, 358, 360. The petition was sent by the Congress under cover of a letter

the press together with a signed statement that they were true copies of the petition delivered to Lord Dartmouth.[6] By September 6 the "Olive Branch Petition" had appeared in print and had apparently become a matter of common knowledge to the British public.[7] It was therefore inevitable that the petition would come before Parliament.

Parliament had been prorogued on May 26, 1775; it did not reconvene until October 26.[8] In his speech to both Houses on that day the King gave a veiled reply to the petition of the Continental Congress by declaring:

> "Those who have long too successfully laboured to inflame My People in America by gross Misrepresentations, . . . repugnant to the true Constitution of the Colonies, and to their subordinate Relation to Great Britain, now openly avow their Revolt, Hostility, and Rebellion. . . . The Authors and Promoters of this desperate Conspiracy have . . . meant only to amuse by vague Expressions of Attachment to the Parent State, and the strongest Protestations of Loyalty to Me, whilst they were preparing for a General Revolt. . . . The rebellious War now levied, is become more general, and is manifestly carried on for the Purpose of establishing an independent Empire. . . . It is now become the Part of Wisdom, and (in its Effects) of Clemency, to put a speedy End to these Disorders by the most decisive Exertions. . . ."[9]

In the House of Lords an address in reply to the King's speech was moved in the following terms: "With the utmost abhorrence and indignation we see the real design of those desperate men, who . . .

dated July 8, signed by President John Hancock, to Richard Penn and to London colonial agents William Bollan, Arthur Lee, Edmund Burke, and Charles Garth. It contained a request that they present the petition to the King "with all convenient expedition after which we desire it may be given to the public. We likewise send you our second application to the equity and interest of our fellow subjects in Great Britain, and also a declaration setting forth the causes of our taking up arms, both of which we wish may be immediately put to press and communicated as universally as possible" (Arthur Lee Papers, 2:59). But only Richard Penn and Arthur Lee were disposed to assume such responsibility. Edmund Burke refused to be involved in view of the fact that he had not been authorized to do so by the Assembly of New York. See Burke to Arthur Lee, August 22, 1775, *Life of Arthur Lee*, I, 42–3.

[6] Arthur Lee Papers, 2:59a.

[7] An intercepted letter written by William Strahan in London to Benjamin Franklin, September 6, 1775, digested in the *Dartmouth Manuscripts* (II, 374), cites Strahan as saying of the petition: "it appears to be written in loose terms and after he (Franklin) was convinced that words and arguments were of no use."

[8] Parliament was prorogued on July 27 and again on September 14. *Journals of the House of Commons*, XXXV, 394–6.

[9] *Ibid.*, XXXV, 397–8; see also *Parliamentary History*, XVIII, 695–6.

leave no doubt of their traitorous purpose to induce the colonies to shake off the controul of the supreme legislature. . . ." The Marquess of Rockingham sought to insert in the address an amendment to read: "That . . . the disorders and discontents in the British colonies rather increased than diminished by the means which have been used to suppress and allay them"; that this was largely due to lack of information supplied to Parliament by the Ministry; that with the fullest information once supplied, the whole of the late proceedings of Parliament will be reviewed so that "the alarming and dangerous expedient of calling in foreign forces" may be avoided as well as the "still more dreadful calamity of shedding British blood by British hands."[10] This amendment was strongly supported by the opposition to the administration.

In the debate that followed, the Earl of Coventry supported the doctrine that Parliament was "the supreme legislature over the colonies"; at the same time he condemned "the madness and absurdity of expecting to reduce them by mere measures of coercion, so as to answer any one rational purpose of sovereignty, commerce, or finance." There was, he declared, "no alternative left, but either to relinquish all connection with the colonies, or to adopt conciliatory measures; the idea of conquering them was wild and extravagant. . . ." Lord Lyttelton also supported the idea of reconciliation by advocating the repeal of "all the Acts respecting America, passed since the year 1763." In turn the Bishop of Peterborough, Dr. John Hinchcliffe, recommended the American petition to the King as a basis for reconciliation; admitting that on the surface it was manifestly "a refined piece of political subtlety," yet, he insisted, it demonstrated that "the bulk of the people [of America] do not even now wish for a total separation, whatever may be the object of some among the leaders who direct their councils."[11] The Dukes of Manchester and Richmond, both known supporters of Rockingham, upheld his efforts

---

[10] *Ibid.*, XVIII, 705–9.

[11] Parenthetically, it should be noted that on November 7, 1775, the petition of the Continental Congress to the King came before the House of Lords. On the 10th, Richard Penn was questioned closely on the state of American affairs; the Duke of Richmond then moved that "the said Petition affords Ground of Conciliation of the unhappy Difference subsisting between the Mother Country and the Colonies. . . ." In the course of the debate the Earl of Dartmouth admitted that in its wording the petition was "unexceptionable, but there was every reason to believe that the softness of the language was purposely adopted to conceal the most traitorous designs." When the House divided on this motion 33 were in favour of it as against 86. See *ibid.*, XVIII, 895–936.

to amend the address. Nevertheless, the amendment failed to win approval.

In the final voting, the address was supported by 76 votes, including 10 proxies, with 33 opposed to it. Whereupon nineteen of the Lords united in the following formal protest against the rejection of the amendment:

> "1.) . . . we cannot, as Englishmen, as Christians, or as men of common humanity, consent to the prosecution of a cruel civil war, . . . We have beheld with sorrow and indignation . . . attempts made to deprive some millions of British subjects of their trade, their laws, their constitution, their mutual intercourse, and of the very food which God has given them for their subsistance. . . . 2.) . . . this unnatural war, thus commenced in oppression, and in the most erroneous policy, must, if persevered in, be finally ruinous in its effects. . . . 3.) . . . Great Britain, deprived of so valuable a part of its resources, and not animated, either with motives of self-defence, or with those prospects of advantage and glory, which have hitherto supported this nation in all its foreign wars, may possibly find itself unable to supply the means of carrying on a civil war, at such a vast distance, in a country so peculiarly circumstanced, and under the complicated difficulties which necessarily attend it. . . . 4.) . . . we conceive the calling in foreign forces to decide domestic quarrels, to be a measure both disgraceful and dangerous; and that the advice which ministers have dared to give to his Majesty, . . . of sending to . . . the dominions of the crown of Great Britain, a part of his electoral troops, without any previous consent, recommendation or authority of parliament is unconstitutional. . . . 5.) . . . the ministers, who are to be entrusted with the management of this war, have proved themselves unequal to the task, and in every degree unworthy of public trust."[12]

In the House of Commons the address in reply to the King's speech was framed to conform to the one approved in the House of Lords.[13] In moving the address John Dyke-Acland, a new member representing Collington in Cornwall, reportedly declared "the future fate of the British empire and of ages yet unborn" to be at stake, for it was apparent that America was "rising from her subordinate relation to this country, to the undisguised assertion of independence and em-

---

[12] For the debates in the House of Lords see *ibid.*, XVIII, 705–29, especially pp. 726–8 for the protest.

[13] For the address see *ibid.*, XVIII, 795–8; see also *Journals of the House of Commons*, XXXV, 399–400.

pire. . . . The question is now, therefore, . . . do [you] gentlemen chuse to acquiesce in the independence of America, or to enforce their submission to this country by vigorous measures?" After the motion had been seconded by former Governor Lyttelton of South Carolina, Lord John Cavendish moved that the address be amended in words identical with those used in the amendment proposed in the House of Lords. In seconding this move Sir James Lowther "condemned the address throughout." Wilkes, Lord Mayor of London, when supporting the seconding of the motion, is reported to have denounced the ministers "who have precipitated the nation into an unjust, ruinous, felonious, and murderous war." Also in support of the motion, George Johnstone, late Governor of West Florida, delivered an extremely long speech denying that the Americans were aiming at independence and asserting that "they wish for nothing more than a constitutional dependence on Great-Britain, according as they have subsisted from their first establishments. . . . I maintain that the sense of the best and wisest men in this country, are on the side of the Americans." Finally, Johnstone pointed out, should Great Britain succeed in conquering the Americans, it would be necessary to "establish a military despotism in the colonies, which the revenues of an oppressed people never can pay." General Conway likewise condemned the war made by the King's servants on the Americans "as cruel, unnecessary, and unnatural" and called it "a butchery of his follow subjects . . ." He was joined by Charles James Fox, who argued that, far from the colonials desiring independence, "to be popular in America it was necessary to talk of dependance on Great Britain, and to hold that out as the object in pursuit." Nevertheless, the amendment to the address was voted down by 278 to 108. The following day, October 27, an attempt was made to recommend it to the further consideration of the committee of the whole House. This brought on another spirited debate, but the effort to recommit was defeated when but 72 voted for it as against 176 opposed.[14]

The address as finally approved by the members of the House

---

[14] For the debate in the House of Commons see *Parliamentary History*, XVIII, 729–95. It should be noted that, especially in the debate on the address, the speeches of the opposition to the administration are given chief emphasis. As the address of the House embodied the views of the majority, it is fortunate that the position of the minority was so clearly stated and from so many angles. In the case of the major address by former Governor Johnstone, it is clear that it was carefully prepared with the idea of future publication in mind. The report of the debates in both Houses of Parliament presented in the *Annual Register, 1776* (pp. 55–75), also stresses the arguments of the opposition.

of Commons asserted that their fellow subjects in America had been "seduced from their Allegiance by . . . the most wicked and insidious Pretences, [for] they have been made the Instruments of the Ambition and traiterous Designs of those dangerous Men, who have led them Step by Step to the Standard of Rebellion, and who have now assumed the Powers of Sovereign Authority, which they exercise in the most despotic and arbitrary Manner, over the Persons and Properties of this deluded People." The address also affirmed "that the rebellious War now levied is . . . manifestly carried on for the Purpose of establishing an independent Empire" and finally pledged the House's fullest support in putting down the revolt.[15]

The opposition to the Ministry, despite defeat in both Houses of Parliament over the address, fought doggedly on every issue relating to America. On November 1 the question of employing foreign troops without the express consent of Parliament was raised in the House of Lords by the Duke of Manchester. His Lordship was strongly opposed to the use of Hanoverians to garrison Gibraltar and Minorca in order to relieve British forces from those places to serve against the Americans. Accordingly, he moved: "That bringing into any part of the dominions of the crown of Great Britain, the Electoral Troops of his Majesty, or any other Foreign Troops, without the previous consent of parliament, is dangerous and unconstitutional." In support of the motion, the Duke of Grafton held up the Bill of Rights as a precedent for preventing the Crown from taking such action. Others —including Lord Lyttelton, the Earl of Effingham, who had resigned his military commission rather than serve against the Americans, Lord Camden, the Duke of Richmond, and the Earl of Shelburne— also spoke in favour of the motion, each in turn condemning the illegality of bringing foreign troops into the King's dominions. Nevertheless, the motion was lost by a vote of 32 to 75.[16] On November 3, when Lord Barrington presented to the House of Commons his estimate of the charges for supporting five battalions of Hanoverian troops at Gibraltar and Minorca,[17] Sir James Lowther (following up the lead set by the opposition in the House of Lords) moved: "That the introducing the Hanoverian Troops into any part of the dominions belonging to the crown of Great Britain, without the consent of parliament first had and obtained, is contrary to law." He

---

[15] *Journals of the House of Commons*, XXXV, 404.
[16] *Parliamentary History*, XVIII, 798–816.
[17] *Journals of the House of Commons*, XXXV, 419–20.

argued that such a measure should be considered "a most dangerous weapon in the worst hands which any weapon can be lodged in." Governor Johnstone strongly seconded the motion in a speech as vigorous and almost as long as the one he had delivered against the address to the King; he took his stand upon the violation of the Act of Settlement passed in the reign of William III. The motion was also supported by Serjeant Adair, Burke, and General Conway among others. Nevertheless, the motion failed by a vote of 81 in favour to 203 against.[18]

Edmund Burke had delivered his great speech on conciliation with the colonies on March 22, as was discussed earlier. On November 16, while presenting a petition from various inhabitants of Wiltshire calling attention to their serious economic situation,[19] he seized the occasion to present the draft of a bill which, if adopted by Parliament, "he was confident, both from the nature of the thing, and from information which did not use to fail him . . . would restore immediate peace" between the mother country and America.[20] The bill laid down the premise that the basis of colonial discontent was taxation of the colonies by Parliament. It therefore provided that no tax should be levied on them by this body other than the "levy of duties and taxes for the regulation of trade and commerce," which duties when collected would be placed at the disposal of the general assembly of the colony where they were raised; it also gave legal recognition to the Continental Congress by authorizing the King to empower the Governors in America to require that the assemblies send deputies to the Congress "with full powers to bind their said several provinces, to all acts done by a majority of voices in the said general meeting . . ."; it likewise provided for the complete repeal of the partially revoked Revenue Act of 1767, the Boston Port Act, the Act for the Impartial Administration of Justice, and the Act for Better Regulating the Government of Massachusetts Bay; finally, it included a provision for general amnesty in the conflict which had already taken place in America.[21] Burke introduced the bill with a luminous speech concerned with the various methods brought forward to settle the American crisis. He was backed by such able speakers as Sir George

---

[18] *Parliamentary History*, XVIII, 818–37.
[19] *Journals of the House of Commons*, XXXV, 447.
[20] *Parliamentary History*, XVIII, 963–78.
[21] *Ibid.*, XVIII, 978–82.

Savile and Lord John Cavendish, and a number of other eloquent supporters.

In his address Burke had given the reasons for not adopting the means of reconciliation most "frequently suggested . . . by several friends and well wishers to America"—principally, repeal of the Declaratory Act of 1766—explaining that this "was a thing impossible; for it was nothing less, than to make the legislature accuse itself of uttering propositions that were false, and making claims that were groundless." He predicated this on the reasons for passage of the Act and "the perfect acquiescence of the colonies under it; until by the renewal of the scheme of actual taxation their apprehensions were roused, and they were taught to look with suspicion and terror upon the unlimited powers of the British legislature."[22] Former Governor Thomas Pownall now made a devastating attack on Burke's proposals. Denying that there had been any such acquiescence of colonials in the Declaratory Act or the other legislation passed in 1766 relating to the colonies, he quoted the following excerpt from the journals of the Continental Congress:

> "After the repeal of the Stamp-Act, having again resigned ourselves to our antient unsuspicious affections for the parent state, . . . in hopes of a favourable alteration in sentiments and measures towards us, we did not press our objections against the above mentioned Statutes [that is, the Declaratory Act of 1766, the act of 1766 imposing rates and duties payable in these colonies, and the Revenue Act of 1767] made subsequent to that repeal."[23]

He also cited the petition sent to the House of Commons by the New York merchants in 1766 requesting repeal of most of the trade regulations,[24] as evidence that the colonials had been far from content, adding,

> "they not only were not, in fact, but they could not on the principles from which they opposed our system, be content. They objected to all laws laying duties for the express purpose of a revenue. . . . Many laws prior to this period, gave and granted duties, and appropriated them to the purpose of revenue."

---

[22] *Ibid.*, XVIII, 975.

[23] *Journals of the Continental Congress*, I, 92.

[24] This petition is to be found among the Shelburne Papers, 51:659–63, Clements Library; it was forwarded by Governor Moore to the Earl of Shelburne under cover of his letter dated December 10, 1766. Unfortunately, it is not presented in the *New York Colonial Documents* series; it has, however, been dealt with in Volume XI in this series, Chap. 2.

Pownall then pointed out that the Navigation Act of 1672 (25 Charles II, c. 7) was an act laying duties as a regulation of trade; but, he argued, the system was changed by the comprehensive trade act of 1696, not in 1764; revenue officers were appointed for the colonies and the revenue so derived on duties became part of the royal revenue, and, finally, by the Civil List Act of 1714 (1 George I, st. 1, c. 1), these revenues were directed to be used to form a fund for the civil list.[25] Then, referring to Burke as a supporter of both Rockingham and the program of his administration, Pownall characterized the bill before the House as "ready to repeal every Act, except the Acts of the administration of that gentleman's friends. The Declaratory Act is not to be repealed. The Revenue Act of the 6th George 3 is not to be repealed." Then, to show how far Burke's plan failed to meet the demands of the colonials, he referred again to the attitude of the Continental Congress toward the Declaratory Act by quoting the words of complaint issued by that body: "What is to defend us against so enormous, so unlimited a power?" He therefore concluded that the Burke bill was not sufficiently comprehensive to meet the needs of the current situation, which called for "some great and general system" for changing the administration of colonial government.[26] When the debate ended at about four o'clock the following morning, the Burke bill failed of approval by a vote of 105 in favour and 210 against it.

When the news had reached Great Britain that all the older North American colonies, including Georgia, were now in open rebellion, Lord North on November 20 asked leave of the House of Commons to bring in a bill to prohibit all trade and intercourse with them. His motion proposed the repeal of the temporary Boston Port Act and the two temporary acts restraining the trade of the colonies in rebellion, and sought authority for His Majesty to appoint commissioners with power to grant general or particular pardons and to re-

---

[25] *Parliamentary History*, XVIII, 986–7. The acts referred to above do not throw definite light on Pownall's statements, which seem to have been based upon directions issued from the office of the Lords Commissioners of the Treasury. For the view that the Treasury officials were short-sighted in not realizing that financially independent colonies, such as the older American colonies were by the 1770's, "would not easily submit to domination and would be able to resist force with force," see Dora Mae Clark: *The Rise of the British Treasury* (New Haven, 1960), Chap. 6. Professor Clark concludes this work (p. 197) with the comment: "In the years between 1766 and 1776 the Treasury bore the major responsibility for measures inciting to revolution."

[26] For Pownall's address see *Parliamentary History*, XVIII, 984–9.

ceive the submission of any province or colony and thereafter re-store free exercise of trade to its inhabitants.[27] At the same time the chief minister indicated that he was ready to move the repeal of the tea duty and "suspend every exercise of the right of taxation, if the colonies themselves would point out any mode by which they would bear their share of the burden and give their aid to the common defence." His speech emphasized two points of constitutional importance, both bearing on his position as the King's chief minister:

"The first was that the king had an undoubted right of naming his own servants: the second, which formed the happiness of this country, that if the people by their representatives did really disapprove the measures of any minister, to that degree they would not go along with him; the king, however much he might approve such minister, could not carry on business by him, and must part with him."

He then declared that, although the issue over taxation had arisen before he was involved in it as a minister, "unless the King dismissed him, or a majority of the House, disapproving his conduct, desired his dismission, he would not give up the conduct of this business to any body else."

Charles James Fox criticized the proposal to cut off all trade with America, asserting that it was "a declaration of perpetual war," and moved to strike out all words having to do with the stoppage of colonial trade and with the appointment by the King of royal commissioners. But when the House divided over the amendment, it drew but 64 yeas as against 192 nays.[28] From the second reading of the Prohibitory Bill to its passage in the House on December 11, by a vote of 112 to 16,[29] it was bitterly and doggedly objected to by the opposition. For example, on December 7 David Hartley, an opponent of war and strongly against slavery, pleaded at length with the House for suspension of hostilities and "a treaty of pacification." In a series of abortive motions, he sought leave to bring in a bill that would restore the government of Massachusetts Bay to its conditions under the charter; another bill that would "establish the Right of Trial by Jury in all Criminal Cases to all Slaves in North America: and to annul all Laws of any Province repugnant thereto";

---

[27] *Journals of the House of Commons,* XXXV, 451.

[28] *Ibid.,* XXXV, 451; *Parliamentary History,* XVIII, 992–1000.

[29] *Journals of the House of Commons,* XXXV, 486.

a third bill "to establish a permanent Reconciliation between Great-Britain and its Dependencies in North-America"; a fourth bill "for a free Pardon, Indemnity, and Oblivion" to all arrayed in arms against the Kingdom; and finally an address to the King suggesting that

> "when the present unhappy Dispute in North America shall be brought to an amicable Termination, . . . His Majesty should be graciously pleased to give Orders, that Letters of Requisition be written, in the accustomed Manner to the several provinces . . . to make Provision for the Purposes of protecting, defending, and securing said Colonies and Plantations."[30]

When the Prohibitory Bill reached its second reading in the House of Lords on December 15, strong but futile opposition was voiced by the Dukes of Manchester and Richmond and the Earl of Shelburne. It was, the Duke of Manchester insisted, "founded in the most aggravated injustice . . . involving the innocent and guilty in one common punishment" and giving encouragement "to the subjects of one part of this great empire to destroy and pillage the other." The Duke of Richmond denounced it as "a most unjust, oppressive, and tyrannical measure," and further asserted: "I do not think the people of America in rebellion, but resisting acts of the most unexampled cruelty and oppression." Echoing these sentiments, the Earl of Shelburne declared that "the colonists are not in a state of rebellion, but are armed in support of their just, their inalienable and constitutional rights, thus openly invaded and attacked." Nevertheless, the bill, with certain amendments, was approved by a vote of 78 to 19. Eight peers immediately signed a strong protest, however, charging among other things that the bill by its declaration of war against the colonies treated them as a foreign nation and thus might bring about their permanent separation from the parent state.[31]

When the Prohibitory Bill, with the amendments, was returned to the House of Commons,[32] David Hartley—in the course of a fruitless attempt "to adjourn the consideration" of the amendments for six weeks—prophetically stated his hopes that the unremitting

---

[30] *Ibid.*, XXXV, 479–80; *Parliamentary History*, XVIII, 1042–56.

[31] For the debate in the House of Lords on the bill and the signed protest against it see *ibid.*, XVIII, 1065–94.

[32] For the Lords' amendments to the bill see *Journals of the House of Commons*, XXXV, 493–4.

opposition to the bill by certain members of Parliament would "remain as a memorial, that some of us, at least, lament this final separation of America with an affectionate regret."[33] With the royal assent given on December 22, the bill became law. In its preamble the Act stated that whereas many persons in the thirteen named colonies had set themselves "in open rebellion and defiance to the just and legal authority of the king and parliament of Great Britain, . . . have . . . engaged his Majesty's troops, and . . . have usurped the powers of government", all trade and commerce with them was prohibited on pain of forfeiture of all vessels and cargoes "as if the same were the ships and effects of open enemies." All ships violating this prohibition after January 1, 1776, were to be subject to capture as prizes and their crews should be subject to service in the royal navy unless under certain options they were put ashore at some place not in rebellion. A final clause provided that the King could commission persons to grant pardons to individuals and groups, and by proclamation to declare any colony, district, or place to be at peace with His Majesty, in which case the act would no longer apply.[34] A state of war was thus declared to exist with the thirteen older North American colonies.

Before turning to consider the resort to open hostilities in North America, one final step taken by Parliament must be noted. This was the approval accorded by Parliament to a series of treaties entered into by the King with the Duke of Brunswick on January 9, 1776, and with the Landgrave of Hesse-Cassel on January 15 and February 5, 1776, by which Brunswick was to furnish 4,300 and Hesse-Cassel a total of 12,668 troops to serve with the British army in America.[35] When presenting the three treaties to the House of Commons on February 29, 1776, Lord North moved that they be referred to the committee of supply and "urged the necessity of the

---

[33] *Parliamentary History*, XVIII, 1103–5.

[34] For the Prohibitory Act (16 Geo. III, c. 5) see *Statutes at Large* (Pickering), XXXI, 135–54.

[35] For translations of these three treaties see *Journals of the House of Commons*, XXXV, 564–76. It should be noted that in subsequent treaties the number of troops furnished by the Duke of Brunswick was increased to 6,000; the contribution of the Landgrave of Hesse-Cassel finally amounted to about 17,000; the rulers of other German states also signed treaties to supply limited numbers of men. In all about 30,000 Germans were provided for the British army during the war. See Max von Eelking: *Die deutschen Hülfstruppen im nordamerikanischen Befreiungskrieg, 1775–1783* (2 vols., Hanover, 1863), translated and abridged by J. G. Rosengarten as *German Allied Troops in the North American War of Independence, 1775–1783* (Albany, 1893); see also E. J. Lowell: *The Hessians . . . in the Revolutionary War* (New York, 1884).

measure, and the great effects he expected from it." In the debate on the motion, David Hartley again launched a vehement protest against the entire conduct of the Ministry toward the colonies. Referring to the conciliatory proposals offered by the Ministry the previous year, he declared that it was now clear nothing was meant by "the proposition, insidious as it was," but destruction and bloodshed, and added:

> "This year again, your pretext is a pretended commission to offer peace, at the same time tying up the hands of the commissioners from making any offer but of unconditional submission, with an army of foreign mercenaries sent close upon their heels, to lay waste the whole country with fire and sword. Sir, my opposition to this unjust American war, is so total and absolute against every part of it, that I hardly know in what terms to express my aversion to any one part more than to every other; yet I think, Sir, if there could remain any measure exceeding every preceding one in disgrace and barbarity, it is this of introducing foreign troops."

It is, moreover, not without deep significance that Lord Barrington, Secretary at War, in supporting the motion to approve the treaties, revealed "that recruits could not be procured on any terms"—thus, by inference, indicating the reluctance of the British to enlist in a war against their fellow subjects who had taken up arms to defend their liberties. When the debate ended at two o'clock the morning of the following day the motion was approved by a vote of 242 to 88.[36]

When the treaties came before the House of Lords on March 5, 1776, the Duke of Richmond moved that the members implore the King to give immediate orders "for stopping the march of the Hessian, Brunswick, and Hanau troops, and for a suspension of hostilities in America, in order to lay the foundation of a speedy and permanent reconciliation between the great contending parts of this distracted empire." In the debate on the Richmond motion, the Earl of Carlisle (who, in 1778, was to head the commission sent by Lord North to America "to treat, consult, and agree upon the means of quieting the disorders") urged, in support of coercive measures being applied to America, "that the number of hands required to carry on our manufactures, the little use of new levies,

---

[36] See *Parliamentary History*, XVIII, 1167–85; see also *Journals of the House of Commons*, XXXV, 606.

and the desire every friend to his country ought to have to put a speedy determination to the present unhappy troubles, create an evident necessity for the employment of foreigners, in preference to native troops." The majority of the peers seem to have shared this point of view. Nevertheless, the opposition continued its eloquent pleas. In the course of the debate the Earl of Coventry, emphasizing the opinion he had expressed earlier in the session, declared that he would continue to deem unwise the measures being pursued toward America. He saw the destruction of the Empire as inevitable in view of

> "the increasing power, wealth, and population of the colonies. . . . It is in the body politic as in the natural body, the seeds of dissolution are contained in the vital principles of both. . . . If you look on the map of the globe, and view Great Britain and North-America, and compare the extent of both; if you consider the soil, the harbours, rivers, climate, and increasing population of the latter, nothing but the most obstinate blindness and partiality can prevail on any man to entertain a serious opinion that such a country will long continue under subjection to this. . . . [Therefore,] instead of meditating conquest, and exhausting our strength in an ineffectual struggle, we should vote a thanksgiving, and wisely abandoning all wild schemes of coercing that country, we should leave America to itself, and wish to avail ourselves of the only substantial benefit we can ever expect to derive from it, the profits of an extensive commerce, and the strong support of a firm and friendly alliance for mutual defence and assistance."

In the final vote, the motion for halting the movement of the troops was lost by a vote of 32 to 100.[37] It need only be added that the decision to employ German troops in America intensified the conviction of colonials that they had at least the moral support of the British people, who, by their failure to respond to the call of the government to bear arms against their American co-nationals, had made necessary the employment of foreigners in what had become a civil war.

---

[37] *Parliamentary History*, XVIII, 1188–1228.

CHAPTER XIV

Independence

ETURNING now to the course of events in America, by June
1775 the colonies were fully committed to war. On the 17th
British forces captured the fortifications dominating Boston
that had been erected by the Americans at Breed's Hill. But the
manœuvre was at a fearful cost.[1] Nevertheless, the army was held
in the town under siege by Washington's continental forces.

Late in June the Continental Congress decided on the invasion
of Canada, but it was September before the expedition moved
forward and cleared the way to Montreal. On November 13 the
American leader, General Montgomery, entered the city without
resistance. He then moved down the St. Lawrence to Quebec to
join another American force, under Benedict Arnold, which under
conditions of great hardship had moved up the Kennebec and
down the Chaudière to where it empties into the St. Lawrence a
little above Quebec. By November 14 Arnold's forces had crossed
the river and encamped on the already famous Plains of Abraham.
On December 2 the two forces joined. Governor Carleton, when
confronted by the enemy, took all necessary steps to defend the
powerfully walled city and refused to surrender. Montgomery, now
in command of the united colonial forces, finding himself unable
to break the walls with the artillery at his command, decided to
storm them. The attempt, made on the night of December 30, failed
miserably. Montgomery was dead, Arnold wounded, and half of
their men killed, wounded, or taken prisoner. Still the depleted
American force held its position outside the walls. However, with

---

[1] For an account of the battle at Breed's Hill, at which Dr. Joseph Warren lost
his life, see John Cary: *Joseph Warren* (Urbana, Ill., 1961), pp. 220–3.

the arrival of a British fleet on May 6, 1776, the Americans, wracked by disease and short of supplies, raised the siege and retreated to Montreal. Forced to give up this city, too, they were back at Lake Champlain by June 1776.[2] Nor did the attempt of the Continental Congress to win the French Canadians over to the American cause by persuasion succeed any better.

While the Americans were still in control of Montreal and camped before Quebec, Congress voted on February 15, 1776, to send to Canada two of its members, Benjamin Franklin of Pennsylvania and Samuel Chase of Maryland, together with two other Marylanders, Charles Carroll of Carrollton (an ardent patriot and a Catholic fluent in the French language) and his cousin John Carroll (a member of the Jesuit order before its suppression by Pope Clement XIV in 1773). The mission of this group was to persuade the French inhabitants to join the American Union.[3] The commission arrived in Canada in April. Finding themselves faced with the hostility of Bishop Briand of Quebec and the general satisfaction of the people with the Quebec Act, and soon realizing that nothing could be accomplished, the Americans returned home.[4] Thus the British were left with only thirteen colonies in revolt.

When the year 1776 began, the purpose of the colonial rebellion was still considered by most Americans to be simply an attempt to gain recognition of their claim to the rights belonging to all subjects of the British King. It is clear, however, that some had already gone much further in their thinking, especially such Massachusetts Bay men as Samuel Adams, John Adams, and the late Dr. Joseph Warren. Yet these radical leaders were slow in winning converts. Many potent influences were still persuading Americans that their welfare could be best guarded within the folds of the great British Empire—once colonial demands had been met. But peace had given place to war.

It was now evident that if the objectives of the struggle were widened in some form that could gain general acceptance, enormous potential advantages might accrue to the patriotic cause. Yet the

---

[2] For detailed accounts of the military expedition to Canada see "Notes of Witnesses' Testimony concerning the Canadian Campaign," *Papers of Thomas Jefferson* (Boyd), I, 433–54.

[3] See *Journals of the Continental Congress*, IV, 151–2, 219.

[4] For Charles Carroll's account of the fruitless Canadian trip, see "Journal of Charles Carroll of Carrollton," published as an appendix in Kate M. Rowland: *The Life of Charles Carroll of Carrollton, 1737–1832* (2 vols., New York, 1898).

Continental Congress, which had assumed the responsibility of carrying on the war, was bound by the instructions the delegates had brought from their respective colonial congresses or conventions, none of which called for a declaration of independence from the mother country.[5] Nevertheless, it was clear that something was needed at this critical juncture to alter American thinking—something to substitute in place of the traditional and continuing loyalty to the King, as so fully expressed the preceding year in the petition of the Congress to George III. What was wanted was a new concept of loyalty which, roughly expressed, might be stated as loyalty, not to a person, but to a country—to America, to its people and its land.[6] This new and startling idea was promulgated with amazing effectiveness by a publication that issued anonymously from the Philadelphia press on January 10, 1776, under the title *Common Sense: Addressed to the Inhabitants of America.*

The author of *Common Sense*, Thomas Paine, was unknown beyond a small circle of acquaintances in Philadelphia. He carried no credentials to speak for any group and had only arrived in Philadelphia from England late in 1774. Born at Thetford in 1737, reared in a Quaker home, and having received an indifferent education, Paine had successively tried the occupations of staymaker, privateersman, school usher, grocer, unordained dissenting preacher, and excise man, in all of which he was a failure, as he had likewise been in marriage. It had been his good fortune at this juncture to meet in London Benjamin Franklin, whose advice to go to the colonies he had followed. Through the good offices of Franklin's friends he had secured an editorial post on the *Pennsylvania Magazine.* His articles on a variety of topics immediately attracted attention, for the one thing he could do well was write. Moreover, he had deep convictions and did not hesitate to voice them. True to his Quaker upbringing, he abhorred slavery and, in an article on the slave trade, called on Americans to consider "with what consistency, or decency they complain so loudly of attempts to enslave them while they hold so many hundred thousands in slavery." But his chief indictment was against Great Britain for permitting and even supporting this nefarious trade.

---

[5] For the instructions to the delegates to the Second Continental Congress see *Journals of the Continental Congress*, II, 13–21, 45, 240–1.

[6] For an excellent recent study of this subject see Max Savelle: "Nationalism and other Loyalties in the American Revolution," *American Historical Review*, LXVII, 901–23.

In an article that appeared in the *Pennsylvania Journal* on October 18, 1775, entitled "A Serious Thought by Humanus," he reflected on this crime against mankind. "I hesitate not for a moment to believe that the Almighty will finally separate America from Britain," he declared. "Call it Independence or what you will, if it is the cause of God and humanity it will go on."

Paine now set to work on what was to prove to be his masterwork on the cause of American independence—*Common Sense*. When submitted to cold scholarly analysis, the work may be found to be filled with superficialities, exaggerations, distortions, and plain misstatements of fact. Nevertheless, its publication in 1776 struck the public like a thunderbolt. In it, Paine solemnly charged that the "Cause of America is in a great measure the Cause of all Mankind"; heroically, therefore, the people of this country must fight the world-battle for freedom. On the subject of the traditional forms of government, he asserted that "the palaces of Kings are built upon the ruins of the bowers of paradise," and further, that "Government by Kings . . . was the most prosperous invention the Devil ever set on foot for the promotion of idolatry." With "all men being originally equal," he claimed, "no one by birth could have a right to set up his own family in perpetual preference to all others forever." George III was denounced as the "Royal Brute of Britain," who "hath wickedly broken through every moral and human obligation, trampled nature and conscience beneath his feet, and by a steady . . . spirit of insolence and cruelty procured for himself an universal hatred." This was, then, a struggle to be freed from the institution of monarchy, and that monster wearing the royal crown. Paine therefore called upon Americans to treat without mercy those who deserted the common cause to support this enemy of mankind. "A line of distinction should be drawn between English soldiers taken in battle and [Tory] inhabitants of America taken in arms. The first are prisoners, but the latter traitors. The one forfeits his liberty, the other his head." Such was the heart of *Common Sense*.[7]

Within three months of its publication, an estimated 120,000 copies of *Common Sense* had been sold.[8] As to its effect, in the

---

[7] For Paine, see M. D. Conway: *The Life of Thomas Paine* (2 vols., New York, 1892) and Hesketh Pearson: *Tom Paine, Friend of Mankind* (New York, 1937); see also *The Complete Writings of Thomas Paine* (ed. P. S. Foner, 2 vols., New York, 1945) and *Writings of Thomas Paine* (ed. M. D. Conway, 4 vols., New York, 1894–6).

[8] E. C. Burnett: *The Continental Congress* (New York, 1941), p. 131.

words of Benjamin Rush, who was one of the signers of the Declaration of Independence, it "burst from the press with an effect which has rarely been produced by types and papers in any age or country."[9] General Charles Lee, writing to Washington on January 24, said: "Have you seen . . . *Common Sense?* I never saw such a masterly, irresistable performance. It will, if I mistake not, in concurrence with the transcendent folly and wickedness of the Ministry, give the coup-de-grâce to Great Britain."[10] Benjamin Franklin later asserted that the pamphlet had "prodigious effects."[11] There can be little doubt that this was true. Yet it is equally true that as time passed and perspectives changed some men at least came to see the pamphlet in a different light. For example, John Adams declared, in writing to Jefferson on June 22, 1819: "What a poor, ignorant, malicious, short-sighted, crapulous mass is Tom Paine's 'Common Sense.' . . . And yet history is to ascribe the American Revolution to Thomas Paine!"[12] In seeking the cause for the remarkable influence of *Common Sense* the point must be re-emphasized that men act, as a rule, not in the light of what is true, but according to what they are led to believe or want to believe is true. They act on feelings not intellect, and Paine stirred up feelings.

While *Common Sense* was gradually changing men's minds on the question of American independence and their attitude toward monarchy, the majority of delegates in the Continental Congress apparently continued to act as though separation from the mother country were not an objective. On January 24, 1776—when, after some hesitation, it was agreed "to prepare an address to the inhabi-

---

[9] *Letters of Benjamin Rush* (ed. L. H. Butterfield, 2 vols., Princeton, 1951), I, 95–6n. Dr. Rush, as is well known, advised Paine on the writing of the pamphlet.

[10] *American Archives,* 4th ser., IV, 839.

[11] Franklin to M. Le Veillard, April 15, 1787, *Writings of Benjamin Franklin* (ed. A. H. Smyth, 10 vols., New York, 1905–7), IX, 562. See E. C. Burnett: *op. cit.,* pp. 131–7, for the great impact of *Common Sense* on the thinking of colonials.

[12] *Works of John Adams* (ed. C. F. Adams, 10 vols., Boston, 1850–6), X, 380–1. An English reformer who had perhaps an even stronger influence than Paine upon John Adams and Jefferson was James Burgh, whose *Political Disquisitions* (3 vols., London, 1774; Philadelphia, 1775) was read eagerly by colonials. The work, a severe and sustained denunciation of the corruption in England's political and social life, contrasted this demoralization with the noble simplicity of manners and disciplined character of public life to be found in America—especially in New England—although Burgh had never been there. Burgh himself was not a revolutionist, but he was made to appear so by the American radicals who quoted him out of context. See Oscar and Mary Handlin: "James Burgh and American Revolutionary Theory," *Massachusetts Historical Society Proceedings,* LXXIII, 38–57.

tants of the United Colonies," in answer to the speech the King had delivered before Parliament on October 26, 1775—the members chose as the drafters John Dickinson and James Wilson of Pennsylvania, William Hooper of North Carolina, James Duane of New York, and Robert Alexander of Maryland, none of whom was identified with the more extreme position taken by the members from Massachusetts Bay and Virginia.[13] This long, carefully framed address, while a severe indictment of the constitution of the British Empire and especially of the powers that Parliament sought to exercise over the colonies, most explicitly denied that Americans were attempting to establish "an independent Empire." Such an imputation, in fact, was declared to be unjust, and the following part of the address to the King by the Congress of the preceding year was cited:

> "We have not raised Armies with the ambitious Designs of Separating from Great Britain, and establishing independent States. . . . We are accused of aiming at Independence. But how is this Accusation supported? By the Allegations of your Ministers, not by our Actions. Give us Leave, most solemnly to assure you, . . . the Object we have ever had in View [is] a Reconciliation with you on constitutional Principles, and a Restoration of that friendly Intercourse, which to the Advantage of both we till lately maintained."[14]

When the address was finally submitted to Congress by the committee on February 13, it was ordered to lie on the table.[15] By that date, in view of the rapidly changing public attitude toward independence, such an address was manifestly no longer desirable or appropriate. In fact, on the 16th of the month, a committee of the whole Congress took into consideration the question of throwing American ports open to the trade of other nations[16]—certainly a long step toward declaring independence. The question was

---

[13] *Journals of the Continental Congress*, IV, 87. According to Richard Smith, a New Jersey delegate to the Congress, most of January 24 was taken up "on a Proposal to address the People of America . . . informing them of our Transactions and of the present State of Affairs, much was said about Independency and the Mode and Propriety of stating our Dependance on the King, a Com^ee was appointed to draw the Address ("Diary of Richard Smith," *American Historical Review*, I, 495).

[14] For the "Draft of an Address of the Continental Congress to the People of the United States, 1776," which was in the handwriting of James Wilson, see *ibid.*, I, 684–96. This was edited for publication by Herbert Friedenwald. The document also appears in *Journals of the Continental Congress*, IV, 134–46.

[15] *Ibid.*, IV, 146.

[16] *Ibid.*, IV, 154.

finally put to a vote on April 6, when it was agreed to permit the importation in foreign vessels of goods from all other parts of the world except Great Britain, Ireland, and the British West Indies.[17] But during the discussions on the 16th it had been strongly argued by George Wythe, a Virginia delegate, that first of all treaties of commerce must be entered into with foreign powers. Yet this raised certain questions, such as: In what role should America approach a foreign court—as subjects of the King of Great Britain or as rebels? "No," he announced. "We must declare ourselves a free People."[18]

While the momentous question now brought into focus was held in abeyance, on March 13 the issue was raised and debated for four hours as to whether Congress should authorize privateers with letters of marque and reprisal to sail against British ships.[19] On the 23rd, in a formal declaration, Congress at length resolved that, in view of designs to reduce colonials "to a state of servile subjection, and . . . whereas an unjust war hath been commenced against them; . . . And whereas the parliament of Great Britain hath lately passed an Act, affirming these colonies to be in open rebellion . . . and . . . their property, wherever found upon the water, liable to seizure and confiscation. . . . Resolved, that the inhabitants of these colonies be permitted to fit out armed vessels to cruize on the enemies of these United Colonies."[20] Such was the answer to the British Prohibitory Act—news of which had reached the Congress late in February—an answer that was another move away from purely defensive warfare and in the direction of independence.

One other step of great importance was taken in the spring of 1776. This was the determination of the secret committee of the Congress to send to France Silas Deane of Connecticut, a member of the First Continental Congress, with the mission of purchasing military supplies. Already certain Frenchmen had mysteriously appeared in America, among them Achard Bonvouloir, Pierre Penet, and Emanuel de Pliarne, all intimating that the French government would look favourably on supplying the needs of the rebelling

---

[17] *Ibid.*, IV, 258.

[18] See "Diary of Richard Smith," *op. cit.*, I, 502–3, and *Adams Papers* (Butterfield), 1st ser., II, 229–30.

[19] "Diary of Richard Smith," *op. cit.*, I, 510–11.

[20] *Journals of the Continental Congress*, IV, 229–33.

colonials.[21] Deane was given a commission on March 1 for his very secret mission.[22] He arrived at Bordeaux on June 6, and by July 14 was in touch with the famous Caron de Beaumarchais. It soon became clear to Deane that the sort of aid the colonials might hope to receive from France would depend upon whether the war was simply a civil war, to be terminated by a reunion with the mother country, or a war for American independence. He sought to assure Beaumarchais, and through him the French minister Vergennes, that it was in fact a war for independence.[23] Upon the basis of this assurance, plans were laid for funnelling to the colonies various types of war material in secrecy and by various instrumentalities and seaports.

Despite all the hesitations on the part of Congress, Deane was correct in his analysis of the American situation. Although the efforts to conquer Canada and to win over the French Canadians had failed, Washington, by the brilliant manœuvre of fortifying Dorchester Heights, succeeded in bringing sufficient pressure to bear upon the British army in Boston so that Major General William Howe, who had succeeded Gage as commanding officer, decided to evacuate the town. This he did on March 15, leaving for Halifax accompanied by many Loyalist refugees. The psychological effect of this strategic victory upon the thinking of Americans was undoubtedly profound. Not only had the continental army contained the British forces in Boston, but it had been able at length to compel them to give up their hold on this important town, the heart of the revolutionary movement. Further, the only serious uprising of Loyalists to take place in the colonies was crushed on February 27. A force of some 1,600—composed of one-time Scottish Highlanders together with former Regulators and others, under the command of Brigadier General Donald McDonald of the regular army—attempted to cross a bridge at Moore's Creek in North Carolina in an effort to reach the coast, but was repulsed by a contingent of patriots under Colonel James Moore.

---

[21] E. C. Burnett: *The Continental Congress*, pp. 141–2.

[22] See the secret committee of the Congress to Silas Deane, with enclosure, March 1, and special instructions to Deane from the committee of March 3, 1776, *Deane Papers 1774–1777* (New-York Historical Society *Collections* for 1886), I, 116–19 and 123–6. The members of the secret committee were Benjamin Franklin, Benjamin Harrison, John Dickinson, Robert Morris, and John Jay.

[23] See Deane's letters to M. Conrad, A. Gerard, and Beaumarchais dated respectively July 18 and 20, *ibid.*, I, 146–54.

Complete independence from Great Britain now became the aim of an increasing number of colonials. The Provincial Congress of South Carolina, meeting at Charleston, resolved on March 23 to authorize its delegates to the Continental Congress both collectively and independently "to concert . . . and execute, every measure which they or he, together with a majority of the Continental Congress, shall judge necessary, for the defense, security, interest, or welfare of this Colony in particular, and of America in general."[24] Three days later it took a bold step in the direction of repudiating all its ties as a royal colony with the government of Great Britain, when it approved the draft of a "Constitution or form of Government." The plan, framed by a committee under the chairmanship of John Rutledge, provided for a General Assembly (in place of the Commons House of Assembly), with power to elect a Legislative Council; these two bodies were in turn authorized to choose by ballot "a President and Commander-in-Chief, and a Vice-President of the Colony." The document, consisting of thirty-four articles, dealt with all phases of the government of South Carolina, which, however, was still denominated a colony.[25]

On April 13 the Provincial Congress of North Carolina, meeting at Halifax, went even further than had that of South Carolina. It resolved unanimously "That the delegates for this Colony in the Continental Congress be impowered to concur with the delegates of the other Colonies in declaring Independency, and forming foreign alliances. . . ."[26] Two days later the Provincial Congress of Georgia repudiated "the unwise and iniquitous system of administration obstinately persisted in by the British Parliament and Ministry against the good people of America. . . ." It thereupon resolved, on the basis that all power originates in the people, to provide, as had South Carolina, for the election of a President by ballot; however, in this instance it was to be by vote of the Congress itself; there was also to be created a Council of Safety to advise the President and to act with him to fill all local offices; a judiciary system with election of the officials by the Congress was also provided.[27] Yet there was no declaration of independence. Georgia, like South Carolina, was still called a "colony." But the thread that held these

---

[24] See the minutes of the South Carolina Provincial Congress, *American Archives,* 4th ser., V, 605.

[25] *Ibid.,* V, 609–14.

[26] *North Carolina Colonial Records,* X, 512.

[27] *Revolutionary Records of Georgia* (ed. A. D. Candler, 3 vols., Atlanta, 1908), I, 274–7.

more southern provinces to Great Britain was very fragile indeed.

On May 6 a convention of delegates met at Williamsburg, Virginia. The Old Dominion, then as in the past, was a key colony. Whatever action was taken there would profoundly influence the decision of other colonies. Richard Henry Lee, impressed with this fact, wrote from Philadelphia to Patrick Henry on April 20 respecting the approaching convention: "Ages yet unborn, and millions existing at present, must rue or bless that Assembley, on which their happiness or misery will so eminintly depend. Virginia has hitherto taken the lead in great affairs, and many now look to her with anxious expectation. . . ."[28] The decision that Lee was ardently hoping would be made by the convention came on May 15, when, among other resolves, it was agreed unanimously "That the delegates appointed to represent this colony in General Congress be instructed to propose to that respectable body to declare the United Colonies free and independent states absolved from all allegiance to, or dependence upon, the crown or parliament of Great Britain. . . ."[29] Even before the news of this decision had reached him in Philadelphia, John Adams wrote to James Warren: "Every Post and every Day rolls in upon Us, Independence like a Torrent."[30]

While the Virginia convention was still deliberating, the Continental Congress on May 10 had come to the decision—doubtless under the influence of the steps already taken by the provincial congresses of the Carolinas and Georgia—to recommend that the colonies "adopt such government as shall . . . best conduce to the happiness and safety of their constituents in particular, and America in general." On the 15th it was decided to publish this resolve, together with a preamble proposed by John Adams.[31] This decision,

---

[28] *Letters of Richard Henry Lee* (ed. J. C. Ballagh, 2 vols., New York, 1911–14), I, 176–80.

[29] Edmund Pendleton, who drew up this resolve, it would appear, had prepared an earlier resolution to present to the Virginia convention proposing that it declare the colony "discharged from any allegiance to the crown of Great Britain." For this rejected resolution and the resolution that was approved see D. J. Mays: *Edmund Pendleton, 1721–1803* (2 vols., Cambridge, Mass., 1952), II, 107–9. In this connection see also the illuminating paper by S. E. Morison: "Prelude to Independence: The Virginia Resolutions of May 15, 1776," *William and Mary Quarterly*, 3rd ser., VIII, 483–92.

[30] *Warren-Adams Letters, 1743–1777* (Massachusetts Historical Society *Collections*, LXXII), I, 249.

[31] For the resolve and Adams's proposed preamble, added later, see *Journals of the Continental Congress*, IV, 342 and 357–8.

vastly important as it was, was not enough; a further step was needed. Meanwhile, pursuant to the instructions from the Virginia convention mentioned above—giving its delegates authority to propose to the Continental Congress the final move for severing all connections between the thirteen colonies and Great Britain—on June 7 Richard Henry Lee moved three resolutions:

> "That these United Colonies are, and of right ought to be, free and independent States, that they are absolved from all allegiance to the British Crown, and that all political connection between them and the State of Great Britain is, and ought to be, totally dissolved. That it is expedient forthwith to take the most effectual measures for forming foreign Alliances. That a plan of confederation be prepared and transmitted to the respective Colonies for their consideration and approbation."[32]

Although the New England colonies had long been prepared for these momentous steps and had been the first to wage war with the King's troops, they had—for this very reason and also on account of the open advocacy of independence by their chief and most weighty spokesman, John Adams—wisely held back, to let the representatives of other colonies take the lead. Now that Virginia had spoken and the other Southern colonies, exclusive of the provinces of East and West Florida, seemed prepared to support its resolves, all that was needed was a commitment to the cause of independence by the five Middle colonies: New York, New Jersey, Pennsylvania, the Lower Counties on the Delaware, and Maryland. To gain time to bring this about, the Congress voted that consideration of the first resolve be postponed to July 1 "and that in the mean time . . . a committee be appointed to prepare a Declaration to the effect of the said first resolution."[33]

According to Jefferson, the chief arguments against an immediate declaration, as voiced by James Wilson and John Dickinson of Pennsylvania and Robert R. Livingston of New York, among others, were:

> "That the people of the middle colonies . . . were not yet ripe for bidding adieu to [the] British connection but that they were fast ripening & in a short time would join in the general voice of America.

---

[32] *Ibid.*, V, 425; *Papers of Thomas Jefferson* (Boyd), I, 298–9.
[33] *Journals of the Continental Congress*, V, 425–6n and 428.

. . . That if the delegates of any particular colony had no power [as a result of the nature of their instructions] to declare such colony independent, certain they were the others could not declare it for them. . . ."

The Congress should therefore wait for a time—a Pennsylvania convention would soon take place; a New York convention was then sitting; the following Monday, conventions would meet in both New Jersey and the Delaware counties.[34] Nevertheless, it was agreed on June 11 that Thomas Jefferson, John Adams, Benjamin Franklin, Roger Sherman, and Robert R. Livingston should form a committee to prepare a declaration so that it might be at hand when the time came to take action.[35]

Meanwhile, the Virginia convention not only issued its "Declaration of Rights" on June 12 but also, after a number of drafts had been presented and considered, adopted a constitution on June 29, 1776, whereby a new form of government, "the Common Wealth of Virginia," was to supplant the old colonial system. The preamble to the constitution contained a long catalogue of the misdeeds of George III, who had endeavoured to pervert the government of Great Britain "into a detestable and insupportable Tyranny. . . ." To escape from his "Acts of Misrule" it was deemed necessary to ordain a future form of government for Virginia.[36] The constitution therefore provided for a General Assembly made of a House of Delegates and a Senate; the executive authority was entrusted to a Governor and a Privy Council or Council of State, both to be chosen annually; provision was also made for other offices of state.

The day before Virginia adopted its new constitution, the committee appointed by the Continental Congress to prepare a declaration of independence reported.[37] The task of drafting this document had wisely been assigned to Thomas Jefferson, although he was the next-to-youngest member of the committee. He had already proved his great ability as a polemical writer and, in addition, he hailed from that most strategic colony, Virginia, which had taken

---

[34] Jefferson's "Notes of Proceedings in the Continental Congress," *Papers of Thomas Jefferson* (Boyd), I, 309–10.

[35] *Journals of the Continental Congress*, V, 431.

[36] For various drafts, three of them by Jefferson, and the constitution as adopted, see *Papers of Thomas Jefferson* (Boyd), I, 329–86.

[37] *Journals of the Continental Congress*, V, 491–502. For an interpretation and analysis of the evolution of the independence movement as a concomitant to the development of the powers of the Continental Congress, see Herbert Friedenwald: *The Declaration of Independence* (New York and London, 1904).

the lead in working for such a declaration. If the declaration were designed, among other things, to influence the more conservative Americans, it certainly would have been inappropriate for John Adams—long held in suspicion as a revolutionist not only by members of the Congress but also by many outside this body—to have received the assignment. Nor would the choice of Benjamin Franklin have been any more appropriate, for a variety of reasons, among them his representation of a colony so openly and seriously divided on the great issue of independence as Pennsylvania. Further, the action of the Congress in placing Jefferson's name so properly at the head of the committee doubtless had influenced the committee itself to turn over to the Virginian the labour of making a draft of what was to become the most famous of American documents.[38] Consideration of the draft of the Declaration of Independence was, however, postponed until July 1. By this date Congress had been notified that "the deputies of Pennsylvania, met in provincial conference," had expressed "their willingness to concur in a vote of Congress, declaring the United Colonies Free and Independent States";[39] the New Jersey Congress on June 21 had also empowered its delegates to the Continental Congress to use their discretion about joining with the other delegates "in declaring the United Colonies independent of Great Britain, entering into a Confederacy for Union and common Defence, making Treaties with foreign Nations . . . and to take such other Measures as may appear to them and you necessary. . . ."[40] Likewise, the members of the Maryland

---

[38] For John Adams's account of why Jefferson was chosen see *Adams Papers* (Butterfield), 1st ser., III, 335–7; for a more extended account see Adams to Timothy Pickering, August 6, 1822, *Works of John Adams*, II, 512–14n. For the drafting of this document see J. H. Hazelton: *The Declaration of Independence: Its History* (New York, 1906); Carl Becker: *The Declaration of Independence. A Study in the History of Political Ideas* (New York, 1956); J. P. Boyd: *The Declaration of Independence: The Evolution of the Text* (Princeton, 1945); and *Papers of Thomas Jefferson* (Boyd), I, 413–33.

[39] *Journals of the Continental Congress*, V, 478. But the Pennsylvania delegation was sharply divided. John Dickinson, Robert Morris, Thomas Willing, and Charles Humphrey were opposed to a declaration, as had been James Wilson. Wilson, however, now joined with Franklin and John Morton to favour it. With pressure brought to bear upon Dickinson and Morris to absent themselves from the Congress, on July 2 a vote of three to two in the Pennsylvania delegation in support of the Lee resolve was secured. See Thomas McKean to Cæsar Rodney, [September?] 22, 1813, *Letters of Members of the Continental Congress*, I, 534–5; see also McKean to Alexander James Dallas, September 26, 1796, *ibid.*, I, 533–4.

[40] *Journals of the Continental Congress*, V, 490. In his "Autobiography" John Adams made the following statement: "Friday June 28, 1776 a new Delegation appeared from New Jersey. Mr. William Livingston and all others who had hitherto

convention voted on June 28 to withdraw the earlier instructions to their deputies in the Congress and to empower them "to concur with the other United Colonies, or a Majority of them, in declaring the United Colonies free and independent States."[41] On June 14 the House of Assembly of the Lower Counties on the Delaware had given leave for its delegates to join with the other colonies "in forming such further compacts between the United Colonies, . . . and in adopting such other measures as shall be judged necessary for promoting the liberty, safety, and interests of America. . . ."[42] But the three delegates were sharply divided in their views on an immediate declaration, with Thomas McKean and Cæsar Rodney in favour of it and George Read opposed. Rodney, Speaker of the House of Assembly, was detained in the colony on public business until July 1. Apparently warned by McKean that his presence in the Congress was absolutely necessary, he rode to Philadelphia through a storm to be on hand by July 2.[43] By July 1 only the New York deputies to the Congress were still forbidden to cast a vote in favour of independence, as the result of their instructions dated June 11 from the third Provincial Congress.[44] On June 29 a great British fleet had appeared in the outer harbour of New York, under command of Admiral Viscount Richard Howe, and on July 2—the very day that Congress had decreed American independence—Lieutenant General Sir William Howe, who now commanded the British Forces in North America and who had brought his army from Halifax to join his brother, began landing troops on Staten Island.[45] Nevertheless, the newly elected Provincial Congress—from which all Loyalists had been eliminated—in a brief session held at White Plains on July 9, unanimously resolved: "That the reasons assigned by the Continental Congress for declaring the United

resisted Independence were left out. Richard Stockton, Francis Hopkinson, and Dr. John Witherspoon were new Members" (*Adams Papers* [Butterfield], 1st ser., III, 395).

[41] *Journals of the Continental Congress*, V, 504.

[42] For these instructions see *Pennsylvania Journal*, June 19, 1776. These are reprinted by W. T. Read in his *The Life and Correspondence of George Read* (Philadelphia, 1870), pp. 164–5.

[43] Rodney to Thomas Rodney, July 4, 1776, *Letters of Members of the Continental Congress*, I, 528, and *Letters to and from Caesar Rodney, 1756–1784* (ed. G. H. Ryden, Philadelphia, 1933), pp. 94–5n.

[44] *Journals of the Continental Congress*, V, 505n.

[45] See Governor Tryon to Lord George Germain, July 8, 1776, *New York Colonial Documents*, VIII, 681. Sir William succeeded Gage on October 10, 1775, with the local rank of "General in America."

Colonies Free and Independent States, are cogent and conclusive; and, that while we lament the cruel necessity which has rendered that measure unavoidable, we approve the same, and will, at the risque of our lives and fortunes, join with the other colonies in supporting it."[46]

It was on July 1 that Richard Henry Lee's motion of June 7 in favour of a declaration of independence occupied the attention of the delegates, as Congress resolved itself into a committee of the whole "to take into consideration the resolution respecting independency."[47] The draft of the declaration also came before the committee. On July 2 the Lee resolution was approved.[48] The following day the draft of the special committee's declaration was given further consideration. It was on the 4th of July that formal approval was registered of "A Declaration by the Representatives of the United States of America, in General Congress Assembled."[49]

In analyzing the Declaration of Independence, it should be borne

---

[46] See *Journals of the Continental Congress,* V, 560. For an excellent account of the movement for independence in the Province of New York see C. L. Becker: *History of Political Parties in the Province of New York, 1760–1776* (Madison, Wisc., 1909, reissued in 1960), pp. 250–73.

[47] *Journals of the Continental Congress,* V, 504. On that day, according to Jefferson, South Carolina and Pennsylvania voted against the approval of the Lee resolves, the Delaware delegation was divided, and that of New York felt it could not participate in a vote. Edward Rutledge of South Carolina, who had been strongly opposed to a declaration before a united government could enter into foreign treaties, asked (again following Jefferson's account) on July 1 that the declaration be postponed until the next day, when he thought his colleagues, although disapproving of the resolves, would vote for it. See "Notes of Proceedings in the Continental Congress," *Papers of Thomas Jefferson* (Boyd), I, 314. Rutledge's attitude on June 8 is made clear in his letter of that date to John Jay. See *Letters of Members of the Continental Congress,* I, 476–7.

[48] *Journals of the Continental Congress,* V, 507. The New York delegation did not participate in this vote or the vote on the 4th on the grounds of not being authorized so to act.

[49] *Ibid.,* V, 510. It was not until August 2 that the declaration was engrossed on parchment and signed. See *ibid.,* V, 626. The title was changed to read: "The Unanimous Declaration of the thirteen United States of America." Whether the original document which came from the committee and was approved on July 4 was also signed on that day is not clear. See J. H. Hazelton: *op. cit.,* pp. 193–219 and 495–543; and *Papers of Thomas Jefferson* (Boyd), I, 304–8. Dr. Boyd analyzes with great care the implications of Jefferson's "Notes of Proceedings in the Continental Congress," in which the author of the Declaration of Independence wrote that on July 4 it "was reported by the commee., agreed to by the house, and signed by every member present except Mr. Dickinson" (*ibid.,* I, 315). For Bernhard Knollenberg's defence of Dickinson for his unwillingness to vote for independence at this particular juncture, see "John Dickinson vs. John Adams, 1774–1776," American Philosophical Society *Proceedings,* CVII, 138–44.

in mind that the document was designed for certain specific purposes, chief among which was the aim of welding the American people into unity. Highly emotional in tone, the Declaration sought to erase any thought that the type of government that had existed under George III was suited to the needs of those who had been his colonial subjects. "The history of the present King of Great Britain," it declared, "is a history of repeated injuries and usurpations, all having in direct object the establishment of an absolute Tyranny over these States." These injuries and usurpations were thereupon set forth at great length, all pointing an accusing finger no longer at the Ministry and Parliament, as had been the earlier practice, but at the King.[50] "He has combined with others to subject us to a jurisdiction foreign to our constitution, and unacknowledged by our laws; giving his Assent to their Acts of pretended Legislation." In fact, it is hard to realize that the same Congress that had voted in 1775 to petition the King in terms of greatest devotion to him to save the colonies from the abuse of power by Parliament could now turn upon him as the very symbol of an iniquitous ruler. But this aspect of fomenting rebellion was only one facet of the great statement.

On the other hand, the nobility of concept and expression of much of the Declaration remains unsurpassed. For example, it would be hard to improve upon the language expressing the doctrine of popular government:

> "We hold these truths to be self-evident, that all men are created equal, that they are endowed by their Creator with certain unalienable Rights, that among these are Life, Liberty and the pursuit of Happiness.—That to secure these rights, Governments are instituted among Men, deriving their just powers from the consent of the governed.— That whenever any Form of Government becomes destructive of these ends, it is the Right of the People to alter or to abolish it, and to institute new Government, laying its foundation on such principles

---

[50] The question may be asked whether it was Jefferson, alone or in concert with other Virginians, who fastened upon the idea of castigating the King as a method for weaning the colonials from their basic loyalty as British subjects. For, as has been made clear, it was Jefferson who took the lead in drafting the preamble to the Virginia constitution, adopted on June 29, and in drafting the Declaration of Independence; for another view of the rise of feeling against the King see Stella F. Duff: "The Case Against the King: The *Virginia Gazettes* Indict George III," *William and Mary Quarterly*, 3rd ser., VI, 383–97. See also W. F. Dana: "The Declaration of Independence as Justification for Revolution," *Harvard Law Review*, XIII, 319–43.

and organizing its powers in such form, as to them shall seem most likely to effect their Safety and Happiness."

And, as a synthesis of the ideas of fundamental law, public rights, libertarian thought, and political philosophy, from Sophocles to Blackstone and Aristotle to Locke, the document remains a world classic.[51] Finally, as Dr. Boyd has pointed out, "the greatness of the Declaration lay in the very fact that it expressed what Adams himself said was in the minds and hearts of the people."[52]

Nevertheless, the Declaration of Independence did not speak the minds and hearts of all Americans. Thousands of them were still loyal to the King and devoted to the British connection. For example, Governor Tryon of New York, while on board ship off Staten Island, wrote to Lord George Germain on July 8:

> "On Saturday last I received the Militia of the Island at Richmond Town, where near four hundred appeared, who chearfully, on my Recommendation, took the Oath of Allegiance & fidelity to his Majesty. Tomorrow I am to have another muster for the inlistment of Voluntiers to form a Provincial Corps for the defence of the Island. . . ."[53]

These men, along with others from various parts of the colonies, who, earlier or later, were prepared to go out and battle the rebels,

---

[51] See Carl Becker: *The Declaration of Independence* . . . Chap. 2; C. F. Mullett: *Fundamental Law and the American Revolution, 1760–1776* (Columbia University Studies in History . . . No. 385, New York, 1933); and J. P. Boyd's masterly study *The Declaration of Independence* . . . , Chap. 1, "Backgrounds."

[52] See Jefferson's own defence of "the great apologia of the American Revolution" in response to criticism of it by Timothy Pickering, John Adams, and Richard Henry Lee (*ibid.*, p. 2), wherein is also cited Jefferson's explanation of his task (written to Henry Lee on May 8, 1825) as having been: "Not to find out New principles, or new arguments, never before thought of . . . but to place before mankind the common sense of the subject, terms so plain and firm as to command their assent, and to justify ourselves in the independent stand we [were] impelled to take. Neither aiming at originality of principle or sentiment, nor yet copied from any particular and previous writing, it was intended to be an expression of the American mind" (*Writings of Thomas Jefferson* [ed. P. L. Ford], 10 vols., New York, 1892–9, VII, 407). For a discussion of the purpose of the Declaration as an expression of a minority group's attempt to win over a majority, and therefore requiring broad statements made in familiar phraseology, see Herbert Friedenwald: *op. cit.*, Chap. 8.

See also Carl Becker's argument that the Declaration was primarily intended "to proclaim to the world the reasons for declaring independence . . . as a formal justification of an act already accomplished" (*The Declaration of Independence* . . . , p. 5). See further the illuminating article by P. F. Detweiler: "The Changing Reputation of the Declaration of Independence: The First Fifty Years," *William and Mary Quarterly*, 3rd ser., XIX, 557–74.

[53] *New York Colonial Documents*, VIII, 681.

as they called their enemies, were generally the ordinary run of men, so far as evidence is obtainable. However, what proportion of Americans were prepared to lay down their lives in the King's service is difficult to determine. A leading authority on the New York Loyalists arrived at the conclusion that at least 3,500 men in that state served with the British army and navy or in the Loyalist militia as against 17,781 embodied in the American regular forces and another 23,852 in the militia supporting the revolutionary American Union, or 41,633 altogether.[54] But New York was exceptional in its loyalty to the King, and the same authority suggests that in all the other colonies combined no larger number of people flocked to the royal standard.[55] Still another authority on the Loyalists concludes that "50,000 soldiers, either regular or militia, were drawn into the service of Great Britain from her American sympathizers."[56] Whatever the correct figures may be, it cannot be questioned that the War for American Independence took on all the characteristics of a civil war in many parts of the country—especially in New York and in the more southern colonies—with all the horrors that such wars involve when friends and neighbors are set against one another in deadly combat.

In addition to the Loyalist combatants, there were vastly greater numbers of colonials hostile to the revolutionary movement. They stood aghast at the acts of terrorism performed by bands of rioters and vandals—the tarring and feathering of people or the meting out to them of other physical abuse and humiliation, and the destruction of their property. These were men and women whose sole offence was the affirmation of their loyalty to one whom all Americans earlier had been glad to acknowledge as their King. To people of such conservative tendencies the patriotic cry of liberty was a mockery, when hand in hand with it went acts of violence designed to deprive them of all liberty because they disagreed on the great issue of the day. The Quakers, with few exceptions, were loyal, but their deep

[54] A. C. Flick: *Loyalism in New York during the American Revolution* (New York and London, 1901), pp. 112–13.

[55] *Ibid.*, pp. 180–2, in which Dr. Flick estimates that 95 per cent of the people of New York professed loyalty to the King, Empire, and British constitution before the Declaration of Independence; thereafter, he concludes, 90,000 out of a population of 185,000 were Loyalists, and of this number 35,000 emigrated, while the remainder accepted the inevitable.

[56] C. H. Van Tyne: *The Loyalists in the American Revolution* (New York, 1929), pp. 182–3. Van Tyne, it should be pointed out, leans heavily at this point on Flick's figures. J. R. Alden: *The American Revolution, 1775–1783* (New York, 1954), p. 87, considers the above figures too high.

religious scruples would not permit them to take up arms; in the same category could be placed the Moravians, the Mennonites, the Dunkards, the Amish, and other pietistic groups, as well as the Anglican clergy in the Northern colonies and many of them in the Southern colonies. In addition to the office-holders under the Crown, most of whom were loyal, there were merchant princes of the seaports, humble frontiersmen, lawyers, planters, farmers, shopkeepers, artisans, labourers, in fact all categories of people from the very rich to the very poor, from the highly educated to the illiterate,[57] who refused to join with the patriots for reasons that each considered sufficient—whether based on devotion to their King or self-interest. For there was concern over worldly possessions on the part of some, who feared the anarchy that might follow a successful revolt or the confiscation of property that might succeed a suppression of the rebellion by the might of Great Britain.[58] Although many of those not bearing arms gave of their substance to the King's cause, it would appear that most of them refrained from any open support of the British, preferring to live quietly while awaiting the outcome of the struggle. The total number of Loyalists, from the ardent to the timorous, may never be known. In his recent study, Professor William H. Nelson takes the view that "in the West and in the tidal region of the Middle Colonies Loyalists and neutrals may have formed a majority of the population."[59]

---

[57] See E. B. Greene: *The Revolutionary Generation, 1763–1790* (*History of American Life*, IV, New York, 1943). For authoritative short biographies of Harvard graduates who became leaders in the American Revolution, both patriot and Loyalist, see C. K. Shipton: *Biographical Sketches of Those Who Attended Harvard College . . . 1731–1750*, Vols. IX–XII of *Sibley's Harvard Graduates* (Boston, 1956–62).

[58] In the above connection see L. W. Labaree: "The Nature of American Loyalism," American Antiquarian Society *Proceedings*, LIV, 15–58; see also, by the same author, *Conservatism in Early American History* (New York and London, 1948), Chap. 6, "The Tory Mind," and especially W. H. Nelson: *The American Tory* (Oxford, 1961).

[59] W. H. Nelson: *op. cit.*, p. 87. Among the writings of Loyalists see Thomas Hutchinson: *Strictures upon the Declaration of the Congress at Philadelphia; In a Letter to a Noble Lord* (London, 1776) and his *Diary and Letters* (ed. P. O. Hutchinson, 2 vols., London, 1883–6); Samuel Seabury: *Letters of a Westchester Farmer* (ed. C. H. Vance), Westchester County Historical Society *Publications*, VIII; Joseph Galloway: *A Candid Examination of the Mutual Claims of Great Britain and the Colonies* (New York, 1775) and *Historical and Political Reflections on the Rise and Progress of the American Rebellion* (London, 1780); *Peter Oliver's Origin of the Rebellion* (San Marino, Calif., 1961); Jonathan Boucher: *A View of the Causes and Consequences of the American Revolution* (London, 1797) and *Reminiscences of an American Loyalist, 1738–1789* (ed. Jonathan Boucher, Boston and New York, 1925); *Samuel Curwen, Journal and Letters* (ed. G. A. Ward,

But the Loyalist cause did not prevail, whereas the Declaration of Independence did. It was an announcement to the world that a new nation had come into existence. The great task of creating the instrumentalities that would be adequate to realize the immediate aims and the more distant aspirations of the American nation do not lie, however, within the scope of this series. Nor are we here concerned with the bitter trials awaiting the patriots after the initial wave of exaltation over the proclamation of independence had re-

Boston, 1842). Among studies of individual Loyalists the following are of importance: Lorenzo Sabine: *Biographical Sketches of Loyalists of the American Revolution* (2 vols., Boston, 1864); J. K. Hosmer: *Life of Thomas Hutchinson* (Boston, 1896); J. E. Alden: "John Mein, Scourge of Patriots," Colonial Society of Massachusetts *Transactions*, XXXIV, 571–99; J. A. Thompson: *Count Rumford of Massachusetts* (New York, 1935); L. H. Gipson: *Jared Ingersoll* . . . (New Haven, 1920); H. C. Van Schaack: *Life of Peter Van Schaack* (New York, 1842); R. H. Spiro, Jr.: "John Loudon McAdam in Revolutionary New York," *New-York Historical Society Quarterly*, XL, 29–54; E. P. Alexander: *A Revolutionary Conservative: James Duane of New York* (New York, 1938); Catherine Fennelly: "William Franklin of New Jersey," *William and Mary Quarterly*, 3rd ser., VI, 361–82; O. C. Kuntzleman: *Joseph Galloway, Loyalist* (Philadelphia, 1941); E. H. Baldwin: "Joseph Galloway, the Loyalist Politician," *Pennsylvania Magazine*, XXVI, 161–91, 289–321, 417–42. The following works, in addition to those already mentioned, are useful for an examination of American loyalism in the thirteen colonies, moving from north to south: W. H. Siebert: "Loyalist Troops of New England," *New England Quarterly*, IV, 108–47, "The Exodus of Loyalists from the Penobscot," Ohio State University *Bulletin*, XVIII, No. 26, and "Loyalist Refugees of New Hampshire," *ibid.*, XXI, No. 2; O. G. Hammond: *Tories of New Hampshire in the War of the Revolution* (Concord, 1917); J. H. Stark: *The Loyalists of Massachusetts and the Other Side of the American Revolution* (Boston, 1910); E. A. Jones: *The Loyalists of Massachusetts* . . . (London, 1930); G. A. Gilbert: "The Connecticut Loyalists," *American Historical Review*, IV, 273–91; Epaphroditus Peck: *Loyalists of Connecticut* (Connecticut Tercentenary Commission, *Historical Publications*, No. 31); W. H. Siebert: "Refugee Loyalists in Connecticut," Ohio State University *Bulletin*, X; G. W. Kyte: "Some Plans for a Loyalist Stronghold in the Middle Colonies," *Pennsylvania History*, XVI, 177–90; O. T. Barck, Jr.: *New York City during the War for Independence* (New York, 1931); W. C. Abbott: *New York in the American Revolution* (New York, 1929); Ruth M. Keesey: "Loyalism in Bergen County, New Jersey," *William and Mary Quarterly*, 3rd ser., XVIII, 558–76; E. A. Jones: *The Loyalists of New Jersey* . . . (New Jersey Historical Society *Collections*, X); W. H. Siebert: "Loyalists of Pennsylvania," Ohio State University *Bulletin*, XXIV, No. 23; H. B. Hancock: *The Delaware Loyalists* (Historical Society of Delaware *Papers*, new ser., 3); I. S. Harrell: *Loyalism in Virginia* . . . (Durham, N.C., 1926) and his "North Carolina Loyalists," *North Carolina Historical Review*, III, 575–90; R. O. DeMond: *The Loyalists in North Carolina During the Revolution* (Durham, N.C., 1940); C. A. Ellefson: "James Habersham and Georgia Loyalism, 1764–1775," *Georgia Historical Quarterly*, XLIV, 359–80, and by the same author: "Loyalists and Patriots in Georgia During the American Revolution," *The Historian*, XXIV, 347–56; W. H. Siebert: *Loyalists in East Florida, 1774–1785* (2 vols., De Land, Fla., 1929); W. H. Siebert: "Loyalists in West Florida and the Natchez District," *Mississippi Valley Historical Review*, II, 465–83. See also, in general, A. E. Ryerson: *Loyalists of America and Their Times* . . . (Toronto, 1880); Moses Tyler: *Literary History of the American Revolution* (2 vols., New York, 1897) and his "The Party of the Loyalists in the American Revolution," *American Historical Review*, I, 24–45.

ceded and before the British government was forced in 1783 to sign a treaty of peace, acknowledging that the King's once loyal subjects were now citizens of the thirteen states of the American Union and no longer dependent upon the Crown and Parliament.

Despite the loss of the thirteen older North American colonies, the British Empire remained powerful and continued to count vast territories and commercial enterprises within the scope of its far reaches.[60] These dependencies were of vital importance to the mother country, especially during the period when Americans were challenging the authority of the British government to pass laws that would bind them and dispose of their property. Therefore, to round out this series in its broader purposes and bring to a balanced conclusion this study of the Old Empire, there will be presented in the volume to follow an account of the course of events down to the Declaration of Independence in those parts of the Empire that did not revolt.

---

[60] In this connection the student should consult V. T. Harlow: *The Founding of the Second British Empire, 1763–1793* (2 vols., London, New York, and Toronto, 1952, 1964), I, Chap. 1, "The Old Empire and the New."

Index

A NOTE ABOUT THE AUTHOR

LAWRENCE HENRY GIPSON is Research Professor of History, Emeritus, at Lehigh University. After receiving a bachelor of arts degree from the University of Idaho, he entered Oxford as the first Rhodes Scholar from the state of Idaho; there he gained a degree in the Oxford Honour School of Modern History. He was later a Bulkley Fellow in the graduate school at Yale, where his doctoral dissertation, *Jared Ingersoll: A Study of American Loyalism in Relation to British Colonial Government*, received the Porter Prize as the best work in literary form presented by a student in any division of the University during the preceding year; it was also awarded the Justin Winsor Prize by the American Historical Association. Since then he has written and published many works relating to colonial history (including twelve volumes of his *magnum opus*; the final volume is in preparation). During the academic year 1951–2 he occupied the Harmsworth Chair in American History at Oxford; he also has been a member of the board of editors of the *American Historical Review,* was a founder of the Conference on Early American History, and is a past president of both the Conference on British Studies and the Pennsylvania Historical Association. He is the Honorary Consultant in American Colonial History to the Library of Congress for the period 1965 through 1967. Many prizes and honors have come to him as a result of his writing, including, in 1962, the Pulitzer Prize in History for Volume X of *The British Empire before the American Revolution* and, most recently, his election as Honorary Fellow of Lincoln College, Oxford University.

July 1965

A NOTE ON THE TYPE

THE TEXT of this book is set in *Caledonia*, a typeface designed by W(ILLIAM) A(DDISON) DWIGGINS for the Mergenthaler Linotype Company in 1939. Dwiggins chose to call his new typeface Caledonia, the Roman name for Scotland, because it was inspired by the Scotch types cast about 1833 by Alexander Wilson & Son, Glasgow type founders. However, there is a calligraphic quality about this face that is totally lacking in the Wilson types. Dwiggins referred to an even earlier typeface for this "liveliness of action"—one cut around 1790 by William Martin for the printer William Bulmer. Caledonia has more weight than the Martin letters, and the bottom finishing strokes (serifs) of the letters are cut straight across, without brackets, to make sharp angles with the upright stems, thus giving a "modern face" appearance.

  W. A. Dwiggins (1880–1956) was born in Martinsville, Ohio, and studied art in Chicago. In 1904 he moved to Hingham, Massachusetts, where he built a solid reputation as a designer of advertisements and as a calligrapher. He began an association with the Mergenthaler Linotype Company in 1929, and over the next twenty-seven years designed a number of book types for that firm. Of especial interest are the Metro series, Electra, Caledonia, Eldorado, and Falcon. In 1930, Dwiggins first became interested in marionettes, and through the years made many important contributions to the art of puppetry and the design of marionettes.

Composed by The Haddon Craftsmen, Inc., Scranton, Pa.,
printed and bound by The Kingsport Press, Inc., Kingsport, Tenn.
Typography and binding design by
W. A. DWIGGINS